SONGS OF SHIPS & SAILORS

Not since Joanna Colcord published *Roll and Go* in 1924 have we seen such a comprehensive compilation of songs from the sea as this one. Julia Lane and Fred Gosbee have brought forth not just the songs, but so much important contextual information, such as a map of the location of singers, the source of the song, the melody to which the song is sung, and editorial notes that compare songs with other known versions, or similar songs known by different names. This is a book that will be a treasure to singers, but also to folklorists, ballad scholars and historians. The authors have exceeded their goals to create a song book. They have created a volume that will stand proudly on library bookshelves next to books by Phillips Barry, Fannie Eckstorm, Joanna Colcord and other ballad scholars.

  Pauleena MacDougall, Ph.D., Former director Maine Folklife Center, author & editor

One of the very best books on historic songs of the sea. There are many such books, but few achieve such a high level throughout, with such attention to musical detail and such precise writing. The lengthy introduction itself is invaluable to anyone interested in historic music, the sea, and Maine.

  Dr. Stephen Sanfilippo, Ph.D. Maritime History, educator, performer, author & editor

[This book is] the result of extraordinary detailed transcribing and deciphering of songs rescued from obscurity in an all but forgotten archive. The songs are then illuminated by Julia and Fred's long, deep study of the music and history of the state of Maine and the British Isles… It is filled with surprises and delights. I know it will certainly delight lovers of music and of Maine.

  Van Reid, Award-winning author and creator of *The Moosepath League*, Viking Press

A profoundly significant and scholarly contribution to the world of folk song, this book should be read by anyone who is interested in the traditional music of rural America. In-depth and clearly presented, these Anglo European folk songs are expertly collected, written and exhibited by folk singers and researchers Julia Lane and Fred Gosbey. This book exhibits a treasure trove of painstakingly collected folk songs that have migrated from Anglo Europe to Maine. The song examples are artfully presented and shown in the context of the culture from which they come.

  Stuart P. Gillespie Jr., Composer, choral director, Maritime Historian and singer at Mystic Seaport (1972–85)

Pick this up, you won't put it down. Whether you're a singer or just a lover of lore, you'll find herein a fruitful feast of ballads and broadsides, some familiar (with a local twist), some wholly new, and all with deftly written notes as to the history behind them. A labor of love as ever you'll find, this volume reflects years of meticulous research into the annals of Maine's "songstory," with song after song brought to light (and life) along with detailed information as to its origins and evolution. What a gold mine of material! Every Maine music teacher must have a copy! Send one to the teacher nearest you! Julia Lane and Fred Gosbee have managed to corral an exhaustive list of songs into a volume that's readable and user-friendly.

  Janie Meneely, Musician, promoter, journalist (former editor *Chesapeake Bay Magazine*)

BYGONE BALLADS OF MAINE, VOLUME I

SONGS OF SHIPS & SAILORS

Compiled & Edited by
Julia Lane & Fred Gosbee

LOOMIS HOUSE PRESS
NORTHFIELD, MINNESOTA

Copyright © 2021 Julia Lane

All rights reserved. No part of this book may be reproduced in any form by any electronic or mechanical means including information and retrieval systems without permission in writing, except by a reviewer who may quote brief passages in a review.

However, the melodies and lyrics of the included songs are explicitly retained in the public domain, and may be freely performed, recorded, and repurposed.

All illustrations are from public domain sources and remain in the public domain. Special thanks to the Internet Archive (archive.org) where most of them were sourced.

Cover image "View of Portland Harbor, ca 1853, detail." Collections of Maine Historical Society

ISBN 978-1-935243-79-3 (paperback)
ISBN 978-1-935243-78-6 (hardcover)

Publisher's Cataloging-in-Publication data

Names: Lane, Julia, editor. | Gosbee, Fred, editor.
Title: Songs of ships and sailors / compiled and edited by Julia Lane and Fred Gosbee.
Description: Includes bibliographical references and index. |
Northfield, MN: Loomis House Press, 2021.
Identifiers: LCCN: 2021949294 |
ISBN: 978-1-935243-78-6 (hardcover) | 978-1-935243-79-3 (paperback)
Subjects: LCSH Sea songs. | Folk music–New England. | Folk songs, English–New England. | BISAC MUSIC / Genres & Styles / Folk & Traditional | HISTORY / Maritime History & Piracy | HISTORY / United States / State & Local / New England (CT, MA, ME, NH, RI, VT)
Classification: LCC M1977.S2 S66 2021 | DDC 784.6/8/6238--dc23

CONTACT:
Julia Lane & Fred Gosbee / Castlebay Music
PO Box 168, Round Pond Maine 04564
207-529-5438
castlebay@castlebay.net
www.castlebay.net

Melodies for the songs in this book can be heard at
http://castlebaycds.com/bygone_ballads_1_sound.html

*This book is dedicated to all intrepid seafarers, sung and unsung,
and their families, who call Maine their home,
and in memory of Sandy & Bobby Ives*

Special thanks to Gordon Bok, Jim Douglas, Pauleena MacDougall,
James Nelson, Lisa Null, Stephen & Susan Sanfillipo,
Kathy Westra-Stephens, Hilary Warner-Evans, Steve Woodbury,
Claire Curtis, and Sandy Guibord.

We are very grateful to the staff at the following institutions:
The American Folklife Center, Library of Congress, Washington, DC
The Bangor Public Library, Bangor, ME
The Maine Folklife Center, University of Maine, Orono, ME
The Fogler Library, University of Maine, Orono, ME
The Davis Family Library, Middlebury College, Middlebury VT
The Houghton Library, Harvard College, Cambridge, MA
The Maine State Library, Augusta, ME
The Maine Historical Society, Portland, ME
The Portland Public Library, Portland, ME

Contents

Foreword	vii
Author's Note	ix
Introduction	xiii
About the Sources	xvi
The Songs	1
Glossary of Nautical Terms and Expressions	257
Index of First Lines	262
Subject Index	265
Index of Song Sources	269
Biographies of Collectors and Major Sources	284
Bibliography	292
About the Authors	295

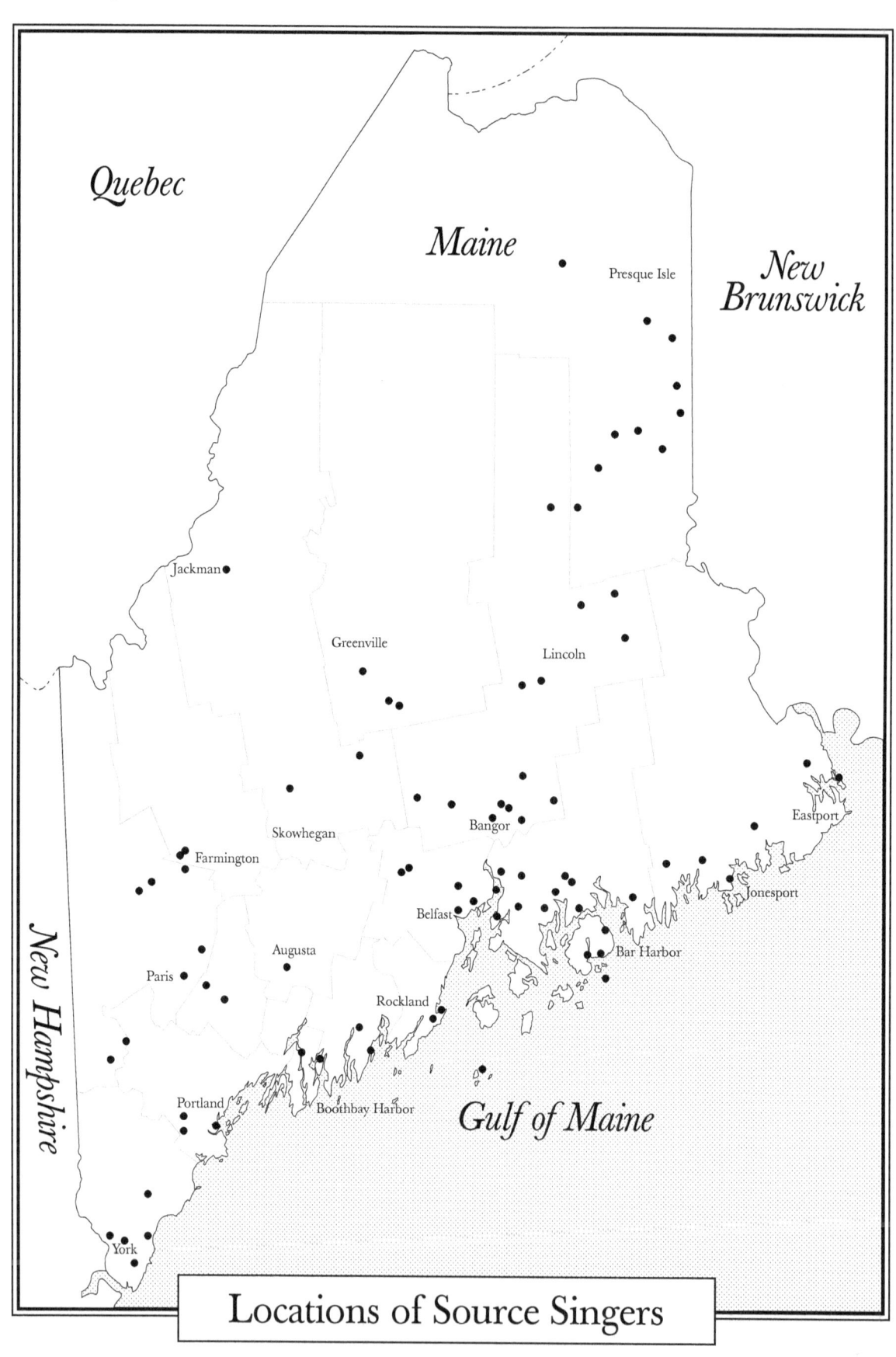
Locations of Source Singers

Foreword

For the more than 50 years I've been listening to, participating in, presenting, and performing traditional folk music I've known the names of Helen Hartness Flanders, Eloise Hubbard Linscott, Carrie Grover, and Fanny Hardy Eckstorm. These New England women have long been associated with their published collections of songs and ballads that offer a glimpse into the people, pastimes and occupations of a long-ago New England.

These collecting women were not only fascinated with the old songs, but also determined to share them with a wider audience. The books they published nearly a century ago became "go to" resources for folksingers and folklorists interested in the New World progeny of older ballads and broadsides from the British Isles. Flanders, Linscott, Grover, Eckstorm and other song-finders tramped all over New England, knocking on strangers' doors looking for these songs, competing with one another to discover new singers, and painstakingly writing down the lyrics (and sometimes the tunes) offered by the people they encountered.

In the late 1970s I was lucky to have a chance to meet Massachusetts native Eloise Hubbard Linscott. I joined my former husband, Joe Hickerson, on a business trip where he hoped to encourage Mrs. Linscott to donate her original manuscripts, notes, and field recordings to the Library of Congress Archive of Folk Song, of which Joe was then Head.

On a very hot New England summer day, Mrs. Linscott treated us to a home-made midday "dinner" of chicken and dumplings while regaling us with tales of her collecting adventures. My favorite was the story she told about the day Vermont-based collector Helen Flanders arrived at Linscott's suburban Boston doorstep. Brandishing a copy of Linscott's book, *Folk Songs of Old New England*, Mrs. Flanders warned her perceived rival in no uncertain terms to "stay out of Vermont!" As Mrs. Linscott told us with a grin: "I went to Vermont on my very next trip!"

Regardless of their rivalry, the songs Flanders, Linscott, and their contemporaries tracked down likely would not have survived but for these women's determined passion for song-finding. Though not trained scholars, they shared the delight of interested amateurs in unearthing cultural treasure. They did it at a time when women, nice women, simply didn't leave their homes to do things like that. We all owe them a debt.

Though I have known about Flanders, Linscott and their contemporaries for years, I did not realize until recently that for every song they included in their well-known collections, hundreds of songs they unearthed were never published. Until now.

Thanks to another intrepid woman and amateur song-finder, my friend and neighbor Julia Lane of Round Pond, Maine, more than 250 never-before-published songs from those early women collectors have been brought to light in this volume.

Both Julia and her husband, Fred Gosbee, are singers and native Mainers who perform and record together as the duo Castlebay. Both of them delight in finding and sharing songs that reflect the history and culture of our state and region.

Julia, like the women collectors who inspired her, developed an interest in traditional songs as a child. In recent years, she has taken that interest to a new level by knocking on the doors of archives from the Library of Congress in Washington, D.C., to university libraries and local historical societies all over New England to locate and listen to the previously unpublished Maine ballads and songs you find here. Julia listened to and transcribed hundreds of scratchy recordings; pored over the earlier collectors' handwritten notes about the people who sang them; talked her way into historical archives usually only available to university-affiliated scholars; and dug deeper to discover how these fascinating maritime songs might have found their way to the repertoires of Maine singers, some of whom lived far from the coast. Julia's work, like that of her predecessors, is a tribute not only to her fascination with Maine history and music, but also to her dogged determination over more than a decade of effort to make sure these songs and the times they celebrate are not lost.

Both Julia and Fred are also my favorite kind of amateur historians—not just passionate about the old songs, but also knowledgeable about a host of things that reflect the kind of Maine-born New Englanders they are. Whether it's putting up rose-petal jam made from flowers picked from her beautiful garden (Julia), or hand-hewing a new mast for a historic sailing ship (Fred), this couple has studied—and accomplished—the kinds of things the old songs celebrate. They've done it because those things fascinate them, and because they want to share their skills and knowledge with you. So, enjoy this book. Learn some fascinating maritime history. Sing the songs. Tell your friends. You won't be sorry.

Kathy Westra Stephens
Owls Head, Maine, June 2021

Author's Note

I have always been interested in alternate expressions of historical experience. Historians may record events that occur as humans travel the road of time, but it is song and story, art and literature that record true human experience. Growing up with artists, musicians and writers around me, I learned the possibility for variety in the telling of a tale. Arguments can be made that these things are, by their nature, subjective and not "fact." I would counter that personal reality is "fact" to the individual and even to groups that live through an experience together. People act and react in their world as a result of their notion of reality. The personal story provides valuable insight for the listener / reader. Even within a family children will report different relationships with the same parents and family members will report different experiences of the same events, though they will agree on many details. Truth is discovered when these different stories are expressed and compared.

For me, songs, ballads and stories told with music are a true and immediate expression of experience often created out of a need to speak and pass on the story. As with a journal entry, they can be direct, raw and forceful or filled with nuance and innuendo. But rhythmical cadence sets the unfolding pace and the music carries an emotional layer not evident in the words alone. Rather than being ephemeral, they can be transferred easily without the need for physical manifestation, and can be changed, either intentionally or not, as they pass through an individual filter. These changes can reflect additional cultural, religious and political bias. Like skills and knowledge traditionally passed from master to apprentice without benefit of codification, the individual edits and innovates as resources and environment dictate.

When I was small, I would, like all children, make physical artistic representations of my thoughts and experiences. In addition, I created stories and songs that reflected my world both real and imaginary. When I heard and read those made by authors, both celebrated and anonymous, I began to explore this world of vernacular expression. There was a very good library nearby and I started spending a good deal of time in the "special collections" reading volumes containing the harvest of intrepid collectors. I realized that these things were part of my cultural identity, and perhaps even my own personal history with versions possibly being sung by my ancestors. At the time, I was finding very little that had been gathered in my home region of New England. I found this curious, as my grandfather made sure I knew that "our people" had arrived in the early 17th century, but I attributed this to Puritan suppression. As a scion of an embarrassingly mono-ethnic family, the Anglo-Celtic matter became a focus. As a singer, I learned songs which spoke to me. Intrigued by the variant versions of a ballad, I would seek the "truth" of the story by comparing them with actual recorded history when possible. I also discovered that the official, sanctioned histories were rife with bias.

The works of J.R.R. Tolkien became of particular interest. As I read them, I realized that the incredible world he created was not just his fantastic imagination but directly based on ancient balladry and myth. His deep knowledge of these sources allowed him to process them and bring them forward to create a complete, timeless and meaningful experience for his readers. Seeking to read his sources for myself, I decided I needed to travel to Oxford and perhaps meet the master himself. Although Tolkien died before I could do this, I was able to negotiate an early graduation from 12th grade and arrange a "gap" semester in England where I thought to take up my own collecting project. Though I was fortunate to be in an environment with resources that allowed me to follow my muse, my passion was barely tolerated by family and peers and, at age 17, there were numerous obstacles to this adventure which I allowed to discourage me.

While immersing myself in the legacy of the old ballads, I began writing my own songs, reflecting personal experience. Feeling that experience to be somehow incomplete, I sought to live in the world inhabited and experienced by the makers of the old ballads. I left college after two years and came to live in Maine, the place where "my people" had landed and lived for over 300 years. I realized that I needed to engage more fully with the elemental aspect of the land that had sustained my ancestors. Although my grandparents had sought opportunities elsewhere, like migrant birds our family had always returned seasonally to reconnect with the place and with relatives. When we were small, my older brother and I would go hang around the fishermen's co-op down by the shore where the elder fishermen would hold court, telling jokes and stories and surreptitiously supervising our adventures around the docks. Returning to this place seemed to be the next step, so I married a local fisherman, homesteaded a small farm and raised two children. All this informed not only my own songs that came out of that time, but my interpretation of the ballads I had learned.

My grandparents had also returned to retire in Maine. As I cared for my grandfather after my grandmother's early passing, I found that he had recorded the stories told by my great-uncle Frank who had been one of the elder fishermen in the co-op. As I listened to the familiar voice on the tape, it struck me that there must be other recordings made for the same reason that my grandfather had made this one—to make an audio record of the person and their life experience. Hearing the actual voice telling stories and singing songs added dimension to the old photos and family anecdotes. I began to seek collections and resources that might contain these recordings. Unfortunately, in 1976, this material was very difficult for a non-credentialed low-income rural person to access.

As time and life went on, I became more confident that music was my calling and developed a career as a songwriter and singer of songs particularly from the Anglo-Celtic tradition. Always researching and seeking connections between the contemporary and the ancient, I developed relationships with others on the same quest. Somewhere along the way, and I honestly don't remember when or how, I acquired a copy of *British Ballads from Maine* by Phillips Barry, Fanny Eckstorm and Mary Smyth, published in 1929. This was a pivotal, revolutionary event that justified all the work I had done and hoped to do.

Upon devouring this tome, I realized that Fanny Eckstorm and her friend Mary Smyth were forces to be reckoned with. I subsequently found their previous book, *Minstrelsy of Maine* in which they clearly outline their mission to document the ballads of ordinary people, made directly from their own experiences or those around them. Collectors have sometimes viewed the songs themselves as trophies. Like some genealogists looking for golden apples on the family tree, they value them only for the "proof" they provide of an aristocratic past. To them, the singers are merely vehicles and as such the collectors have neglected to record their specific biographies. In many cases, we only know the singer's name, the location and date of the recording event. Eckstorm and Smyth sought to honor the singers who, as messengers from an earlier time, brought these songs forward to help us understand their lives and those of previous generations. Many of them were people the women knew personally in their own community. Phillips Barry recognized the importance of this and supported their efforts to publish which had been denied them as women. Inspired by this encouragement, they ranged throughout Maine, networking with various sources, all the while performing the social duties expected of the women of their time in spite of personal tragedy or limitation. Elsewhere, Helen Hartness Flanders and later, Eloise Linscott took up the torch and expanded the quest into the rest of New England. They corresponded with Eckstorm and Smyth, comparing versions and sources. It was these women who did the lioness's share of field work in the area. Phillips Barry did some work himself but was largely an enthusiastic promoter and provider of resources. In the work of these women, not only documenting the songs themselves but valuing the people who sang them, I hear the voice of my Uncle Frank on my grandfather's recording. There were later collectors in Maine who worked under the tutelage of Dr. Edward (Sandy) Ives out of the Maine Folklife Center in Orono, but the early work, pre-1950, was most inspirational to me because of the dedication of the collectors and the obstacles they had to surmount. It also represents material which is less influenced by the popular media which has since replaced vernacular culture.

As much as I loved, and still love, the "root music" of the old world, it struck me that these newer manifestations are equally valid for what they tell us about changes in social priorities and human response to historic events and environment. I began corresponding with fellow musicians in Scotland, several of whom were regarded as traditional music "vectors" in Dumfries and Galloway. They became intrigued when I sent them copies of songs that had been contributed to Fanny Eckstorm by Mrs. James McGill whose family had come from that region. Several of the songs were unique versions that were no longer sung there. Our friends wanted to include these in a local school project about emigration but needed more information about Mrs. McGill and her journey to America. My partner, Fred Gosbee, and I approached Pauleena MacDougall who was then director of the Maine Folklife Center, asking if she had any more information than was included in *British Ballads from Maine*. Coincidentally, Dr. MacDougall was working on editing Eckstorm's second volume which had been missing for 70 years. She was also curious, especially since Mrs. Eckstorm identified the singer only as "Mrs. James McGill" and not by her given name! We decided to do a road trip to archives in the museum just across the Canadian border in St. Andrews, New Brunswick, close to Mrs. McGill's hometown of Chamcook. Upon arriving at the museum we were greeted by the director, Marguerite Garnet. We had informed her of our mission and expected to be shown a file of documents (this was before the internet). Ms. Garnet made a phone call and then informed us that we would need to "go to another building." We followed quizzically as she led us down several back streets to a small house. As she knocked on the door, she announced "Well, her name was Margaret Waterston, and this is her daughter, Betty!" The door was opened by an an elderly woman who invited us in. She was amazed and delighted that anyone would be interested in her mother and her songs. Betty was a small girl when Fanny Eckstorm had arrived with her recording equipment and remembered being banished from the room while her mother sang "The Trooper and the Maid" as it was deemed unseemly for young ears. She provided many details of both her parents' lives and the sources of their songs. Unfortunately, none of us had thought to bring a recording device as we never imagined we would find a live source! Pauleena valiantly scribbled notes as Betty talked, and we vowed to return to record her. Sadly, she passed away before we could do that. Fred and I were able to take Margaret Waterston McGill's songs back to her home country where we taught them to the children of Dumfries and Galloway. It seems that Margaret had retained some songs that had been lost in the region! The kids then performed them in a gala concert honoring the emigrants who had sought their fortune in America. As sad as I was to miss recording Betty, the experience reinforced my mission to bring the songs and singers to the attention of the present generation.

Much of Eckstorm's work, particularly, appears only as text manuscript as she was not able to transcribe the tunes. *Minstrelsy of Maine* contains only lyrics. As a musician, I have felt compelled to re-integrate the music with the lyrics as it completes the ballad's purpose by providing a landscape for the lyrics. Ethnomusicologist Georg Herzog, a friend of Phillips Barry, did transcriptions for *British Ballads from Maine* but I have only located a fraction of the other tunes. Until recently, it was almost impossible to gain access to the source recordings made by various collectors before the advent of audio tape. Thankfully innovations in technology have made them available, albeit on a limited basis, as institutions are variously welcoming. Strangely, history seems to be repeating itself as I have tried to navigate the rapid changes in media and format without losing information! How frustrating it must have been to have to learn to use different kinds of recording equipment in the many different environments where singers were found. The patience of the collectors as they respectfully interviewed and encouraged their informants is evident and laudable. They obviously valued not only the material but the people presenting it. In listening to the field recordings transcribed in this book, as difficult as they are to physically hear and understand, I have felt the presence of the singers not only when they sang for the collectors, but as they communicate with me. I somehow feel them urging me to carry on the legacy they embody, reminding us of the value of their personal experience. There are still many which are not available. I look forward to someday listening to, and perhaps learning, those which I have not yet been able to hear.

I am deeply indebted to so many for their direction and inspiration but most especially to Fred Gosbee without whom, truly, none of this would have been possible.

Julia Lane
Round Pond, ME
May 20, 2021

Introduction

Music has always been important part of daily life for all people both at work and leisure. Singing, in particular, is not only an avenue for self-expression and shared experience, but a kind of social glue. In addition, the songs sung by and about people preserve much of what we know about their lives, their lore and history. The transfer of these songs through generations reveals much about social priorities, morality and lifestyles. Lyrics and melodies are retained or adapted according to the times through which they pass. Some withstand the rigors of time and are a testament to the strength of their story or the enduring beauty of the music.

Culture is honed and refined by the movement of people, changing resources, and the passage of time. As populations re-locate, both the home culture and the experiences of the immigrants in their new home inform their family stories, songs, and folkways. These folk traditions give us a window into the lives and concerns of our ancestors. They also enrich our perspective of our own lives and our relationships to each other and our environment.

The songs collected in the northeast of North America are sometimes more closely connected to their origins across the Atlantic than those in other regions of the country since the people who brought them came earlier to this continent. There are also versions that reflect both the seafaring and woods logging traditions of the area, imbuing a distinct regional personality. The often timeless subject matter allows us to see ourselves in a broader human context. We can consider how, and how much, our lives and culture have changed or stayed the same since these songs came to Maine. Both the singer and the listener can reflect upon how things have changed or stayed the same as well as the similarities and differences between cultures. We connect not only across the centuries and geographic boundaries but also across contemporary socio-economic divisions. We believe that publication of these songs is important to illustrate and promote understanding of both the threads of cultural individuality and the weave of community with other regions.

In writing this book, our goal was to create a songbook, not an archive. Our intention is to create a resource for singers, educators, and folk music enthusiasts to help carry forward the traditions interrupted by modern media. The educational value of these songs is indisputable. They can easily enhance an integrated curriculum as well as entertain an audience. We believe that content which is interesting, engaging, educational and accessible will assure the transfer of the songs. Notably, the sources were largely unaccompanied and it is evident that it is the song itself that is important, not the accompaniment. Individual singers added fascinating nuances, creating a personal style. We have not provided accompaniment, though this may incorporated in the presentation of the song. The singer is encouraged to be inspired by the songs, make them their own, and pass them on.

Julia Lane gleaned these songs from various historical collections and manuscripts made in Maine before 1950 to reduce the influence from radio and popular recordings. We have examined hundreds of journals, newspapers, letters, logs, audio recordings — even a genealogy! It is an Anglo-Celtic collection, not by design or prejudice, but for lack of collected material from other traditions. We are also presenting those not previously published with both words and melodies. A complete list of documented titles and sources is printed in an appendix.

As singers and storytellers ourselves, we feel it is important to not only honor a source, but also the singer who passes it along, the audience who receives it and the story itself. With that in mind, we have selected representative versions to create an engaging but usable resource, seeking complete stories and tunes with musical integrity. This process of restoring, or "mending" as Robert Burns called it, is time honored and, indeed, part of the folk process. It is this process that created the rich variations which we find in the genre. In his introduction to *The Maine Woods Songster* (1937), esteemed folklorist Phillips Barry said: "In preparation of a scientific work, the editor must publish his recordings exactly as they were taken down from singer or reciter... The editor of a practical work, however, has the right and is under the duty to make both singable and understandable the songs he edits... to fill a 'hole in the ballad' or to make sense of nonsense."

The mutation of material through this "folk process" presents several challenges. We often find renditions of songs within these collections that have differences in lyrics and melodies, although the story itself remains recognizable. Some are regional, with the song varying according to location, and some are personal reflections of the singer's own experience, memory, or bias. In all cases, if the song in the archive was incomplete, we sought other versions, from the same locale as the source if possible, to complete the story or to provide an appropriate tune where needed. The singers' own words remain as intact as possible. The accompanying comments note any additions from other sources. We retained archaic language where it occurs, as well as some of the pronunciation such as "love-lye" rather than "lovely." Regarding profanity, such filtering seems to have been done by previous collectors and even the singers themselves, perhaps because most collectors were women. In addition, overt racist language is rare.

In the written manuscripts, collectors have sometimes assumed these verses to be poetry composed by the writer. Closer scrutiny, and knowledge of the genre, reveals that they are existing songs recorded by the writer as a reflection of their experience. In his book *Songs the Whalemen Sang*, collector Gale Huntington presents a wealth of these extracted from journals kept on long voyages. Although some are personal creations, most are either lyrics from songs important to the writer or parodies of songs known to them. Singers commonly kept small notebooks containing their favorite song lyrics to use for reference. Although these verses were meant to be sung, tunes were rarely transcribed, probably due to space constraints or the inability to write the music. Sometimes a melody is designated on the page, in which case we can find it from other sources. If not, we matched the words with another musical version of the song found as geographically close to the source as possible or used a historically appropriate tune.

The audio recordings have their issues, not only regarding the quality of the sound but also the technology on which the content is recorded and played. Initially, mechanical recordings were made as vibrations were incised on wax cylinders, aluminum discs, or wire devices. Many parallel techniques were developed and applied to different situations, introducing their own idiosyncrasies. Portability was a factor in making field recordings. Various collectors used different devices throughout their careers, resulting in an assortment of recorded media. Through time, recordings have become compromised from being transferred through further changes in technology and delivery systems. The environment has affected the media with heat, cold, dust, and age reducing the clarity of the originals. Interpretation of the indistinct sound is a challenge. Sometimes, our transcriptions vary from those previously done as we hear words, phrasing, and references not familiar to other transcribers from different backgrounds. Finally, inefficient documentation has reduced the integrity of the collections.

And then, there are the singers themselves. In the face of rapid change in the late 19th and early 20th century, collectors tried to preserve a tradition that was, itself, fading. The singers were often elderly, selected as a source because the collectors believed their versions of the songs would be more historically valuable. However, their voices and memories are not always strong and clear, and their accents and archaic use of language are often inscrutable. Keys wander as the singer becomes tired. The songs preserved on these recordings display a range of diversity as each individual interpreted the piece. Differentiating style, ornament, and interpretation from fatigue or forgetfulness is sometimes a challenge. One man, who recorded a song at two different times, used completely different tunes while retaining the same lyrics. On another recording, a woman changed tunes four times during the singing of one song. Still another man uses the same tune for all the songs he sings! Again, quoting Phillips Barry, regarding the singer of folk songs, "Acting in response to the universal instinct of man to sing, he takes them as he finds them, and makes them his own, shaping them according to the subconscious dictates of his own fancy."* We might also note here the 18th-century tradition of improvisation in the interpretation of music. The myriad of printed collections of tunes and songs meant for the "talented amateur" clearly leave the tempo and accompaniment to the discretion of the musician with directions like "faster for dancing; slower for singing." Like Robert Burns and Thomas Moore, poets would often use popular tunes as a vehicle for their words, and church hymnals adapted well-known melodies for the word of God. In addition, lyrics vary between one publication and another. So, there is a precedent, beyond personal ability and memory, to adapt a song for contemporary use.

All of these factors have produced a flawed and incomplete but intriguing documentation of social heritage. We are sometimes left only with shadows and whispers beckoning across time. We have tried to clarify these faded images in the same way a photo is retouched to bring it into focus. We only claim copyright on our transcriptions of the songs and have tried to be clear about changes made to them, giving credit to sources as we know them. Readers may be interested in seeing or hearing alternate or original versions of these songs. They are welcome to contact us or can refer to the supplemental and source materials in the appendices at the end of the book.

* "The Transmission of Folk-Song," Phillips Barry, *The Journal of American Folklore*, Vol. 27, No. 103 (Jan.–Mar. 1914), pp. 67–76.

About the Sources

During the latter part of the 19th century and in the early 20th, people became aware of the value of vernacular songs and began collecting and cataloguing them. The most famous collection, *The English and Scottish Popular Ballads*, was compiled by Frances James Child and published between 1892 and 1898. The contents became known as "Child Ballads" and are a standard to which other collections are compared. In Maine, two women, Fanny Hardy Eckstorm and Mary Winslow Smyth, who were inspired by Child's work, became very active collectors in the early 20th century. Fanny traveled with her father, a fur trader, through the inland woods camps while Mary worked on the coast finding a wealth of ballads in that region. As neither woman was a musician, their volume *Minstrelsy of Maine* (1927) contains only lyrics. Their work attracted the attention of Harvard professor Dr. Phillips Barry and together they collaborated to publish a collection of Maine versions of Child ballads called *British Ballads from Maine* in 1929. A second volume, latent for 80 years, was recently edited and updated by Dr. Pauleena MacDougall of the University of Maine and musician Fred Gosbee. It was published in 2011 by the Maine Folklife Center in Orono, ME.

During their collecting journeys in Maine, Eckstorm, Smyth, and many others found numerous other vernacular songs which do not fit Francis Child's criteria yet are interesting in their depiction of personal and community experience. Songs about epic weather events, murders, marriage, victories and defeats make the stories in modern media pale by comparison. These songs appear not only in the manuscripts made by collectors, but also in journals, letters and newspapers of the time. Small volumes of lyrics called "chapbooks" or "songsters" were popular in the personal libraries of farmers, sailors and woodsmen who would sometimes refer to them while singing. Some of these survive in the archives of the many historical societies throughout the state. Local stories written in rhyme and set to music can also be found. Eckstorm and Smyth shared these with Phillips Barry and together they founded the Ballad Society of the Northeast which published a journal featuring their findings. Many of the songs appear in their book *Minstrelsy of Maine*. Barry also compiled *The Maine Woods Songster* which "mended" versions of songs collected by Eckstorm and Smyth. Credit must also be given to one of their informants, Susie Carr Young of Brewer, who contributed a wealth of personal family songs – many dating back to the 18th century – as well as helping to track down source singers.

In the meantime, Joanna Colcord of Searsport published her book *Songs of American Sailormen* in 1924 which documented the songs she heard while onboard her father's ship as it traveled the globe. Although most of her songs are from the international crews that worked the ship and cannot be classified as strictly Maine songs, she does include several collected by Eckstorm and Smyth. Another collector, Roland Palmer Gray, head of the English Department at the University of Maine Orono, published his anthology *Songs and Ballads of the Maine Lumberjacks* the same year and also includes some of Eckstorm's findings.

Through her association with Phillips Barry, Mrs. Eckstorm became acquainted with Helen Hartness Flanders, a collector from Vermont. Flanders had established a newspaper column in her hometown newspaper, the *Springfield Union*, which solicited contributions of folksongs from readers. She inspired Eckstorm to publish a similar column in the *Bangor Daily News* which included material collected in Vermont as examples of the songs she sought. These articles became a forum for people to send in those they knew and to discuss them. This collaboration inspired Flanders and her partner Marguerite Olney, who previously had been working in Vermont, to expand their search to Maine. Flanders and Olney went on to record some 900 songs in the state adding to their vast collection of New England music. This amazing work is currently housed at Middlebury College in Middlebury, VT. For her part, Eckstorm envisioned an eventual "continuous district" with collectors throughout the Northeast, including Canada, working "sympathetically."* Although there have been various institutions established for the purpose of documenting folksongs throughout the region, full cooperation has yet to be achieved.

Some songs have been preserved by the families themselves as in *The Kneeland Miscellany*, written in 1917 by Frank and Bertha Kneeland of Searsport, and *A Heritage of Song* (1955) by Carrie Grover of Gorham. The *Miscellany* is, in fact, a very entertaining genealogy which includes 100 songs sung throughout their lives by Frank's parents James and Amanda. There are songs for every occasion, some learned at the "singing schools" of the day, some on the battlefields of the Civil War, onboard ship, or at home with the family on the farm. The music notation is not included because it was assumed that everyone knew the melodies. The presence of these songs in the context of their daily lives is a testament to the pervasiveness of vernacular song in the community. Carrie Grover's book reflects a similar experience, including songs from both sides of her family, ranging from tragedy to mirth, history to fiction. Happily, Mrs. Grover, being also a fiddler, provides the tunes. In both of these collections, there is very little of a religious nature, possibly because the pervasive religious traditions of the time and region reserved these songs for the Lord's Day.

It is interesting to note that, with the exception of Carrie Grover, virtually none of the collectors were themselves musicians and their attempts at transcription of the tunes is often inscrutable. Early on, Barry arranged for the help of noted ethnomusicologist George Herzog in transcribing while in the field. Later, recording machines were acquired and transcriptions were made after the fact by Samuel Bayard. These are meticulous and often obscure the melody in an effort to chronicle the style of the singer. In his introduction to his collection of transcriptions, he eloquently described his understanding of the traditional singers' style and the difficulty in transcribing an ephemeral art. Helen Flanders' publications relied on Marguerite Olney for the transcription duties while Eloise Linscott engaged friends to create simple arrangements for publication.

---

* Fannie Hardy Eckstorm, interviewed by Miles L. Hanley, Associate Director of the Linguistic Atlas of New England, in the summer of 1934. NA1297.

These manuscripts and recordings are archived in several places. Much of the original work of Eckstorm and Smyth was in possession of Phillips Barry at the time of his death in 1937 and is included in his collection at the Houghton Library at Harvard and the Library of Congress. The Fogler Library at the University of Maine in Orono holds Fanny Eckstorm's personal papers, which include those of Mary Smyth. Roland Palmer Gray's work is also there while Joanna Colcord's papers are at the Penobscot Marine Museum in Searsport. Helen Flanders' entire collection is at Middlebury College in Middlebury, VT and the raw audio files can be found online at Archive.org. The recordings of Horace Beck can be found at the Library of Congress, while his papers and dissertation are at various other libraries. Dr. Edward "Sandy" Ives' recordings and papers can be found both at the Library of Congress and the Maine Folklife Center in Orono, ME which he founded. Carrie Grover was recorded by Alan Lomax as well as Eloise Linscott and their work is at the Library of Congress. Linscott's other recordings and papers are also available there. Grover's work is now showcased in a new interactive website created by Julie Mainstone Savas (https://carriegroverproject.com/) and PDF copies of each song in her collection, as well as some original recordings can be heard there.

In addition, there are personal journals, letters, chapbooks, local newspapers, and publications archived in historical societies and slumbering in family attics which continually yield delights and surprises! We would be grateful for any that the reader would care to share with us.

The Songs

The Sea Ballads

Songs and stories about seafaring have a timeless and universal appeal. Our earliest bardic sagas have intrepid ocean journeys at the core of the plot. The lore of island nations, such as the British Isles and Ireland, is enriched by this theme and so it is not surprising to find a wealth of these songs in the tradition of people with that ancestry. The songs presented here are "ballads" or story songs gathered from the singing of ordinary people, songs that eased the tedium of isolation both at sea and on shore. Rather than the curt and rhythmical shanties that helped coordinate arduous work, these are melodious and romantic, often epic tales of human endeavor, both tragic and humorous.

Maritime culture and experience are integrated into the fabric of New England's history and lore. Much of the region's lingo, in fact, includes terms and references to things nautical. People are asked to "hit the deck" to make something "ship-shape," or "hang onto the rigging" in case they go to "wrack and ruin." If a person is "between wind and water," they might "plumb the depths" to "sound out" the situation and make sure everything is "above board." The sea and its elemental mystery, as well humanity's experience with it, provide a setting for compelling stories, which, in the folk tradition, form the basis for songs and ballads passed between populations and generations. In collections of songs made in the Northeast are found not only vernacular songs of personal tragedy and triumph, but also ancient ballads of romance and intrigue, many of which have references to the sea and life upon it. In the case of the older ballads, these were often passed down through generations of families as oral heirlooms, reminding people of their ancestors' connections with the sea.

Although those who were directly engaged with the maritime economy made and enjoyed songs related to their livelihood, these songs also appear throughout the region, on the coast as well as inland and in the mountains. While ocean travel provided connection with the world at large and all it had to offer, the romance of this notion also fueled the imagination of those less able to enjoy its reality. In addition to their timeless entertainment appeal, the sharing of these songs was partially a result of seasonal migration between shore and forest. Seamen jumped ship and fishermen hauled their boats to go work in the lumberwoods during the winter, taking their songs and stories with them. Then, in the spring, a reverse migration occurred as people left the woods and came to the shore, taking to the sea again. As the singers migrated, the songs were a commodity exchanged between ship's fo'c'sles, logging camps, and home kitchens. Friends and family would gather to hear a new song then carry it with them to another venue, renewing that mysterious bond with the sea and those who venture out on it. Interestingly, we have found very few, if any, songs which originated in the woods passing into the tradition of the seafaring community.

As time has passed, new technology and lifestyles have made us less dependent on seafaring. Yet the sea itself still intrigues us and the adventures of those who have engaged with it still provoke romance and inspiration. Simply, the stories of the experience of humans in an elemental environment are as timeless as love and loss, tragedy and hope. These songs provide a window into those journeys and adventures of heart and spirit.

The Jolly Sailors

Oliver Jenness, York, ME 1941
Helen Hartness Flanders Collection
Transcription © 2019 Julia Lane

I dearly love the hearts so bold and the truth to you I'll write
And plowing the ocean true is all my heart's delight.
I hate the sight of a landlubber who will always stay at home
And a-workin' in the cornfield is all that he can do, do,
Is all that he can do.

And when the sun goes down at night they eat beside their plow
And they say "We can no longer work so it's home we will go now,"
And when they do get home at night they tell the girls sad tales
Of the long and tedious job they've had a-digging grass and weeds, weeds,
A-digging grass and weeds.

And when darkness does come on it's into bed they'll crawl
While we poor jolly sailors stand many a bitter squall.
And when the wind begins to blow and darkness then comes on
Our captain he cries out "Brave boys, all up from down below, below!"
All up from down below!

And when we do all crowd on deck our goodly ship to guard
Our captain he cries out "Brave boys, down with topgallant yards!"
But when we do get on the shore we make the taverns roar.
And when our money is all gone we'll go to sea for more, more,
We'll go to sea for more.

Given the migratory quality of the Maine workforce from the sea to the farm or the woods, it is interesting to find a song like this that pokes fun at the landsman. A timeless subject, we can trace the theme to several ballads from the 1600s such as "In Praise of Saylors" circa 1630 or "The Fair Maid's Choice or The Seaman's Renown" from 1650. Others from Maine include "The Sailor's Come-All-Ye" and "The Schooner Fred Dunbar." We have adjusted the verses to accommodate the uneven lines sung by Mr. Jenness.

The Sailor's Come-All-Ye

Susie Carr Young, Brewer, ME 1925
Fannie Hardy Eckstorm Collection
Tune collected by Gale Huntington
Transcription © 2019 Julia Lane

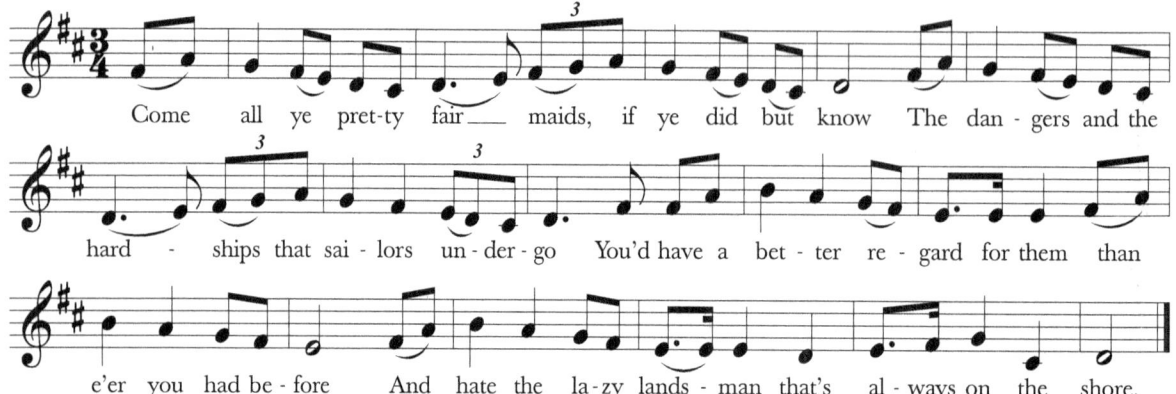

Come all ye pretty fair maids, if ye did but know
The dangers and the hardships that sailors undergo
You'd have a better regard for them than e'er you had before
And hate the lazy landsman, that's always on the shore.

They are always with the pretty girls, telling to them fine tales,
Concerning all the hard day's work that's done in their cornfields;
'Tis pulling of the weeds and grass, 'tis all that they do know,
While we, like jovial seamen, boys, go plow the ocean through.

Soon as the sun it does go down, aside they'll throw their plow,
Saying, "Our day's work's done, me boys, no more we will do now."
Soon as the night is dark as pitch, 'tis into bed they'll crawl,
While we, like jovial seamen, boys, stand many a bitter squall.

Soon as eight o'clock it does come on, the winds begin to blow,
Our Captain he commands us all: "All hands from there below!
All hands from there below, my boys, stand by our ship to guard!
Aloft, aloft, me lively lads, send down th' t'gans'l yard!"

The seas they run full mountains high and toss us up and down,
In the midst of all these dangers we are 'fraid our ship will drown;
But don't let that discourage us, boys, we'll see the girls again,
For the might of all America, we'll cross the raging main.

We'll sail to all parts of the world that ever yet was known,
We'll bring back gold and silver, 'tis when we do return;
We'll make our country flourish, me boys, more'n ever it did before,
And when our money's all spent and gone, we'll cross the seas for more.

Susie Carr Young heard this from her grandmother who died at age 75 in 1868. She contributed it to Fannie Eckstorm who printed the words in her *Minstrelsy of Maine* in 1927. Joanna C. Colcord published the words in *Songs of American Sailormen* (Norton, 1924, 1938) p. 137. Also called "Hearts of Gold," the tune was collected by Gale Huntington, who found the words in an 1832 journal of the Salem whale ship *Bengal*. It is another of the career songs descended from "In Praise of Saylors" circa 1630 or "The Fair Maid's Choice or The Seaman's Renown" printed in *Thomas Lanfiere's Bagford Ballads* 1650–74. Other songs of this lineage include "The Jolly Sailors" (Oliver Jenness) and "The Schooner *Fred Dunbar*" (Amos Hanson).

A Sailor Walking in His Garden

Albert E. Conray, Ellsworth, ME 5/14/1942
Helen Hartness Flanders Collection
Transcription © 2016 Julia Lane

A sailor walking all in his garden,
A pretty fair damsel he chanced to spy.
He stepped up to her the more to view her
Saying "Fair lady, can't you fancy I?"

"I have a sailor out on the ocean
And seven long years he's been gone from me
And seven more I will wait for him
And if he's alive he'll return to me."

"If seven long years he's been gone from you
He must be dead or else he's lost!"
"Oh, if he's alive I dearly love him
And if he is dead I'm in hopes he's at rest."

He put his hands all in his pocket,
His fingers being both neat and small.
He pulled out the ring that was broke between them
And when she saw it, oh, she down did fall.

He picked her up all in his arms;
He gave her kisses one, two and three
Saying, "I am your own beloved young sailor
Just lately returned from the raging sea!"

Oh, now she is living with her sailor
And she has got her heart's delight
And she rides out and takes her pleasure
Dressed in her silk from morn till night.

Most often this is sung as "The Fair Maid All in her Garden" or "Long Lost Johnny Reilly" and is commonly found in collections from the 19th century. Except for the first line, these words are pretty much identical to those songs. Mr. Conray must have felt it was important for the sailor to have a garden (and house?) of his own in which to live happily with his sweetheart.

The *Flying Cloud*

Harry Cole, Springfield ME 3/1934
Fannie Hardy Eckstorm Collection
Jack McNally, Stacyville, ME 7/11/1942
Tune; Jerry Desmond, Bridgewater, ME 7/11/1940
Helen Hartness Flanders Collection
Transcription © 2018 Julia Lane

My name is Edward Hallahan as you may understand.
I belong in the county of Waterford in Erin's happy land.
When I was young and in my prime kind fortune on me smiled.
My parents doted on me, I being their only child.

My father bound me to a trade in Waterford's old town,
He bound me to a cooper there by the name of William Brown.
I served my master faithfully for eighteen months or more,
When I shipped on board the *Ocean Queen* bound for Bermuda's shore.

When I reached Bermuda shore I fell in with Captain Moore,
Commander of the *Flying Cloud* belonging to Trimore.
So kindly he requested me on a slaving voyage to go,
To the burning sands of Africa where the sugar cane doth grow.

The *Flying Cloud* was as fine a ship as ever swam the seas,
Or ever hoisted a main topsail before a lively breeze.
Her sails were like the drifting snow on them there was no stain,
And eighteen brass nine-pounder guns she carried abaft her main.

Oh, the *Flying Cloud* was a Spanish ship of five hundred tons or more,
She would outsail any other ship I ever saw before.
I have oftentimes seen our gallant ship as the wind lay abaft her wheel,
With the royal and the skysail set aloft sail nineteen by the reel.

We sailed away without delay till we came to the African shore,
And eighteen hundred of those poor slaves from their native Isle sailed o'er.
For we marched them all along our decks and stored them down below,
And eighteen inches for a man was all we could allow.

The very next day we sailed away with our cargo of slaves,
'Twould have been much better for those poor souls had they been in their graves;
For the plague and fever came on board and swept half of them away;
We dragged the dead up on the decks and threw them in the sea.

We sailed away without delay till we came to the Cuban shore.
We sold them to a planter there to be slaves forevermore;
The rice and coffee fields to hoe beneath the burning sun,
To lead a long and wretched life till their career was run.

And when our money it was all gone we put to sea again.
Then Captain Moore he came on board and said to us, his men:
"There is gold and silver to be had if with me you will remain:
We will hoist aloft a pirate's flag and we'll scour the raging main!"

We all agreed, excepting five and those we had to land,
Two of them being Boston men and two from Newfoundland.
The other was an Irishman belonging to Trimore,
Oh, I wish to God I had joined those men and returned with them on shore.

We robbed and plundered many a ship all on the Spanish Main,
And many's the widow and orphan child in sorrow must remain,
For we made their crews to walk the plank and gave them a watery grave;
For the saying of our captain was: "A dead man tells no tales."

Chased we were by many a ship down on the Spanish Main
By frigates and by men-o'-war, liners and brigantines.
They poured their hot shot after us; their cannons roared full loud
'Twas all in vain, none on the Main could outsail the *Flying Cloud*.

'Twas then we spied a British ship, her dungeon holes* in view.   [the *Diogenes* hove]
She fired a shot across our bows, a signal to heave to
We paid to her no answer but flew before the wind
When a chain shot cut our mizzenmast we were forced to fall behind.

"Prepare for action!" was the word as she drew up 'longside
And soon acrost our quarterdeck there ran a crimson tide.
We fought till Captain Moore was slain and eighty of our men,
When a bombshell set our ship on fire. We were forced to surrender then.

At length to Newgate we were brought, bound down in iron chain,
For robbing and plundering merchant ships down on the Spanish Main.
It was drinking and bad company that made this wretch of me,
Now, let young men a warning take and a curse to piracy!

So fare you well you green shady bowers and the girl I left behind
Whose voice like music in my ears is ringing in my mind.
I shall never kiss her ruby lips nor squeeze her lily-white hand,
But I must die a scornful death in a strange and foreign land.   [last two words spoken]

* In verse 13 the odd term "dungeon holes" appears in several versions. The meaning of this was unfamiliar to all maritime historians we contacted but some versions have the line as "the Dungeon hove in view." In 1926, retired seaman Joseph Mc-Ginnis contacted collector R. W. Gordon about *The Flying Cloud* saying "I gave Miss J.C. Colcord the words and music… The name of the man-o'-war I gave her was the *Dungeness*. I thought at the time it was the wrong name. I have come to the conclusion since that it was the *Diogenes*." Given this, we have chosen to offer the name as an alternative lyric. Interestingly,

Songs of Ships & Sailors

there was, in fact, a slave ship called *Diogenes* in 1836 that was captured by the British ship *Leveret* but this event doesn't fit the story of the song.

We found the reference to "liners" in verse twelve to be puzzling, but it turns out that ships called liners were in service by 1837. They were initially sailing ships with auxiliary power, then steamships with auxiliary sails, and finally, by the end of the 19th century, steamships with no sails.

Although there is no definitive record of the actual ship and the characters, and there is some thought that it may actually combine two earlier songs. Joseph McGinnis contributed the song to collector Joanna Colcord saying he had learned it in 1883 in the ship's foc'sle. It also became a favorite in the lumber camps of the Northeast. We have nine Maine versions and it was recorded by all the collectors represented in this collection. Horace Beck wrote an extensive essay about *The Flying Cloud* in his unpublished thesis.

In the days when a singer's place as storyteller was highly valued, this song was a favorite to pass a long evening. Indeed, *The Flying Cloud* was a *tour de force* of many singers and would prove their worth to the gathering. It has all the epic elements required for this high status in the repertoire. Though versions vary, there is surprising consistency of detail from one to the other. We have created a composite and have used Mr. Desmond's tune as it is unusual, being completely different from the common one. The speaking of the last line is a common practice in ballad singing both in New England and Scotland.

We have also included a copy of the usual tune as transcribed by Samuel Bayard in his attempt to notate Mr. Frank Tracy's singing style as an example of the ornaments and liberties taken by a traditional singer. After the death of Phillips Barry in 1937, Samuel Bayard took on the task of transcribing the recordings made by Barry. The following, regarding the process of transcription, is quoted from *Folk Tunes from the Phillips Barry Collection*; transcribed from Dictaphone recordings by S. P. Bayard, Harvard College Library, June 1942.

> "…no written record can convey the really essential qualities of traditional singing; the smooth melodic flow, combined with vigorous rhythmical force and frequently interrupted by sudden, effective pauses; the deliberate and "uncircumscribed" manner of delivery; and the peculiar slight emphasis on occasional tones which bring out their full melodic value—all these combining with the ornamental turns introduced by individual singers to produce an effect which cannot be learned from paper.… Each of these transcriptions is meant to furnish a record (as nearly complete as possible) of an individual's rendition of a folk air."

To illustrate his point, here is Bayard's attempt to capture the ornamented singing of Frank L. Tracy of Brewer, ME. (1932)

Adieu Ye Banks & Braes of Clyde

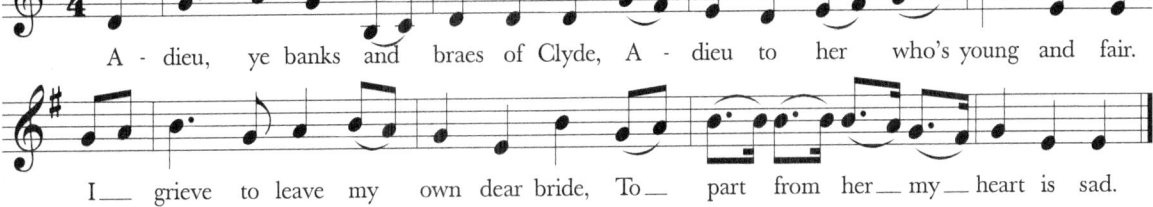

Adieu, ye banks and braes of Clyde,
Adieu to her who's young and fair.
I grieve to leave my own dear bride,
To part from her my heart is sad.

CHORUS:
    I grieve to leave my comrades all,
    I grieve to leave my native shore.
    My aged parents I do adore,
    And my bonnie, bonnie lassie on the banks of Clyde.

My barque is hauled out in the bay,
The wind blows fair; I must away,
Away to sail o'er the briny deep.
Adieu ye banks and braes of Clyde.

The sun is sinking in the west,
The birds sit on the mulberry tree,
All Nature seems prepared for rest
But alas, there's none prepared for me.

The drums do beat and the warpipes play,
The signal's given; I must away,
Away to sail o'er the deep blue sea,
Farewell ye banks and braes of Clyde.

This song is reminiscent of the popular "Farewell to Nova Scotia," sharing a similar tune and some lyrics. Both songs can be traced to "The Soldier's Adieu," a late 18th century Scottish folk song first printed in 1803 in a Glasgow newspaper and attributed to Robert Tannahill. No doubt Scottish immigrants to Maine and Maritime Canada brought the song with them. Frank Kneeland recorded the songs he heard from his father, James.

The Capture of the *Crown*

Henry Chamberlain, Round Pond, ME 1929
Phillips Barry Collection
Adaptation © 2010 Fred Gosbee
Tune: Traditional
Transcription © 2018 Fred Gosbee

On the twenty-sixth of April, or so it does appear,
The brave boys of Bristol fitted out a privateer
In command of Captain Tucker, a sloop both neat and trim,
And we set out to sail the seas all for to take the *Bream*.

CHORUS:
 So, cheer up me lively lads and never be it said
 The brave boys of Bristol were ever yet afraid!

We cruised the shores for several days and nothing did appear
At length our brave commander resolved to homeward steer.
It was on a Friday morning, and clear was the sky
And as we were returning, a sail we did espy.

Then up rose our bold commander and to his men did say
"My boys, be all stout-hearted and do not fail today!
Our enemy's before us and after her we'll run
For I'm resolved to take her before the setting sun."

Then we bore away for her and up to her did come
We hauled down our foresail and gave her a gun.
'Twas broadside and broadside we showed her Yankee play
'Til our enemy got frightened and tried to run away.

We shot away their halliards and down their colors come
We drove them from their quarters and down below they run.
Their captain he stepped forward and waving of his hand
He cried "I must surrender; this I can no longer stand!"

We tried to bind her to our lee but much to our chagrin
We found we had no grappling hook to seize and pull her in
'Til Collamore stepped up and swung the anchor o'er his head
"Captain, shall I let her fly?" The Bremen Monster said.

Then we heisted out our boats and on board of her did go
We made them all prisoners and ordered them below
We heisted Yankee colors and hauled the British down
And when we did examine her, she proved to be the *Crown*.

"Now," says our brave commander "we'll bring our prize ashore
For we're the boys that fear no noise, tho' cannons loudly roar!
And quickly we will clear the coast of all these British boys
For we will fight 'em till we die, and never mind their noise!"

Now we have fought this privateer till she is overcome.
And God bless Captain Tucker this day for what he's done!
Likewise his officers and all his jolly crew
God grant that they may prosper in everything they do!

During the War of 1812, the Maine coast saw much maritime action due to the area's proximity to then British Canada. Local men were pressed into service by the British, farms and supplies were raided and smuggling was rampant. One ship in particular, the *Bream*, was raising havoc by burning the ships it captured. In Bristol, the citizens of the town decided to take matters into their own hands and mustered the sloop *Increase* and crew to be commanded by local hero Commodore Samuel Tucker. A highly successful captain in the Revolutionary War, he had retired to Bremen, and was 66 years old in 1813. His practiced tactic of outmaneuvering his adversary paid off when he won this battle with the British ship *Crown*, fought near Pemaquid in Long Cove. There were only a few volleys of small arms fire during the battle. The British captain surrendered and he and his crew were taken to the jail in Wiscasset. During the transfer, the captain made his escape dressed as a woman.

Embellishing the facts of the conflict, "The Capture of the *Crown*" was written by "a citizen of Bristol" and the text appears in *The Life of Commodore Samuel Tucker*, by John H. Sheppard (Boston, 1868). A version of this song was sung for Phillips Barry by H. H. Chamberlain of Round Pond in 1929. Tucker's granddaughter, then 80 years old, still lived in the village at that time and may have been his source. Local Bristol / Bremen oral history tells of Peter Collamore, aka the "Bremen Monster," using the anchor as a grappling hook. His verse has been added by Fred Gosbee to the original lyric (italics). This tune is an early 19th century version of "The Bonnie Ship the *Diamond*," popular at the time, which fits it perfectly.

The Black Cook

Charles Finnemore, Bridgewater, ME 5/8/1942
Helen Hartness Flanders Collection
Transcription © 2018 Julia Lane

Come all jolly sailors I pray give attention
Concerning a doctor who lived in Cork town,
Who by some young seamen was duly outwitted
And fifty bright guineas was forced to pay down.
There were some jolly tars with their comrades a-grogging,
Their money being spent and their credit far gone;
From Wexford street down to the dock they had wandered
Saying, "We're bound that we'll have some whiskey or fun."

Now the cook of our ship, being a stout able fellow,
A stout able fellow; his color was black.
For wit and for wisdom he always was ready
To find a receipt to get all the change back.

Bygone Ballads of Maine, Volume I

He says, "My brave boys, now, I've heard people saying
A corpse can be sold quite readily here.
Now take me alive, roll me up in me hammock
And sell me to buy us the whiskey and beer."

Now, the sailors being glad to accept of his offer
Away to the town where the doctor did dwell,
And into his ear, so gently did whisper,
Saying "Doctor, we've got a fine corpse for to sell."
"Fine corpse!" cried the doctor, like one in amazement,
"Oh, where did you get him? Come, tell to me, pray!
Go bring him to me; I will buy him quite ready,
And fifty bright guineas to you I will pay!"

Now, the sailors being glad to accept of his offer
Away to the ship they so boldly did steer.
If you pay attention to what I now I mention,
The best of my story you are going to hear.
They took the black cook, rolled him up in his hammock
He being a man both sturdy and strong,
And under his coat, in the way of protection,
They placed a big knife about twelve inches long.

Twelve o'clock it arose and the streets being empty
The sailors set off with the black on their back.
When they came to the room where the doctor resided
It's in a dark room they concealed the poor black.
The doctor he paid the bold seamen their money
They told him the cook he had died while on sea
Rather than to have his dead body to bury,
"We've sold him to you; now he's out of our way."

Now, the doctor went off for his tools to dissect him,
But soon he returned with his saw in his hand.
For when he went up with his knife to dissect him
The black with his cutslash before him did stand.
The doctor was forced to retreat in a hurry
And soon of his bargain began to lament.
The cook he went off with his comrades a-grogging
And the rest of the night it was merrily spent!

We surmise that this song, given the subject matter, predates the U.K. Anatomy Act of 1832. Prior to this time, a corpse for educational dissection could only be legally obtained if the unfortunate person had died without last rites or was executed for a heinous crime. Hence, a specimen was extremely valuable. Coincidentally, since a corpse had no legal status, removal of a body from a grave, or body snatching, was not in itself illegal and providing bodies to researchers this way was a lucrative business. (Only the body was removed from the grave as actual robbing of grave goods was a crime.) In Scotland, the unscrupulous duo Burke and Hare began by selling exhumed bodies then progressed to obtaining bodies by hastening people to their demise. They were eventually apprehended, executed and themselves dissected. Incidents like this, combined with the "Resurrection Riots," which were public reactions to lack of regulation of the body snatchers, led to legislation which facilitated the donation of cadavers by families for science. Eventually the practice of embalming made the freshness of the corpse irrelevant.

Songs of Ships & Sailors

Bold Dighton

Charles Finnemore, Bridgewater, ME 5/7/1942
William Merritt, Ludlow, ME 1941 in italics
Helen Hartness Flanders Collection
Transcription © 2019 Julia Lane

Come all British seamen that plows the rough main,
Pay heed to my ditty, the truth I'll explain.
It's of a misfortune in the sad time of war
And how we escaped the bold French at Basseterre

There were some British seamen, five hundred or more,
Shut up into prison on the Guadeloupe shore;
Shut up in small compass, being sorely distressed
By painful diseases and famine oppressed.

There was a bold hero from Santa Luce came,
He was generous and wealthy, called Dighton by name,
Had the heart of a lion and the soul of a prince,
To us his kind offerings he soon did advance.

He came to our prison, he mourned our sad fate,
Launched out his gold to relieve our sad state;
Five hundred bright guineas he paid out, I am sure,
Which quick did relieve us in that distressed hour.

*At this generous action the French did complain
And they soon bound our hero in fetters and chain
And down in a dungeon with us for to lay
But of his fetters and chains we soon set him free.*

*Then up speaks bold Dighton saying, "You take my advice
If you only prove constant, it'll be done in a trice.
It's down in the harbor the Tiger does lay
She's a stout and fine coaster all fit for the sea!"*

*"Our captain's onshore and there's all things onboard
There's plenty of cannon, pike, pistol and sword.
If you'll only prove constant and stand by my side
We'll board 'er tonight boys and sail the next tide."*

Then out of our prison we all rushed amain!
Two small guns were fired and the French guard was slain
And down to the *Tiger* we all fought our way.
We broke both our cables and ran out to sea.

*It caused a sad rumpus, it being midnight
The Frenchmen bawled out in a terrible fright,
"Mon Dieu! Les Inglis!" Drums beat and bells tolled
While our hero shouted, "Freedom! for each valiant soul!"*

Their batteries being open, then on us did play,
Their shots flew like hail as we got underway.
They shattered our spars as we sailed from the shore
To bid them "good night" we a broadside did pour.

Being out of all danger, we thought ourselves clear
And for that misfortune we paid very dear.
For early next morning the Lion *we spied!*
The Lion, *a corvette, bore down on our side.*

She supplied us with broadside which grieved our hearts sore,
Which caused the fierce *Tiger*'s big guns for to roar!
With twenty-six eighteens the *Lion* did howl,
With eighteen brass nines the *Tiger* did growl.

Broad arms to broad arms in port we did lay
Till at length our broadsides cut their mainmasts away.
"Oh now," says bold Dighton, "If you're tired of this fun,
You've now got your choice boys, to fight or to run!"

But a run from the corvette our crew seemed inclined;
To save blood and slaughter that was their design,
But at that very moment, the grapples did pierce
And then sword and pistol were our only resource.

Then, up spake brave Bold Dighton, like a hero did feel.
His eyes glanced with fury like bright burnished steel
Saying, "Every man's life now depends on his sword!
It's freedom or death, boys let's all jump on board!"

Then over her bulwarks we jumped in a row!
One strike from his broadsword laid three Frenchmen low.
Drums beat and pikes rattled and swords loudly clashed
Till the blood on our deck like salt water did splash.

All the French on their knees and their weapons let fall
It's on us for quarter, oh, then they did call.
We soon gave them quarter at the point of our sword;
In order to save them we took them onboard.

To convey the French home then our Tiger *we gave,*
Our crew being so gen'rous, so valiant and brave,
And down to Antiguo the Lion we bore
And early next morning we all jumped on shore.

"And now," said Bold Dighton, "this battle is o'er!
Let the French learn a lesson and teach it on shore.
Go home to your country, tell your friends be aware
You're better for future each prisoner of war."

Drink a health each seaman, each seaman of fame,
And each crowned with laurels returned home again!
May the fair of this country some gratitude show
To the sons of the ocean who fight the proud foe.

Here's a health to Bold Dighton, he's a true honest friend.
May glory pursue him and honor attend
And when that he dies may all you seamen draw near;
Come kneel at his tombstone and let fall a tear.

Songs of Ships & Sailors

During the Napoleanic wars in the early nineteenth century the French expanded their influence to the West Indies putting both British and American interests at risk there. The historic record is filled with accounts of various skirmishes and battles for control over the many islands of the region. This event evidently occurred during the time when the French held Guadaloupe and imprisoned both British and Americans. We have not found any specific official record, maybe because Dighton, whoever he was, was not a military person, but seemingly a concerned merchant who tried to free the prisoners with "500 bright guineas."

An apparent veteran of this engagement, Mr. P. Russell, published multiple versions of his story, perhaps seeking compensation for his ordeal. He released his first draft with five other autobiographical poems. The first begins "Russell's adventures — I was born in New Hampshire, in Hillsborough County," and the last is titled, "The Escape from Basseterre."

Separate broadsides by Russell followed:

In 1806, "GUADELOUPE – RUSSEL (P.) The escape from Bassaterre — The author was second in command, in this memorable action — and composed the following lines, while a prisoner in the Moro Castle; at which place he lay in irons for the space of six months."

In 1810, "The lines on this sheet were composed by P. Russell: who has received eleven wounds under the American flag, who has endured seven captivities, and remained two full years in irons, on cold stone, in a dungeon, in the Moro Castle, (in the island of Cuba) without once beholding the light of the sun."

In 1814, "The lines on this sheet, were composed by the unfortunate Russell, while laying in irons in the Moro-Castle, who has been prevented from obtaining a livelihood in the ordinary pursuits of life, from wounds received in battle."

And finally, in 1829, "BOLD DIGHTON — Being the account of an action fought off Guadaloupe, in 1805, where ninety-five Americans, and near three hundred Britons made their escape from the prison at that place."

The song, also known as "The *Tiger* and the *Lion*" was popular in New England and the Maritimes. We have at least three versions from Maine.

Basseterre, St Kitts

The Crocodile

Frank L. Tracy, Brewer, ME 10/7/1941
Helen Hartness Flanders Collection
Transcription © 2015 Julia Lane

Come all you landsmen list to me, to tell you the truth I'm bound,
What happened to me in going to sea and the dangers that I found.

Shipwrecked I was on the coast of Pee-ru and cast upon the shore,
Where I resolved to travel on the country to explore.

I travelled east and I travelled west till I came to the Atlantic Ocean
'Twas there I saw a wonderful sight that looked like the earth in motion.

And steering up right close 'longside, I saw 'twas a crocodile
From the end of his nose to the tip of his tail he made three hundred mile.

This crocodile, you'd plainly see, was not of the common race
I had to climb a very tall tree before I could see his face.

While I was up aloft so high there blew a gale from the south
I lost my holt and down I fell, right into this crocodile's mouth.

He quickly closed his jaws on me, and tried to gain a victim,
But I run down his throat, you see, and that's the way I tricked him.

'Twas there I travelled five months or more till I got into his maw
There I found rum kegs, quite a few, and a thousand dollars in store.

This crocodile was getting old; Alas one day he died.
He was six months in getting cold he was so long and wide.

His hide was ten miles thick I'm sure or somewhere's thereabouts
For I was full six months or more in cutting my way out.

Now if my story you disbelieve if ever you cross the Nile
Right where he fell you'll find the shell of the wonderful crocodile.

There is historic documentation of the sighting of sea serpents along the Maine coast, but this aquatic comic ditty comes from the colonial "Darby Ram" song family and is derived from "The Great Sea Snake" (*Jack Reeves Comic Songster,* 1835) also appearing as "The Wonderful Crocodile" in *Modern Street Ballads* by John Ashton, 1888. Some of these songs date back to ancient ritual songs involving supernatural "spirit animals," however there seems to be a 19th century fashion of musical tall tales probably for use in the music halls of the time (See the "Sailor's Tale," "The *Irish Rover,*" and "Blow Ye Winds") Other versions of "The Crocodile" were sent to Fannie Eckstorm by Susie Carr Young of Brewer, ME, and Thomas Edward Nelson of Union Mills, NB, in January 1929. Mr. Tracy was previously recorded singing this song by Phillips Barry on July 11, 1932 and it is virtually the same.

Rockweed

Susie Carr Young, Brewer ME 1930
Phillips Barry Collection
Transcription © 2019 Julia Lane

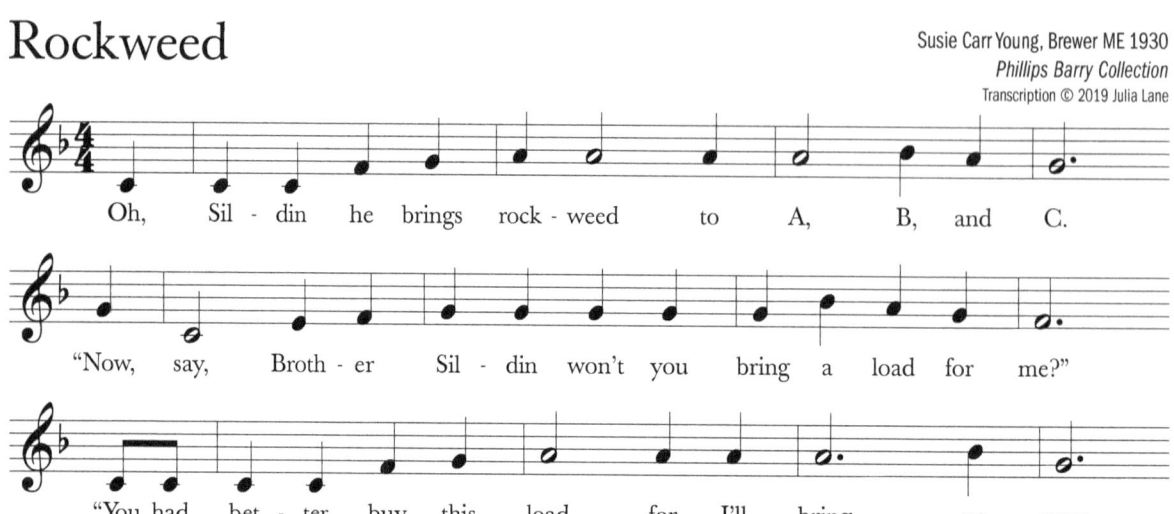

Oh, Sildin he brings rockweed to A, B, and C.
"Now, say, Brother Sildin, won't you bring a load for me?"

"You had better buy this load for I'll bring no more.
The rockweed is a-growing scarce along the dock and shore!"

Mrs. Young said that her brother sang this as a small boy. We speculate that he may have heard a street song from a vendor of rockweed which was used for garden fertilizer. The notion that seaweed, which generally grows abundantly, could be scarce is wry "super-humor."

Our Ship Lays in the Harbor

Graham Wilson, Cherryfield, ME 9/25/1940
Helen Hartness Flanders Collection
Add'l Lyrics: 1813 Broadside
Transcription © 2019 Julia Lane

Our ship lays in harbor just ready for to sail.
May heaven be your guardian, love, till I return again!
Till I return again! May heaven be your guardian, love, till I return again!

Says the father to the daughter, "What makes you so lament?
Is there no man in all this world that can give your heart content?"   [Repeat as before]

Said the daughter to the father, "I will tell you the reason why:
You have sent that man to sea that could me satisfy."

"If that's your inclination," the father did reply,
"I wish he may continue there, and on the seas may die!"

Then like an angel weeping on the rock side every day,
She waited for her own true love returning from the seas.

When nine long years were over and ten long tedious days,
She saw the ship come sailing in with her true love from the seas.

"Oh, yonder sits my angel! She's waiting there for me,
Tomorrow to the church we'll go, and married we will be."

The church it being over and they were strolling home,
They met her honored father and several gentlemen.

Says the father to the daughter, "Ten thousand pound I'll give,
If you'll forsake your sailor lad and come with me and live."

"No, it's not for your gold that glitters nor your silver that does shine
For I am married to the man I love contented in my mind."

For some reason, this fragment, collected by Mrs. Flanders from Mr. Wilson, is titled "In London Lived a Merchant" in her collection. The name is wrong—these are the last three verses of "Our Ship Lays in the Harbor," a broadside from 1813 that became part of many songbooks throughout the nineteenth century. The lyrics in italics are from Mr. Wilson.

Songs of Ships & Sailors

George Reily

Hiram Virgin, Mexico, ME 11/13/1941
Eloise Hubbard Linscott Collection
Transcription © 2017 Julia Lane

On a bright summer's morning, the weather being clear,
I strolled for recreation down by the river clear
Where I overheard a damsel most grievously complain
All for an absent lover that plows the raging main.

I being unperceived did unto her draw near
Where I lay down in ambush the better for to hear
Her doleful lamentations and melancholy cries
Whilst sparkling tears like crystal were streaming from her eyes

Crying, "O cruel fortune to me has proved unkind
As my true love has left me no comfort can I find!"
While she was thus lamenting and grieving for her dear
I saw a gallant sailor who unto her drew near.

With eloquence most complaisant he did address the fair
Crying, "Sweet and lovely fair one, why do you mourn here?"
"All for an absent lover," the fair one did reply,
"Which causes me to wander for to lament and cry.

"It's three long years and more that his absence I have mourn'd
And now the war is ended he has not yet returned."
"Why should you grieve for him alone?" the sailor he did say
"Perhaps his mind is alter'd or chang'd some other way.

If you will but forget him and fix your mind on me
Till death doth demand me to you I'll faithful prove!"
To which this fair maid answered, "Sir that can never be!
I never can admire any other man but he.

"He is the darling of my heart none else can I adore
So, take this as an answer and trouble me no more."
Then said the gallant sailor, "What is your true love's name?
Both that and his description I wish to know the same."

"George Reily was his name sir, he was a man both neat and trim
So manly in proportion that few could equal him
With the ringlets down his shoulders, the fairest yellow hair
And his skin for whiteness exceeds the lily fair."

"Fair maid, I had a messmate; George Reily was his name
I'm sure from your description that he must be the same.
It is really most surprising that he was so unkind
As to leave so fair a creature in sorrow here behind.

"Three years we spent together on board the old *Belflew*
And such a gallant comrade before I never knew.
It was on the twelfth of April near to Port Royal Bay
We had a tight engagement before the break of day

"Between Rodney and DeGrasse where many a man did fall
Your true love he fell by a French cannon ball.
Whilst weltering in his blood your generous lover lay
With falt'ring voice and broken sighs these words I heard him say,

"'Farewell, my dearest Nancy were you but standing by
To gaze your last upon me contented would I die!'"
This melancholy story it wounded her so deep
She wrung her hands in anguish and bitterly did weep.

Crying, "My joys are ended if what you say be true
Instead of having pleasure I've naught but grief in view!"
On hearing which his person no longer he conceal'd
He flew into her arms and his person did reveal.

Now these constant lovers did each other embrace.
He kiss'd the bright tears from her cheeks and wiped her lovely face,
Crying, "My dearest Nancy with you I'll ever stay
I'll never more depart till my mainmast's cut away!"

The lyrics here are as noted by Eloise Linscott in her unpublished manuscript for *A Yankee Pedlar's Pack*. Her recording of Mr. Virgin only includes verse 8 (italics) and is quite different from what she apparently intended to publish. It appears that her transcription may be adapted from the *Forget-me-not Songster* (1840). She has, however, combined several verses perhaps for clarity of the story. The action in verses 10 and 11 describes the Battle of the Saintes, April 12, 1782 in the West Indies where the British and French forces were vying for control of the islands there. The French Rear-Admiral Comte DeGrasse, who had helped George Washington to prevail at Yorktown in the Battle of the Chesapeake in September 1781, was soundly defeated and taken prisoner by the British Admiral Sir George B. Rodney. Another song, "Rodney's Glory," tells the story in full. An English ship-of-the-line called *Barfleur* (*Belflew*?) is mentioned in descriptions of naval military action in the Caribbean during this time.

Songs of Ships & Sailors

True Lovers Bold

Mrs. Guy R. Hathaway, Mattawamkeag, ME 6/14/1932
Fannie Hardy Eckstorm Collection
Tune: Carrie Grover, Gorham, ME 1953
Transcription © 2019 Julia Lane

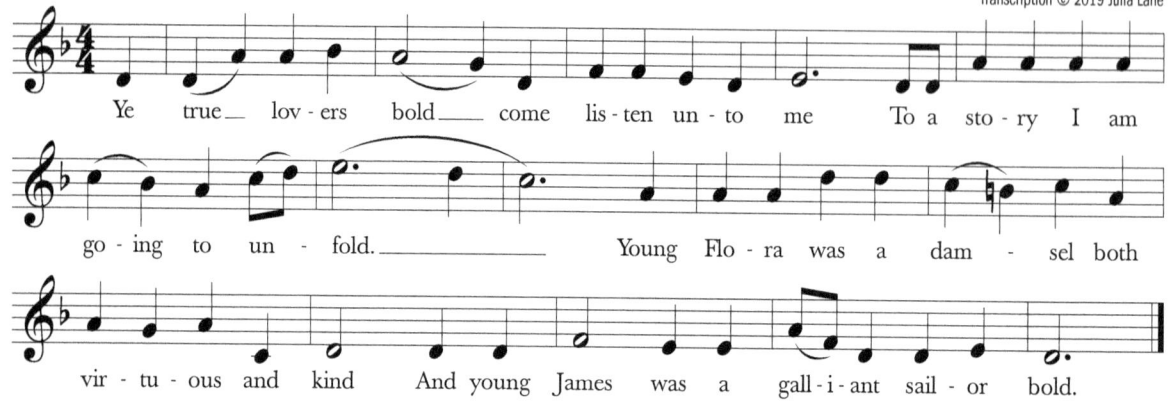

Ye true lovers bold, come listen unto me
To a story I'm going to unfold.
Young Flora was a damsel both virtuous and kind
And young James was a gall-i-ant sailor bold.

"It's adieu to lovely Flora," one morning he did say,
"I am forced, I am called to go away,
Unto some foreign shore where the cannons loud do roar
In battle where the stormy winds do blow."

Like a maiden in despair she tore her yellow hair,
Saying, "Along with you I will go
Unto some foreign shore where the cannons loud do roar
In battle where the stormy winds do blow!"

"Oh no, no, my lovely Flora, I'm sure you must be mad,
To venture your sweet life upon the deep;
Instead of going aloft, upon your pillow soft,
Contented at home you might be."

"Oh, you need not persuade, for I am not afraid.
Alone with you I'll go off to some foreign shore
Where it's loud the cannons roar
In battle where the stormy winds do blow!"

Six years lovely Flora she sailed o'er the sea;
Respected by all her ship's crew,
And it never yet was said that young Flora was a maid
In her trousers and jacket so blue.

On occasion she would fight from morning until night,
Hard to, to the battle she would go
She would stand by her gun, do her duty like a man,
In battle where the stormy winds do blow!

Bygone Ballads of Maine, Volume I

At length they were discharged and they both were enlarged,　　　　[enlarge = to set free]
Straightway unto the captain he did go,
Saying; "Here behold a maid, that never was afraid
In battle where the stormy winds do blow!"

Now the captain did stare when these words he did hear,
He looked on her with surprise;
And he shouted with delight as he gazed on her so bright
And the tears fell in torrents from his eyes.

"Ye true lovers bold, here is fifty pounds in gold
To see you get married I will go,
And you can in joy be blessed, upon your pillow rest;
Stay at home when the stormy winds do blow!"

Not commonly found, this is a variant of a mid-19th century British broadside ballad "James and Flora" published by H. Such (London) among other printers. It is also known as "The United Lovers." One of the "Warrior Women" ballads, the subject is similar to "The Rose of Britain's / Breton's Isle." According to Linda Grant De Pauw in her book *Seafaring Women*, the presence of women on board British warships was more common than presumed. Although this text appears in the bulletin of the Ballad & Folk Song Society of the North East (Vol. 8, 1934), we print the version here as found in the collection of Fannie Eckstorm as it contains some extra verses. Both indicate the tune was transcribed by Barry but we have not been able to locate it and so use that written down by Carrie Grover, titled "James and Florence" in her book *Heritage of Song* (1955).

Black-Eyed Susan

Charles Finnemore, Bridgewater ME 10/29/1943
Helen Hartness Flanders Collection
Transcription © 2016 Julia Lane

All on the Downs the fleet lay moored, their streamers waving in the wynd,
When Black-Eyed Susan came on board saying, "Where shall I my true love find?
Tell me, ye jovial sailors, tell me true, if my sweet Willie,
If my sweet Willie sails among your crew."

Willie, who high upon the yard, rocked with the billows to and fro,
Soon as her well-known voice he heard, he sigh'd and cast his eyes below.
The cords glide swiftly thro' his glowing hands and quick as lightning,
Quick as lightning on the deck he stands.

"Oh, Susan, Susan, lov-lye dear! My vows will ever true remain.
Let me kiss off those falling tears, we only part to meet again.
The noblest captain of all that British fleet might en-vye Willie,
Might en-vye Willie's lips those kisses sweet.

"Believe not what the landsmen say. They'll tempt with doubts thy constant mind.
They'll tell thee sailors when away, in every port a mistress find.
Yes, yes! believe them when they tell thee so, for thou art present,
For thou art present wheresoe'er I go.

"If to fair India's coast I sail thine eyes are seen in diamonds bright.
Thy breath is Africa's spicy gale, your skin is ivory so white.
The pleasant breezes where so e'er they blow, they bring me mem'ries,
They bring me mem'ries of my lovely Sue."

The bo's'n gave the dreadful word. The sails their swelling bosom spread.
No longer could she stay on board. He turned, she sighed, and hung her head.
Her little boat unwilling rowed to land. "Adieu," she cried,
"Adieu," she cried and waved her lily hand.

An especially elegant song, "Black-Eyed Susan" was written for a ballad opera by John Gay (1685–1732) no later than 1723. Although several settings of the song appeared in the early 18th century, it is that by the bass singer Richard Leveridge (1670–1758), written for *The Village Opera* (1729), which gained the most favor and was printed in Chappell's book *Popular Music of the Olden Time* (1856). This seems to be the version most widely sung. Verse 3 is not in the original song and the last two lines of verse 5 are unique to this version which Mr. Finnemore learned from his father. We think it is rather extraordinary to find such a song essentially intact in the woods of Maine.

Roving Jack Tar

Text: Mrs. Avery Olmstead, Brewer, ME 3/1934
Fannie Hardy Eckstorm Collection
Tune: Susie Carr Young, Brewer, ME 1930
Phillips Barry Collection
Transcription © 2019 Fred Gosbee

Come old folks! Come young folks! Come and listen unto me.
Would you wed a saucy sailor boy just returned from the sea?
Would you wed a saucy sailor boy just returned from the sea?

"Oh, you're ragged, sir, and you're dirty, and you smell so strong of tar,
So begone, you saucy sailor lad, you roving Jack tar!"
So begone, you saucy sailor lad, you roving Jack tar!"

"If I'm ragged, love, and I'm dirty, and I smell so strong of tar,
I have silver in each pocket, love, and gold I have in store." (2x)

And when she had heard of this, down on her bending knees she fell,
Saying, "Kind sir, I accept your offer now, for a sailor I love well." (2x)

Oh, these factory girls they are pretty, but changeable in their mind,
You can hug them, you can kiss them, too, but their love you ne'er can find. (2x)

Once more I'll sail the raging sea where the big fish they do swim,
And since you've refused my offer, love, some foreign maid shall wear the ring. (2x)

Variations of "The Saucy Sailor," of which this is one, were widespread across the Anglo-Celtic lands with the popular theme of the slighted sailor having the last word. A broadside was published in 1781. Fannie Eckstorm collected this song in March 1934 from Mrs. Avery Olmstead of Brewer, as sung by her brother Capt. Perleston Quinn. The lyrics are almost identical to those of Vernon Mayo of Menardo, ME, as collected by Flanders in September 1942, except he does not repeat the last two lines. The tune and first verse are from Susie Carr Young's manuscript in Phillips Barry Collection. See also "Early, Early in the Spring" sung by Frank Kneeland, recorded by Flanders.

The Sailor and the Sea Captain

Charles Finnemore, Bridgewater, ME 5/7/1942
Helen Hartness Flanders Collection
Transcription © 2016 Julia Lane

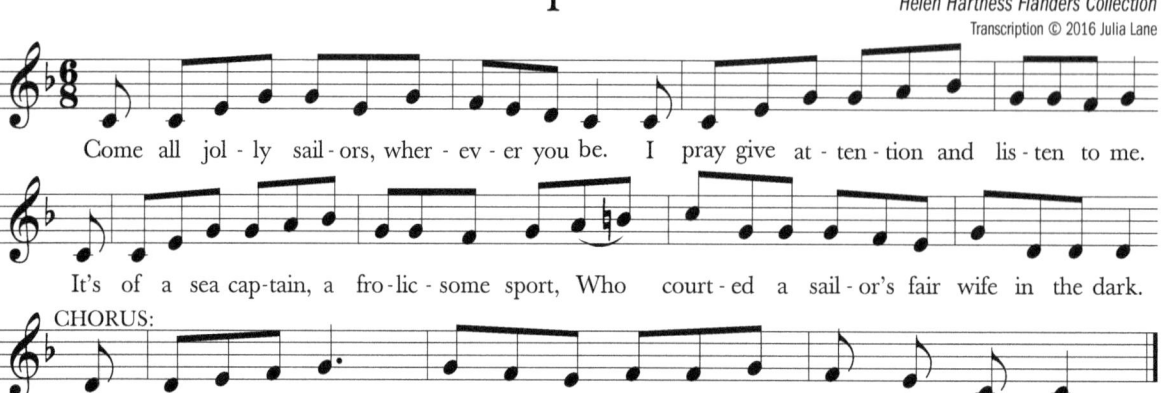

Come all jolly sailors, wherever you be,
I pray give attention and listen to me,
It's of a sea captain, a frolicsome spark,
Who courted a sailor's fair wife in the dark.

CHORUS:
    Sing derry aye day,
    Fol the dol laddie, sing whack fol the day.

It's of a young sailor, Jon Hahnsen by name,
He had a fair and frolicsome dame.
She went onboard her husband to see;
"Oh, good!" said the Captain, "A partner for me!"

The supper being over, their pleasures was o'er
And all of the ladies was ordered onshore.
While all the poor sailors onboard they must stay,
Well, the captain should go this fair charmer to see.

Now, Jack, he mistrusted that something was wrong;
At the close of the evening he gently went home
And under the bed himself did convey
To hear what the captain to his wife might say.

"Here's fifty bright guineas, my joy and delight,
If you will consent to lie with me tonight!
Your husband shall have a promotion at sea
Sure, I'll use him more kindly than I did agree!"

The sight of the gold so delighted the dame
She quickly consented to play at the game
And off to bed this gay couple did go
And the game that they played was the "Up and Ti-yo!"

This tiresome game soon caused them to sleep
When out from under the bed Jack did creep.
He put on the captain's bright britches and coat
His wig and his waistcoat to make up the joke!

Now, Jack he was dressed from the top to the toe
And off to the captain's house he did go.
And when he got there he rapped so bold
In the captain's bright coat of the scarlet and gold.

The waiting maid came and she brought him a light
But Jack didn't seem for to get in a fright;
"Oh, where is your mistress?" She answered "In bed!"
"Oh, open your parlor door quickly!" Jack said.

Now, feigning to be drunk Jack staggered in.
The captain's wife scolded him, "Where have you been?
It's the day long with the girls you will stroll
At night you will come home as drunk as a fool!"

But Jack turned around, give the candle a puff
And she turned her back over all in a great huff.
He jumped into bed, as a sailor would do,
He reefed 'er, he hauled 'er till he brought her to!

He reefed 'er, he hauled 'er, he tickled her knee!
At length this fair damsel began to grow pleased;
With captain's wife all night Jack did lay
And he laid in her arms till the broad break of day.

But when she awoke and saw this strange face
She drew a long breathe, made a pitiful case.
"Oh, lady," said Jack, "Don't get in a fright!
Your husband was kissing my wife all last night!"

She listened while Jack his story he told
And laughed all that her two sides could hold.
"Go hitch up my horses, I vow and protest,
And we'll go see that rogue in his tarpaulin vest!"

The horses was ready and off they did go
And Jack and his lady they cut a fine show
And when they got there the first words was spoke,
"Oh God!" said the captain, "Jack, pull off my coat!"

"Here's fifty bright guineas, Jack, pull off my coat!
And don't to the rest of the sailors report
For many an old sailor's been cuckold you know
But here's four jolly cuckolds stand here in a row!"

This song is based on a broadside "The Merry Wives of Wapping," which dates from 1680 and refers to the unsavory docksides of London where lodgings were provided for seamen and where ships were outfitted. Also called "Tit for Tat," it was written out in 1780 by Thomas Nixon, a musician from Framingham, MA. Apparently Nixon collected the street songs which contained vulgar words that Boston publisher Nathaniel Coverly deemed unprintable in 1811. As a result, nineteenth century versions are less racy. Horace Beck also collected this as "Jack Simpson, the Sailor" from Dale Potter of Kingman, ME, in 1950.

The Basket of Eggs

Sadie Murphy Harvey, Monticello, ME 9/30/1941
Helen Hartness Flanders Collection
Transcription © 2015 Julia Lane

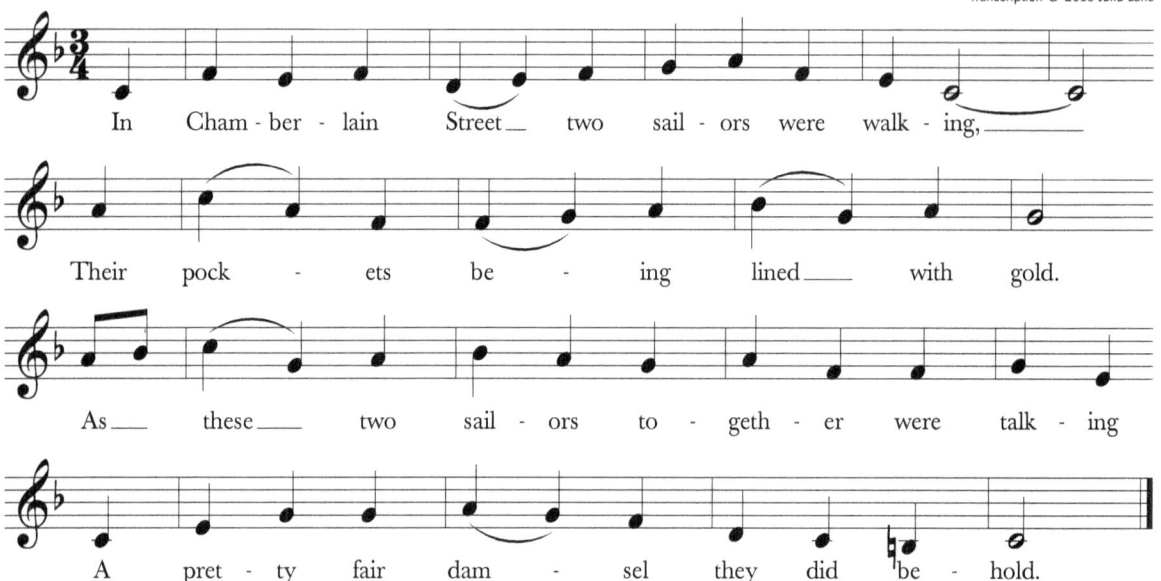

In Chamberlain Street two sailors were walking,
Their pockets being lined with gold.
As these two sailors together were talking
A pretty fair damsel they did behold.

One of the sailors spied a basket
As she sat down to take her ease
And offering to carry it one of them askéd her
Her kind answer was, "Yes, if you please!"

One of the sailors picked up the basket
"It's full of eggs; I pray you take care.
And if perchance you should overwalk me
At the halfway house, pray leave them there."

The halfway house was soon walked to;
The halfway house was soon passed by
But still this fair maiden she steppéd on lightly
And on the sailors she cast her eye.

These two sailors called into an ale house.
They called for beer and a glass of wine
Saying, "Oh, what fools women are in this country.
A woman has left her eggs behind!"

"Pray, tell the landlord to bring on some bacon
For we have eggs all for to broil."
But when this young sailor he opened the basket
Instead of the eggs he found a young child!

One of the sailors set down to fretting.
"To fret," said the other "It is all in vain.
Here's fifty bright guineas I'll give to the maiden
If any women it will obtain."

A woman was standing by the fire
To hear what the sailors would have to say.
She said, "I'll take the baby as soon as its mother
If down the money you will pay."

He paid her over and down the money,
"You see, kind sir, I hope I'm free.
But to tell you the truth, without further conclusion,
The daddy of the child you be."

"If this be you, my lovely Nancy,
  That I danced with last Easter Day?"
"Oh yes, then, kind sir, and since you've had your fancy,
  Oh, now the fiddler you have paid!"

Here is one of a number of songs depicting the clever maiden outwitting the sailor ashore including "Bung Yer Eye," sung by the singer's husband Murchie Harvey, and the popular "Quare Bungo Rye." This version (called by the singer "The Sailor Song") describes quite an elaborate and clever retribution for a night of indiscretion. It dates from an early 1700's English ditty originally involving a miser and featuring a clever country lass. Mrs. Harvey says she learned the song as a child from a woman whose father worked in a lumber camp.

Jack Tar's Frolic

David N. Poor, Portland, ME c.1842
Tune: Susie Carr Young
Phillips Barry Collection
Transcription © 2019 Fred Gosbee

Come all you sailor boys
That delights in sailors' noise
There's nothing to compare to but laughter!
When a sailor comes on shore
With his gold and silver store
There's no one can get rid of it faster.

For the first that Jack craves
Is a light and chamber bed
And good liquors of every sort
And a pretty girl likewise
With those black and rolling eyes
Then Jack Tar is pleased to the heart.

The landlady's daughter she comes in
Oh, she looks so neat and trim
Ready to wait on Jack when he calls.
Ready to wait on him
When she finds him in good trim
Marks him down two for one at the bar.

This rig it does run on
Till Jacks money is all gone
Then the old bird begins for to frown
With her damned old squinted eye
And her nose turned all awry
Saying "Sailor, 'tis high time to be gone!"

Now Jack he understands
There's a ship for to be manned
And to the East or West Indies she is bound
With a sweet and pleasant gale
Oh, she spreads a lofty sail
And bids adieu to the girls of this town.

Every seaport town had taverns and other places that exploited the weary sailor's need for entertainment, often to the sailor's chagrin and bankruptcy. The words to this song can be found on page 16 of a transcription of the sea journal of David N. Poor of Portland, ME, begun in 1842. David Poor follows these lyrics with the words "Not respectfully yours, David N. Poor." Mr. Poor was born in 1818 and died in 1909, working most of his life in the coasting trade along the eastern North American seaboard. Susie Carr Young has the last verse noted in her musical transcription, titled "Sailor Song," and so we have used her tune, slightly revised, to suit Poor's lyric.

The Banks of Newfoundland 1

Mrs. Annie V. Marston, West Gouldsboro, ME 1926
Phillips Barry Collection
Transcription © 2019 Julia Lane

You may all bless your happy lots that you are safe on shore.
You do not know what howls and blows that 'round poor seamen roar.
You do not know what hardships that we were forced to stand
For fourteen days and fourteen nights on the banks of Newfoundland.

Our vessel never sailed before across the distant sea.
She was well rigged and fitted out before she sailed away.
She was made of good and seasoned wood, but she could not well withstand
The hurricane that struck us on the banks of Newfoundland.

On the morning of the twelfth day our provisions they gave out.
On the morning of the thirteenth the lots were cast about.
The lot fell to the captain's son, a youth both brave and gay.
But some, thinking that relief might come, spared him another day.

On the morning of the fourteenth we told him to prepare.
We gave to him one hour to offer up a prayer.
But Providence proved kind to us, kept blood from every hand,
For an English vessel hove in sight on the banks of Newfoundland.

O, when they took us from the wreck, we were more like ghosts than men.
We were all able seamen that did our vessel man.
They took us and they fed us and they brought us safe to land.
But the captain lost both feet by frost on the banks of Newfoundland.

"The Banks of Newfoundland" is the title of at least six different songs. These are not variations on a single tune, but entirely different songs with different airs and lyrics. All share a common theme—the dangers of fishing or sailing off the coast of Newfoundland—but none are very similar. The most popular of these was based on an old British song telling of the hardships suffered by convicts being transported to the penal colony called Van Dieman's Land, modern Tasmania. This version, however, is not as widely collected, though it appears both in Maine and across the ocean in Ballycastle, Northern Ireland. The theme of a dire situation resulting in the need for cannibalism shows up in a number of North Atlantic shipwreck ballads. The true story of the 1740 passage of the *Sea Flower* from Northern Ireland to Boston chronicles just such an event, complete with the timely rescue. In addition to Mrs. Marston, the song was collected from Mabel Worcester of Hanover, ME, in 1967 as recorded at the Maine Folklife Center in Orono, ME.

Songs of Ships & Sailors

Bracey on the Shore

Mrs. Enoch Bulger, Big Cranberry Island, ME 9/3/1926
Fannie Hardy Eckstorm Collection
Tune: Traditional
Transcription © 2018 Julia Lane

It was of a young sea captain, on Cranberry Isle did dwell.
He took the schooner *Arnold*, I suppose you all know well.
She was a tops'l schooner and hailed from Calais, Maine.
They took a load from Boston to cross the raging main.

CHORUS:
    Bracey on the shore, Bracey on the shore,
    Bold and undaunted stood Lew Bracey on the shore.

He arrived to Cranberry Island and anchored off the Point.
The wind was to the east'ard, a-blowin' feather-white.
The *Arnold* dragged her anchor and drifted on the Bar.
They tried all means to get her off, but couldn't move a spar.

They had a little Miss on board; I do not know her name.
They took her out of prison, all down to Calais, Maine.
They say she was part Indian, but that I do not know
But when the *Arnold* struck adrift, it proved her overthrow.

They say that Captain Boardman has just arrived in town!
He says that Captain Bracey is the biggest rogue he's found.
Up speaks the other gentleman and says, "We'll have to stop
For she's loaded with gin bottles from her keel up to her top!"

Cynthy took a firkin full and lugged them 'way 'round home
To decorate her cupboard all in the northeast room.
She says "Now dearest Lewis, pray do not drink no more
For folks are talking very bad all down along the shore!"

They say that Mrs. Howard has got a case of gin
She deals it out for medicine to cheat the eyes of men.
Aunt Darkis says "I Vanny! I think it's very good
To have a little whisky when Amos is cutting wood!"

He has left Cranberry Island and gone to Calais, Maine
He's bought a pay-tent cookie to travel all through Maine
They say he paid five hundred—I think it's very dear!
He'd better took the money and laid it out in beer.

The way he's got his living is smuggling tea and gin,
Across St. Stephen River up to Bar Harbor, Maine.
And now it's Captain Bracey, I'll tell you what to do;
It's leave off drinking whiskey and hugging the women, too!

A local song, it was written in the 1870s to the popular Irish tune "Brennan on the Moor." It's about a wreck which occurred on "Jimmy's Point" on the Big Island, about one half mile from the captain's home. The incident revealed the makings of a "first class scandal" aboard. This text was taken down from the recitation of Mrs. Enoch Bulger, Big Cranberry Island, Sept. 3, 1926 with some additions from fragments previously taken down from her brothers, Capt. Archie S. and George Henry Spurling of Little Cranberry Island.

Fannie Hardy Eckstorm says in *Minstrelsy of Maine* (circa 1926): "For many years this very local song has been one of the most popular songs on the Cranberry Islands, and it is still sung especially on winter nights when the men are gathered round the stove in the store. It is said that the Spurling brothers can sing forty verses of it. Nevertheless, when asked for it by the collectors, no one could remember any of it and it was only by heroic efforts that a few stanzas could be pieced together."

Songs of Ships & Sailors

Sail Away

Amos Hanson, Orland ME
Sung by his daughter, Mrs. Hattie Hanson Soper 1932
Phillips Barry Collection
First transcription by S. Bayard
Transcription © 2019 Julia Lane

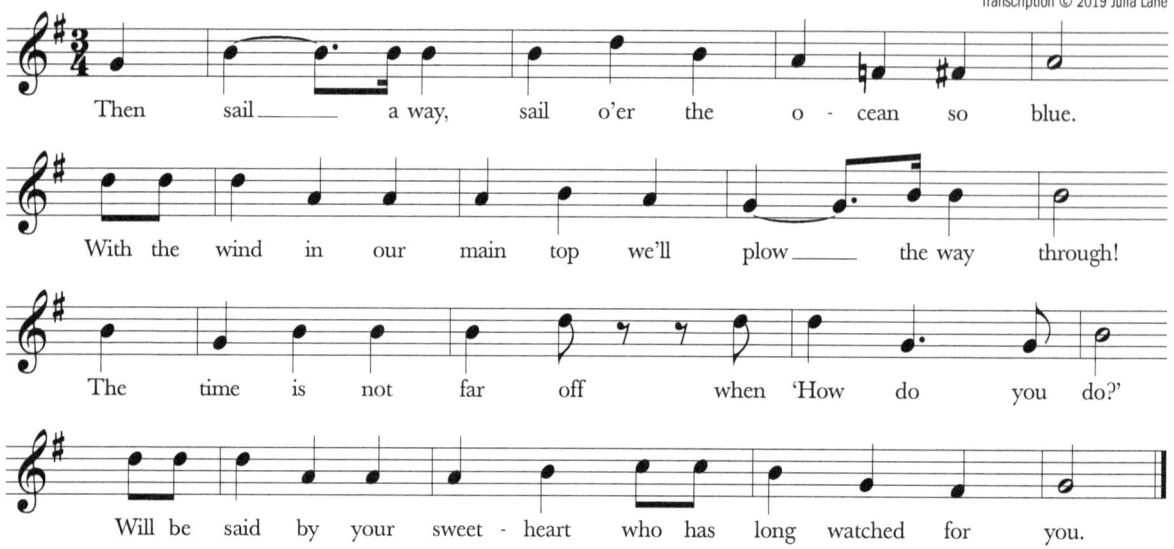

Then sail away, sail o'er the ocean so blue.
With the wind in our maintop we'll plow the way through!
The time is not far off when 'How do you do?'
Will be said by your sweetheart who has long watched for you.

Only one verse and the tune were found in Barry's collection, with the alternate title "Bagaduce Bay," and published in the newsletter of the Ballad & Folk Song Society of the North East (1933 p. 16), with no other longer transcriptions available. Amos Hanson was a fisherman songwriter from Orland, ME, who sailed out of Bagaduce Bay and wrote songs based on his adventures and the people in the area. His daughter, who sang the song for Eckstorm, told her, "It was composed when the author was a very young man." (see "The Schooner *Fred Dunbar*" and "A Trip to the Grand Banks")

The Bold Privateer

Susie Carr Young, Brewer ME 1930
Phillips Barry Collection
Additional lyrics: traditional
Transcription © 2019 Julia Lane

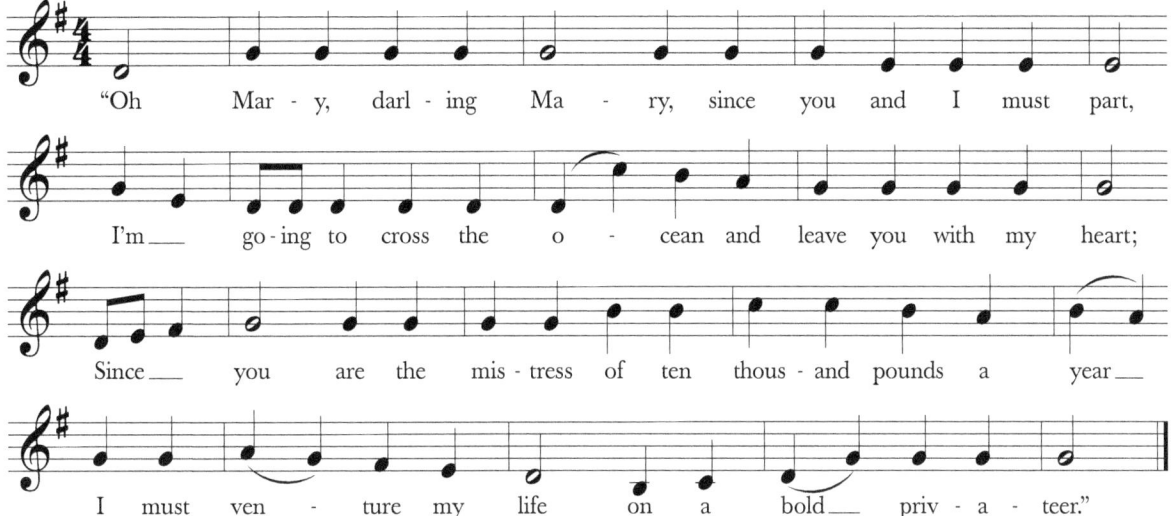

Oh Mary, darling Mary, since you and I must part,
I'm going to cross the ocean and leave with you my heart;
Since you are the mistress of ten thousand pounds a year
I must venture my life on a bold privateer.

Oh, Willie, darling Willie, stay at home if you can,
Many a man has lost his life since this cruel war began.
You had better stay at home where the girls they love you dear
And not venture your life on a bold privateer.

Your father and your mother both show me a great spite,
Likewise your brother has threatened my life.
I'm in hopes that soon from their anger I'll get clear
If I once set my foot on board of the bold privateer.

Oh, Mary, darling Mary, ten thousand times adieu
Our good ship lies at anchor will all her jolly crew,
We'll run up our colors till our purpose we make clear
We will soon let them know that we are the bold privateer.

And now this war is over and God has spared our lives,
Some men are returning to their sweethearts and their wives,
But I am returning to the arms of my dear
For I ventured my life on board of the bold privateer.

Despite its national popularity on stage and in print in 19th century America, "The Bold Privateer" does not seem to be included in the Maine repertoire to any extent. The tune and the italicized lyrics are a fragment from Susie Carr Young which is the only example we have found. We have filled out the verses from published broadsides.

False Nancy

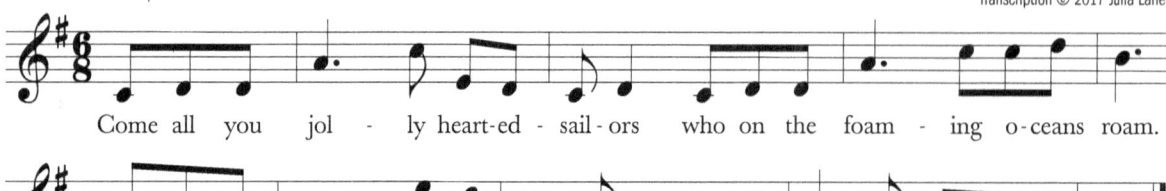

Annie Marston, West Gouldsboro, ME circa 1925
Phillips Barry Collection
Transcription © 2017 Julia Lane

Come all you jolly-hearted sailors who on the foaming oceans roam.
For sev'n long years I courted Nancy thinking one day to make her my own.

A chain of gold I gave unto her and a costly wedding ring likewise.
The chain of gold she fond accepted but the wedding ring she did despise.

The chain of gold she wore about her; she wore it about her neck in view
Saying "Be gone you young tarry sailor for I can have a better man than you."

I went unto her tender mother thinking she might stay my friend
But she proved more cruel than my jewel and for an officer did send.

She swore that I had wronged her daughter and punished for it I should be.
For forty days on bread and water that cruel woman confined me.

In a short time after that maid got married to one of the blackguards of the town.
He did not in the least regard her which served to pull her proud spirits down.

As I was walking the streets one morning, I chanced to meet her all on the way;
She, poor soul, in a low condition and I myself in a thriving way.

I turned my head around to view her and these are the words to her did say:
"Oh, many a bright and sunshiny morning turns to a dark and dismal day."

Now all you loyal-hearted lovers turn not your first true love away;
For many a dark and cloudy morning turns to bright and sunshiny day.

A similar story to the "Saucy Sailor" except with a much more satisfactory ending. Carrie Grover sang this as "The Tarry Sailor" and published it in her *Heritage of Song* (p. 141). Also known as "The Rambling Beauty," variants from Scotland in the Gavin Greig collection seem to be the only ones to use the name "Nancy" which implies that this version has Scottish origins.

Why Don't My Father's Ship Come In?

Charles Finnemore, Bridgewater ME, 10/29/1943
Helen Hartness Flanders Collection
Transcription © 2015 Julia Lane

It was on one summer's evening as I lay down to sleep,
I heard a boy of six years old at his mother's knee did weep,
Saying, "Once I had a father dear who did me kind embrace
And if he was here he would wipe those tears rolled down dear mother's face.

"Where is that tall and gallyant ship that took him out to sea?
With white sails reaching to the sky, filled with a summer's breeze
While other ships come sailing in splitting the ocean's foam
Why don't my father's ship come in or why don't he come home?

"More well do I remember him when he took me on his knee
Here is the garden fruit he brought from that fair India tree,
I think I see him coming now, waving his hat, in hand,
'God bless you both' was his last words, as he sailed from our land."

"My boy, your father long tarries, beneath the deep blue sea,
Your father's tall and gallyant ship, you never more will see,
Your father's tall and gallyant ship was sank beneath the waves,
There is many the tall and gallyant ship, sails over your father's grave.

"There is a burden from him brought, I hold it to my side,
There is a home for you and I that lives beyond the skies,
There is a burden from him brought, I fold it to my side."
They cast their eyes to Heaven, the son and mother died.

These lyrics first appear as "The Questioner" in the diary of Theophilus Richmond who was the ship's surgeon aboard the *Hesperus* in 1837–38. He had received a melancholy letter which "being too long to describe in prose, I shall attempt it (for the lack of other matter) in verse." First published in 1837 in *The Thompsonian*, a medical manual, the poem quickly became popular and was printed in a variety of publications. It eventually acquired new verses and a tune as well as various titles such as "The Sailor's Child" and "The Gentle Boy." Variations were widely published in periodicals throughout the 19th century. Other Maine versions were sung by Amanda Kneeland of Searsport and George Dalton of Brewer both called "What Makes my Father Stay So Long?"

Songs of Ships & Sailors

The British Man-O'-War

Charles Finnemore, Bridgewater, ME 10/28/1943
Helen Hartness Flanders Collection
Transcription © 2018 Julia Lane

It was down by Colvin's garden for pleasure I did stray.
I overheard a sailor and a rich lady gay.
He says, "My lov-e-lye Susan, I now from you must go
To cross the briny ocean on a British Man-O'-War."

O, Susan fell to weeping and unto him did say,
"Love, would you be so venturesome to throw yourself away
You know when I am twenty-one I shall receive my store
Jolly sailor, do not venture on this British Man-O'-War."

"O Susan, lov-e-lye Susan, the truth to you I'll tell.
The British flag insulted is, old Eng-e-land knows it well.
The British flag insulted is so like a jolly tar,
But I'll face the walls of Chiney on a British Man-O'-War."

"O sailor, lov-e-lye sailor don't face the proud Chinee!
You'll find they are as treacherous as any Portuguee
And by some dead-i-ly dagger you might receive a scar!
So change your inclination from this British Man-O'-War."

"O Susan, lov-e-lye Susan, the truth to you I'll tell.
The British flag insulted is, old Eng-e-land knows it well.
The British flag insulted is so like a jolly tar,
I'll fight for love and Susan onboard of a Man-O'-War."

The sailor took his handkerchief; he cut it fair in two,
Saying, "Keep one half of this for me; I'll do the same for you.
I may be crowned with honor so like a jolly tar
I'll fight for fame, and Susan, on a British Man O'-War!"

"O Susan, lov-e-lye Susan, the time will quickly pass.
Come down to yonder alehouse and we'll have a parting glass.
My shipmates they are waiting there to row me from the shore
All for England's glory on a British Man-O'-War."

A few more words together then he let go her hand.
The jovial crew so merr-i-lye their boat did launch from land.
The sailor waved his handkerchief just like a jolly tar
And Susan blessed her sailor on a British Man-O'-War.

Also known as "Lovely Susan," several details in this song give clues to its English origins as well as connections with historic events. Susan's concern that her sailor lover might be injured by the "woeful dagger" of the "proud Chinee" reveals currency with the Opium Wars between England and China from 1839–1842. Susan goes on to declare "You'll find they are as treacherous as any Portuguee." This slur against the Portuguese was based in public resentment resulting from the Portuguese Governor of Macao's reluctance to permit his government becoming involved in the war. Interestingly, there are several Maine versions, appearing in Eckstorms's *British Ballads from Maine, Second Series* which change the timing of the action. In 1924, Dr. Lewis Freeman Gott of Bernard, ME, places the event during the battle of Vera Cruz in the Mexican-American war of 1847 saying "I will face the walls of Vera Cruz in a Yankee man-o-war," but still retaining the negative connotations of the Portuguese as follows: "The Spanish are as treacherous as any Portuguee." Another is clearly a Civil War version. "Fair Susie," was taken down by Mary W. Smyth, August, 1925, from the singing of Mr. Horace E. Priest of Sangerville, ME. He learned it from Mr. Everett York of Medway, ME, in a lumber camp forty years previously, and sings "To face the guns of the Merrimack on the Yankee man-of-war." See also "The Jolly Roving Tar" for a "female sailor" variant.

The Bold *Princess Royal*

Lyrics: Frank Matthews, Eastport ME 10/1927
Phillips Barry Collection
Tune: Carrie Grover, Gorham, ME 10/30/1941
Eloise Hubbard Linscott Collection
Transcription © 2017 Julia Lane

On the fifteenth of April we sailed from the strand
In the bold *Princess Royal* bound down to Newfoundland.
We sailed from the eastward, to the westward bore we
With forty brave seamen our ship's company.

We had not been sailing but days two or three
When a sailor from the foretop a strange sail did see
"Sail Oh! Sail Oh!" He loudly did cry
"From the peak of her mizzen black colours do fly!"

Then up speaks our Captain, saying "What shall we do?
If this proves a pirate he will soon fetch us to."
"Oh no!" says our Chief Mate, "It shall not be so!
We will shake out our reefs, boys, and from him we'll go!"

Scarce one hour after he ranged alongside
With a loud speaking trumpet "Whence are you?" he cried.
Up speaks our commander and answers him so:
"I am out from Babaira, I am bound for Burdo."   [La Guaira, Bordeaux]

"Then back your main topsails and heave your ship to!
I'm an old coasting pilot; I've a message for you."
"If I back my main topsails, if I heave my ship to
It will be in some harbor, not alongside of you!"

He chased us to windward that very same day.
He chased us to leeward, but we gave him no play.
He chased us to windward that very same day
But we shook out our topgallant sails and from him went away.

We shook out our royals and skysails also.
We rigged out our stunsails and from him did go.
He fired a shot at us thinking it might prevail
But the bold *Princess Royal* soon showed them her tail!

Now we are safe boys, the Pirate is gone!
Here's a breaker of whiskey and a keg of good rum!
Go down to your grog, boys, and drink with good cheer
For while we have sea room, there's nothing to fear!

This song of an encounter with pirates may be based on the following account. On June 21, 1789, nine days out from Falmouth (England) on her way to New York (some accounts say Halifax), HM mail packet *Princess Royal* was hailed and pursued by a brig, the French privateer *Aventurier*. The two ships exchanged fire and the *Aventurier* gave chase. The *Princess Royal* was outmanned, with a crew of thirty-two men and boys and seventeen passengers as opposed to the *Aventurier*'s eighty-five men and boys. The packet was also outgunned, with only six cannons to the brig's sixteen. However, the English ship held off the privateer for two hours, eventually damaging the stern of the *Aventurier* enough to make her move off. While the French ship limped back to Bordeaux for refitting, the *Princess Royal* continued on her course. There are numerous variants of the song in the tradition. The tune is from Linscott's recording of Carrie Grover in 1941.

The Lass of Mohee

Mrs. W. H. Smith, Houlton, ME 9/23/1940
Helen Hartness Flanders Collection
Transcription © Julia Lane 2015

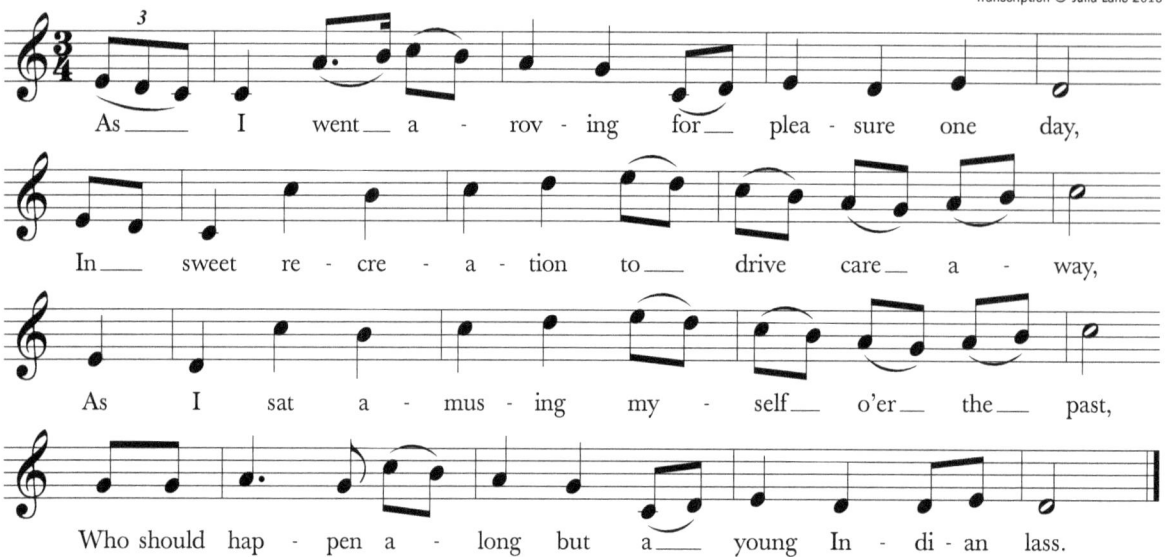

As I went a roving for pleasure one day,
In sweet recreation to drive care away,
As I sat a-musing myself o'er the past,
Who should happen along but a young Indian lass.

She sat down beside me and she squeezed my hand,
Saying, "You are a stranger from some foreign land,
And if you will go with me, you are welcome to come
For I live by myself in a snug little home."

Just as the sun was setting all o'er the salt sea,
Alone I did wander with the Lass of Mohee.
Together we rambled, and together we roamed,
Till we came to the cottage in the cocoanut grove.

The fondest expression she made unto me,
Saying, "You are a stranger from some foreign counteree
And if you are willing to stay here with me,
I'll learn you the language of the Isle of Mohee."

I said, "My pretty fair maid, that never can be
For I have a sweetheart in my own counteree
And I would not forsake her, for her poverty
For she has a heart as true as the lass of Mohee.

The last time that I saw her it was down on the sand,
As our ship was leaving, she wavéd her hand;
Saying, "When you get over to the girl that you love,
Think of the lass of Mohee and the cocoanut grove."

New I am safe landed on my own native shore,
And friends and relations come 'round me once more
And of all that comes 'round me and all that I see
There's none to compare with the lass of Mohee.

This Indian girl was handsome, she was modest and mild.
Her actions and behavior were gracious and kind;
When I was a stranger she took me to her home
Now I think of the lass of Mohee as I wander along.

"The Lass of Mohee" was extremely popular both onboard ship and in the woods camps with at least fifteen versions found in Maine. The earliest versions are called "The Indian Lass" and may have originated as a colonial tale of the European stranger encountering a friendly indigenous woman. Some variations are called the "Miami Lass" and may refer to the Miami tribe in Ohio, though more probably Florida as it is coastal. As sailors traveled to the Pacific, particularly on whaling vessels, the lass became a resident of "Mohea / Mohee" probably Maui. The romance of the story varies with the fellow being faithful (or not) to his sweetheart at home, and she waiting for him (or not) whereupon he either reminisces about the Indian lass or actually returns to her. More recent tunes resemble "On Top of Old Smokey" but there are several beautiful alternatives. "The Lakes of Ponchartrain" is a landsman's variant of this song.

Dublin Bay

Mrs. Rosalie Wood, Bangor ME 1875
Phillips Barry Collection
Tune attributed to Barker 1863
Transcription © 2019 Julia Lane

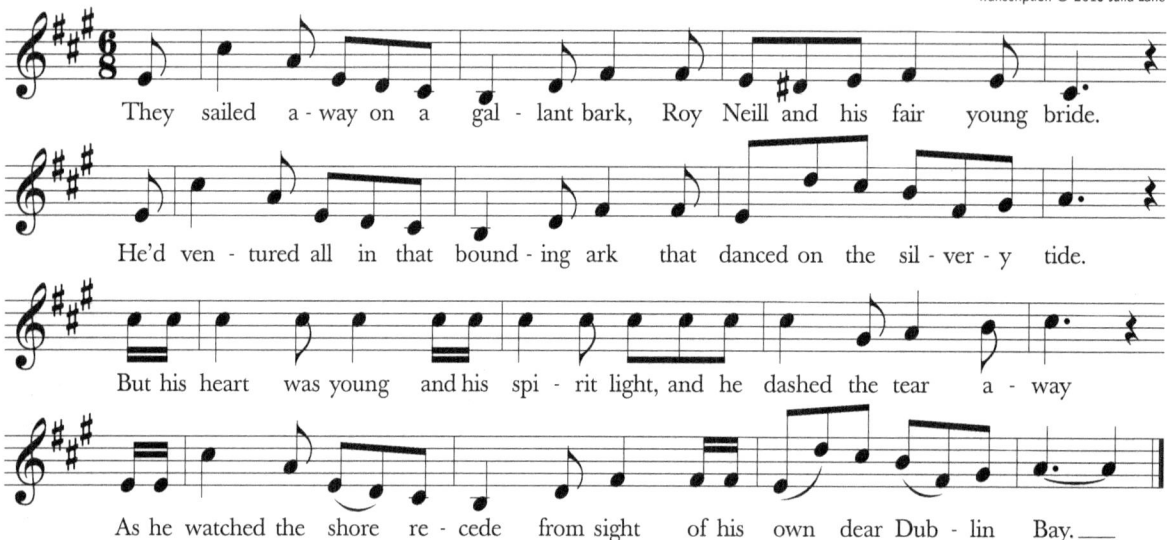

They sailed away in a gallant bark, Roy Neill and his fair young bride.
He'd ventured all in that bounding ark that danced o'er the silvery tide.
But his heart was young and his spirit light, and he dashed the tear away
As he watched the shore recede from sight of his own sweet Dublin Bay.

Three days they sailed, and a storm arose, and the lightning swept the deep,
And the thunder crash broke the short repose of the weary sea boy's sleep.
Roy Neill, he clasped his weeping bride, and he kissed her tears away.
"Oh! love, 'twas a fatal hour," she cried, "when we left sweet Dublin Bay!"

On the crowded deck of the doomed ship some stood in their mute despair;
And some, more calm with a holy lip, sought the God of the storm in prayer.
"She has struck on a rock!" the seaman cried, in the breath of their wild dismay.
And the ship went down, and the fair young bride that sailed from Dublin Bay.

Clearly an immigration ballad, the words are credited to "Mrs. Crawford" in the 1847 collection, *Songs of Ireland and other Lands*. By 1863, the tune, if somewhat incongruous, had been transcribed and attributed to one "Barker" and published in the *New Naval Song Book*. It appears in several collections of dance tunes as "Roy Neill." The 1875 manuscript given to Phillips Barry includes only the lyrics.

The Missing Ship

Harold W. Castner, Damariscotta ME 1930
from a poem by John Malcolm (1824)
Music not attributed
Transcription © Julia Lane 2018

Her mighty sails the breezes swell and fast she leaves the less'ning land.
And from the shore the last farewell is waved by many a snowy hand.
And weeping eyes are on the main until its verge she wanders o'er, But from that hour of parting pain, Oh! She was never heard of more! Oh! She was never heard of more!

Her mighty sails the breezes swell and fast she leaves the less'ning land.
And from the shore the last farewell is waved by many a snowy hand.
And weeping eyes are on the main until its verge she wanders o'er,
But from the hour of parting pain, Oh! she was never heard of more!

In her was many a mother's joy, and love of many a weeping fair
For her was wafted, in its sigh, the lonely heart's unceasing prayer
And oh!, the thousand hopes untold of ardent youth, that vessel bore
Say, were they quench'd in ocean cold? For she was never heard of more!

When on her wide and trackless path of desolation, doom'd to flee,
Say, sank she 'mid the blending wrath of racking cloud and rolling sea?
Or, where the land but mocks the eye, went drifting on a fatal shore?
Vain guesses all; her destiny is dark—she ne'er was heard of more!

The moon hath often changed her form, from glowing orb to crescent wan;
Mid skies of calm, and scowls of storm, since from her port that ship hath gone;
But ocean keeps its secret well, and though we know that all is o'er,
No eye hath seen, no tongue can tell her fate; she ne'er was heard of more!

Originally a poem titled "Lines on a vessel" written by James Malcolm of the Orkney islands in 1824, it was set to music in 1841, first appearing in the *Literary Souvenir* magazine without a composer attribution. A clipping in the scrapbook of Harold Castner at Skidompha Library, Damariscotta, ME, features the poem with a note, "The Ship *Norris*." The *Norris* was built in Damariscotta by Elbridge Norris and launched in September 1874 a week before his death. She was commanded by Captain Joseph Barstow of Alna. Late in 1894, the ship sailed from Newport News, VA, for Barcelona, Spain, then disappeared without a trace in the mid Atlantic. We have found several other connections with midcoast Maine regarding passengers onboard; Mr. Castner must have felt this song to be a fitting tribute to the ship and the local families touched by her loss.

Songs of Ships & Sailors

The Jolly Sailor Boys

A.W. Collins, Lewiston, ME, 1910
Phillips Barry Collection
Transcription © 2018 Julia Lane

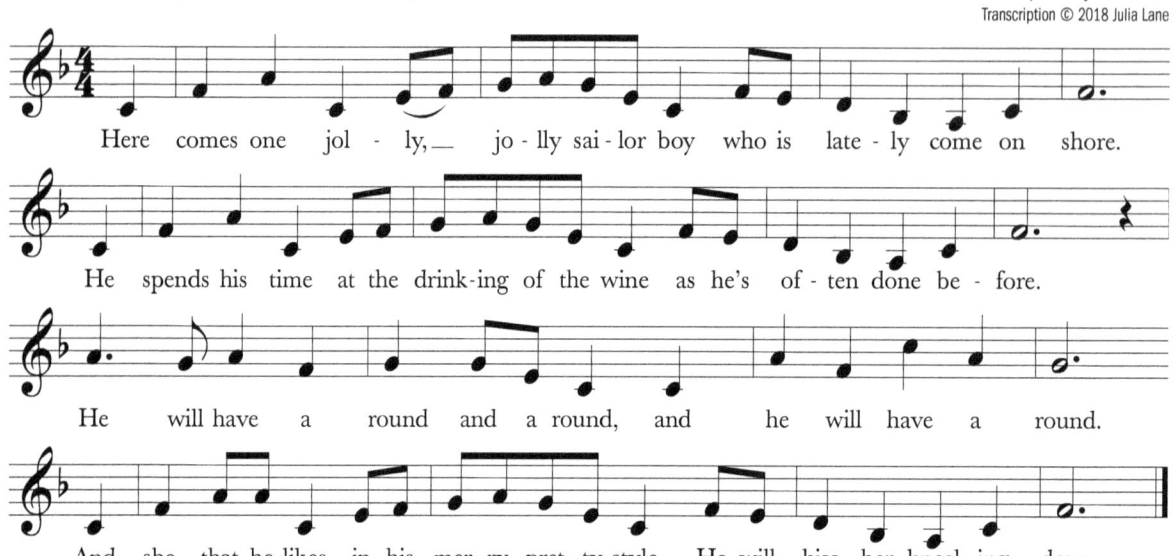

Here comes one jolly, jolly sailor boy
Who is lately come on shore.
He spends his time at the drinking of the wine
As he's often done before.
He will have a round and a round,
And he will have a round.
And she that he likes in his merry, pretty style
He will kiss her kneeling down.

Here come two jolly, jolly sailor boys, etc.

Here come three jolly, jolly sailor boys, etc.

Here come four jolly, jolly sailor boys, etc. *(ad infinitum)*

This courting / play-party song and dance is found widely as a children's game throughout North America and was, no doubt, brought here in Colonial times. It has its origins in "We be three poor mariners," printed in Ravenscroft's *Deuteromelia* song collection in 1609, and is a descendant of King Henry VIII's *Mirth or Freemen's Songs*. Although this version implies a "round" of ale or liquor, the original sings "Shall we go dance a round, a round, a round." Included with the song, sent to Phillips Barry in 1910, were dance instructions as follows:

> Children join hands and form a ring. The "sailor boy," whilst stanza 1 is being sung, walks about in the ring. At the end of the stanza he drops a handkerchief in front of one of the children in the ring, who then becomes another "sailor boy." During the singing of the second stanza the two "sailor boys" walk together. At the close of the second stanza the second "sailor boy" chooses a third, and so on.

Another version, "We are the Jolly Sailor Lads," was sung by Lorenzo Hooper of South Berwick, ME in 1941 and recorded by Helen Flanders.

The *Roving Lizzie*

Charles Finnemore, Bridgewater ME, 10/28/1943
Helen Hartness Flanders Collection
Transcription © 2016 Julia Lane

'Twas in the month of September from St. Daniels we set sail.
May the heavens guide and guard us from a sweet and pleasant gale.
We are called the *Roving Lizzie*; Bold Donnelly, our captain's name.
We are bound down from Maguire, all o'er the Spanish main.
    We are called the *Roving Lizzie*; Bold Donnelly, our captain's name.
    We are bound down from Maguire, all o'er the Spanish main!

We had not been sailing more days than two or three
When a man from the mizzen, a strange sail he did see
With a black flag under her middle peak come bearing down this way
"Why, dammit that's a pirate!" Bold Donnelly he did say.
    With a black flag… etc.

When we came up to her, they steered right up alongside
With a loud speaking trumpet "Where are you from?" he cried
"We are called the *Roving Lizzie*, Bold Donnelly's our captain's name
We are bound down from Maguire, all o'er the Spanish main."

"O haul back your main topsail and bring your ship under my lee."
"I'd see you be dammit!" said Donnelly, "I'd rather sink at sea!"
Then up went our two British flags their hearts to terrify
With our big guns and our small arms, why dammit, we did let fly.

They had twelve twelve-pounders and a crew of a hundred men
And the time the action did begin, it was just about half past ten.
We fought with six six-pounders and a crew of twenty-two
And twenty-five minutes by the watch the Spaniard cries "It won't do!"

Now this great prize we have taken along Columbia's shore
We sail to a port in Amerikay, the city called Baltimore
We'll drink a health to Bold Donnelly, likewise his able crew
We fought and beat the Spaniards with his number twenty-two.

Also called "Bold Daniels," this song is relatively rare, being found mostly in New England, the Upper Midwest, and the Canadian Maritimes. There are four versions documented in Maine. It was allegedly sung by Capt. William Solomon Loud, an early settler of Muscongus Island in Bristol, ME. In Mr. Finnemore's version, the destination is "Maguire," a corruption of La Guayra, Venezuela, which was sacked by pirates in 1743. This variant is unusual in its use of profanity, which we have found to be rare in the collections we have examined, and that the hero is Bold Donnelly. In most versions he is Bold Daniels. Regarding any historical connection, the only vessel we could find documented is an 1886 Nova Scotian fishing schooner, *Roving Lizzie,* 10.79 tons with a crew of 5. We can safely speculate that the schooner may have been named for the song rather than the reverse.

Songs of Ships & Sailors

The Ship's Carpenter

Arthur Walker, Littleton, ME 9/1/1942
Helen Hartness Flanders Collection
Transcription © 2016 Julia Lane

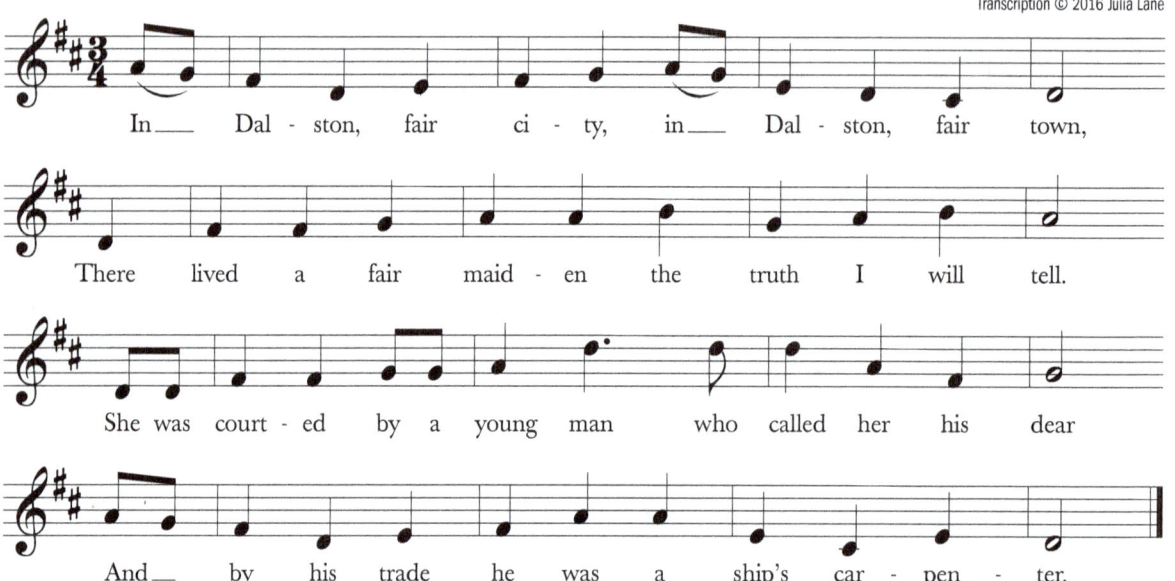

In Dalston, fair city, in Dalston fair town,
There lived a fair maiden the truth I will tell.
She was courted by a young man who called her his dear
And by his trade he was a ship's carpenter.

One morning, one morning before it was day
He went to Pretty Polly and these words he did say
"Arise, Pretty Polly and come along with me
Before we get married our friends we'll go see."

Now he led her through valleys, over hillsides so steep
Which caused pretty Polly to mourn and to weep
Saying, "Billy, dear Billy, you led me astray
The purpose my innocent life for to take."

"Yes it's true, yes it's true, it's true what you say
For all of last night I was digging your grave;
The grave you stand over which you're standing by."
Which caused Pretty Polly to weep and to sigh.

"Oh Billy, dear Billy if you'll spare my life
I'll live in shame if I can't be your wife.
I'll sail the world over to set you free
If you will but pardon my baby and me."

"No pardon," says Billy, "No pardon to extend!"
Then instantly taking a knife in his hand
He ripped and he tore her; the blood from her flew
And into the grave her fair body he threw.

Now he covered her over so safe and secure
He said that this lady would never be found.
He went aboard of a Spanish ship to sail the world round
Not thinking this murder would ever be found.

Oh, they had an old steward with courage so bold
And late that night he went in the ship's hold.
He met this fair damsel, to him she did appear
And she held in her arms a baby so dear.

He was merry with liquor and ran to embrace,
Enchanted at once by her beautiful face,
And when that woman she vanished away
To the captain he hurried without more delay.

Oh, the captain he summons this noble ship's crew
He said, "Oh, my boys I'm afraid some of you
Have murdered some damsel before you came away
And she is here now to haunt me on the sea!"

"And if he is here and the truth he deny
We'll hang him up the foremast so high
But if he confesses, his life we won't take
But land him on the first island we make."

Up speaks a bold sailor, he said, "It's not me"
Up speaks another he said, "It's not me"
And up speaks another he said, "It's not me"
So they all said this to the ship's company.

Oh, Billy he started to the cabin with speed
He met this fair damsel; she made his heart bleed.
She ripped him, she tore him, she split him in three
Just because he had murdered her baby and she.

And now, to the crew, this ghost she did say
"That since I have taken this murderer away
May the heavens protect you and may you all be free
That you arrive safe in your own counteree!"

Based on a garland called the "Gosport Tragedy," this song has its roots in the town of Gosport, near Portsmouth, England. The original broadside of 34 verses was printed about 1730 and uses the names Molly and Willie. It was later condensed into a shorter 19-verse version called "The Cruel Ship's Carpenter," and became very popular in Canada, England and the U.S. around 1900, making a revival in the 1960s. We have found 8 versions of this ballad in the Maine tradition. It was called "Pretty Polly" by F.E. Buzzell in Barry's collection circa 1925, "Willie and Molly" by Annie Syphers of Monticello, ME, in 1941 and is related to the song "Handsome Harry." Professor David Fowler (University of Washington) did extensive research to see if the ballad was based on an actual event and his interesting essay appeared in *Southern Folklore Quarterly* in 1979. While Professor Fowler could not find evidence of the crime he did find several historical elements—the name of the ship (*Bedford*), the name Charles Stewart, the circumstances of the ship's deployment, the death onboard of the carpenter—which appear in the original broadside. This song does not appear in Francis Child's *The English and Scottish Popular Ballads*. He did include a related song, "The House Carpenter," a version of which appears on page 198.

The Gallant Brigantine

Hanford Hayes, Staceyville, ME 9/1940
George Dalton, Brewer, ME 6/24/1941
Helen Hartness Flanders Collection
Transcription © 2016 Julia Lane

As I roamed on shore one Sunday from my gallant brigantine
In the Islands of old Jamaica, where I've so lately been.
And tired of my ramberling, not caring where I went,
Up to some rich plantation, my steps I slowly bent.

Where there's orange leaves, they deck the trees in green and yellow spots;
I filled my mind so keenly with melancholy thoughts,
And tired of my ramberling, I sat me down to rest
And I thought all on my native home, the home I love the best.

Where people lives in harmony and labor at their ease,
While I am bound by foolishness to plow the raging seas,
While I am bound by foolishness to labor night and day,
And I sang a song of old Ireland, to drive dull care away.

My song it being ended, my mind it felt at ease,
I rose to pull some oranges that hung upon the trees.
When there I spied a female form that filled me with delight.
She wore the robes of innocence; her dress it was snowy white.

Oh, her dress was snowy white, likewise her mantle, it being green,
She had a silken shawl hung 'round her neck, her shoulders for to screen.
Her hair hung down in ringlets, as black as any sloe.
And a dark blue eye attracted me; her cheeks were like the rose.

I kinderly saluted her, "Good morning, pretty maid!"
And with a kind reception, "Good morning, sir," she said;
I kinderly invited her to set down and chat awhile,
And I told her many's a hard old yarn that caused her for to smile.

Before I rose to go away I gave her to understand
That my name was Harry Redmond; I was a married man.
And three days before I'd left the shore, my troubles, they began.
The wife I loved from all above, run away with another man.

And 'fore she rose to go away she did me thus address,
"Call in and see my husband; he'll treat you to the best."
It was then she introduced me to a noble-looking man,
Who kinderly saluted me and took me by the hand.

I said I was a sailor that's lately come on shore.
"I belong to yonder brigantine lies anchored in the bay."
The wine being on the table and dinner was served up soon.
We three sat down together, to spend a jovial afternoon.

Also called "The Isle of Jamaica," this is related to "The Lass of Mohea" and "Lakes of Ponchartrain" and is the old story of a stranger treated kindly by a local woman and her family. There was regular trade between New England and the Caribbean, particularly for molasses, a prime ingredient for rum or "New England Tea." Vast sugar cane plantations were owned by white aristocrats and worked with slave labor. To complete the story, we have combined the versions of two informants recorded by Flanders.

Robin Hood's Bay

Frank Matthews, Eastport, ME 1927
Phillips Barry Collection
Transcription © 2020 Julia Lane

In Robin Hood's Bay a fair damsel did dwell.
She was courted by a sailor who did love her well.
He promised he would marry when he did return.
Mark his sad misfortune; this young man was drowned.

For then these poor sailors they put out to sea
In a terrible gale that chanced for to be.
Oh, the winds they did whistle and the wild waters roar
Which drove them poor sailors far from the sea shore.

Then these poor sailors they swam for their lives!
Some they had sweethearts and others had wives
But this poor young sailor he chanced to be one;
Marked his sad fortunes; a watery tomb.

When these sad news this young girl did hear
She wrung her white hands and she tore out her hair
Crying, "All you wild billows bring my love back on shore
That I may behold his sweet features once more!"

As she was strolling in Robin Hood's Bay
She espied a dark object come a-drifting her way.
She stopped and she gazed, brought herself to a stand;
She knew it was her true love by a mark on his hand.

She hugged him and kissed him o'er and over.
She cried and she kissed him a dozen times o'er
Crying, "I am contented to die by your side!"
One more kiss on his cold lips; broken hearted she died.

In Robin Hood's churchyard, this young couple does dwell
And o'er their grave is a covering this story does tell
So come all you young sailors who pass by this way,
Think of this young sailor of Robin Hood's Bay

The 1927 handwritten manuscript from the Phillips Barry collection at Harvard's Houghton Library, submitted by Frank Matthews, is simply titled "Sea Song" with "Sailor's Return" crossed out, and "Robin Hood's Bay" underlined. English collector Kidson titles it "The Drowned Sailor" while others call it "Stow Brow" and "Scarborough Sands." Robin Hood's Bay is a fishing village on the Yorkshire coast. Some historians speculate that the song may have antecedents in a lament inspired by a woman's discovery of her drowned lover, one Captain Digby, published as a broadside in 1671. We have used the tune collected by Frank & Anne Warner from Tink Tillet of Wanchese, NC (Outer Banks) in 1940 and published in their book *Traditional American Folk Songs*.

The Lowlands of Holland

Carrie Grover, Gorham ME 1953
Mr. Murray, Holden, ME 1914
Fannie Hardy Eckstorm Collection
Adaptation & Transcription © 2011 Julia Lane

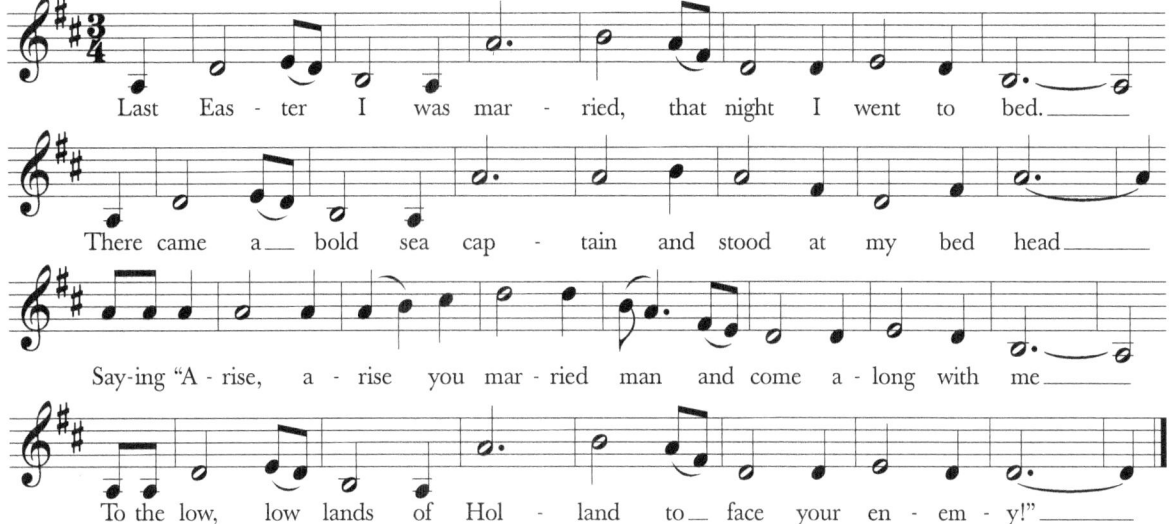

Last Easter I was married, that night I went to bed
There came a bold sea captain and stood at my bed head
Saying "Arise, arise you married man and come along with me
To the low, lowlands of Holland to face your enemy!"

I clasped my arms about my love imploring him to stay
But still this bold sea captain said "Arise and come away!
Arise, arise you married man and come along with me
To the low, lowlands of Holland to face your enemy!"

The Lowlands is a cold place, and a place where grows no green,
Neither flowers nor habitations for a stranger to dwell in.
But they say that money is plenty as the leaves upon the tree
My curse rest on that captain that parted my love and me.

Said the mother to the daughter, "Dear, why do you thus lament?
There are men enough in our town to make your heart content."
"There are men enough in our town, but there's not one for me
For I never had but one true love and he has gone from me."

"No sash shall go about my waist, nor comb come in my hair
Neither fire, coal, nor candlelight shine in my chamber more
And never will I married be until the day I die
Since cruel waves and angry winds have parted my love and me."

The "Lowlands of Holland" refer to the Netherlands, which were in conflict with Britain from James I in the early 1600s to the mid 1800s. A series of Anglo-Dutch wars were fought over the course of 200 years and the song was adapted to include current details. The earliest printed version is a 1684 broadside, "The Seaman's Sorrowful Bride," where the woman laments that "Holland's land doth me withstand and parts my love and I," but there is no mention of a military conflict or the press gang. David Herd's *Scots Songs* (1776) has an equally simple variation set to the tune which is most commonly used. In 1780 in Connecticut, during the Fourth Anglo-Dutch War (1780–1784), the song appears in a notebook written by Thomas Fanning with this lyric: "To the lowlands of Holland to fight in Germany." In Phillips Barry's Collection, we find

Songs of Ships & Sailors

Mrs. Lewis Pierce's Songbook from 1845 in Maine which has this:

> A noble chieftain came and stood at my bed feet
> Saying, "Arise, my noble warrior and go along with me
> Into the lowlands of Holland to fight for Germany"

This detail suggests participation in a mercenary Scotch Brigade of the Dutch States Army which was "borrowed" for use in America and implies that the man's service is voluntary and laudable. These versions also include a shipwreck as the source of the woman's despair rather than the fact that he has been a victim of the press gang— a later addition. Officially, the Dutch did not use impressment to swell their ranks; however, the British were notorious for sending representatives of the armed forces to range through villages and towns recruiting or "pressing" men into service. What better place to find a likely candidate than at a wedding? This practice continued on both sides of the Atlantic until the War of 1812, when British ships were harassing Maine's coast; the later versions of the song include this element. Neither Fanning nor Pierce reference the beauty of the destination as do some later versions ("Sugarcane is plentiful and tea grows on each tree"). This motif, which seems to be restricted to later Scottish and Irish variants, may refer to the Dutch territories in both the East and West Indies that were a source of conflict in the early 19th century.

The two complete Maine versions of this song that we have are basically identical except for the third verse, which came from the singing of Mr. Murray in 1914 and was transcribed by Fannie Eckstorm's brother W. M. Hardy (above, in italics). It includes a bleak description of the destination and has a chorus cursing the captain, which is unusual. Although we have few Maine examples of the song, it was apparently well known, as evidenced by Dan Golden's autobiographical rewrite for a lumberman taking leave of his sweetheart to work in the woods:

> Oh, the night that I was married, Oh, and laid on marriage bed,
> Up rose John Ross and Cyrus Hewes and stood at my bedhead
> Saying, "Arise, you married man and come along with me
> To the lonesome hills of Suncook to swamp them logs for me!"

His song process is well documented in *Minstrelsy of Maine,* pp 133–39. Before singing for Mrs. Eckstorm, the singer said "My name is Daniel H. Golden. When you write anything about me again, you will put in my name, won't you? I was born in Paisley, Scotland, and I come to this country in 1865." It makes sense, then, that he would use a Scottish song as his template. Most tunes are variants of "Miss Admiral Gordon's Strathspey" originally found in the *Caledonian Pocket Companion* (1750). Mrs. Grover is the only singer from Maine to provide a tune and the version in her book *A Heritage of Song* (p. 50) echoes this. She was recorded by Alan Lomax at Washington, D.C., in 1941.

The Sailor's Tale

David Kane, Searsport, ME 1945
Helen Hartness Flanders Collection
Transcription © 2018 Julia Lane

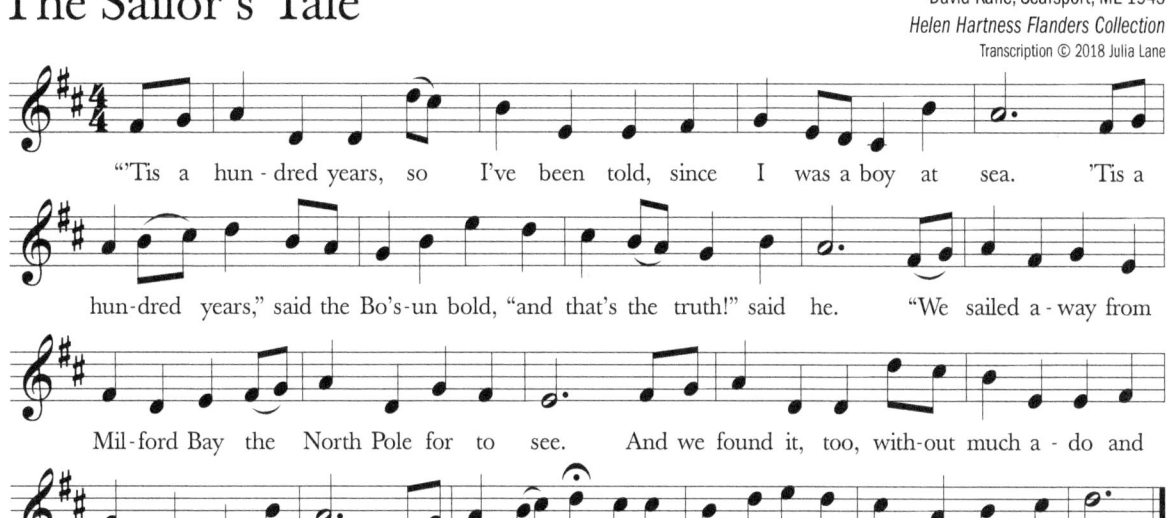

" 'Tis a hundred years, so I've been told, since I was a boy at sea.
'Tis a hundred years," said the Bo's'n bold, "and that's the truth!" said he.
"We sail'd away from Milford Bay the North Pole for to see.
And we found it, too, without much ado and that's the truth!" said he.
"We found it, too, without much ado and that's the truth!" said he.

"We sail'd and sail'd and one fair moon a great whale we espied
So we took a rope and a long harpoon and we struck him in the starboard side.
Then away and away went the great big whale and away and away went we
Tied fast to his tail, to the North we did sail and that's the truth!" said he,
"Tied fast to his tail, to the North we did sail and that's the truth!" said he.

"But when we came to the great North Star an iceberg we did see
Said the Captain, 'I have come thus far I am not going back!' said he;
So we tickled the tail of the great big whale with a tenpenny nail did we,
And we sailed right through that iceberg blue and that's the truth!" said he,
"And we sailed right through that iceberg blue and that's the truth!" said he.

"And there the North Pole we did see and we anchored the whale astern.
But he gave us a whack that sent us back or I mightn't have been spinnin' this yarn.
Now messmates all," said the Bo's'n bold "If the North Pole you would see
Just you take a sail at the tail of a whale and that's the truth!" said he.
"Just you take a sail at the tail of a whale and that's the truth!" said he.

Although some claim this is a "stamp & go" work shanty, it was in fact a collaboration between two of the 19th century's more successful commercial ballad writers. Frederic Edward Weatherly (1848–1929) was an English lawyer, author, lyricist and broadcaster. He is estimated to have written the lyrics to at least 3,000 popular songs, including the sentimental ballad "Danny Boy." James Lynam Molloy (1837–1909) was an Irish composer, poet, and author who began writing songs in 1865. His work came particularly in demand during the 1870s as his songs were sung in London theaters. "Love's Old Sweet Song" (1884) was a best seller, especially popular among sailors. His songs, like Weatherly's, gained such popularity in the early 20th century that some passed into oral tradition. This song was published in 1881 as "The Boatswain; or The Tale of a Whale" by J. L. Molloy, words by F. E. Weatherly. It prompted the editors in *Punch Magazine*, May 28, 1881 to comment on "New Naughtycal Music" saying "We notice that Mr. J. L. Molloy has produced a new song called 'The Boatswain's Story.' Glad to hear it, and still more glad to hear that J. L. M., for whose music we have a sincere regard, is continuing the series with *The Mate's Whopper, The Swab's Suppression of Fact, The Cabin-Boy's Crammer, The Lie of the Land-Lubber, The Second Lieutenant's Abominable Falsehood, The Coxwain of the Captain's Gig's Disgusting Perversion of the Truth, and The Mate's Mendacity*."

Songs of Ships & Sailors

The Sailor's Grave

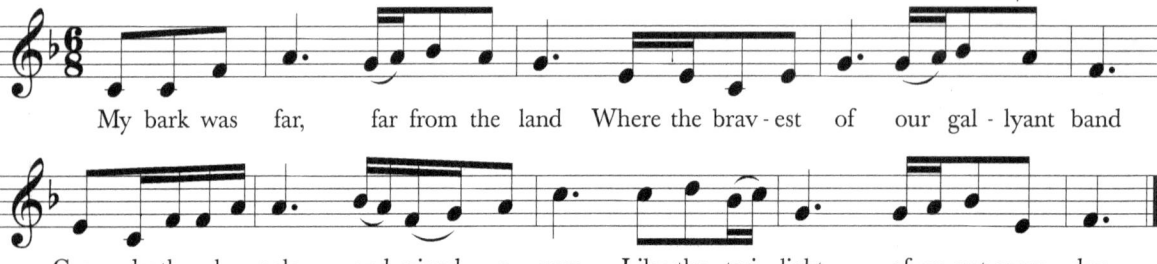

My bark was far, far from the land
Where the bravest of our gallyant band
Grew deathly pale and pined away
Like the twilight of an autumn day.

We watched him through long hours of pain;
Our cares were grave but our hopes in vain.
Death's stroke! He gave no coward's alarms
But smiled and died in his messmate's arms.

We proudly decked his funeral bed
With the British flag upon his breast.
We gave him this as a badge of the brave,
Then he was fit for a sailor's grave.

We had no costly winding sheet;
We placed two round shots at his feet.
He laid in his hammock, as snug and sound,
As a king in his long shroud marble bound.

Cheeks they grew pale, each heart grew weak,
Of the tears that was seen on the brownest cheek.
A quiver was played on lips of pride
As we lowered him down by the ship's dark side.

A splash and a plunge and the task was o'er
And the billows rolled as they rolled before
And it's loud prayer hallowed the wave
As he sank beneath, a sailor's grave.

Before the days of embalming, a corpse would have to be disposed of relatively quickly on site. On board ship, as voyages were often long, it was impractical for remains to be returned to loved ones at home. Hence the body of the deceased would be committed to the depths. Many inscriptions on gravestones in Maine cemeteries indicate that the seafaring person is "lost" at sea. Persons of high station were exceptions, of course, and tradition has it that the term "Nelson's blood," in reference to rum, derives from the story that Admiral Nelson's remains were preserved in a cask of rum after the battle of Trafalgar. "The Sailor's Grave" was quite popular, being distributed as sheet music from 1845 with words by Eliza Cook and music by John C. Baker. We have five traditional examples collected in Maine.

The Spanish War

Mr. H.H. Chamberlain, Round Pond, ME 1925
Fannie Hardy Eckstorm Collection
Transcription © 2018 Julia Lane

Yankee Dewey sailed away
On an armored cruiser.
He took along for company
Of men and guns a few, sir.

CHORUS:
   Yankee Dewey, ha, ha, ha!
   Dewey you're a dandy.
   With men and guns and cruiser too,
   You're certainly quite handy.

He sailed away for the Philippines
With order for to snatch them;
He smashed the Spaniards right and left
Where he could catch them.

Yankee Dewey done it, too,
He done it so complete, sir,
That not a single ship was left
Of all that Spanish fleet, sir.

After the sinking of the USS *Maine* in Havana, Cuba, the U.S. was committed to the Spanish-American War, which included defending American interests in the South Pacific. Admiral George Dewey prevailed at the Battle of Manila Bay in the Philippines on May 1, 1898. A historically decisive victory, the Spanish fleet was effectively decimated while a single crewman was lost on the American side. This parody of the patriotic song "Yankee Doodle" underscored the sentiment of the time. The words are attributed to Ina Libby in *Spanish American War Songs–a complete collection of newspaper verse during the recent war with Spain* edited by Sidney Witherbee and published in 1898 (p. 555).

Songs of Ships & Sailors

Root, Hog, or Die

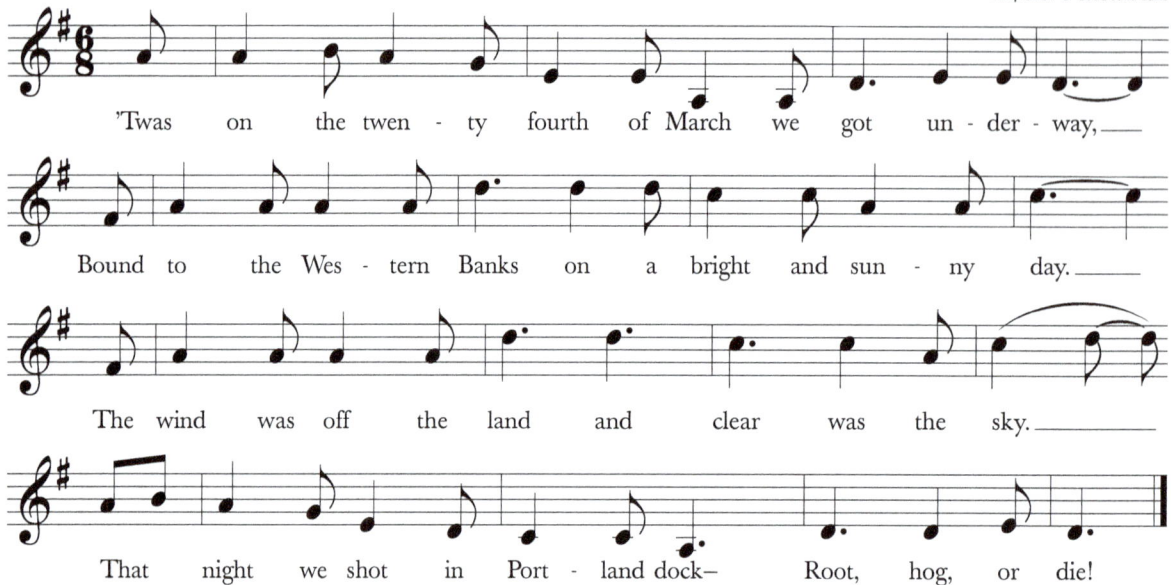

Capt. Archie Spurling, Isleford ME, 1925
Fannie Hardy Eckstorm Collection
Tune collected by Alan Lomax
Adaptation © 2018 Julia Lane

'Twas on the twenty-fourth of March we got underway,
Bound to the Western Banks on a bright and sunny day.
The wind was off the land and clear was the sky.
That night we shot in Portland Dock — Root, hog, or die!

Now, boys, bring down your stores and fix them all complete;
Bring up your fishing lines and fix your fishing fleets.
The Captain came on board and "Ready!" was the cry:
"We'll move down Hog Island Roads — Root, hog, or die!"

Now, boys, bring up your water casks and carry them up on shore,
And fill them up with water till they will hold no more;
Then hoist up the boat, boys, we'll have another try
To get up on the Western Bank — Root, hog, or die!

We hoisted up our sails and the wind began to blow.
We cleared up our decks and then went below,
We tumbled in our bunks but scarce shut an eye,
When 'twas, "Turn out and reef, boys — Root, hog, or die!"

We tumbled from our bunks, regard to no brain*
One says unto the other, "I wonder if it rains,"
"It rains like the devil," the other quick replied,
"And we will have to oil up — Root, hog, or die!"

Now we've got her close fore and aft, and we will go below,
The wind is to the eastward and like the devil it does blow,
We beat about and banged about and never saw the sky,
At last we shot in Port Latoun — Root, hog, or die!

We bargained with old Carter for to get some wood;
He said he had a-plenty and that 'twas very good;
He said he had a team he would send down by and by,
And help us get it to the boat—Root, hog, or die!

By 'n by the thing he called a team came rambling through the field,
'Twas nothing but a goose pen tied on to a pair of wheels,
And as for the driver, I would rather be he than I,
Whoa! gee! drive them straight!—Root, hog, or die!

And now I've sung you all about his farm and his stock,
I'll sing you about his girls, for he has quite a flock;
He's got one, she stands full eight feet high;
She doesn't favor wearing hoops—Root, hog, or die!

Now I says unto the cook, "Make haste and bear a hand,
And we will take a walk on this Nova Scotia land."
As we were going up the road, two girls we did espy,
Sitting down upon a log—Root, hog, or die!

Now I wish you'd seen the cook, I think likely 'twould ha' made you stare,
For I thought he was as bashful as Timothy, I declare,
But if those rocks could speak as well as you and I,
Someone would be jealous at home—Root, hog, or die!

Although the phrase "root, hog, or die" appears in print in the 1834 biography *Life of David Crockett*, it is, no doubt, a common phrase from early Colonial times, when pigs were turned out into the fields and forests to fend for themselves, thus creating a colloquial term for self-reliance. There are numerous variants of this song for just about every hardscrabble occupation imaginable—including circus roustabouts! It first appears in 1854 as a patriotic broadside, then as a popular minstrel song in 1856. In 1858 it describes the hardships of gold miners, then makes its way through the Civil War, out West with the cowboys and in modern times as a football chant. This deep-sea fishing version, from *Minstrelsy of Maine* by Eckstorm and Smyth, was taken down in 1925 from the singing of Captain Archie S. Spurling of Islesford, ME, who learned it as a bosun on board a fishing schooner fifty years prior. It features an encounter between fishermen and landsmen and echoes the bothy tradition of poking fun at members of the crew. Regarding the tune, we did find a version by Lena Bourne Fish of Jaffrey, NH recorded by Flanders, but her tune did not fit these lyrics. The tune in Lomax's book *Folksongs of North America* p. 333 seems to suit and so we have fit the lyrics to that.

*Note: "regard to no brain" is the original phrase; its meaning is inscrutable.

Pretty Polly of Topsham

Susie Carr Young, Brewer, ME 1925
Phillips Barry Collection
Transcription © 2020 Fred Gosbee

Come all ye fair gallants, fair gallants attend.
A story, a story to you I will tell.
'Tis of a young sea captain, wherein he took delight,
And he courted a lady whose beauty was bright.
He had not courted her past twelve months, no more,
When his own business called him from the shore.
He went unto his Polly all for to take his leave,
Saying, "Polly, pretty Polly, I pray thee, don't grieve."

"For I'm going to cross the ocean my fortune to restore,
Where the seas are in motion and the foaming billows roar
And if unto America I never do return,
Here I leave you, pretty Polly, in Topsham to mourn."
Past months two or three he had not been away,
When a young minister came there for to stay;
In viewing of her features, she looked so brisk and bold,
He made love unto her, as I have been told.

Saying, "Polly, pretty Polly, if you can fancy me,
I will make you as happy as happy can be;
But if to any other young man 'tis you are engaged,
I pray you prove true to the vows you have made."
" 'Tis I am engaged, and the truth I will tell,
'Tis I am engaged, but I don't like so well;
He will be at home, and it is by and by,
And then you will see how quick him I'll deny."

This young man came home at last, as I have been told.
He brought home fine riches and fine stores of gold;
He brought home fine ribbons and fine silks so gay,
To adorn pretty Polly on her wedding day.
Saying, "Polly, pretty Polly, since I have been to sea,
Have you seen any other you love better than me?"
Then she turned herself round with a high and haughty air,
Saying, "Priest Ellis I love better, I suppose you don't care!"

Saying, "Polly, pretty Polly, since I must free my mind,
I think you are the falsest of all womankind;
Since I have been so constant, and you have proved untrue,
Farewell, pretty Polly, I bid you adieu.
'Tis I will go a-rambling, go rambling for rest,
In hopes to relieve my poor tortured breast;
'Tis I will go a-rambling, like some dove around the shore,
And I never will go near my false Polly any more."

This text and melody are from Susie Carr Young of Brewer as sung by her mother and grandmother and found only in her family. According to Phillips Barry in the *Bulletin of the Folksong Society of the Northeast* (2:16–17) this song is allegedly a true story referring to Topsham, ME. "Priest Ellis" is Reverend Jonathan Ellis who married Mary Fulton of Topsham. The text also appears in the *Anthology of American Folk Poetry* by Duncan Emrich.

Fifteen Ships on Georges Banks

Lyrics: Henry Bunker, Cranberry Island, ME 7/1924
Fannie Hardy Eckstorm Collection
Tune: Margaret Hallett, Lubec, ME 1963
Maine Folklife Center Collection
Transcription © 2017 Julia Lane

Come all you bold undaunted ones who brave the winter cold
And you that sail on Georges Banks where thousands have been lost.
Come all you sad and grieving mothers and wives and sweethearts too,
Likewise you loving sisters who bade them last adieu.

I pray you give attention and listen unto me,
Relating to those noble men who were drowned in the sea.
'Twas on the first of February, in eighteen sixty-two,
Three vessels sailed from Gloucester with each a hearty crew.

The course they steered was east-southeast, Cape Ann passed out of sight;
They anchored on the Banks that night with everything all right.
But on the twenty-fourth that night the gale began to blow
The sea rose up like mountaintops which proved their overthrow.

The thought of homes and loving ones did fill their hearts full sore,
For well convinced were all those men they'd see their homes no more.
No tongue can e'er describe the sea; the sky was thick with snow;
Fifteen sails did founder there and down to bottom go.

One hundred and forty-nine brave men so lately left their land,
Now sleep beneath the Georges Bank those rough and shifting sands.
One hundred and seventy children those men have left on shore,
With seventy mournful widows their sorrows to endure

I hope they will be reconciled and not give up to grief,
For there's a widow's God above, and He will give relief.
There are many in the Army and in the Navy too,
Who mourn and grieve in private who will sympathize with you.

Bygone Ballads of Maine, Volume I

You will at times think of home, of days that's past and gone,
When by their sides their husbands sat, and cheerful was their song.
For you they left their native shore, for you the sea did roam;
'Twas love and duty called them forth to leave their happy home.

So now adieu to Georges Banks, that place I now despise,
For many a storm I've braved out there and heard the widows' cries
So bid adieu to Georges Banks, dry up your tearful eyes,
Prepare to meet your God above and dwell beyond the skies.

The area called Georges Banks in the North Atlantic has historically been a rich fishing ground, often attracting a hundred ships at one time hoping to share the bounty. In the 19th century, Gloucester, MA was the home port for many of the fishing schooners that ventured forth. The work was hard and dangerous, but men from throughout the region signed on to make their fortunes. In February 1862, the schooners headed out to the Banks as usual with upwards of 70 ships anchoring near each other. On Monday the 24th, a fierce gale slammed out of the northwest without warning. *The Fishermen's Memorial & Record Book* of 1873 reported, "Not having sufficient warning of the blow, they were unable to heave up" resulting in "fearful collisions… Nearly every boat would lose booms, masts, cable and anchors or were so badly stove up as hardly to be able to get back to shore." 120 men and 15 vessels were lost, leaving 70 widows and 140 fatherless children. There is a memorial in Gloucester to the tragedy, but at least half of the casualties came from other communities in coastal New England. We can be sure that many of the victims were from Maine.

This song was originally published in a book titled *Ballads and Songs of the Sea compiled by Procter Brothers and respectfully dedicated to the hardy fishermen of Cape Anne, Gloucester 1874* on page 21 thus: "On the loss of the Georges Vessels, in 1862 by Captain Peter Sexton." The lyrics in italics are from the original poem. Julia found a manuscript of another song "in progress" in the Boothbay Historical Society which details the loss of 25 fishermen from the region in 1851, many of whom sailed on Gloucester schooners. This is one of three variants of the Procter Brothers song collected in the Bar Harbor area during 1924–26 by Eckstorm and Smyth for their *Minstrelsy of Maine* (p. 281). Others were from M. C. Cilley, Southwest Harbor and Mrs. Mary L Cotton, of Orland. We are grateful for the tune provided by Margaret Hallet of Lubec and recorded by Pauline Lewis for the Maine Folklife Center Collection.

The Jovial Sailor & His Beautiful Queen

Delia Quimby/Susie Carr Young, Brewer, ME 1925
Phillips Barry Collection
addl. lyrics from Helen Creighton Collection
Transcription © 2019 Julia Lane

Come all ye fair ladies and gentlemen bold,
I'll tell you as true a story as ever was told.
Concerning a fair lady of old Yarmouth town
She was famed for her beauty, her wealth and renown.

As she was a-walking one day on the street
A jovial young sailor she happened to meet.
He was light, brisk and airy as he passed her by;
She wavéd her handkerchief and she bade him draw nigh.

"What is your name, sir, and what is your trade,
And in what part of America have you lately surveyed?
And where is your last place you made your abode,
And what is the reason for traveling this road?"

"Willie is my name, I'm a sailor by trade,
And in all parts of America I have lately surveyed,
In the city of New York I have made my abode,
And I hope it's no harm I am traveling this road?"

"Willie, I'll have you to stay here and tarry,
And perhaps by your countenance some girl you might marry,
And perhaps some great fortune may increase your store,
For Willie, I want you to wander no more."

"I would not leave rambling for thousands or more,
You can see by my rambling I have money in store,
I have gold in my pocket and silver likewise."
Like an innocent girl the tears came from his eyes.

"O Willie, I'll have you for to marry me,
I've men and rich servants for to wait upon thee,
And a coach and six horses at your leisure may ride,
And Willie, I'll have you to make me your bride!"

To the church they did go on the very same day,
And there they got married without further delay,
A handsomer couple you never have seen
Than Willie the sailor and his beautiful queen

An alternative title for this song is "It's of a Rich Lady." Although undoubtably a broadside ballad, there is little evidence for this song outside New England and Maritime Canada. The first two verses (in italics) and this tune are from Delia A. Quimby of Brewer, ME, as dictated to Susie Carr Young in 1925, with the remainder being from Nova Scotia collector Helen Creighton's *Maritime Folk Songs* (p. 53). A popular song in the region, these lyrics were sung to Creighton by Mr. Grace Clergy of Petpeswick, NS, in 1951.

The Captain and the Squire

Dale Potter, Kingman, ME 1947
Horace Beck Collection
Tune from collection of Len Graham, Northern Ireland
Transcription © 2019 Julia Lane

It's of a sea capting, a sea capting of late.
He married a lady with a fine estate.
And before they were married he was bound for the sea,
And before they were bedded, he was called away.

CHORUS:
  They had rowdy dum dum, they had rowdy dum day!

Now the capting being gone, 'twas the squire's intent
To go see this lady he was fully bent
So with his butler and his footman and his coachman so fine
He went up to the lady to bid her be kind.

He stepped up to this lady and gave her a kiss,
He says, "A slice of your loaf it will never be missed."
He threw his arms around her and gave her another
"It will do you no harm, it will make you a mother."

At last she consented so to bed they did go.
The cook and the butler they followed also.
With the coachman and housemaid it was all of the same
And the footman slept up in the garret with Jane.

Now six months was over and seven months being come
This lady began to grow thick round the waist.
When eight months was over and nine had gone
And the very same night, the sea captain came home.

He stepped up to his lady all her to embrace
He said, "My fair jewel, you grow thick 'round the waist."
"It is fat, it is fat," this fair lady did say.
"Would you have me as lean as when you went away?"

(I've had rowdy dum dum etc)

He then took his lady and went out in the hall.
She opened her mouth and loud she did bawl.
"The colic, the colic, the colic," she cried.
"I'm so sick with the colic I'm afeard I shall die!"

They sent for the midwife and when she got there,
She ordered the cook for some tea to prepare.
The cook she made answer all in the next room,
"I'm so sick with the colic that I cannot come!"

They sent for the doctor and when he got there
He delivered this lady with a beautiful heir.
The cook and the housemaid, they all stood the same.
Both one of them all, it was all the same.

"Well, well," says the captain, "as sure as I live
All for this joke's sake I will freely forgive.
But tell me my lady, tell me if you can
Do all these four babies belong to one man?"

"No, no," says the lady, "the squire got me beguiled
And each of his servants gave my maids a child."
"No matter" says the capting, "No matter for that!
That night I went away I had a bit of old hat!"

I found this in Horace Beck's unpublished dissertation. One of many songs that he collected from Dale Potter, its roguish nature probably kept it from being included in any of his many books. Also known as "The Colic." The earliest version, "The Young Squire's Frolic," was printed as a broadside by Burbage and Stretton, Nottingham, between 1797 and 1807. "The Roving Sea Captain" was also collected by Len Graham in Northern Ireland and appears on his recording *It's of My Rambles*.

The Fate of Franklin

Will Merritt, Ludlow, ME 1941
Helen Hartness Flanders Collection
Transcription © 2015 Julia Lane

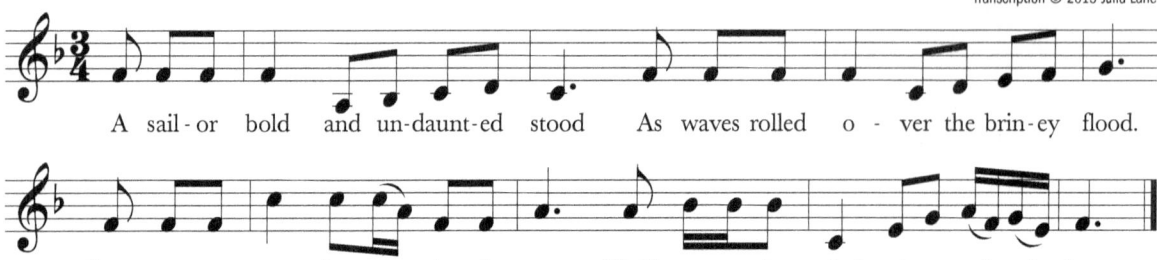

A sail-or bold and un-daunt-ed stood As waves rolled o-ver the brin-ey flood.
Come pay at-ten-tion to what I say: 'Twill put you in mind of a sail-or's dream.

A sailor bold and undaunted stood
As waves rolled over the briny flood.
Come pay attention to what I say:
'Twill put you in mind of a sailor's dream.

We were homeward bound one night on the deep
When in my hammock I fell asleep
I dreamt a dream which I thought was true
Concerning Franklin and his brave crew.

As we drew near to old England's shore
I heard a lady so sad implore
She wept aloud and she seemed to say
"Alas, my Franklin's so far away!"

"It's seven long years since that ship of fame
It bore my Franklin across the main
With a hundred sailors with courage true
To find a northwestern passage through."

"To find a passage around the Pole
Where lightning flashes and loud thunder rolls
It's more than any man can do
With a heart undaunted and courage true."

"There was Captain Kelly of Sedgewick town
And Captain Osburn of high renown
And Doctor Tate like many more
That's long been cruising the Arctic shore."

"Oh, they sailed east and they sailed west
From Greenland's Island where they thought best
They met with hardships and vainly strove
With mountains of ice where their ship was stove."

"In Baffin's Bay where the cold wind blows
The fate of Franklin nobody knows.
Five hundred pounds would I freely give
To know on earth does my Franklin live."

"But alas he's gone like many more
That's left their home to return no more.
God help the widows who sorely weep
For loss of husbands drowned the deep."

John Franklin entered the British Navy at age 14 in 1800, then turned to surveying in 1819 and joined a three-year expedition mapping the Arctic. After a hiatus serving in the Mediterranean and as Lt Governor of Van Dieman's land (Tasmania) he returned to seek the Northwest Passage, setting sail on May 19, 1845. Two ships, the HMS *Erebus* and HMS *Terror*, carried 134 chosen men and enough supplies for three years. They were spotted in Baffin Bay on July 26 by passing whalers, then vanished without a trace. After three years with no word from the expedition, the British Admiralty offered £10,000 for information about their fate, and his wife, Lady Franklin, financed many ships to continue the search. At least 15 rescue parties combed the Arctic until 1859 when Capt. Leopold McClintock found various artifacts including a written account secured in a cairn. This described the ship becoming frozen in the ice in 1846 and Franklin's death in 1847. The remaining men tried to make their way to the Hudson Bay Company's outpost, but according to an interview with an Eskimo woman, "they fell down and died as they walked." The mystery has intrigued generations of historians and archeologists. In 2014 and 2016, expeditions discovered the underwater wrecks of the *Erebus* and the *Terror* south of King William Island. Various theories about the actions and fate of the crews are being proven and debunked as these wrecks and their artifacts are examined.

Regarding the song itself, a poetry competition sponsored by Oxford University in 1860 yielded a variety of epics about Franklin and his fate. Some describe the voyage in detail, others wax eloquent and emotional but are less informative. The most popular, similar to this version, originate in a broadside that may have been penned and circulated by Lady Franklin herself. Mr. Merritt said he learned this song from his mother who was born in Scotland. The last two lines from another version have been added to complete the verse.

Ten Thousand Miles Away

Tune: Capt. Archie Spurling, Southwest Harbor, ME circa 1930
Phillips Barry Collection
Lyrics attributed to Joseph B. Geoghegan 1897
Transcription © 2019 Julia Lane

Sing Ho! for a brave and a valiant bark and a brisk and lively breeze,
A jovial crew and a captain, too, to carry me over the seas,
To carry me over the seas, me boys, to my true love so gay.
She has taken a trip on a gallant ship ten thousand miles away.

CHORUS:
    So blow the winds, heigh-ho; a-roving I will go,
    I'll stay no more on England's shore, so let the music play!
    I'll start on the morning train, to cross the raging main,
    For I'm on the move to my own true love, ten thousand miles away.

My true love, she is beautiful, my true love she is young;
Her eyes are as blue as the violet's hue, and silvery sounds her tongue
And silvery sounds her tongue, my boys, but while I sing this lay,
She is doing grand in a distant land, ten thousand miles away.

Oh! that was a dark and dismal day when last she left the strand
She bade good-bye with a tearful eye, and waved her lily hand
And waved her lily hand, my boys, as the big ship left the bay
"Adieu" says she, "Remember me, ten thousand miles away."

Oh! if I could be but a bo's'n bold, or only a bombardier,
I'd hire a boat and hurry afloat, and straight to my true love steer
And straight to my true love steer, my boys, where the dancing dolphins play,
And the whales and the sharks are having their larks, ten thousand miles away.

Oh! the sun may shine through a London fog and the Thames run bright and clear,
The oceans' brine be turned to wine, and I may forget my beer
And I may forget my beer, my boys, and the landlord's quarter-day;
But I'll never part from my own sweetheart, ten thousand miles away!

In his *Shanties from the Seven Seas* Stan Hugill says that this was originally a shore ballad sung by street singers in Ireland in the early nineteenth century. The song has been passed from singer to singer as a traditional working shanty, though it later became popular in music halls. *The Scottish Student's Song Book* gives the author as "J. B. Geoghegan"—Joseph Bryan Geoghegan (1816–1889) who was manager of the Star and Museum Music Hall in Bolton, Lancashire. The reference to "ten thousand miles" may refer to the distance between England and Australia, with the separation of the lovers being a result of penal transportation. Several of the variant texts indicate this possibility:

Oh, dark and dismal was the day when last I saw my Meg,
She'd a Government band around each hand and another one 'round her leg.

Songs of Ships & Sailors

The Brave Seaman

Kathleen Clark, Pembroke ME 1928
Traditional tune set by Kris Paprocki, Pembroke, ME © 2014
Transcription © 2018 Julia Lane

The waves dash high against the rocks with a mighty thund'ring roar
And the strong wind buffets the whitecaps and sweeps the long rough shore.

CHORUS:
>Hurrah for that noble seaman! May his name be praised in song!
>May he enter the gates of heaven and dwell with the happy throng!

Far out on the rocky headline comes a distant whistling sound.
A ship in distress gives its signal as over the rocks it bounds.

Up high on the steep rocky ledge a man watches anxiously.
"I must save them!" he cries aloud as he gazes on the raging sea.

He buttons his sea coat round him; his face is drawn and white.
His thoughts are of his comrades at sea on that stormy night.

He launches his boat in a hurry; he steers for that dangerous reef.
The wind and waves dash 'round him. He must bring them quick relief

As he nears the sinking vessel he throws the lifeline out.
The men are drawn to safety and are soon within the boat.

Kathleen Clark was a 15-year-old sophomore at Pembroke High School when she wrote "The Brave Seaman." It was published in 1928 in the Pembroke High School students' literary journal, *The Pennamaquan Guide*. The poem was found in the archives of the Pembroke Historical Society in 2012 by Susan Sanfilippo, the society's curator. In 2014, it was set to music and arranged by Kris Paprocki, music teacher at the Pembroke Elementary School, using the 19th century hymn tune "Nettleton." Pembroke's proximity to the dangerous rocky shores of Quoddy Head would ensure Miss Clark's awareness of the subject of her poem.

The Tarry Sailor

Charles Fennimore, Bridgewater, ME 5/7/1942
Helen Hartness Flanders Collection
Transcription © 2016 Julia Lane

I came on shore in the month of May,
So careless-lye I went a-walking,
I over heard my own true love
Along with her father talking
Saying, "Jack, your true lover came on shore,
He is the lad you do adore,
Now, silly Nancy your tricks give o'er,
Don't you wed with a tarry sailor."

Then up steps Jack as nimble as a bee
And he said, "My love-lye Nancy
Do you think I have just returned from sea
To my heart's delight and fancy?
I have been where the raging billows roar
And oft times faced my daring foe;
Come answer me quick-er-lye yes or no,
Will you wed with a tarry sailor?"

Her father he was a-standing by
And at Jack was a-gawking
He said, "Young man you might as well be gone
As to stand here and be a-talking,

For I tell you my daughter is too young
And sailors they have a flattering tongue,
So quit my presence and be gone
She'll not wed with a tarry sailor!"

Then Jack stepped up as nimble as could be
And he said, "My lovely Nancy,
Do you think I have just returned from sea
With both my pockets empty?"
When on the table, so I've been told,
He placed five thousand in shining gold,
He slipped it into her apron fold,
"Take this from a tarry sailor!"

The old man he was a-standing there
When he saw Jack act so clever.
"Now since you have given her all your store
O now Jack, you may have her.
And since you've given her all your store
I'll double it and ten times o'er,
I'll double it and ten times o'er
Although you're a tarry sailor."

The "Tarry Sailor" in this song indicates British origin, as sailors on Royal Navy ships wore their long hair in a queue held out of their eyes with an application of pine tar. (American sailors cut their hair short in a "crew cut.") This also explains the "shining gold" which was, no doubt, his share of the prize money gained during a victorious sea battle or two. There is a broadside called "Tarry Sailor" circa 1810, but the story does not include the father nor the happy ending. A more likely source is a song called "The Sailor's Courtship" found in several Scottish chapbooks from the early 19th century. A later version, "Jack the Sailor," appears in Frank Kidson's *English Peasant Songs* (1929).

Poor Old Man

Mr. Charles Creighton, Thomaston, ME 1911 via Professor S. P. Chase
Roland Palmer Gray Collection
Tune from Joanna Colcord Collection
Transcription © 2019 Julia Lane

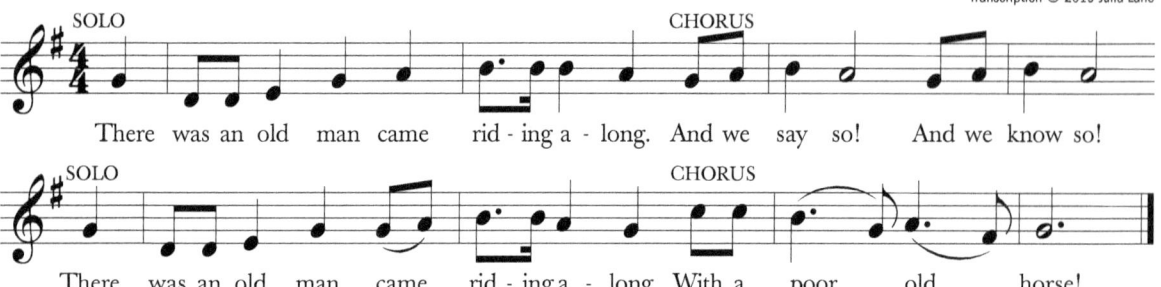

There was an old man came riding along
    And we say so! And we know so!
There was an old man came riding along
    With a poor old horse.

Says I, "Old man, your horse will die."
    And we say so! And we know so!
Says I, "Old man, your horse will die."
    This poor old horse!

And if he dies, we'll tan his hide
    And we say so! And we know so!
And if he lives, we'll take a ride
    This poor old horse!

From Saccarapp to Portland Pier
    And we say so! And we know so!
He's carted rock for many a year,
    This poor old horse!

And now worn out with sore abuse,
    And we say so! And we know so!
Salted down for sailors' use
    This poor old horse!

Similar to the "Old Horse" song, Roland Palmer Gray was given this song by a fellow University of Maine professor, S. P. Chase, in 1911 who wrote it down from the singing of Mr. Charles Creighton, of Thomaston, ME. Mr. Creighton was a sailor and his father was a sea captain. He said that the song was "once in general use along the New England coast." Given the call and response structure of this version, it seems likely that it was used as a work shanty as in Joanna Colcord's book. Mr. Creighton's son, James A. Creighton, printed a similar version in *The Bowdoin Quill*, December, 1910, XIV, (p. 230-231) Other versions of the song declare "Poor Old Man!" as the second chorus.

The Sailors' Alphabet

Oliver Jenness, York, ME 1941
Helen Hartness Flanders Collection
Transcription © 2016 Julia Lane

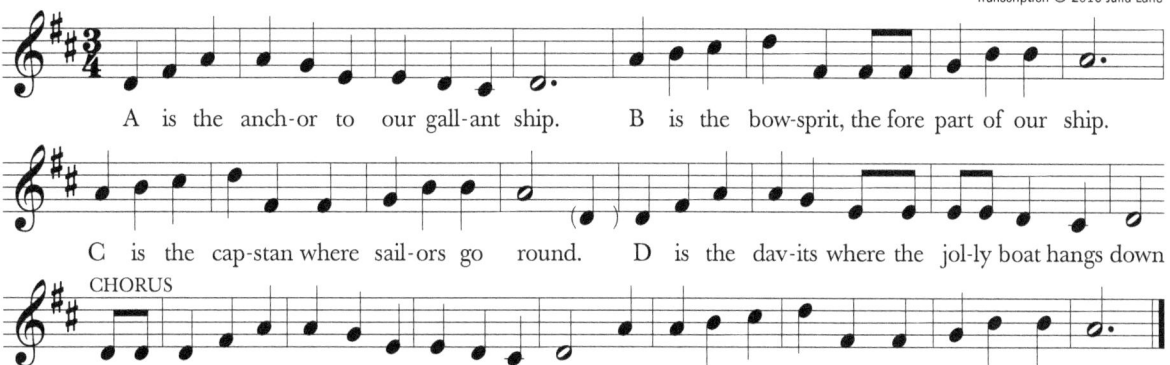

A is the anchor to our gallant ship.
B is the bowsprit, the forepart of our ship.
C is the capstan the sailors goes round.
D is the davits where the jolly boat hangs down.

CHORUS
    To me hi deera derrow, an diddle o down.
    Give sailors their grog and there's nothing goes wrong.

E is the ensign, the red, white and blue.
F is the fo'c'sle where dwells our ship's crew.
G is the gangway where the mate takes his stand.
H is the halliards we hand over hand.

I is the iron that bound our ship round.
J is the jib-boom on the bowsprit is found.
K is the keel the lower part of our ship
and L is the lanyards that's never to slip.

M is the mainmast, through the deck rove.
N is the nasty old cook with his stove.
O is the orders we have to beware.
P is the pumps that cause sailors to swear!

Q is the quadrant, the sun for to take.
R is the rigging that's never to break.
S is the sailors to our gallant ship.
T is the tops'l that's never to split.

U is the ugly ol' skipper of ours.
V is the varnish to rub on our spars.
W is for water, the salt sea so brine.
and X is the letter I can't bring to rhyme.

    So I've sung you a song called the sailor's alph'bet—
    Excepting three letters I'll have to omit.
    Excepting three letters I can't bring to rhyme
    And I'll sing you the verses another fine time.

There are many, many alphabet songs found in print from 1671 and onwards. Originally made to teach children the alphabet, by the 19th century there were a number of occupational alphabets—shepherds, soldiers, bargemen, lumbermen—which list tools and activities of each trade in alphabetically ordered rhyme. It is difficult or impossible to know if the "Sailor's Alphabet" or the "Lumberman's Alphabet" is the older song. We can be quite sure, however, that the "Housewive's Alphabet," the "Vietnam Alphabet," the "Cockney Alphabet," the "Socialist's Alphabet," and the "Folkie's Alphabet" are more recent inventions. Fannie Eckstorm collected a version from Mr. Fred Phippen of Islesford, ME, in 1925 and we have filled in with his lyrics for the few instances where those of Mr. Jenness were indistinct.

Songs of Ships & Sailors

The Sinking of the *Royal George*

Amanda Crockett Kneeland, Searsport, ME
Kneeland Miscellany 1914
Melody by G. F. Handel 1725
Transcription © 2017 Julia Lane

Toll for the brave, the brave that are no more.
All sunk beneath the wave fast by their native shore.
Eight hundred of the brave, whose courage well was tried,
Had made the vessel heel and laid her on her side.
It was not in the battle; no tempest gave the shock.
She sprang no fatal leak, she ran upon no rock.
His sword was in the sheath, his fingers held the pen
When Kempenfeldt went down with twice four hundred men.

Kempenfeldt is gone; his victories all are o'er
And he and his eight hundred shall plow the wave no more.
Help weigh the vessel up, once dreaded by our foes
And mingle with the cup the tear that England owes,

Her timbers yet are sound and she may float again
Full-charged with England's thunder and plow the raging main.
But Kempenfelt is gone, his victories are o'er;
And he, and his eight hundred, shall plow the wave no more.

The *Royal George* was launched in 1756 and had a distinguished career in the Seven Years' War. At the time of her sinking in 1782, she was the flagship of Admiral Richard Kempenfelt, and was anchored in the harbor of Portsmouth for minor repairs. Besides the Admiral and crew of 800 men there were 300 women and children on board, but there were only 200 survivors. The plan to raise the ship was not a success, and the wreck was finally blown up more than fifty years later. Kneeland says "This song was a favorite of Grandfather and Grandmother Crockett and is among Mother's earliest recollections. It is the poem written by William Cowper, commemorating the sinking of the British frigate, *Royal George*, near London, on August 29, 1782." In addition to providing the lyrics for rousing tavern songs, as in Ritson's 1813 publication, this kind of heroic poetry was often part of required elocution classes in public school. The text for "The Sinking of the Royal George" appears in *The Fisherman's Ballads and Songs of the Sea* published by the Procter Brothers in Gloucester in 1874. The song is found in *The Scottish Students' Songbook* by Colin Miller published by Bayley and Ferguson, London, 1891.

The wreck of the *Royal George*

The Gay Spanish Maid

Hanford Hayes, Stacyville, ME 5/5/1942
Helen Harness Flanders Collection
Transcription © 2016 Julia Lane

A gay Spanish maid at the age of sixteen
Through a meadow she roamed far and wide.
And beneath a beech tree she sat down for to rest
With her gay gallyant youth by her side,
With her gay gallyant youth by her side.
And beneath a beech tree she sat down for to rest
With her gallyant youth by her side.

"Our ship sails tonight, oh my darling," says he
"And with you I can ramble no more.
And when all in the house are retired to rest
Will you meet me tonight, love, onshore?
Will you meet me tonight, love, onshore?
And when all in the house are retired to rest
Will you meet me tonight, love, onshore?"

When all in the house had retired to rest
Jeanette, she stole out the hall door.
With her hat in her hand she ran down in dry sand
And sat down on a rock by the shore.
And sat down on a rock by the shore.
With her hat in her hand she ran down in dry sand
And sat down on a rock by the shore.

Bygone Ballads of Maine, Volume I

The moon had just risen far over the sea
And the earth and the heav'ns seemed to meet,
When a voice from the ocean made answer to her
And it broke on the shore at her feet,
And it broke on the shore at her feet.
When a voice from the ocean made answer to her
And it broke on the shore at her feet.

That night passed away with a terrible storm
And the wind through the rigging did howl,
When far over the sea came a murmuring wave
And our ship she was lost in the storm,
And our ship she was lost in the storm.
When far over the sea came a murmuring wave
And our ship she was lost in the storm.

Oh, now we will turn to that ship on the sea
And the gallyant young sailor so brave.
He jumped on a plank and escaped from the wreck
Whilst the rest met a watery grave,
Whilst the rest met a watery grave.
He jumped on a plank and escaped from the wreck
Whilst the rest met a watery grave.

Oh, now we will turn to the maid on the shore.
When she heard of her boy in the storm
She died like a rose that was nipped by the frost
And she left him in silence to mourn,
And she left him in silence to mourn.
She died like a rose that was nipped by the frost
And she left him in silence to mourn.

In the 19th century, Maine had one of the highest standards of living in the world. As such, families might be comfortable enough to afford a piano or pump organ around which friends and family would gather to sing hymns or the many composed "parlor songs" of the time. These songs were often published in bound books which resided on many pianos in both urban and rural homes. Lyrics would be eagerly memorized by singers and shared in other settings with very little variation from the published song. "The Gay Spanish Maid" is of one of these. We have six Maine versions all very consistent with each other.

The Bold Pirate

Composite from Baker & Little Cranberry Islands, ME 1924
Fannie Hardy Eckstorm Collection
Tune from James Brown, South Branch, New Brunswick 1963
Transcription © 2019 Julia Lane

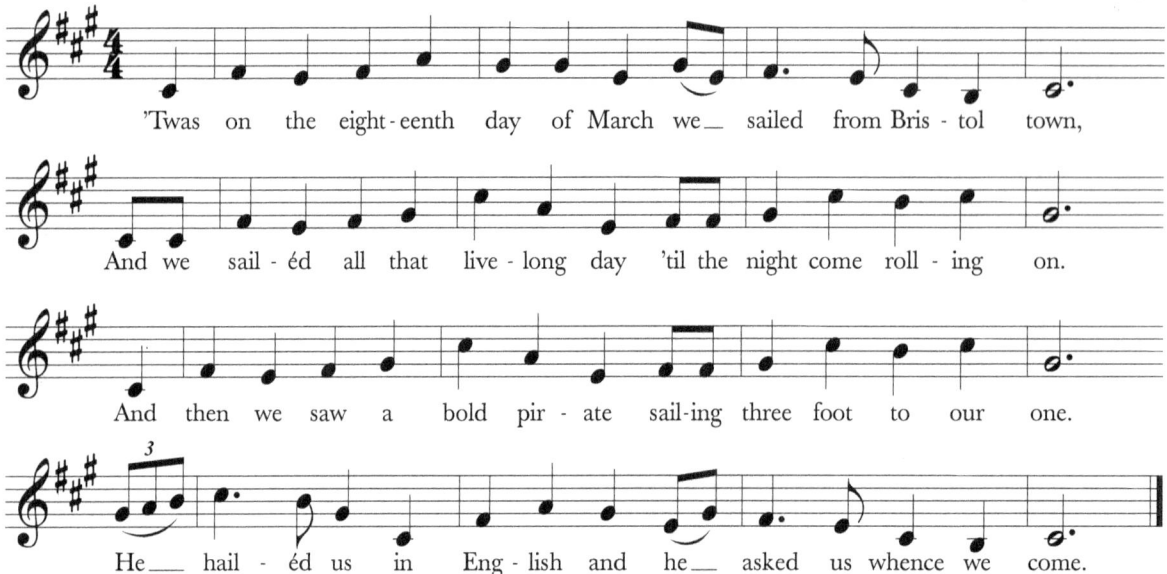

'Twas on the eighteenth day of March we sailed from Bristol Town,
And we sailéd all that livelong day till the night come rolling on.
And then we saw a bold pirate sailing three foot to our one.
He hailéd us in English, and asked us whence we come.

We told him we was from Bristol Town, and on our course was bound,
And askéd of him the reason why he ran us so fast down.
Up spoke this bold old pirate, "I soon will let you know!
Haul down your fore and main courses and let your ship lie to."

Then up spoke our brave commander, and says, "No such thing can be
While we have twenty-eight brass guns to bear us company.
Besides, we have three hundred men, all British seamen bold.
Who value more their honor than a miser does his gold."

Then this bold pirate boarded us with three hundred of his men;
With pistols, pikes and cutlasses we soon did slaughter them.
He hauléd down our ensign flag, thinking our royal ship to take;
We ran them such a rig, my boys, made their very hearts to ache.

Then this bold pirate boarded us with the remainder of his men;
By the word of our commander bold, we soon did slaughter them.
And out of that five hundred men we reducéd them to three,
And down on their knees for mercy cried, but none it was their due.

Then this bold pirate strove from us, and tried to run away;
But a broadside from a rounded gun caused him to stay.
We heisted out our boats from the buoys and boarded her immediately;
And there we saw their bold commander with both legs shot off to his knees.

We took her all in tow, my boys; what a glorious sight to see!
We towed her in to the sight of land beside the Bristol quay,
Where each one had his fortune made and we all got safe on shore.
We'll drink to our success, me boys, and plow the seas no more.

Eckstorm & Smyth collected this in 1924 on Baker & Little Cranberry Islands, ME, from three ladies, Mrs. Nathan S. Stanley, Mrs. Harriet Taylor & Mrs. Phoebe Stanley, all over eighty years old. They said they learned it as children from their father, Joseph Gilley, which makes the song at least a century old when they sang it for the collectors and it is probably older. In 1819 the United States passed a federal statute against piracy to protect the commerce of the United States, and amended it in 1820 to include outlawing participation in the slave trade. The melody comes from James Brown, South Branch, NB, as recorded by Dr. Edward (Sandy) Ives in 1963 and published in *Folksongs of New Brunswick*, 1989 (p. 128)

Songs of Ships & Sailors

The Ship That Never Returned

Frank & James Kneeland, Searsport, ME 1914
The Kneeland Miscellany
Judson Carver, W. Jonesport, ME 8/20/1942
Helen Hartness Flanders Collection
Transcription © 2018 Julia Lane

On a pleasant morn as the waves that rippled
'Neath a calm and gentle breeze,
A ship set sail with a cargo laden
For a port beyond the seas.
There were sweet farewells and kind words spoken
While a form they yet discerned.
Though they knew it not, 'twas a sad parting
Of the ship that never returned.

CHORUS:
    Did she never return? No, she never returned
    And her fate is yet unlearned.
    For years and years there's been fond ones watching
    For the ship that never returned.

Said a feeble youth to his anxious mother
"I must cross the wide, wide sea.
They say, perchance, in a foreign climate
There is health and strength for me."
A ray of hope 'mid a maze of danger
And her heart for her youngest yearned
She sent him forth with a smile and a blessing
In the ship that never returned.

"Only one more trip," said a gallant captain
As he kissed his weeping wife.
"Only one more bag of the golden treasure
That shall last us all through life
Then we'll settle down in a cozy cottage
To enjoy the rest I've earned."
But alas, poor man! he sailed commander
Of the ship that never returned.

Another song lyric documented in the 1914 *Kneeland Miscellany*, this tune was sung in August 1942 for Helen Flanders by Judson Carver of West Jonesport, ME, who says he learned it as a young man on a fishing schooner. We added the chorus from the standard version to accommodate Kneeland's lyrics. A popular song, it was also sung to Phillips Barry by Mrs. Nell Spurling of Great Cranberry Island around 1930. Written by Henry Clay Work in 1865, it became a standard parlor song and was widespread particularly in the U.S. In her notes, Fannie Eckstorm reminds readers of "Radio listeners who have heard Bradley Kincaid, the Kentucky mountain boy and his hound dog guitar," singing the song. The tune formed the basis of "The Wreck of the Old 97," about a train which was wrecked on the run from Washington to Spencer, NC, near North Danville, VA, in 1902. This was recorded by Vernon Dalhart in 1924, and many others afterward, becoming the first million selling country music hit. Later, the melody was adapted for "Charlie on the M.T.A," created in 1948 as a campaign song for Walter O'Brien protesting the administration of the Massachusetts Transit Authority with a story of a man who couldn't get off a Boston subway train for lack of fare. The Kingston Trio recorded that song in 1959 and it became a hit the same year.

Goodbye, Annie Darling

Annie Tate Moore, Ellsworth Falls, ME 6/22/1941
Helen Hartness Flanders Collection
Transcription © 2016 Julia Lane

FIRST VERSE AND CHORUS:
Goodbye Annie Darling, I leave you in sorrow
Tomorrow the parting must be.
I'll the sail the seas over, I'll cross the wide ocean
I'll sail the seas over from thee.

I go, Annie darling, but leave thee in sorrow;
I go for thy sake, far away;
Then bid me good-bye with a smile, on the morrow.
And cheer me with blessings, I pray.

I'll think of thee ever, and pray for thee only,
As over the waters I roam;
I'll tarry not, darling, and leave thee all lonely;
But hasten again to my home.

Out, out on the ocean, away o'er the billow,
My heart on its purpose still bent;
My brow shall find rest, when I seek my lone pillow.
In knowing that thou art content.

Cheer up, Annie darling, break off from thy sorrow
'Tis sad that our parting must be;
But give me thy smile, when I leave thee, tomorrow,
To sail the seas over for thee.

Mrs. Moore only provided the first verse, which is actually the chorus to the song. The rest of the song is from Alfred Lord Tennyson's poetic story, "Enoch Arden," which tells of a fisherman turned merchant sailor who leaves his wife Annie and three children to go to sea with his old captain. He returns to find she has married his childhood rival. Also called "Farewell Song of Enoch Arden," or "I'll Sail the Seas Over," the first musical setting was published in 1851. Several theatrical plays and musicals subsequently have been made based on the poem.

'Twas Early, Early in the Spring

Frank Kneeland, Searsport, ME 10/1941
Helen Hartness Flanders Collection
Text from the *Kneeland Miscellany* 1914
Transcription © 2016 Julia Lane

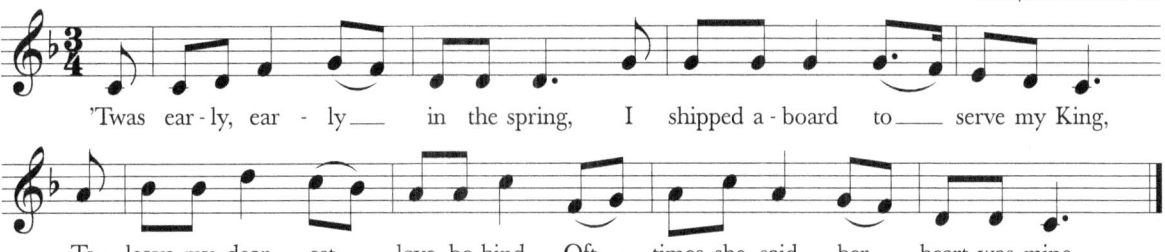

'Twas early, early in the spring,
I shipped aboard to serve my King,
To leave my dearest love behind.
Ofttimes she said her heart was mine.

As I was sailing o'er the sea
I took each fair opportunity
To write a letter to my dear
Not one word from her did I hear.

At length I came to her father's house
I gave a rap and aloud did call.
Her father made me this reply
"My daughter's married more equally."

"My daughter's married, kind sir, you know,
My daughter's married long time ago!
My daughter's married for the term of life;
Go you, young man, seek another wife!"

Curse be on gold and on silver, too!
Curse be on the girl that won't prove true!
Curse be on the girl that will promise me
Then forsake her vows for such richery!

Forevermore I do intend
The briny ocean to be my friend
I'll sail the seas till the day I die;
I'll split the waves that roll mountains high!

This is directly related to the "Saucy Sailor," with the same theme of the disappointed sailor returning to sea. With the reference to serving the king, this is either pre-Victorian British or pre-Revolutionary and indeed there are precedent versions from that time. There are several other songs with the same title, but they seem to be versions of "The Sailor's Bride."

Songs of Ships & Sailors

The Ship of Revolution

Albert E. Conray, Ellsworth ME 5/14/1942
Helen Hartness Flanders Collection
Transcription © 2018 Julia Lane

'Tis of a ship of revolution, a ship of great fame.
Captain Bendigo commands her, if you wish to know his name.
We sailed from Jamaica, and to Bristol were bound;
On the northwest of Cuby this pirate we found.

Then we'll heist our lofty topsail, hoping from them to steer.
On the northwest of Cuby lay this bold priverteer.
Then we'll heist our lofty topsail, hoping from them to run.
When we found that this rovier gained two leagues to our one.

Then it's up 'longside of us, this proud rovier come,
With a loud speaking trumpet, saying, "Where are you from?"
"I sailed from Jamaica and to Bristol we're bound."
"Then I'll ask you the reason why you sailed so fast around?"

"The reason is very plain, I will soon let you know.
I will cut down your lofty topsail and I'll lay your ship low."
"Oh, no," said our capting, "that never can be!
For I'll wheel my ship 'round about and I'll go under your lee!"

The first time they boarded us with a hundred brave men,
With the rattlings of the big arms we soon killed all of them
They compelled down upon us, our lives, our ship to take,
But we gave them such a dose, my boys, that it made their hearts ache.

The second time they boarded us with fifty more men,
With a rattlings of small arms, we soon killed all of them.
They compelled down upon us; they could no longer stay,
Like faint-hearted men, my boys, like cowards run away.

We wheeled our ship round and we follow them close.
With a hundred pound of powder we soon gave them another dose.
From a hundred-seventy and two we reduced them to twenty-two,
And only twenty-eight of us were in our jovial ship's crew.

We have found no evidence of this specific song anywhere else; it may be an amalgam of "Bold Daniels" and "The Bold Pirate." It is a typical pirate/privateer encounter, probably dating from the early 1800s when the navies of several nations, particularly the U.S. and Britain, began an anti-piracy campaign primarily around Cuba and Puerto Rico. They were effective in their efforts as piracy declined significantly after 1825. The "ship of revolution" may indicate that the ship had been used during the Revolutionary war.

The Rose of Breton's Isle

John West, Harmony, ME, 1971
Collected by Fred Gosbee
Transcription © 2019 Fred Gosbee

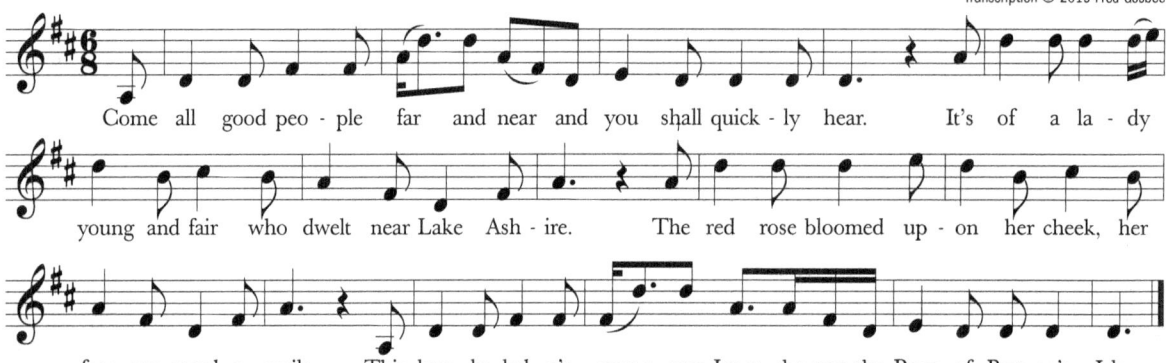

Come all good people far and near and you shall quickly hear.
It's of a lady young and fair who dwelt near Lake Ashire.
The red rose bloomed upon her cheek, her face appeared a smile.
This lovely lady's name was Jane; she was the Rose of Breton's Isle.

She was her mother's only child, her father's pride and joy
But at sixteen she fell in love with her father's 'prentice boy.
Young Edward he was not content till her heart he did beguile
"By all above!" he cries, "I love the Rose of Breton's Isle!"

When her old father came to know that courting this couple were
He flew into a furious rage and terribly did swear
Saying "If disgrace you bring on me, I'll send you many a mile
Prepare this day to cross the main from the Rose of Breton's Isle!"

Young Edward he did board a ship to sail across the main.
While Jane at home did weep and moan her bosom filled with pain.
She dressed herself in sailor's clothes and in a little while;
On board the ship with Edward went the Rose of Breton's Isle.

When they arrived quite near to Spain the enemy gave the alarm
And by a ball, young Jane did fall; it shattered her left arm.
The sailors ran to render aid while Jane in anguish smiled
"Behold the maid!" cried Edward, "She's the Rose of Breton's Isle!"

Young Edward he was not content but troubled in his mind
And when Jane had recovered again they went back across the main;
Back to old England they did steer all in a little while.
Home again came Edward with the Rose of Breton's Isle!

Now her old father being dead, most glorious to relate,
With all his money willed to Jane, likewise his large estate!
Married they were while the bells did ring and villagers did smile
And happy lived young Edward with the Rose of Breton's Isle.   [last line spoken]

Transcribed from memory by Fred Gosbee who heard his grandfather, John West of Harmony, ME, (born 1899) sing this song in the 1970s. John learned this song when he worked in the lumber camps of Maine and New Brunswick prior to 1922. Fred surmises that he used "Breton's Isle" and "Lake Ashire" (Britain's Isle and Lancashire) because he was from Canada. As was often done by traditional singers of Maine he spoke the last few words of the song.

Another shorter version, with the more usual title "The Rose of Britain's Isle," was sung by Jack McNally of Stacyville for Helen Flanders in 1942.

The Jolly Roving Tar

Text: Unattributed from *Eckstorm Collection*
Tune: Carrie Grover, Gorham, ME, Oct. 30, 1941
Eloise Hubbard Linscott Collection
Transcription © 2013 Julia Lane

It was in the town of Liverpool, all in the month of May.
I overheard a damsel alone as she did stray.
She did appear like Venus or some sweet lovely star
As she walked the beach lamenting for her jolly roving tar.

"Oh, William, gallant William, how can you sail away?
I have arrived at twenty-one and am a lady gay!
I will man one of my father's ships, and face the Chinese war
And cross the briny ocean with my jolly roving tar."

"Come all you jolly sailors and push the boat ashore
That I may see my father's ships and see they are secure.
Provisions we have plenty, and lots of grog in store,
So drink good health you sailors for my jolly roving tar!"

Oh, they took her in the longboat, they rowed her from the land
And as the sailors rowed away she waved her lily hand
Saying "Adieu ye maids of Liverpool I am going away afar
I am going to cross the ocean with my jolly roving tar!"

Not to be confused with the popular "Get up Jack, John sit down!", this is related to the "British Man-O'-War" or "Lovely Susan," the difference being that in this variant Susan joins her William on the ship to fight beside him. Carrie Grover sang one verse of this song (the last) in 1941 for Eloise Linscott. An unattributed lyric transcription was found in the Eckstorm Collection at the Fogler Library in Orono, ME. This setting combines the two. Although there were several early 19th century printings of broadsides in England, this song is found largely in traditional collections from New England, the Canadian Maritimes and Northern Ireland.

Songs of Ships & Sailors

The Tall Young Oysterman

Johnson 1925
Phillips Barry / Eckstorm Collection
Tune transcribed by Bayard 1942
Transcription © 2019 Julia Lane

There was a tall young oysterman, lived by the river side.
His shop was built upon the bank, his boat was on the tide.
The daughter of a fisherman, that was so tall and slim,
Lived over on the other side right opposite to him.
    A-singing Tol de rol de riddle diddle rye-de-o.

It was this pensive oysterman that saw a lovely maid,
One moonlight evening, a setting in the shade,
He saw her wave her handkerchief, as much as if to say,
"There's plenty time for courting, and daddy's gone away."
    And they sang etc.

Up rose this pensive oysterman, and to himself, said he,
"I'd better leave my boat behind for fear that folks should see,
I've read it in a story book that for to kiss his dear,
Leander swam the Hellespont, and I will swim this here."
    And he sang etc.

Then he popped into the waves, and then he crossed the stream,
And then he clamber'd up the rocks all in the moonlight's beam,
But the moon that instant shone out bright, be sure it was a sin,
Soon they heard the daddy's step, and he pops in again.
    A-singing etc.

Up spoke the ancient fisherman, "What was that my daughter?"
" 'Twas nothing but a brickbat sir, that I chuck'd in the water,"
"But what is that funny thing that paddles off so fast?"
"It's nothing but a porpoise sir, that's been swimming past."
    And she sang etc.

Out spoke the ancient fisherman, "Get me my harpoon!
I'll get into my fishing boat and fix the fellow soon!"
Down falls the lovely damsel, as falls a slaughter'd flock,
Her hair drop'd round her pallid cheeks like seaweed on a rock.
    A-singing etc.

Alas, for these loving ones, she woke not from her swoon,
And he was taken with the cramp and in the water droon,
But fate had metamorphosed them, in pity of their woe,
Now they keep an oyster shop for mermaids down below.
    And they sing etc.

And for this ancient fisherman that caused their sad fate,
The grief that fill'd his bleeding heart was horrid to relate,
He threw his harpoon on the ground close by his daughters side,
And then he popp'd into the waves, kick'd the bucket and died.
    A-singing etc.

The original "Ballad of the Oysterman" was written by Oliver Wendell Holmes in Boston in 1830 and did not include the last verse. An unattributed broadside was published within six years containing colloquial revisions and verses. The song subsequently appeared in various songsters as a burlesque. There is an extensive discussion in *Minstrelsy of Maine* about vernacular changes made to this song in "How the Folk rewrite a song" (p. 266). This version was sung by one Johnson for Mrs. Eckstorm and Samuel Bayard made the first musical transcription, which we have adapted.

Songs of Ships & Sailors

Fair Lady Leroy

Carrie Grover, Gorham, ME 10/29/1943
Eloise Hubbard Linscott Collection
Transcription © 2013 Julia Lane

It was on a fair morning, a fair morning in May.
The birds were a-singing, all nature seemed gay.
I spied a young couple as they stood by the shore
A-viewing the ocean where the wild billows roar.

He said "My fair damsel you're the girl I adore
And to part with my true love it grieves my heart sore
Your parents are rich, love, and angry with me
And if I tarry with you love, my ruin they'll be."

She dressed herself up in a suit of men's clothes
And straightway unto to her own father she goes.
She purchased a vessel and paid the demand
But little did he know 'twas from his own daughter's hand.

Then back to her true love she quickly did go
"Make haste and get ready, there's no time to lose!"
They hoisted the topsail, they shouted for joy
And over the ocean sailed fair Lady Leroy.

Now, when her old father this news came to know
He went down to the captain through grief and through woe.
"Go find them, go hail them! Their vessel destroy!
For he ne'er shall enjoy the fair Lady Leroy!"

The captain being proud with this message go
He sailed o'er the ocean in search of his foe.
He spied a fair vessel whose colors did fly
He hailed them and found 'twas fair Lady Leroy.

He bad them return to their own native shore
Or a broadside of grapeshot down on them would pour.
But Sally's true lover made him this reply,
"We'll never surrender! We'll conquer or die!"

Then broadside to broadside the grapeshot did pour
And louder than thunder the cannon did roar
But Sally's true lover gained the victory—
Here's a health to all fair maids; may they always go free!

Despite the many versions of this song collected in the U.K., the U.S., Australia, and Canada, we have not found a definitive source! There generally do seem to be two basic varieties, though there are outliers. The "Bright Phoebus" variants, appearing in England and the central coast and midwest of the U.S., tend to have a major melody, with Polly as the name of the heroine and a triumphant return to Boston. The "Fair morning / walking" type, whose melody is minor or modal, has Sally as the heroine with no destination specified. It appears more in northeastern North America and Ireland. There are differences as to whether the Lady Leroy is the ship or the girl. In any case, we are fortunate to be able to include Mrs. Grover's version which not only has a most unusual tune, but emphasizes the independence of the heroine, especially with the last line! Another similar version was sung by Murchie Harvey of Houlton, ME for Flanders in 1942.

The Sons of Liberty

Wynifred Smith, Dixfield, ME 11/12/1941
Eloise Hubbard Linscott Collection
Transcription © 2013 Julia Lane

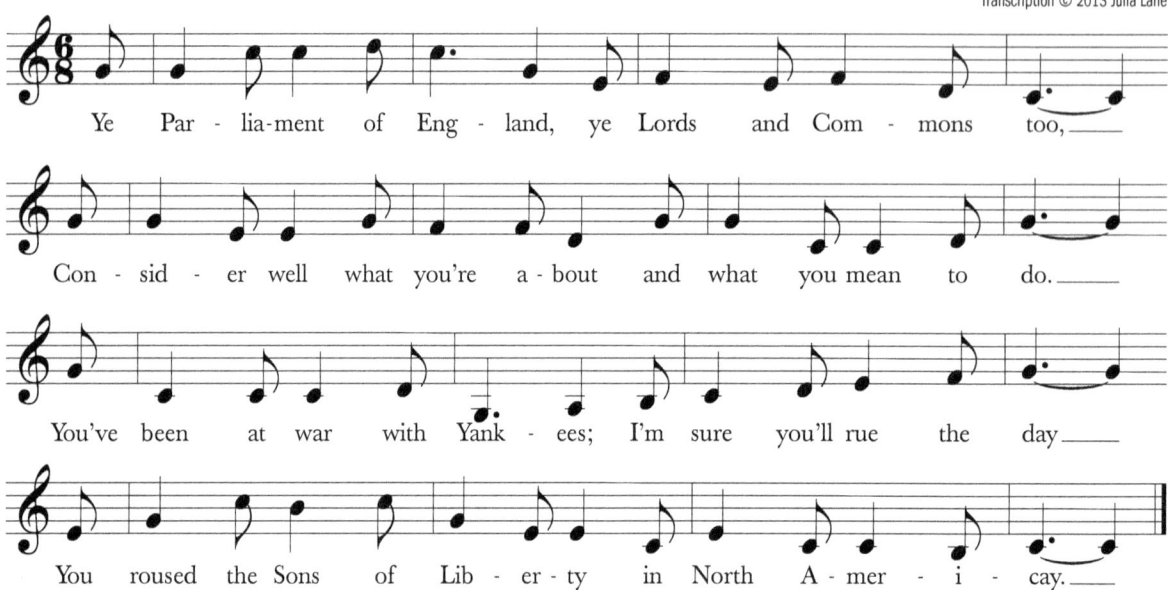

Ye Parliament of England, ye Lords and Commons too,
Consider well what you're about, and what you mean to do.
You've been at war with Yankees; I'm sure you'll rue the day
You roused the Sons of Liberty in North Americay!

You first confined our commerce, and say our ships shan't trade,
You next confined our seamen, and used them as your slaves,
You then insulted Rodgers, while cruising on the main,
And had not we declared war, you'd have done it o'er again.

You thought our frigates were but few, and Yankees would not fight,
Until brave Hull your *Guerriere* took and banished from your sight.
The *Wasp* then took the *Frolic*, you nothing said to that;
The *Poitiers* being of the line, of course she took her back.

The next, your *Macedonian*, no finer ship could swim,
Decatur took her gilt works off, and then he sent her in.
The *Java* by a Yankee ship was sunk, you all must know;
The *Peacock* fine, in all her pride, by Lawrence down did go.

Then next you sent your *Boxer*, to box us all about,
But we had an *Enterprising* brig that beat your *Boxer* out;
We boxed her up to Portland, and moored her off the town,
To show the Sons of Liberty your *Boxer* of renown.

Then upon Lake Erie, brave Perry had some fun,
You own he beat your naval force and caused them for to run;
Whilst Chauncy on Ontario the like ne'er was known before
Your British squadron beat complete, some took, and some run ashore.

Then your brave Indian Allies you styled them by that name
Until they turned their tomahawks and by you savages became
But by your mean insinuation they despised you from their souls
And joined the Sons of Liberty that scorned to be controlled.

Our Decatur in the *Guerriere* soon humbled the Turkish crew
Brought them to submission as he has done to you
The *Essex* in the South Seas, will put out all your lights;
The flag she wore at her masthead was "Free Trade and Sailor's Rights!"

Now lament, you sons of Britain. Far distant is the day
That e'er you'll gain what you have lost in North Amerikay
Go tell your King and Parliament by all the world 'tis known
That British Force by sea or land by Yankees are o'erthrown.

Use every endeavor and strive to make a peace
For Yankee ships are building fast our navy to increase
They will enforce our commerce these laws by Heaven were made
That Yankee ships in time of peace in any port should trade

Grant us free trade and commerce and don't impress our men
Give up all claims of Canada then we'll be at peace again
And then we will respect you and treat you as our friend
Respect your flag and citizens then all these wars will end.

Wearied and outraged by flagrant breaches of agreements regarding shipping during the war of 1812, the Americans gathered their resources to retaliate, including the building of the USS *Constitution*. A warning message to England, this song celebrates the new nation's maritime success against her oppressors. The original can be found in *The American National Songbook, Volume 2, Naval Songs* 1842, by Wm. McCarty. This song, also known as "Ye Parliament of England," appears in *The Kneeland Miscellany* (Searsport, ME, 1914) and was collected by Flanders from the singing of Frank Kneeland in 1941. Musically, the two Maine recorded versions are modal variants of each other. Versions of this song may also be found in Joanna Colcord's *Songs of American Sailormen* and *Songs and Ballads of the Maine Lumberjacks* by Roland Palmer Gray.

Bold McCarty

Charles F. Alley, Jonesport, ME 10/1927
Phillips Barry Collection
Music from Edward D. "Sandy" Ives Collection
Transcription © 2019 Julia Lane

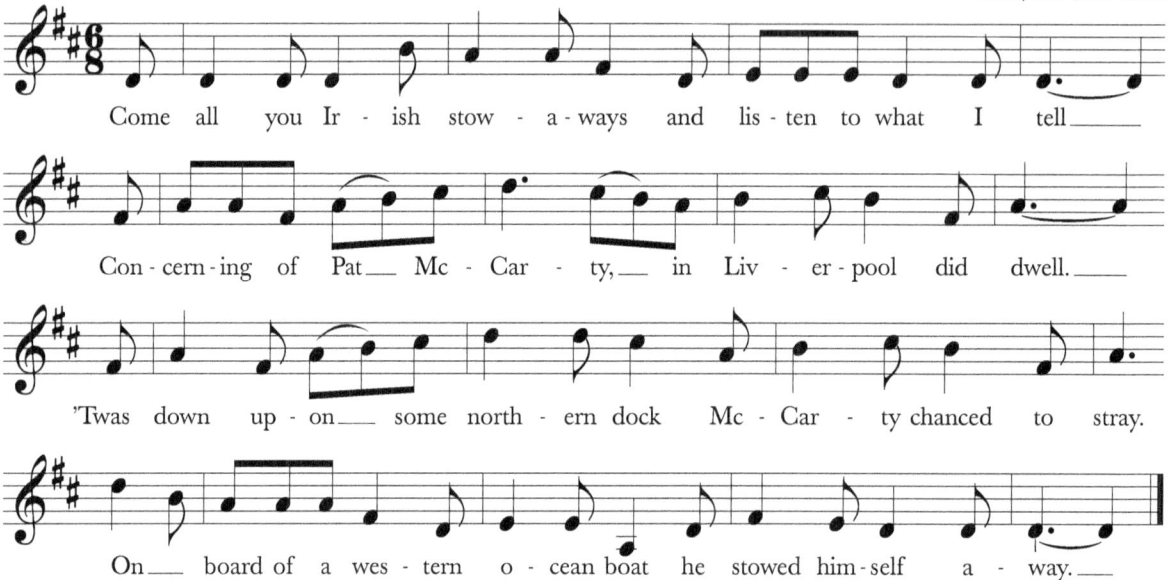

Come all you Irish stowaways and listen to what I tell
Concerning of Pat McCarty, in Liverpool did dwell.
'Twas down upon some northern dock McCarty chanced to stray.
On board of a western ocean boat he stowed himself away.

While sailing down the river to New York we were bound.
McCarty he was going away to leave his native town,
McCarty he was going away to leave his native shore
On board of a western ocean boat, the *City of Baltimore*.

Oh, it's early every morning, boys, our mate he turns us to.
Oh, it's early every morning, boys, we have to put her through.
"Where is that Irish stowaway?" the mate so loud did cry.
"Oh, it's here I am!" cries McCarty, "and what do you want of I?"

"It's true I am an Irishman, the fact I'll not deny,
But before I'll be cornered down by you, I'll fight until I die!
If you're a man of courage bold, before me you would stand
And I'll fight you fair all on the deck of the *City of Baltimore*."

Our mate, he being a cowardly man, before him would not stand
And seizing and iron bowlayin' pin he at McCarty ran.   [belaying]
McCarty, he being a smart young man, soon laid him in his gore –
The bloody 'ruption on the deck of the *City of Baltimore!*

The second mate and bo'sun went to our mate's relief.
McCarty with a hand spike he made them both retreat.
His Irish blood began to boil, like a lion he did roar,
"I'll fight you both on the deck of the *City of Baltimore!*"

Our captain being a Scotchman, MacDonald was his name,
When he saw what McCarty did it's forward then he came.
He took McCarty by the hand and wrung it o'er and o'er,
"I'll make you the bo'sun of my ship, the *City of Baltimore!*"

Also known as "The *City of Baltimore,*" the story of a scrappy immigrant stowaway who prevails against persecution is always appealing. Not finding a melody in any Maine collection, we have combined Alley's lyrics, collected by Barry, with a tune recorded by Dr. Edward Ives for this song in his book *Drive Dull Care Away* (p. 188), a collection of songs from Prince Edward Island.

Handspike = a hardwood bar about four and a half feet long used for turning a windlass. One would make a forbidable weapon!

Captain Kidd

Justin Decoster, Buckfield, ME 1925
Fannie Hardy Eckstorm Collection
Tune: Carrie Grover, Gorham, ME *Heritage of Song* 1955
Transcription © 2019 Julia Lane

Oh my name was Captain Kidd when I sailed, when I sailed.
Oh my name was Captain Kidd when I sailed.
My name was Captain Kidd and God's law I did forbid
And so wickedly I did when I sailed, when I sailed.
And so wickedly I did when I sailed.

I had a Bible in my hand when I sailed, when I sailed.
I had a Bible in my hand when I sailed.
It was my father's command; I sank it in the sand.
I sank it in the sand when I sailed, when I sailed,
I sank it in the sand when I sailed.

I made two solemn vows when I sailed, when I sailed.
I made two solemn vows when I sailed.
I made two solemn vows that to God I would not bow
Nor myself one prayer allow when I sailed, when I sailed,
Nor myself one prayer allow when I sailed.

I murdered Robert Moore when I sailed, when I sailed.
I murdered Robert Moore when I sailed.
I murdered Robert Moore not many leagues from shore;
I left him in his gore as I sailed, as I sailed.
I left him in his gore as I sailed.

I saw three ships from France when I sailed, when I sailed.
I saw three ships from France when I sailed.
I saw three ships from France and to them I did advance
And took them all by chance as I sailed, as I sailed,
And took them all by chance as I sailed.

I saw three ships from Spain when I sailed, when I sailed.
I saw three ships from Spain when I sailed.
I saw three ships from Spain and their ships I did burn.
The crew of them were slain as I sailed, as I sailed.
The crew of them were slain as I sailed.

Farewell the raging main; I must die, I must die.
Farewell the raging main; I must die.
Farewell the raging main, from Turkey, France, and Spain.
I shall never see you again; I must die, I must die.
I shall never see you again; I must die.

Come ye young and old. See me die, see me die.
Come ye young and old. See me die.
Come ye young and old; don't for the sake of gold,
Don't for the sake of gold lose your soul, lose your soul!
Don't for the sake of gold lose your soul!

Capt. William Kidd was arrested in Boston in 1699 and tried in London for deeds of piracy and the murder of his mutinous gunner, William Moore, whom he allegedly crowned with a bucket. Protesting his innocence, he was sentenced on May 9 and hanged on May 23, 1701. Born in Scotland about 1645, Kidd came to New York in the 1660s, becoming a successful ship owner with family and property on Manhattan Island. In the 1690s, Earl Bellomont, the new governor of New York and New England, engaged him to clear the coast of pirates and other unfriendly foreign vessels. Kidd apparently crossed swords with authorities, either turning pirate himself or interfering with extrajudicial arrangements, which resulted in his arrest, conviction, and execution. This popular ballad, composed as a broadside in 1701 in England, passed into tradition here in America with its grim warning not to "lose your soul" to greed and godless behavior. Legends about his alleged buried treasure abound from Florida to Nova Scotia. Mr. Decoster's tune was not recorded so we have used that sung by Carrie Grover in her book *A Heritage of Song* 1955 (p. 34). She was born in Nova Scotia near one place where Kidd's treasure is said to be buried!

Blow Ye Winds, Aye-O

Annie Tate Moore, Ellsworth Falls, ME 6/22/1941
Capt. L. Freeman Gott, Bernard, ME 1925
Phillips Barry Collection
Transcription © 2016 Julia Lane

It was on the fourth of January down in the southern sea.
Our ship lay at anchor near a big coral reef a-waiting for a breeze.
And the captain he was down below and the sailors they were lying all about.
When suddenly from under our bow a jolly little voice piped out,

CHORUS:
Singing, "Blow ye winds aye-o! Blow ye winds aye-o!
Clear way the morning dew and blow ye winds aye-o!"

"There's a man overboard!" our watch cried out, and then they all forward ran
And under the bows on our best bower chain sat perched a big Merman
His hair was red, his eyes were green, his mouth as big as three
And the great long tail he sat upon was a-waggling in the deep blue sea.

Our captain he came up on deck and he gazed at the waters blue
Saying "Come tell me man, just as quick as you can, what favor for you I can do?"
"What can I do, little man, for you? What can I do?" says he
"That you may not bring bad luck to us lest we sink in the salt, salt sea."

Bygone Ballads of Maine, Volume I

"I once was the captain of a gallant ship and proudly sailed," said he,
"But one fatal night the strong winds blew and we sank to the bottom of the sea.
And the stormy sea was dark and cold and I would have drowned," said he,
"But a charming mermaid chanced that way and she taught me how to live in the sea.

"I fell in love with this charming maid with her suit of silvery scales
And we rode away on a honeymoon and we rode on the back of a whale.
I married this charming mermaid and now we have children three,
And we live in a coral house way down in the bottom of the sea.

"You have dropped your anchor in the door of my house so my wife and kids can't get free.
'Twould break your heart to hear them mourn way down in the bottom of the sea."
The Captain smiled and called to the mate, "All hands on deck!" cried he,
"The anchor shall be hove at once and your wife and your chicks set free!"

An irresistibly jolly little song, the earliest record seems to be a broadside circa 1850, probably a product of the music hall entertainments of the time. In her book *Songs of American Sailormen*, Joanna Colcord says "There were many versions of 'Blow Ye Winds,' some too scandalous to print. [It] was a favorite among the comic songs of the forecastle." The first verse, chorus, and the tune here are from Annie Tate Moore of Ellsworth, ME, recorded by Helen Hartness Flanders. Additional lyrics are from Colcord and also Capt. L. Freeman Gott of Bernard, ME, as collected by Phillips Barry in 1925 without a tune. Several versions have been found in Newfoundland and Flanders also collected it from Mrs. John Anderson of Windsor, VT, as sung by her relative from Newfoundland. The song appears in *Vermont Folksongs and Ballads* by Flanders and Brown (1931). We complete the "tale" with lyrics from the original broadside for the last half of the last verse.

Songs of Ships & Sailors

The Schooner *Fred Dunbar*

Composed by Amos Hanson, Orland, ME c. 1850
Mrs. Emory Howard, North Blue Hill, ME 1932
Miss Annie Dunbar, North Castine, ME 4/20/1934
Air recorded June 8, 1934
Fannie Hardy Eckstorm Collection
Transcription © 2019 Julia Lane

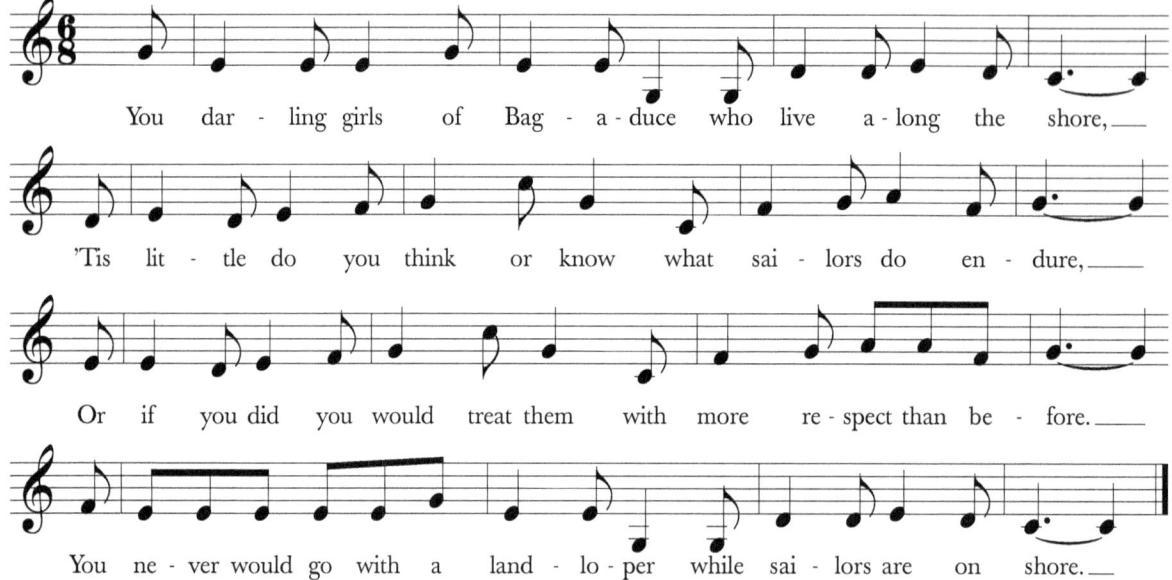

You darling girls of Bagaduce who live along the shore,
'Tis little do you think or know what sailors do endure,
Or if you did you would treat them with more respect than before.
You would never go with a landloper while sailors are on shore.

You handsome girls of Bagaduce, these lines I'm going to write;
I'm going to the Bay Chaleur, it's not my heart's delight.
I'm going to the Bay Chaleur, it's all that we can do,
While these land-loafing fellows will stay at home with you.

Now these Penobscot cowboys, they tell you girls fine tales,
Of the hardships they endure while plowing their cornfields.
They feed the hens and punch the pigs and make their mothers roar,
While we, like jovial-hearted lads go plow the Bay Chaleur.

You handsome girls of Bagaduce, perhaps you'd like to know
The names of all the sailors before we start to go.
Their names and dispositions I'll endeavor to explain
Before we spread our canvas to plow the raging rain.

The first was Hiram Wardwell who runs the *Rory O'More*;
The next was Captain Perkins who roams the golden shore;
They're very much respected by all both fore and aft,
Two better men can not be found on an Androsoggin raft.

There was a little Herman, Leroy and Bill and Oliver Quin, and Steel,
And Amos H. the author who an entry sheep did steal.
The next was little Owen, who loves the girls so well,
The last was young Horatio, we called him the Admiral.

Our Captain's name was Dunbar, our Cook his name was Jim;
Although they are Good Templars they are very fond of gin.
Our Pilot's name was Moody, our Mate, his name was Al;
The first was fond of red rum, the latter of a French gal.

'Twas on the schooner *Fred Dunbar*, well found in fishing gear,
We crowded on the canvas and for Green's Landing we did steer.
And when we came at anchor the sun was getting low;
'Twas there we shipped young Stimpson and Captain Wood Thurlow.

And when we came off Port Margrave we hauled in for our salt;
We took our fiddles and started to have a little waltz.
Twelve of us once started, our songs to the woods did roar;
When I arrived, I was surprised I couldn't count but four.

On the first day of September we came off Cape Marboo;
We took a squall from south-southeast that broke our boom in two.
So galliantly she weathered it, and it was fun to see,
Her walk to the windward, with mainsail down, bound out for Margaree.

The last day of September, a night remembered well,
And how poor sailors fared that night, no tongue can ever tell.
The wind blew hard, the the seas run high and in torrents fell the rain;
I never saw such a night before and hope I shan't again.

Come all you girls of Bagaduce, the time is drawing nigh,
When from our main topmast the Stars and Stripes will fly.
Be ready gallant lasses, put on your other gowns,
For soon you'll see the *Fred Dunbar* come sailing up the Sound.

And now our voyage is ended and we return on shore,
With our pockets full of greenbacks, earned at the Bay Chaleur.
So merrily we will dance and sing, as we have done before,
And when our money is all gone we'll plow the Bay for more.

This song was written by Amos Hanson, a fisherman vernacular songwriter from Orland, ME, who set off on his adventures to Canada from Castine, ME on Bagaduce Bay. It was sung by the fishermen and sailors from the Bagaduce River for years. Hanson's songs are generally very local and from his own experience, incorporating names and adventures of the people around him. They echo the traditions of both the northern logging camps and the bothy ballads of the migrant farm workers in Scotland and Ireland, either celebrating or lampooning one's co-workers. There are several such songs collected in Maine including "The Sailor's Come all Ye" from Susie Carr Young and "The Jolly Sailors" from Oliver Jenness recorded by Helen Flanders. They all seem to be modeled on an ancient predecessor, "In Praise of Saylors" from the 17th century. "The Schooner *Fred Dunbar*" was collected from the singing of Mrs. Emory Howard and her son from North Blue Hill, ME, in 1932 and printed by Phillips Barry in the *Bulletin of the Folk-Song Society of the Northeast* in 1933. We have included all the known verses made for this song including those from "The Girls of Bagaduce" which appear in italics. Both songs are in Fannie Eckstorm's collection. The Bay Chaleur in Quebec is bordered by the Gaspe peninsula in the Gulf of St. Lawrence. Cape Mabou and Margaree are in Cape Breton, NS. Green's Landing is on Isle au Haut, Penobscot Bay. "An entry sheep" was explained as one driven over the bluff and killed by the fall, which the sailors appropriated.

The Dreadnaught

Oliver Jenness, York Village, ME 9/19/41
Helen Hartness Flanders Collection
Transcription © 2016 Julia Lane

The day of our sailing is fast drawing nigh,
And you my dear sweetheart, I'll bid you goodbye.
Good luck to New York and all my friends here.
Bound away in the *Dreadnaught* to the east'ard we steer.

CHORUS:
    Bound away, bound away, where the stormy winds blow.
    Bound away in the *Dreadnaught* to the east'ard we go!

Oh, it's now we are hauling off the Long Island shore
Our captain on deck as was often before
Saying, "Crowd on all sail boys, and let her run free
For the *Dreadnaught* is a clipper and fears not the sea!"

Oh, now we are sailing off the shores of Newfoundland
Where the waters change color and the bottom is sand
Where the fish of the ocean swim about to and fro
Bound away in the *Dreadnaught* to the east'ard we go.

Oh, now we are sailing on the ocean so wide
Where the blue and mighty billows rush against our dark side
With the sails neatly trimmed and the Red Cross to show
Bound away in the *Dreadnaught* to the east'ard we go.

Here's a health to the *Dreadnaught* and her jolly crew,
Likewise Captain Samuels and the officers, too.
You may speak of your packets, Red Line and Black Ball,
But the *Dreadnaught* is the packet that can outsail them all!

This song celebrates the packet ship *Dreadnaught*'s 1860 record run from New York to Queenstown/Liverpool in 9 days and 17 hours during an era when the average passage east was 19 days. It is unusual in that the lyric has the ship sailing "to the east'ard," unlike the more popular English versions which have her sailing west. The *Dreadnaught* was designed and built in Newburyport, MA in 1853 for the Red Cross Line under the watchful eye of Captain Samuel Samuels who declared that he "would sail her to fame or sail her under!" There is some speculation that he may have commissioned the song as well. Since the singer, Oliver Jenness, was from York, ME, only a few miles from place of the ship's origin, we believe this is an older version and closer to the original. The last verse is from another traditional version of the song.

The Jacket of Blue

Hanford Hayes, Stacyville, ME 1942
Helen Hartness Flanders Collection
Transcription © 2016 Julia Lane

It's a ship's crew of sailors you all now shall hear
From Greenland to Liverpool their passage did steer.
There was one amongst them that I wished I never knew.
He is a jolly, jolly sailor who wore a jacket of blue.

Oh, the first time I saw him he had a spyglass in hand.
I tried to talk to him but with me he wouldn't stand
I tried to talk to him but away from me he flew
Oh, my heart it went with him in his jacket of blue.

I said "Noble sailor, I will buy your discharge!
I'll free you from a sailor boy; I'll set you at large
I'll free you from a man-o'-war if your heart will prove true
And I'll never put a stain on your jacket of blue!"

"Oh, you say, noble lady, you will buy my discharge
You'll free me from a sailor boy; you'll set me at large
You'll free me from a man-o'-war if my heart will prove true
But what would my faithful wee Scotch lassie do?

"To stay here with you, lady, that never can be
For I have a wee lassie in my own counteree
I have a wee lassie and to her I'll prove true
For she's never put a stain on my jacket so blue."

I will send for an artist from London or Wales
To take my love's portrait, to take it with skill
I will hang it in my parlor right close to my view
And say I once saw a sailor with a heart that was true.

This has a strong Scottish component as most versions refer to either the sailor or his lassie as "Scotch." Some involve a soldier and describe his "bonnet of blue," which designated a member of the Scottish Highland regiment. In the variant quoted by Roland Palmer Gray in *Songs and Ballads of the Maine Lumberjacks*, the lady is told that the young man's name is Charles Stewart and she remembers "Once a prince of that name wore a bonnet o' blue." The jacket/sailor versions seem most common in the Northeastern U.S. and Canada. An alternate title is "The Ship's Crew of Sailors."

Songs of Ships & Sailors

John Maynard

Charle Finnemore, Bridgewater, ME 10/2/1945
Helen Hartness Flanders Collection
Transcription © 2018 Julia Lane

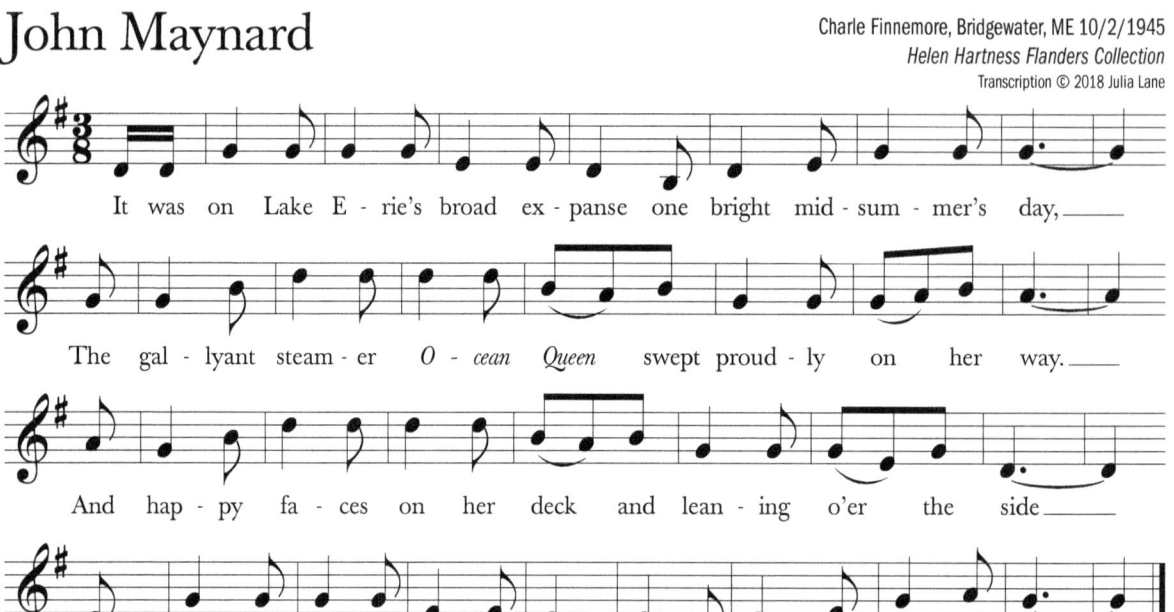

It was on Lake Erie's broad expanse one bright midsummer's day,
The gallyant steamer *Ocean Queen* swept proudly on her way
And happy faces on her deck, and leaning o'er the side
Watched carelessly the feathery foam that flecked the rippling tide.

Now, who beneath that burning sun that smiling bends serene
Could dream the dangers awful vast hung heavy o'er the scene?
Could dream that e'er an hour had sped that frame of sturdy oak
Would sink beneath the lake's dark waves blackened with fire and smoke!

A seaman sought the captain's side, one moment whispered low;
The captain's swarthy face grew pale; he hurried down below.
"Head her southeast!" the captain shouts, above the smothered roar,
"Head her southeast without delay! Make for the nearest shore!"

A sailor, whose heroic name this hour should yet reveal,
By name John Maynard, eastern-born, stood calmly at the wheel.
"Head her southeast!" the captain cried above the smothered roar,
"Head her southeast without delay! Make for the nearest shore!"

The flames approach with giant stride, they scorched his hand and brow;
One arm, disabled, seeks his side, Ah! he is conquered now!
But no, his teeth were firmly set, he crushes down his pain,
One knee upon the stanchion pressed, he guides the ship again.

The flames approached with giant stride, no longer slowly creep,
But creep round that helmsman bold, with fierce, impetuous sweep.
"Hold her! Hold her!" the captain cries "Make for the nearest shore!"
"Hold her! Hold her!" the captain cried "And we will reach the shore!"

But where is he, that helmsman bold? The captain saw him reel,
His nerveless hands released their task, he sank beside the wheel.
The wave received his lifeless corpse, blackened with smoke and fire.
God rest him; Hero never had a nobler funeral pyre!

Though the incident was real, having occurred August 9, 1841, the actual name of the heroic helmsman was Augustus Fuller, age 23, and the ship destroyed by fire was the steamboat *Erie*. The local paper erroneously named him "Luther" Fuller and thus began a strange journey of misinformation. A prose account of "The Helmsman of Lake Erie" was published in the *Maine Cultivator & Hallowell Weekly Gazette* on July 26, 1845 and, for some unknown reason, used the name "John Maynard." After the publication of the same story in the August 30, 1845 issue of the *Baltimore Sun*, a ballad was composed by Benjamin Brown French. French submitted his work to the Baltimore newspaper and it was printed on September 5 of that year. A revised prose sketch was written in 1860 and included in the temperance lectures of John Bartholomew Gough. *The British Workman* (London, England) published an untitled "John Maynard" ballad by the anonymous poet "Josephine" in November 1863. This then accompanied the prose work by Gough. The song given here was originally a poem by Horatio Alger, written in Boston (1875). Having heard an account of the tragedy at a religious meeting in 1866, he penned the opus inspired by the story which gave the hero the name John Maynard. A fourth ballad, "Helmsman of Lake Erie," composed c. 1873 by Epes Sargent, continued to use the name John Maynard. In 1885 the prominent German author, Theodor Fontane, wrote a German language version which is still read and discussed in German schools. The song became particularly popular both in Germany and among German immigrants as many of the passengers were newly arrived from Germany. The original source of the John Maynard name is still in question, though there are a number of research papers dedicated to the subject.

Handsome Harry

Jack McNally, Stacyville, ME 5/9/1942
Helen Hartness Flanders Collection
Transcription © 2016 Julia Lane

I am a sailor by my right
And on the seas take great delight.
Two pretty fair maids I did beguile
Until I had them both with child.

*I promised I'd be true to both
And bound them safe all with an oath.*
To marry both it was not right
So I made but one my wedded wife.

The other being left alone
She says "You false and deluded man
On me you've done a wicked thing
A public shame on you I'll bring!

*"Now you've proved false, I will prove just
And on this earth you'll have no rest!"
And as she spoke it grieved him so
That to the seas he was forced to go.*

This fair one went down to the grove,
While public shame or public show;
She hung herself upon a tree
And two men sporting did her see.

Oh, they went up and cut her down
And in her breast a note was found.
This note was in letters large
"Oh bury me not, I do you charge!

"Here on the ground let my body lie
So's all young men who pass me by
That them by me a warning take
And mark what follows when it is too late!"

As he was sitting on the topmast high
A little small boat he chanced to spy
Saying "Captain, captain, be my defense
There's a mighty spirit coming hence!"

The little small boat it drew 'long side
She was arrayed just like a bride
Saying "Captain, Captain, tell me true
Does Handsome Harry sail in your crew?"

"Now love-lye creature, he is not here
For he has died I do declare!
It was in Havana where he died
It was in Havana his body lies."

"O captain, captain, that is not so!
He's alive and well in your ship below!
Captain," said she, "You must and can
With speed help me to find the man.

"And if you do stand in his defense
A mighty storm I will send hence!
It will cause your sailors all to weep
And send them slumbering in the deep."

Down to the cabin the captain goes
He brings him up to face his foe;
On him she cast her eyes so grim
It made him shake in every limb!

The little boat sailed up 'long side
And he was placed in with his bride.
The boat went up in a flame of fire
Which caused the sailors her to admire!

So, come all you boys to the seas belong
And listen to my mournful song
And you by me a warning take
And mark what follows when it is too late!

The precedent to this song, "The Sailor and the Ghost," also called "The Deceitful Young Man" or "The Dreadful Ghost," was published as a moralistic broadside in 1805. The lurid subject matter and the dramatic ending explain its appeal to the ballad singer and audience. Similar abandonment and ghostly visitations appear in another ballad, called "The Gosport Tragedy," as well as the seduction element of "The House Carpenter," collected by Francis Child. Although McNally's song follows the British broadside very closely, this is an American version with Havana being substituted for St Helen's. The lines in italics are from the 1805 song. Another Maine variant, conveyed by Mrs. Susie Carr Young of Brewer, is more similar to that in the *Forget-me-not Songster* of 1840.

The *Constitution* and the *Guerriere*

Justin De Coster, Buckfield, ME 9/1935
Phillips Barry Collection
Tune: Harry Wass, Addison, ME 8/18/1942
Helen Hartness Flanders Collection
Transcription © 2019 Julia Lane

It ofttimes has been told that the British seamen bold
Could flog the tars of France so neat and handy, O,
But they never met their match, 'till the Yankees did them catch.
Oh, the Yankee boys for fighting are the dandy, O!

Oh, the *Guerriere* so bold on the foaming ocean rolled,
Commanded by proud D'Acres, the Grandee, O,
With as choice a British crew as the rammer ever drew
They could beat the Frenchmen two to one so handy, O.

When this frigate hove in view "Oh," says D'Acres to his crew,
"Prepare ye for action and be handy, O.
On the weather gauge we'll get her and to make the men fight better
We'll give to them gunpowder and good brandy, O."

Now this boasting Briton cries, "Make that Yankee ship our prize,
You can in thirty minutes do it handy, O,
Or in twenty-five I'm sure; If you do it in a score,
I will give you a double share of brandy, O."

Oh, the British balls flew hot but the Yankees heeded not
Until they got a distance that was handy, O.
"When prisoners we've made them with switchel we will treat them
We'll welcome them with Yankee Doodle Dandy, O!"

"Oh," cries Hull unto his crew "We will try what we can do;
If we beat those boasting Britons we're the dandy, O!
The first broad side we poured bro't the mizzen by the board
Which doused the Royal Ensign so handy, O.

Oh, D'Acres he did sigh and to his officers did cry,
"Oh, I didn't know the Yankees were so handy, O!"
The sound told so well that the fore and mainmast fell
That made this lofty frigate look quite handy, O.

"Oh," says D'Acres, "we're undone!" So, he fires a lee gun
And the drummers struck up Yankee Doodle Dandy, O.
When D'Acres came in board to deliver up his sword
He was loth to part with it; it looked so handy, O.

"You may keep it," says brave Hull, "What makes you look so dull?
Have you drank too much of your brandy, O?"
Britons now be still, since we've hooked you in the gill,
Don't boast upon your D'Acres, the Grandee, O!

Launched in 1797, the USS *Constitution* was one of six frigates commissioned for the first U.S. Navy. She is the world's oldest commissioned naval vessel still afloat. During the War of 1812, the capture of the British *Guerriere* by the American *Constitution*, under the command of Captain Isaac Hull, took place on August 19, 1812 some 600 miles east of Boston. During this battle the *Constitution* earned her nickname, "*Old Ironsides,*" as surprised observers noticed that British shot bounced off the ship and declared, "Her sides are made of iron!" After the battle, Captain Hull refused to take the sword of Captain D'acres in surrender. Instead, legend says, he took the gentleman's hat to wear in his next fight against the British. Captain Hull was hailed as a hero and numerous songs were penned in his honor (see "Hull's Victory," page 214). Henry Wass only sang one verse so we have added additional verses from Justin Decoster, the "Bard of Buckfield."

switchel = drink made from vinegar and water.

THE CONSTITUTION IN CLOSE ACTION WITH THE GUERRIERE.

The Fate of *Rena Lee*

Frank Kneeland, Searsport, ME 10/1941
Helen Hartness Flanders Collection
Lyrics from the *Kneeland Miscellany* 1914
Transcription © 2016 Julia Lane

Come all ye bold seamen, pray now attend
To read these few lines that have lately been penned
Concerning the dangers of the salt sea
And the sad destruction of the *Rena Lee*.
Oh, the fate of *Rena Lee*

Seven hundred and seventy bold seamen had we
And ninety brass cannon to bear us company
And as we were a-sailing to our sad surprise
A most terrible storm did begin to arise.
Oh, the fate of *Rena Lee*

The waves looked like fire and rolled mountains high
While over the rigging the salt seas did fly
"Bear away!" said our captain, "and do the best you can
For if the storm increases, we're lost, every man!"
Oh, the fate of *Rena Lee*

We all went to work, our lives for to save.
While our masts and our rigging did beat the salt wave;
"Bear away," cried our captain, "your skill do not spare.
So long as we've sea room, the less we've to fear."
Oh, the fatal **Ramilles**.*

---

* Although the folk process has changed the name of the ship from the historic *Ramilles* to *Rena Lee*, many of the details of the disaster remain in this version of the song. The singer may choose to use whichever ship name they prefer.

A few moments later, to our sad shock
Our good ship, the Rena Lee, she struck upon a rock!
Had you heart like a Turk, I am sure you'd lament
To have heard the sighs and groans as to bottom she went.
Oh, the fate of Rena Lee

All you that are willing to do a good deed.
In relieving the widows in this time of need.
Bear a hand to assist them, and God will you bless
With happiness greater than I can express.
Oh, the fatal Ramilles.

In February, 1760, Admiral Boscawen, with six ships of the line, sailed from Plymouth, England to join the British fleet off Quiberon. A violent storm arose severely damaging the squadron who turned back to Plymouth. Unfortunately, the *Ramilles*, a ship of 90 guns and a crew of over 700 men, was totally wrecked on the shore near Bolt Head in Devonshire. The captain, named Taylor, and the whole of the crew, excepting 26 men, perished in the wreck, one of the most disastrous in the history of the British Royal Navy. A broadside was composed and distributed; the original broadside lyrics appear in italics.

The *Cumberland's* Crew

James Kneeland, Searsport, ME 1914
Text from the *Kneeland Miscellany*
Tune: Traditional, *Edward D. "Sandy" Ives Collection*
Transcription © 2017 Julia Lane

Oh, ship-mates come ga-ther and join in my dit-ty Of a ter-ri-ble bat-tle that's hap-pened of late.

Let each good Un-ion tar shed a sad tear of pi-ty As they think of the once gal-lant *Cum-ber-land's* fate.

The eighth day of March told a ter-ri-ble sto-ry And ma-ny a brave tar to the world bid a-dieu

But our flag it was wrapped in a man-tle of glo-ry By the he-ro-ic deeds of the *Cum-ber-land's* crew.

Oh, shipmates come gather and join in my ditty
Of a terrible battle that's happened of late.
Let each good Union tar shed a sad tear of pity
As they think of the once gallant *Cumberland's* fate.
The eighth day of March told a terrible story
And many a brave tar to the world bid adieu,
But our Flag it was wrapped in a mantle of glory
By the heroic deeds of the *Cumberland's* crew.

On that ill-fated day about ten in the morning
The sky it was cloudless and bright shone the sun.
When the drums of the *Cumberland* sounded a warning
That told every seaman to stand by his gun.
An iron-clad frigate down on us came bearing
And high in the air the base rebel flag flew.
The pennant of Treason she proudly was waving
Determined to conquer the *Cumberland's* crew.

Then up spoke our Captain with stern resolution
Saying, "Boys, by this monster now don't be dismayed.
We swore to maintain our beloved Constitution
And to die for our Country we are not afraid.
We'll fight for the Union. Our cause it is glorious.
To the Stars and the Stripes we will ever stand true.
We'll die at our quarters or conquer victorious!"
He was answered with cheers by the *Cumberland's* crew.

Then our ports we threw open and our guns we let thunder;
Our broadsides like hail on the rebels did pour.
The sailors gazed on filled with terror and wonder
For our shot struck her side and glanced harmlessly o'er.
But the pride of our Navy could never be daunted
Though the dead and the dying our decks they did strew;
The flag of our Union how proudly she flaunted,
Sustained by the blood of the *Cumberland's* crew.

They fought us three hours with stern resolution
Till those rebels found cannon would never avail
For the flag of secession had no power to gall us
Though the blood from our scuppers it crimsoned the wave.
She struck us amidships; our planks she did sever.
Her sharp iron prow pierced our noble ship through.
As slowly she sank on that dark, rolling river,
"We'll die at our guns!" cried the *Cumberland's* crew.

Slowly they sank 'neath Virginia's waters;
Their voices on earth will ne'er be heard more.
They'll be wept by Columbia's brave sons and fair daughters;
May their blood be avenged on Virginia's shore.
In that battle-stained grave they are silently lying
Their souls have forever to earth bid adieu,
But the Star Spangled Banner above them is flying;
It was nailed to the mast by the *Cumberland's* crew.

Columbia's sweet birthright of Freedom's communion
Thy Flag never floated so proudly before
For the spirits of those who have died for our Union
Above its broad folds now exultingly soar,
And when our sailors in battle assemble
God bless our dear Banner, The Red, White and Blue.
Beneath its broad folds we'll cause tyrants to tremble
Or we'll die at our guns — like the *Cumberland's* crew.

One of four versions of this song found in Maine, this recounts the destruction of the frigate USS *Cumberland,* commanded by Lieutenant George Morris, by the ironclad CSS *Virginia* off Newport News during the Civil War. In an effort to delay the development of a rival navy, the Union had scuttled the USS *Merrimack* in Norfolk harbor. As a response, the Confederates raised the ship and had it refitted as an ironclad with a battering ram, renaming her CSS *Virginia,* commanded by Franklin Buchanan. On March 8, 1862, despite never being tested, Buchanan ordered the *Virginia* to engage the Union fleet. When the ironclad brashly steamed into the harbor, the Union sailors watched with dismay as their artillery fire bounced off *Virginia*'s armored hull and her counter-attack accomplished the tragic work of war sinking the *Cumberland*, her colors still flying, and killing 121 sailors. Though *Virginia* had been damaged by the *Cumberland*'s fire, Buchanan then turned his attention to several other Union ships in the harbor, wreaking equal havoc upon them. The following day, the *Virginia/Merrimack* sallied forth from Norfolk and met the Union's own ironclad the USS *Monitor*, which carried a revolving gun turret, engaging in a battle that changed maritime history (See "The *Monitor* and the *Merrimack*"). As was so often the case, broadside songsheets were immediately published and the song quickly became widely sung. In addition, Henry Wadsworth Longfellow composed a very moving poem on the event.

The *Monitor* and the *Merrimack*

Capt. Henry Hunter Chamberlain, Round Pond, ME, 1920
Fannie Hardy Eckstorm Collection
Transcription © 2018 Julia Lane

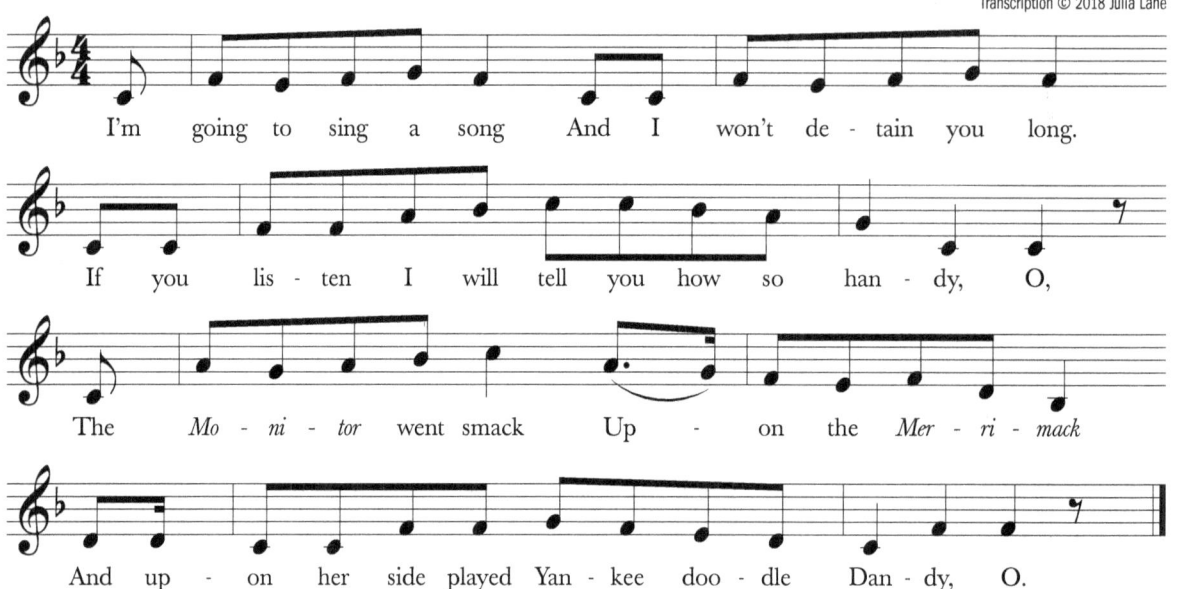

I'm going to sing a song
And I won't detain you long.
If you listen I will tell you how so handy, O,
The Monitor *went smack*
Upon the Merrimack
And upon her sides played Yankee Doodle Dandy, O.

On the Eighth of March
The *Merrimack* slipped out
From Norfolk to take a cruise so handy, O.
She didn't think she'd meet
Anything in all our fleet
Able to give her Yankee Doodle Dandy, O.

Humpty doodle doo,
Jeff Davis how are you?
Our *Monitor* beat your *Merrimack* quite handy, O.
Ericsson,* he's around,
In this world there can't be found
Any people like the Yankee Doodle Dandy, O.

She went rushing 'round
Smashing everything she found
Till the *Monitor* came sailing in so handy, O.
The Warden stopped her fun,
Soon he made her cut and run
While the shells they whistled Yankee Doodle Dandy, O.

For the Yorktown *and the other*
They'd be little bother
To smash and break them both up so handy, O,
For our gunboats they would do
To rip them through and through
While the sailors, they'd sing Yankee Doodle Dandy, O.

Now the *Merrimack* was some
Till the *Monitor* did come
And she opened up her little ports so handy, O.
The shells they did let fly
Till the *Merrimack* did cry,
"Here's the Devil's share or Yankee Doodle Dandy, O!"

To Jeff this ought to show
That this monster is no go
And mechanics in the North are very handy, O,
That he must surrender soon
Or we'll blow him to the moon
With inventions of our Yankee Doodle Dandy, O.

So now, boys, let us cheer
Those lads that know no fear
That worked that little battery so handy, O.
They deserve well of us all
Let us pray that none may fall
May they live long to sing Yankee Doodle Dandy, O!

The first engagement in combat using ironclad warships was the Battle of Hampton Roads in Norfolk, Virginia over March 8-9, 1862. The Confederate ship *Virginia* was built from the remnants of the derelict Union frigate *Merrimack* which had been scuttled in an attempt to prevent development of a Confederate Navy. Stephen Mallory, the Confederate Secretary of the Navy, had other ideas and raised the *Merrimack*'s hull incorporating the still functional engines into a new vessel, an ironclad equipped with a ram. The new CSS *Virginia* succeeded in sinking the USS *Congress* and the USS *Cumberland* though the vessel almost sank when the ram became stuck in the *Cumberland*'s hull. 121 Union seamen drowned in the sinking of the *Cumberland* (see "The *Cumberland*'s Crew") The following day, the Union's ironclad, the USS *Monitor* commanded by John Worden (the Warden), engaged the *Virginia*/*Merrimack* in a lengthy battle which ended in a draw. Both sides claimed the victory. The course of naval history was changed by technical innovations used by both ships. The "Jeff" referred to in the song is Jefferson Davis who served as president of the Confederacy. This cheeky song was published as a broadside by Johnson, a song publisher in Philadelphia, and the lyrics in italics are from that version. The air was noted as "Yankee Doodle Dandy" but the tune currently used for that song does not fit these lyrics. We have used the traditional tune "The Bonnie Lass o' Fyvie-O" which was often used for songs like this as it was also a military fife march. Indeed, this song reminds us of "The *Constitution* and the *Guerriere*" which uses a similar tune.

* Swedish-American inventor and engineer John (Johan) Ericsson was the designer of the *Monitor*.

The Bold Northwestmen

Frank Kneeland, Searsport, ME October 1941
Helen Hartness Flanders Collection
Lyrics from *Kneeland Miscellany* 1914
Transcription © 2015 Julia Lane

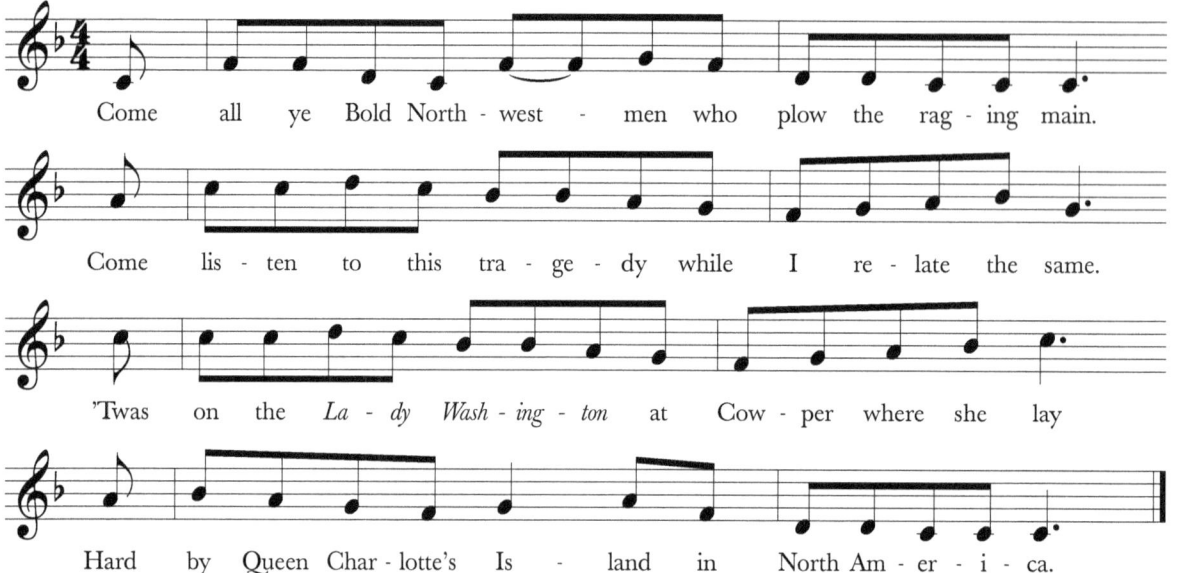

Come all ye bold Northwestmen who plow the raging main.
Come listen to this tragedy while I relate the same.
'Twas on the *Lady Washington* at Cowper where she lay
Hard by Queen Charlotte's Island in North America.

'Twas on November the second day in seventeen-ninety-one
The natives of this country on board of us did come,
And then to buy their furs of them our captain did begin
But mark what followed after before it long had been.

Up upon our quarterdeck our gun chest there did stand,
The keys they being left in them by our gunner's careless hand.
The natives, they perceiving our ship to make a prize,
Thinking we had no other means for to protect our lives.

Up upon our quarterdeck our captain there did stand
With twelve of those bold savages with knives drawn in their hands
All pointing at his body ready to run him through.
If we should offer to resist — Great God! What could we do?

Then into our cabin straightway we did repair
But to our sad misfortune no arms could we find there
Except it were two pistols, one gun and two broadswords
And immediately it was agreed, "Fight them off!" it was the word.

Our powder we got ready; our gun room open lay.
Our souls we did commit to God, our bodies to the clay,
All standing in our cabin waiting for a sign
But there could no sign be given for fear we should be slain.

Then, with what few arms we had we rushed on them with main
And, by our being spirited, the quarterdeck did gain!
And the number that we killed of them was seventy and odd
And as many more were wounded as since we've understood.

Come, all ye bold Northwestmen wherever you may be
Trust not an Indian savage in North America
For they are so desirous your shipping to obtain
That they will never leave it off till the most of them are slain!

This was a favorite song of adventure in both fo'c'sle and woods shanty and is relayed as sung by Mr. Kneeland's father, James. Three versions have been recorded from Maine. As with so many ballads, this tells the story from one point of view. Historic facts are reported as follows: Captain John Kendrick was well known in New England in the late 18th century. He commanded the first expeditions to the northwest attempting to establish a fur trade there. After sailing to China in the sloop *Lady Washington* in 1789, he had her fitted as a brig and made for British Columbia in March 1791. The local American Indians, led by one Chief Koyah, attempted to capture the vessel. Apparently Koyah and Kendrick had had a previous "disagreeable skirmish" for which Koyah was captured and chained in irons. The Indian tradition at the time being one of revenge, the attack described in the songs seems to be one of retribution as Koyah, in various accounts, was said to taunt Kendrick early in the battle by "holding out his leg saying, 'Now put me in irons!'" In another description there appears among the attackers "a woman who was a proper Amazon." She was apparently standing on the main chains "urging them to action with the greatest ardour" and was wounded during the battle. Clearly, there is much more to this story than appears in the song! Although it is generally believed that the ballad was written by an eyewitness, it was not printed as a broadside until 1831. An extensive research paper, "A Ballad of the Northwest Fur Trade," by Judge Frederic William Howay, published in the *New England Quarterly, Vol. I., No. 1* (Jan. 1928 pp. 71–79), quotes from five accounts of the event and fills out the details.

Songs of Ships & Sailors

The Downeast Maid

Susie Carr Young, Brewer, circa 1930
Phillips Barry Collection
First transcribed by George Herzog 1930
Transcription © 2019 Fred Gosbee

'Twas in the pleasant month of May
About the dawning of the day
I overheard a young man say,
"I've lost my fairest jewel!"

Sweet Phoebe was my true love's name,
Her beauty did my heart inflame,
Scarce would you find so fair a dame
Go search Downeast all over.

My love and I we did agree
That we would surely married be.
As soon as I return'd from sea,
We'd seal the solemn bargain.

But Oh! when I returned again,
Death had my sweet companion slain,
The pride and glory of the Plain
In the cold grave mould'ring.

I was forsaken and forlorn,
I wish I never had been born.
How cruel was the dreadful morn
That brought such doleful tidings.

I am undone! What shall I do?
I'll range the earth and ocean through.
I'll dress in some forsaken hue,
And spend my days in mourning.

This appears throughout the Northeast as "Bright Phoebe" and even into the Great Lakes lumber camps as "Sweet Mary Jane." Another Maine singer, Carrie Grover, knew it as "Sweet Caroline" and it appears in her *Heritage of Song*. Only a fragment of lyrics, with a melody titled "Sailor's Love Song," was relayed by Mrs. Young, who claimed it as traditional in her family. Apparently, all the songs are based on a work by the New Hampshire poet Silas Ballou (1753–1837).

According to the writer of Silas Ballou's genealogy, Adin Ballou, "His productions were long in frequent demand throughout a wide rural circle, and not a few of them got into print. He wrote religious hymns, patriotic odes, funeral elegies, festive songs for social celebrations of all kinds, sonnets, acrostics, epitaphs [and] once amused himself by concocting into rhymes all the names of the eight hundred inhabitants of Richmond, which was printed and read to the great admiration of his townsfolk, and their neighbors around."

The original is inscribed thus: "Relating to a disconsolate friend's lamentable bereavement of his betrothed bride, whose name was Phoebe." We have completed Young's fragmented lyrics, which appear in italics, with the Ballou's original verses.

Sur le Bord de L'ile (By the edge of the sea)

Margarita L. Bartley, Jackman, ME 1954
Helen Hartness Flanders Collection
Transcription © 2021 Julia Lane

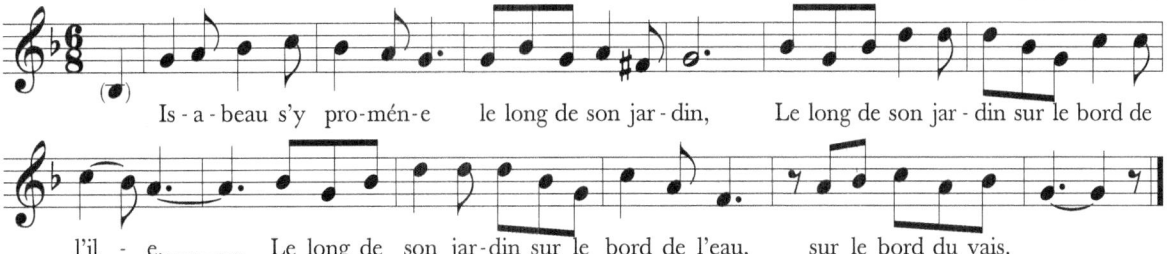

Isabeau s'y pro-mèn-e le long de son jar-din, Le long de son jar-din sur le bord de l'il - e,_____ Le long de son jar-din sur le bord de l'eau, sur le bord du vais.

Isabeau s'y pro-mèn-e le long de son jardin,
Le long de son jardin sur le bord de l'ile,
Le long de son jardin sur le bord de l'eau,
Sur le bord du vaisseau.

Le plus jeu-ne des trente, il se mit chan-ter;
Il se mit a chanter sur le bord de l'ile, etc.

La chan-son que tu chan-tes, je voudrais la savoir;
Je voudrais la savoir sur le bord de l'ile, etc.

Em-bar-que dans mon bar-que, je te la chanterai;
Je te la chanterai sur le bord de l'ile, etc.

Quand eli' fut dans la bar-que, eli' se mit a pleurer;
Eli' se mit a pleurer sur le bord de l'ile, etc.

Qu'avez-vous donc, la bel-le, qu'a vous a tant pleurer?
Qu'a-vous a tant pieurer sur le bord de l'ile, etc.

Je pieur' mon anneau d'or(e), dans l'eau il est tombé;
Dans l'eau-z-il est tombe' sur le bord de l'ile, etc.

Ne pleurez point, la bel-le, je vous le plongerai;
Je vous le plongerai sur le bord de l'ile, etc.

De la premiere plon-ge, il n'a rien ramené;
Il n'a rien ramene, sur le bord de l'ile, etc.

De la seconde plon-ge, l'anneau s'a voltagé;
L'anneau-z-a voltigé ur le bord de l'ile, etc.

De la troisième plonge, le galant s'est noyé;
Le galant s'est noyé sur le bord de l'ile etc.

El-le fit un' ren-con-tre de tren-te matelots;
De trent-e matelots sur le bord de l'ile;
De trente matelots sur le bord de l'eau,
Sur le bord du vaisseau.

The collectors represented in this book concentrated on the Anglo-Celtic song tradition and non English songs were not included in most of the archives we examined. Marguerite Olney did attempt to document some French songs while collecting for Helen Flanders, including this one. Eloise Linscott includes both French and Native American material in her recordings. That being said, there are few examples of French songs relating to the sea. This lovely ballad is an exception. Also known as "Isabeau S'y Promène" this song appears in *Chansons Populaires du Canada (Popular songs of Canada)* by E. Gagnon published in 1865. It is said to have originated in Normandy, France, and may have traveled to North America in the 17th century with the French explorers on the St Lawrence River. The rhythmical cadence and repeated lines might indicate use as a shanty. The song is now found throughout the French speaking world. We have translated it to create this singable English version.

Songs of Ships & Sailors

By the Edge of the Sea (Sur le Bord de L'ile)

Translation ©2021 Julia Lane

Young Isabel went a-walking all in her garden green,
All in her garden green at the island shoreline
All in her garden green by the waterside
With the vessels 'longside.

She met a band of sailors while she was walking there.
While she was walking there at the island shoreline
While she was walking there by the waterside
With the vessels 'longside.

The youngest of the sailors, he sang a song of love.
He sang a song of love at the island shoreline
He sang a song of love by the waterside
With the vessels 'longside.

"Your song is such a sweet one, I'd like to sing it too.
I'd like to sing it too at the island shoreline
I'd like to sing it too by the waterside
With the vessels 'longside."

"If you will come onboard my ship, I will teach you my song.
I will teach you my song at the island shoreline
I will teach you my song by the waterside
With the vessels 'longside."

She went with him onboard the ship but soon began to weep.
She soon began to weep at the island shoreline
She soon began to weep by the waterside
With the vessels 'longside.

"What's wrong, my lovely lady, what makes you so lament?
What makes you so lament at the island shoreline
What makes you so lament by the waterside
With the vessels 'longside?"

"I'm weeping for my ring of gold that in the water fell.
That in the water fell at the island shoreline
That in the water fell by the waterside
With the vessels 'longside."

"Oh, do not cry my lady, I'll get it back for you!
I'll get it back for you at the island shoreline
I'll get it back for you by the waterside
With the vessels 'longside."

He dove into the ocean, returning without the ring.
Returning without the ring at the island shoreline
Returning without the ring by the waterside
With the vessels 'longside.

The next time that he dove down, the ring turned around and round
The ring turned around and round at the island shoreline
The ring turned around and round by the waterside
With the vessels 'longside.

The third time that he dove down, the gallant young man was drowned.
The gallant young man was drowned at the island shoreline
The gallant young man was drowned by the waterside
With the vessels 'longside.

The *Mary L. McKay*

Lyrics by Frederick W. Wallace 1913
Sung by Edmund Henneberry, Devil's Island, NS 1948
Helen Creighton Collection
Adapted by Fred Gosbee 2014
Transcription © 2015 Julia Lane

Oh, come all you hardy haddockers, who winter fishing go,
And brave the seas upon the Banks in stormy winds and snow,
And ye who love hard drivin', come and listen to my lay
Of the run we made from Portland in the *Mary L. McKay*.
We hung the muslin on her, as the wind began to hum,
Twenty hardy Nova Scotiamen chock full of Portland rum,
Mains'l, fores'l, jib and jumbo on that wild December day,
As we passed Cape Elizabeth and slugged for Fundy Bay.

CHORUS
    Storm along! Drive along! Punch her through the rips!
    Don't heed them boarding combers as the solid green she ships.
    'Twould fill your heart with terror and you'd wish you were away
    At home in bed and not aboard the *Mary L. McKay*.

We slammed her by Monhegan as the gale began to scream,
Our vessel took to dancing in a way that was no dream.
A howler o'er the taffrail we steered her East away;
Oh, she was a hound for running was the *Mary L. McKay*.
When we slammed her by Matinicus the skipper hauled the log—
"Sixteen knots, Lord Harry! Ain't she just the gal to jog?"
The half-canned helmsman shouted as he swung her on her way,
"Just watch me tear the mainsail off the *Mary L. McKay*!"

The rum was passing merrily and the gang was feeling grand,
Long necks dancing in our wake from where we left the land.
Our skipper he kept sober for he knew how things would lay,
And he made us furl the mainsail on the *Mary L. McKay*.
Under foresail and her jumbo we tore wildly through the night,
The foaming, surging whitecaps in the moonshine made a sight,
And in this wild inferno, boys, we soon had hell to pay,
We didn't care a hoot aboard the *Mary L. McKay*.

We lashed our helmsman to the box as we steered through the gloom,
A big sea hove his dory mate right over the main boom;
It tore the oilpants off his legs and you could hear him say,
"There's a power of water flying o'er the *Mary L. McKay*."
Our skipper didn't care to make his wife a widow yet,
He swung her off to Yarmouth Cape with just her foresail set,
We passed Forchu next morning and shot in at break of day,
And soon in sheltered harbor lay the *Mary L. McKay*!

From Portland, Maine, to Yarmouth Sound, two twenty miles we ran,
In eighteen hours, my bully boys, now beat that if you can.
The crew said it was seamanship, the skipper he kept dumb
But the force that drove our vessel was the power of Portland rum!

Originally built in Essex, MA, in 1884, the *Effie Morrissey* (as she was then called) had a 30-year career as a fishing vessel and cargo ship running from New England to Nova Scotia. The pride of Bob Bartlett, her captain, the *Morrissey's* speed and maneuverability gained her a reputation which resulted in a ballad by Frederick William Wallace, then a crew member. Originally written in December 1913, "The Log of the Record Run" describes a 225-mile passage made by the *Morrissey* in 18½ hours in gale force winds. It was an instant hit and Bartlett requested a signed copy. Wallace later said, "I altered the name of the schooner to *Mary L. McKay* as I was afraid that to put *Effie Morrissey* in them might incur the displeasure of my shipmates. However, I need not have worried on that score for most, if not all of them, would have been delighted to have been identified with the escapade—so I was told." Printed in the *Canadian Fisherman* in 1914, the story is well entrenched in fishing folklore both in Maine and Nova Scotia and the song has passed into folk tradition.

The *Effie Morrissey* went on to an illustrious career as a cargo ship, an Arctic research vessel, and performing surveys out of Greenland for the U.S. Navy in World War II. Refitted after a galley fire in 1949, the ship was renamed *Ernestina* and worked as a trans-Atlantic packet carrying people and cargo between the United States and the Cape Verde Islands. Eventually, unable to compete with the steamship service, she was put to use plying inter-island trade. In 1975 the new Republic of Cape Verde returned her to the United States as a symbol of their historic ties. *Ernestina* eventually returned to her home port of New Bedford in 1982 now serves as a fully operational museum and educational vessel. She is one of six remaining Essex-built schooners, the oldest surviving transatlantic packet schooner, and one of two remaining Arctic sailing vessels.

The folk process has transmuted the song with many of the variants being the result of ignorance of nautical or local terms and even geography. We recently recorded our version of the original ballad maintaining jargon, geography and details not often included in modern versions. Fred Gosbee has also added a chorus, and an additional verse from the poem.

The *Stately Southerner*

Capt. Archie S. Spurling, Isleford, ME 1927
Tune: Mr. George Kemmer, Isleford, ME 1927
Fannie Hardy Eckstorm Collection
Transcription © 2016 Julia Lane

'Tis of a *Stately Southerner* that carries the Stripes and Stars
With a whistling breeze from west northwest blowing through her pitch-pine spars.
Our starboard tacks we had on board hung heavy on the gale
One autumn night as we rose the light on the Old Head of Kinsale.

It was a clear and cloudless night; the wind blew steady and strong,
And gaily o'er the bounding deep our good ship speeds along.
The dashing billows around doth roar as fiery seas she spreads
While bending low her waist in snow she buries her lee cathead.

There was no sign of shortening sail by him who walked the poop,
And by the weight of her pond'rous jib, her boom bent like a hoop.
Through the groaning of those cross-trees that held the strong main tack
He only laughed as he glanced abaft at the bright and sparkling track.

The mid-tides meet in the channel waves that flow from shore to shore
And the wind held heavy upon the lee from Folkstan to Dunmore.
At the Sterling Light on Tusker Rock where the old bell tolled the hour,
That beacon light that shone so bright was quench'd by the Old Oak Tower.

The night fog had not cleared away that scarce obscured the shore;
A heavy mist hung o'er the land from Erin to Kingshore.
What rises on our weather bow, what hangs upon the breeze?
It's time the good ship hauled her wind abreast of the Saltees.

The nightly robe our frigate wore was her three topsails large;
Her flying jib and spanker and her topsail had been furled.
"Come lay aloft my gallant tars!" The word had scarce been passed
When royals and topgallant yards were crossed upon the mast.

While up aloft upon the yards our sails spread to the breeze,
A ship we spied on the misty tide come bearing down our lee
And by her wondrous press of sail, her long and tapering spars,
We found our morning visitor was an English man-o'-war.

Up spoke their noble Captain, then, as a shot before us passed
"Haul up your flowing courses! Turn your topsails to the mast!"
Those British tars they gave three cheers from the deck of their black corvette
But our patriot bark gave answer with a broadside from the deck.

There was not a cheer from our privateer, nor did our seamen dread
As the starry banner o'er our head from the mizzen peak was spread
Up spoke our noble captain bold, a cloud was on his brow:
He says, "My gallant heroes all, our great distress is now!"

"Out booms! out booms!" our skipper cried, "Out booms and give her sheet!"
And the fastest keel that cuts the deep shot ahead of the British fleet!
Amid a thundering shower of shot, and 'mid the foaming spray,
Down the Channel clear Paul Jones did steer just at the break of day.

The song, which involves the exploits of Captain John Paul Jones in his nautical predations of the coastal U.K. in 1778–79, seems to be a celebration of Jones' seamanship and the merits of the ship more than a specific engagement. The title "*Stately Southerner*" is a confusing mystery, as Jones never commanded a ship of this name. He was most famous for his ship the *Ranger*, a corvette built in Portsmouth, NH in 1777 per order of the new U.S. Congress. In fact, another version of this song is called "Paul Jones and the *Ranger*." A recruiting broadside published at the time declared "The Ship *Ranger* in the Opinion of every Person who has seen her is looked upon to be one of the best Cruizers in America. She will be always able to fight her Guns under a most excellent Cover; and no Vessel yet built was ever calculated for sailing faster." In 1778, Jones was sent to cruise the British coasts to interrupt shipping and engage the British navy. He made good use of the *Ranger* in harassing and outsailing them, much to their annoyance, and earning the reputation of a ruthless pirate. There are a number of English and Scottish songs which refer to him as such. After a raid on Whitehaven, Jones encountered HMS *Drake* off Carrickfergus, Northern Ireland, and defeated her in a bloody and dramatic battle. The geographic details in "The *Stately Southernor*" do not match that location and it would seem if this song were about that event there would be a more detailed description of it. (The Irish song "Young Dobbs" does a good job of this.) In September 1779, Jones, in command of another ship, the *Bonhomme Richard*, went on to defeat a British convoy at the Battle of Flamborough Head in Yorkshire. That engagement is the subject of the song "Paul Jones," also in this collection.

Most of the lyrics were taken down from the singing of Captain Archie S. Spurling of Isleford, ME, with additional lyrics from "The Yankee Man-O'-War" sent in October 1924 by Capt. Lewis Freeman Gott of Bernard, ME and appearing in *Minstrelsy of Maine* by Fanny Hardy Eckstorm and Mary Winslow Smyth, 1927, pp 209–211. According to Horace Beck, Mr. Spurling was also recorded by Wendell Hadlock on Little Cranberry Island "the year before his death." The tune was recorded from Spurling by Mr. George Kemmer of Isleford, ME in 1927. It appears in both *British Ballads from Maine* by Barry, Eckstorm and Smyth, and *Songs of American Sailormen* by Joanna Colcord. Ralph Page printed a 4/4 variant in his *Northern Junket* in 1951 p. 24. We have reordered some of the lyrics to make better sense of the action.

Paul Jones

James Kneeland, Searsport, ME 1914
from the *Kneeland Miscellany*
Tune: *Frank Warner Collection*
Transcription © 2019 Julia Lane

An American frigate, a frigate of war,
With guns mounting forty came from Baltimore
To cruise in the channel of old Eng-e-land.
Our gallant commander, Paul Jones, was the man!

We had not sailed long before we espied
A large forty-four and a twenty likewise.
Paul Jones then he smiled as he sheered alongside
With a loud speaking trumpet "Whence came you?" he cried.

"Whence came you?" he cried, "I hailed you before!
Return me an answer or a broadside I'll pour"
A broadside it came from those bold Englishmen
And the sons of America returned it again.

Paul Jones then said to his men, every one,
"Let every true seaman stand firm to his gun;
We'll receive a broadside from this bold Englishman,
And, like true Yankee sailors, return it again.

"Stand firm to your quarters! Your duty don't shun!
The first one that shrinks, through the body I'll run!
Though their force is superior, yet soon they shall know
What true brave American seamen can do!"

The contest was bloody; both decks ran with gore
And ninety bold seamen lay dead on the floor.
Paul Jones then he smiled in the height of his pride
"If we can't do any better, boys, we'll sink alongside!"

Our shot flew so hot, they could not stand us long,
And the undaunted union of Britain came down.
To us they did strike, and their colors haul down:
The fame of Paul Jones to the world shall be known!

The Alliance bore down, while the Richard did rake,
Which caused the bold heart of poor Pearson to ache.
Our shot flew so hot, they could not stand us long,
And the undaunted union of Britain came down.

Now, all valiant seamen, where'er you may be,
Who hear of this combat fought on the broad sea,
May you all do like them when call'd to the same,
And your names be enroll'd on the pages of fame.

Your country will boast of her sons that are brave,
And to you she will look her from danger to save!
She'll call you, dear sons; in her annals you'll shine,
And the brows of the brave shall green laurels entwine.

And now, my brave boys, we have captured a prize;
A large forty-four and a twenty likewise!
May God bless the mothers who are called on to weep
For their sons who are lain in the ocean so deep.

Paul Jones was a Scottish-born American sea hero who rose to fame in the infant American Navy during the Revolution. He brazenly engaged British ships in their own territory, harassing and interrupting their trade, and became known there as a pirate, especially in Galloway in the Solway Firth where he was born. On September 23, 1779, Paul Jones, with his flagship *Bonhomme Richard* and four others, encountered a fleet of merchantmen off Flamborough Head in the North Sea off Yorkshire. They were escorted by HMS *Countess of Scarborough,* with twenty guns, and HMS *Serapis*, carrying forty-four guns commanded by Captain Richard Pearson. Jones engaged the *Serapis*, and another of his ships, the *Pallas*, engaged the *Countess*. During the battle, Commander Pearson asked Jones if he would surrender, being so much out-gunned, to which Jones replied "Surrender, be damned. I have not yet begun to fight!" The Americans prevailed and numerous songs were written to tell the tale on both sides of the Atlantic. We have added additional lyrics, which appear in italics, from "Captain John Paul Jones's Victory over the British frigate *Serapis* and *Countess of Scarborough*, sloop of war, on the 23d of September, 1779," from *The American National Song Book* by William McCarty (1842).

Green Beds

Arthur Walker, Littleton, ME 8/31/1942
Helen Hartness Flanders Collection
Transcription © 2018 Julia Lane

It's a story, it's a story, it's a story of one
Concerning that bold sailor boy whose name it is John.
Poor Johnny's ofttimes in a house where ofttimes he had been;
Poor Johnny's ofttimes in a house, where ofttimes he had been.

O, Johnny, he being weary, he held down his head.
He asked for a candle, that he might light himself to bed.
"The green beds they are full, John, they have been all this week,
And for fresh lodgings, poor John, you had better seek."

"Call down pretty daughter Polly, and set her down by me;
Call down your daughter Polly, and set her on my knee."
"My daughter, she's engaged, John, she could not come to thee,
Nor would I accredit you to one glass or she."

"How much is it I owe to you, and down it will be paid;
How much is it I owe to you, and down it will be made."
"It's four and twenty shillings, John, you'll owe two years long!"
Well, Johnny he pulled out his two hands full of gold.

The sight of so much money caused this old dame to do;
The sight of so much money caused this old dame to rue,
"You thought I was in earnest, John, but I'm only in jest,
It is by my habitation, I love you, John, the best."

"I'll call down daughter Polly, and set her down by you;
I'll call down daughter Polly and I'll set her on your knee,
For the green beds they are empty, John, they have been all this week
For you and my daughter Polly to take a sound sleep."

"Before I would sleep in your beds I'd lay out by your door,
For when I had no money my fortune it was poor.
But now I've got some money, I'll can make the taverns roar,
With my quarters, jugs and bottles, I can roll along the shore!"

O, down come pretty Polly all with her long face;
She grabbed poor Johnny, she was slender 'round the waist,
"You're welcome home dear Johnny; you're welcome home from sea
The green beds are empty for both you and me!"

"Before I'd sleep in your bed, I'd lie up in a cave;
Before I'd sleep in your bed, I'd lie up in my grave,
For now that I've got money I'll can make the taverns roar,
Without some companion you turned out of doors!"

Now come all you bold Irish boys that plows the raging main
That earns all your monies in cold storms and rain,
I'd have you take care of it, to lay it up in store,
For without some companion you're turned out of doors.

Also known as "Pretty Polly," many versions of this song have been found in the Maine tradition. All include elements of both "The Saucy Sailor," where the seaman tests his sweetheart's loyalty by feigning poverty and "The Wild Rover," where the landlady is duped then asks forgiveness only to be mocked by the patron. The "green bed" seems to signify a place of privilege for affluent travelers at the inn, which may include some female entertainment; perhaps the landlord's daughter. Older traditions show the "green bed" as a springtime fertility ritual. The *Folklore of Jersey* describes a girl selected from the maidens of the village who was made to lie on a bed of greens and receive gifts from suitors. Even the biblical "Song of Solomon" describes the newlyweds' bed as verdant or green.

Jack, the Jolly Tar

Fred Fowler, Hampden, ME 1925
via Susie Carr Young
Phillips Barry Collection
Transcription © 2019 Julia Lane

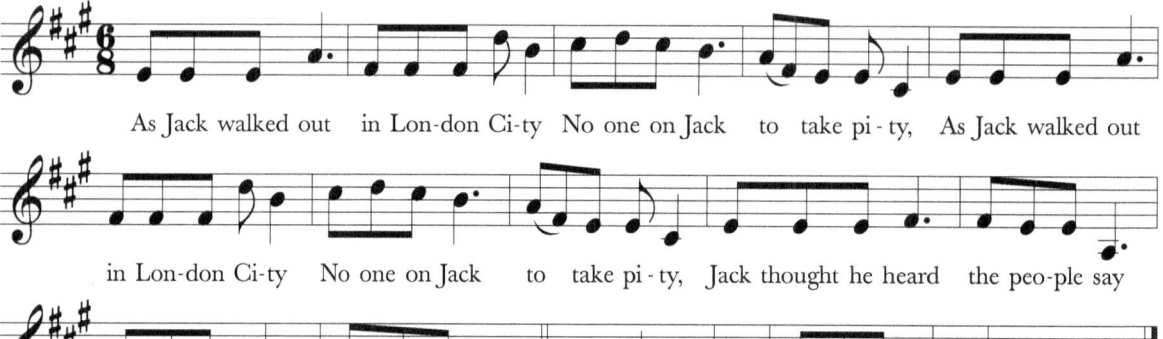

As Jack walked out in London City No one on Jack to take pity, As Jack walked out in London City No one on Jack to take pity, Jack thought he heard the people say That in the streets he'd have to lay. A whang dang diddle-de-dang, fo-lo-lay.

As Jack walked out of London city
No one on Jack to take pity,
As Jack walked out of London city
No one on Jack to take pity,
Jack thought he heard the people say
That in the streets he'd have to lay.

CHORUS:
    A whang dang diddle-de-dang, fol-lo-day.

There was a squire who lived quite handy,
He courted the lawyer's daughter Nancy (2x)
He courted her both night and day
And agreed with her one night to lay.

"I'll tie a string around my finger
And hang it out of chamber window (2x)
You come up and pull the string
And I'll come down an let you in."

She tied a string around her finger
And hung it out of her chamber window (2x)
Jack came up and pulled the string.
And she came down and let him in.

She slipped the string from off her finger
But it dangled from her from her chamber window. (2x)
The squire came up and pulled the string;
The string was pulled but he couldn't get in.

To give the squire a friendly warning,
She arose at daylight the next morning (2x)
There she saw Jack in a striped shirt
His face and hands all covered with dirt.

"How come you here, you saucy fellow?
You've broke my household and robbed me of
    my treasure." (2x)
"I came up and pulled the string,
And you came down and let me in."

"Since it is so, it is no matter
We'll join our hearts and hands together." (2x)
She loved the tarry sailor well,
And told the squire to go to hell.

Another popular story of the clever sailor winning the fair maid, this appears in various forms in several collections of sailor's songs, although not often as a broadside. Other names include "Domeama," "Pull the String," and "The Squire's Lost Lady." It may have been adapted from an 18th century chapbook tale, "The Squire and the Farm Servant." The concluding stanza, collected by Mary Smyth, was sung in a version by Mr. George H. Spurling of Southwest Harbor, ME, circa 1920.

In the Year of '39

Alonzo Lewis, York, ME 10/1/1948
Helen Hartness Flanders Collection
Transcription © 2017 Julia Lane

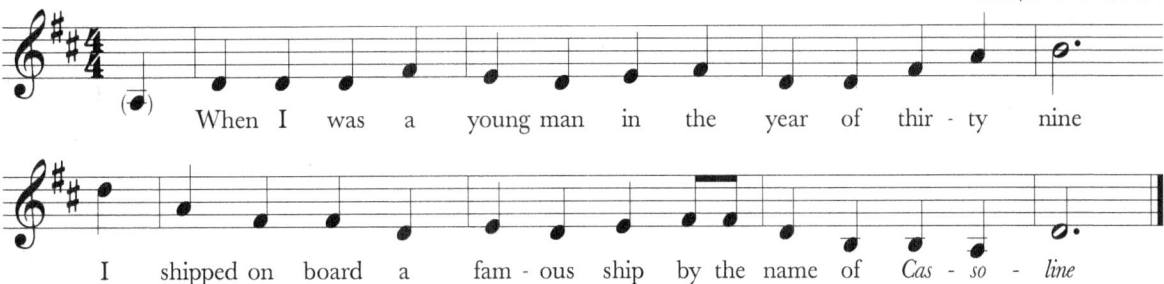

When I was a young man in the year of thirty-nine
I shipped on board a famous ship by the name of *Cassoline*.

She carried twelve guns on each side, that mounted twenty-four,
Commanded by a gentleman by the name of William Moore.

The wind blew up a pleasant breeze and it blew from the northeast.
Our captain says "We'll go my boys and search the raging seas!"

We had not sailed more'n about two days when a ship there hove in sight.
Our captain says "A prize, my boys, if she will only fight!"

And then we bore down on her and found her for to be
A ship belonging unto Cork and bound for Canadee.

She carried twenty-two guns on each side that mounted forty four
With ten to one of our men which grieved our hearts full sore.

And then we head away from her but then to our surprise
When she discharged a whole broadside right in our face and eyes!

Our capting says "We'll fight her now although she is so large,
Although she is a ship of war and we are but a barge."

We fought with them most briskly until our guns grew hot.
Then we run 'longside of her within a musket shot.

There was but eighteen of our men could either go or stand.
Our captain jumped onboard of her and fought with sword in hand.

Of their five hundred and fifty men there was left but twenty-three.
The rest was killed and wounded and buried in the sea.

To Boston Harbor we set sail and brought our prize to land.
Five hundred guineas was each man's share and the money paid in hand.

Despite all the detail included in this account of a sea battle, we have not found any historic evidence of the same. This may be a case where the singer amalgamated two or more songs and perhaps garbled the name of the ship and/or captain. The name Captain Moore appears in another song, "The *Flying Cloud*." Lewis certainly did confuse the melody, as he changed tunes three times throughout the song! The one presented here seems to be his default mode. From the description of the respective size of the ships and crews, the story seems to be the adventure of a privateer. The prize paid in guineas, a British denomination, identifies the account as British, probably pre-Revolutionary War. In any case, the original source remains a mystery. After finishing the song Mr. Lewis said, "I've known that for years; heard the old people sing it, see? Now I'd like for you to play that over, would ye?"

Songs of Ships & Sailors

James Bird

Charles Miner 1814
Susie Carr Young, Brewer, ME 1930
Phillips Barry Collection
Transcription © 2019 Julia Lane

You sons of freedom listen to me,
And ye daughters, too, give ear.
You a sad and mournful story
As was ever told shall hear.

Hull, you know, his troops surrendered
And defenseless left the west,
Quickly then our troops assembled
The invader to resist.

Tender were the scenes of parting,
Mothers wrung their hands and cried;
Maidens wept their swains in secret.
Fathers strove their hearts to hide.

Among the troops that marched to Erie
Were the Kingston volunteers;
Captain Thomas then commanded
To protect our west frontiers.

But there's one among the number,
Tall and graceful in his mien;
Firm his step, his look undaunted.
Scarce a nobler youth was seen.

Mary tried to say, "Farewell, James,"
Waved her hand, but nothing spoke,
"Farewell Bird, may Heaven protect you,"
From the rest at parting broke.

One sweet kiss he snatched from Mary,
Craved his mother's prayer once more.
Pressed his father's hand and left them
For Lake Erie's distant shore.

Soon he came where noble Perry
Had assembled all his fleet;
Here the gallant Bird enlisted,
Hoping soon the foe to meet.

Where is Bird? The battle rages.
Is he in the strife or no?
Is his step yet firm and manly?
Dare he meet the hostile foe?

Ah! behold him, see him, Perry,
In the self-same ship they fight;
Though his messmates fall around him
Nothing can his soul affright.

But behold! a ball has struck him;
See the crimson current flow,
"Leave the deck," exclaimed brave Perry;
"No," cried Bird, "I will not go.

"Here on deck I took my station.
Ne'er will Bird his colors fly,
I'll stand by you, gallant captain
Till we conquer or we die!"

There he fought though faint and bleeding.
Till our stars and stripes arose,
Victory having crowned our efforts
All triumphant o'er our foes.

And did Bird receive a pension?
Was he to his friends restored?
No; nor never to his bosom
Clasped the maid his heart adored.

But there came most dismal tidings
From Lake Erie's distant shore.
Better that if Bird had perished
Midst the battle's awful roar.

"Dearest parents," said the letter;
"This will bring sad news to you;
Do not mourn your first beloved
Though this brings his last adieu."

"I must suffer for deserting
From the brig *Niagara*,
Read the letter, brothers, sisters,
'Tis the last you'll have from me."

Sad and gloomy was the morning
Bird was ordered out to die;
Where's the breast not dead to pity,
But for him would heave a sigh?

See him march and bear his fetters;
Harsh the clank upon his ear;
But his step is firm and manly
For his breast ne'er harbored fear.

Though he fought so brave at Erie,
Freely bled and nobly dared;
Let his courage plead for mercy,
Let his precious life be spared.

See he kneels upon his coffin,
Sure, his death can do no good;
Spare him. Hark! O! God they've shot him!
See his bosom streams with blood.

Farewell, Bird! Farewell forever,
Friends and home he'll see no more;
Now his mangled corpse lies buried
On Lake Erie's distant shore.

James Bird fought on Oliver Hazard Perry's flagship in the Battle of Lake Erie in 1813. Although severely wounded he refused to leave his post and was commended for his bravery by Perry. There are several different stories about what happened next. Apparently, Bird left his post to faithfully follow his commander when Perry was ordered to take command of a frigate on the seaboard. Unfortunately, Bird's action was not appreciated and he was arrested as a deserter and condemned to death. Some officers petitioned to have his sentence changed to imprisonment because of his bravery in the Battle of Lake Erie, but President Monroe refused and Bird was shot and buried on the shore of Lake Erie. In some versions of the story, Perry sends a pardon which came too late. This is unlikely since Perry couldn't countermand a presidential order. The writer, Charles Miner, was a friend of President John Adams and wrote the poem in 1814; it quickly became a popular song. The first verse and tune appear in the manuscript of Susie Carr Young of Brewer, ME, in the Barry collection.

Commodore Perry at the Battle of Lake Erie

Songs of Ships & Sailors

The *Cedar Grove*

Stephen Barlow, Mars Hill, ME 8/30/1942
Helen Hartness Flanders Collection
Transcription © 2018 Julia Lane

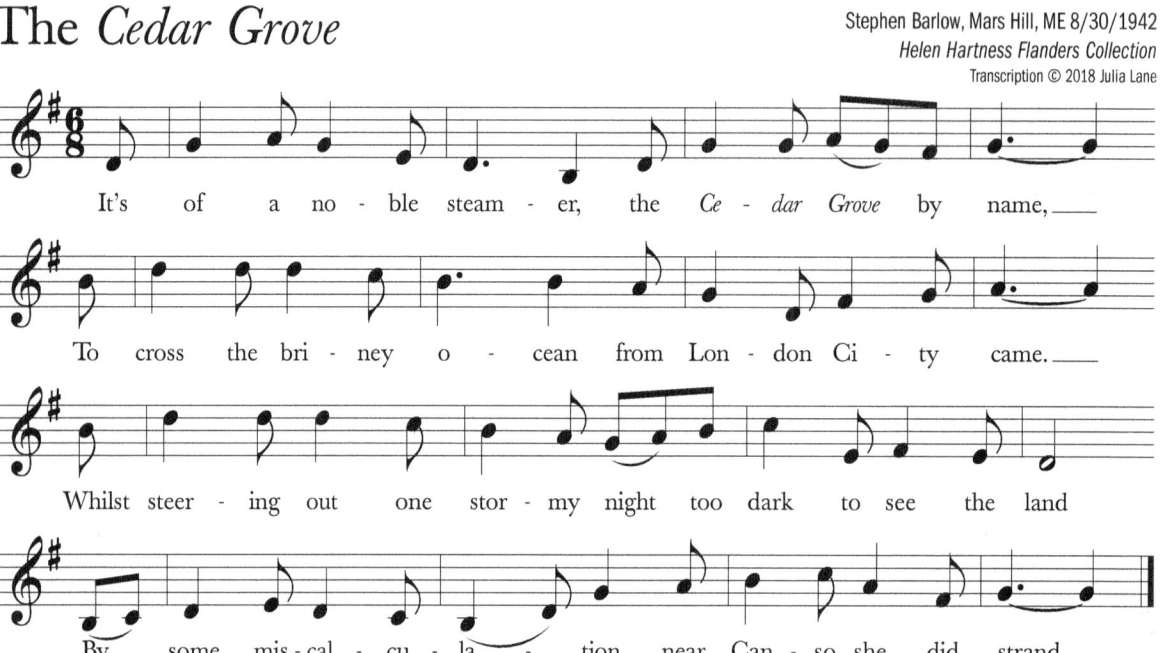

It's of a noble steamer, the *Cedar Grove* by name,
To cross the briny ocean from London City came.
Whilst steering out one stormy night too dark to see the land
By some miscalculation near Canso she did strand.

The sailor at the 'el-m, he knew that he could tell,
He knew they were too near the land by the heeding of the swell.
He thought to give a warning, but no, 'twas not his place
"For discipline it must be observed," he said, "whatever be the case."

The night being dark and stormy, our lookout at his post,
The first he knew of danger was breakers on the coast.
The order it was given our engine to reverse
"Starboard your 'elm!" our captain cried, "Our ship is off her course!"

Straightway into the breakers our noble ship sailed on.
One moment more, an awful crash brought fears to everyone.
Our engineers and firemen were hard at work below
And by their perseverance our ship did backwards go.

Once more in deeper water, and then her fate was sealed.
The waves began to wash her deck and on her side she reeled.
The cabins they began to wash and also down below,
Then through our aft apartments and down our ship did go.

Our brave and gallant captain on maindeck he did stand.
The boats were all got ready and lowered at his command.
Saying, "Engineers and firemen and sailormen also
To save your own dear precious lives into the boats must go!"

The saddest of my story, last still remains.
We had a lady passenger, Miss Farrow was her name;
She was visiting relations in the city of St. John.
She had ventured o'er the deep, but now she's dead and gone.

A sailor said he saw her a cabin door stand by;
He said it grieved him sorely to hear her moaning cries.
He thought to console her and say, "You'll not be lost,"
In a moment more this fair lady in billows she was tossed.

The same sea took our captain and he was seen no more.
The night being dark and stormy our boats still lingered near.
Two engineers were also lost when our noble ship went down
And the body of this lady has never yet been found.

Our cargo was for Halifax and the city of St. John
And to this, the latter port, our good ship did belong.
She was strongly built on the banks of Clyde, three thousand tons or more
But her strength it was no avail on the rocky Canso shore.

November 30, 1882, saw the wreck of the *Cedar Grove*, an iron hulled steamer brig with a 1437 tonnage rating, on Walker's Reef off Saint Andrew's Island near Canso, NS. En route from London to Halifax, the vessel had departed England on November 17 with Capt. Jacob Fritz commanding. The morning of November 30 the weather became rough and the helmsman was rightfully concerned, but maritime discipline dictated that the helmsman could not speak nor be spoken to. A practice designed to prevent distractions here proved disastrous. Of the 23 people on board, 4 perished: Captain Fritz, the lady (Julia A. Fairall of London, England, age 19) and 2 engineers. The remaining 19 were rescued.

The Evergreen Shore

Amanda Crockett Kneeland, Searsport, ME 1914
Lyrics from the *Kneeland Miscellany*
Original hymn 1840 by William Hunter & William Bradbury
Transcription © 2014 Julia Lane

We are joyously voyaging over the main bound for the Evergreen Shore
Whose inhabitants never of sickness complain and never see death any more.

CHORUS:
    Then let the hurricane roar! It will the sooner be o'er!
    We will weather the blast and will land at last
    Safe on the Evergreen Shore!

We have nothing to fear from the wind and the wave under our Savior's command
And our hearts in the midst of the dangers are brave for Jesus will bring us to land.

Both the winds and the waves our Commander controls. Nothing can baffle His skill
And His voice when the thundering hurricane rolls can make the loud tempest be still.

In the thick murky night, when the stars and the moon send not a glimmering ray
Then the light of His countenance, brighter than noon will drive all our terror away.

Frank Kneeland says his mother "learned this of Helen Seavey when they went to school together at the old Center Schoolhouse." Some years later the "Four Center Girls" used to sing it during the intermissions between dances. These girls use to frequent the singing schools which were as popular for the social aspect of their education as for the music. The song appears in 39 hymn books from the 19th century with the earliest lyric found in a broadside dated 1840, attributed to William Hunter. Born in Balleymoney, County Antrim, Northern Ireland in 1811, he emigrated to America with his family in 1817 and went on to become a prolific hymn lyricist. The tune is from William B. Bradbury (1864). Interestingly, the song features in Laura Ingalls Wilder's book *Little House on the Prairie*.

John Riley's Farewell

Hanford Hayes, Bridgewater, ME 9/22/1940, 5/10/1942
Helen Hartness Flanders Collection
Transcription © 2017 Julia Lane

'Twas on a dark and stormy night I heard a fair one say,
"My true love is on the raging main bound for Americay.

"John Riley was my true love's name born in the town of Rae
And he had for to leave his native isle his precious life to save

"My parents they had riches great and Riley he had none
And because I loved my sailor lad they could not him endure."

Up steppéd her old mother and unto her did say
"If you are fond of Riley, you had better send him away!"

"Oh, mama, dear, don't be severe; where would I send my love?
For my very heart lies in his breast as constant as a dove."

"Oh, daughter, dear, I am not severe; here is five thousand pounds,
Send Riley to Americay and there purchase some ground."

As soon as she this money got to Riley she did run,
Saying: "This very night, to take your life, my father has charged a gun.

"Here is five thousand pounds in gold, my mama sent to you,
So sail to Americay and I will follow you!"

As soon as he this money got, those words I heard him say,
"You have my heart, you have my ring till I return this way."

In about six months or better, this maid was wandering by the sea,
John Riley sent a boat onshore and he bore his love away.

The ship was lost, and all were drowned, her father wept full sore;
They found Riley in his true love's arms, all drownded on the shore.

And in her bosom a note was found, those words was written in blood,
Saying: "Cruel was my father; he tried for to shoot my love!"

"Here's a warning to all pretty fair maids, all pretty fair maidens gay,
To never let the lad you love sail to Americay!"

Clearly an Irish immigration ballad, full of drama and tragedy. Another version, sung by Leonard Gilks, also of Bridgewater, is almost identical, but the beginning of the tape is only intelligible from verse 4. The melody is identical, so the initial verses may be presumed to be the same. The song (lyrics only) was also collected by Fannie Eckstorm in 1935 from Pearle Crory of Portage, who heard her 81-year-old father sing it. He said he had learned it "as a child," possibly 1865. Similar lyrics were sung by Sarah Anne O'Neill of Derrytresk, Coalisland, County Tyrone, and recorded by Robin Morton in the singer's home in 1977, though the tune is different.

Songs of Ships & Sailors

Caroline & Her Young Sailor Bold

Henry Bunker, Cranberry Isles, ME 5/1926
Phillips Barry Collection
Transcription © 2019 Julia Lane

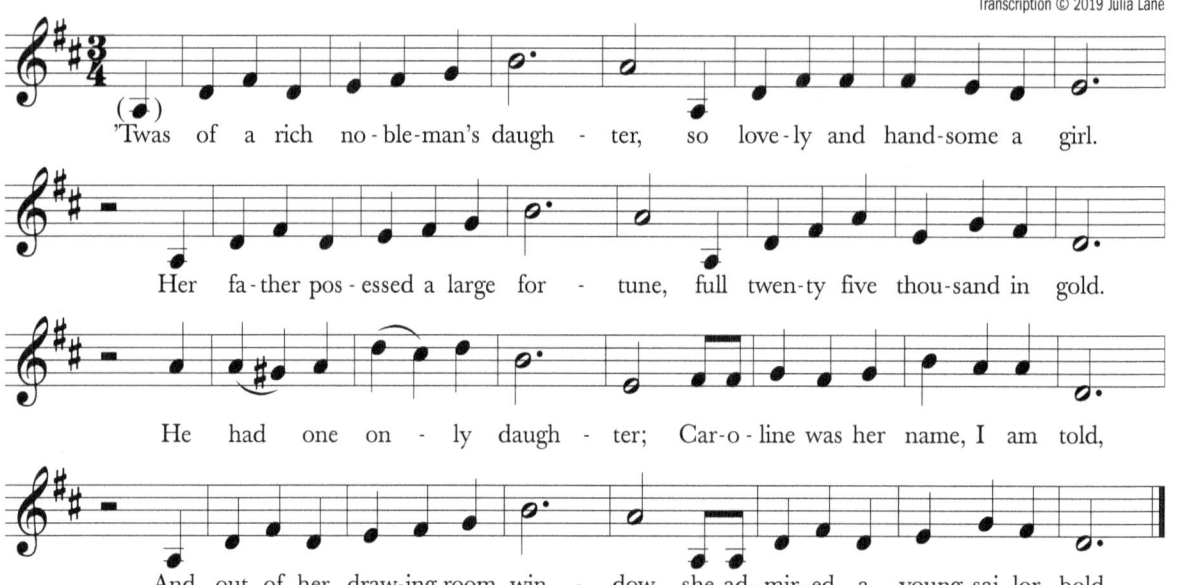

'Twas of a rich nobleman's daughter, so lovely and handsome a girl.
Her father possessed a large fortune, full twenty-five thousand in gold.
He had one only daughter; Caroline was her name, I am told,
And out of her drawing room window she admired a young sailor bold.

Her cheeks were as red as two apples, her eyes were as black as the jet.
Caroline, she watched his departure, went out and with him she met.
Saying: "I am a nobleman's daughter possessed of large fortune and gold.
I'll forsake both my father and mother, to wed with a young sailor bold."

He said, "Oh, my dear honored young lady, be commanded your parents to mind,
For sailors, they are poor dependents, when their true loves are left far behind."
"There's nothing can ever persuade me one moment to alter my mind:
I'll ship and go with my true lover; he never shall leave me behind."

She dressed like a gallant young sailor forsaking both father and gold;
Five years and a half on the ocean she plowed with her young sailor bold.
Five times with her love she was shipwrecked but to him she always proved true.
Her duty she done like a sailor, went aloft in her jacket so blue.

Her father long wept and lamented that his daughter he ne'er should behold,
Till at last she arrived safe in England; Caroline and her young sailor bold.
Straightway to her father she wandered, in her trousers and jacket so blue.
Her father immediately fainted when first she appeared to his view.

Saying: "Father, dear father, forgive me. Forever deprive me of gold.
Grant one more request: I'm contented to wed with a young sailor bold."
They were married and Caroline's fortune was twenty-five thousand in gold
And now they live peaceful and happy Caroline and her young sailor bold.

The dauntless, faithful couple wins again in this song and others like it. They may be based on a more unhappy but true adventure of Anne Thornton, an English girl who dressed as a sailor to follow her beloved to New York. Born in Gloucestershire, Anne Jane Thornton moved with her father to Donegal where he had a profitable store. The family came on hard times and at age 14, having become "strongly attached" to one Captain Burke, the master of a merchantman from New York, she dressed as a sailor and signed on a ship to get free passage to that city. Upon arriving, she found that her betrothed had died a few days earlier so, ever resourceful, she shipped as cook and steward on board the *Adelaide,* which left her, we presume, in northern Maine as one account describes her "having walked from Westport (Eastport?) to St. Andrews, a distance of seventy miles, great part through the woods." There she engaged as a seaman with Capt. McIntyre on board the *Sarah* bound for Belfast, Northern Ireland. She was dutiful and uncomplaining when bullied for not swearing or drinking. One day while performing her personal lavation she was observed and her secret revealed. The captain, feeling obliged to improve her lot, helped her to complete her trick more agreeably and paid her the wages she was owed when they arrived in London, having been diverted from Belfast by a storm. Her case attracted the attention of the Lord Mayor of London who arranged for her passage home. This story is undoubtably the source of the many "female sailor" songs and there is, in fact, an illustrated broadside, *The Female Sailor,* that includes a full description of her adventure.

Songs of Ships & Sailors

The *Irish Rover*

David Kane, Searsport, ME 10/1941
Helen Hartness Flanders Collection
Transcription and adaptation © 2015 Fred Gosbee

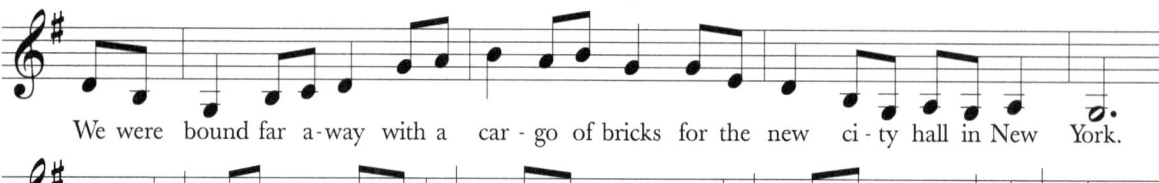

In the year of our Lord fourteen hundred sixty six we set sail from the cove of Cork.
We were bound far away with a cargo of bricks for the new city hall in New York.
We'd a beautiful craft, she was rigged fore and aft and, oh dear, how the trade winds drove her.
She could stand fearful blasts, she had seventeen masts, and we called her the *Irish Rover*.

There was Murphy and Flynn, and McCarthy and Guinn, there was O'Malley, O'Brien and Shay
And Molloy, and McCoy, and McKusker, and Quinn, O'Connell, McGuinness, O'Day
There was Leary and Frye, Joyce, Mulcahey and I, McClough and O'Hara and Grover
And Fitzsimmons and Sly, both from near Athenry in the crew of the *Irish Rover*.

We had one million bags of the best Sligo rags, we had two million barrels of stones
We had three million sides of old blind horses hides, we had four million bundles of bones.
We had five million hogs and six million dogs, we had seven million tons of clover.
We had eight million bales of white billy goat tails in the freight of the *Irish Rover*.

So we sailed seven years when the measles broke out and the ship lost her way in the fog.
The whole of the crew was reduced down to two, just myself and the captain's old dog.
Then we struck Plymouth Rock with a terrible shock, and then, boys, she rolled right over!
She turned three times around and we all got drowned in the wreck of the *Irish Rover*.

This seems to be the earliest recorded version of this popular comic Irish ditty, though we have found references crediting it to J. M. Crofts, a Dublin songwriter circa 1911. Reg Keating, in his website, countysongs.ie, says of his research, "The best I can find is a Joseph Mary Crofts (age 24) who was recorded in the 1911 Census as a 'delph and hardware merchant' living in Dublin at 82 Camden Street, Lower West Side. He could read and write, and was fluent in Irish and English languages." One wonders if all the names in the song might have been his personal acquaintances!

Jenny of the Moor

Susan M. Harding, Hampden, ME 1934
Fannie Hardy Eckstorm Collection
Tune: *Ralph Page Collection*
Transcription © 2019 Julia Lane

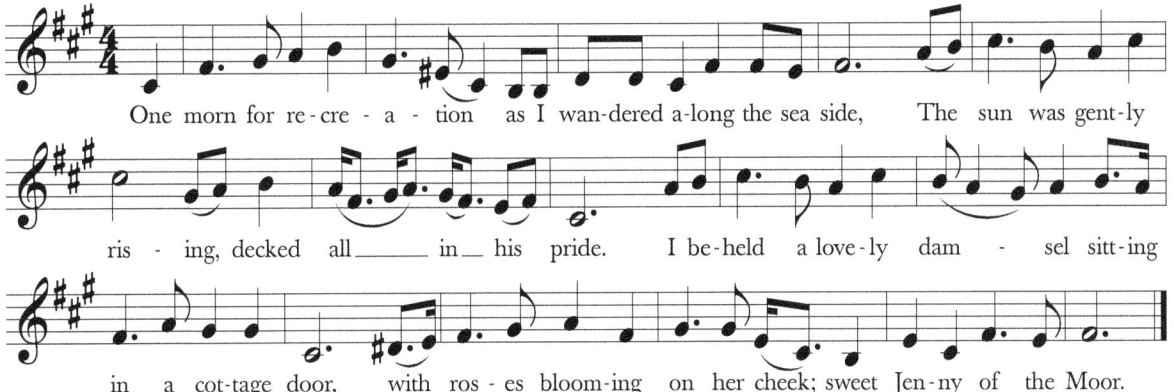

One morn for recreation as I wandered along the seaside,
The sun was gently rising, decked all in his pride.
I beheld a lovely damsel sitting in a cottage door,
With roses blooming on her cheek; sweet Jenny of the Moor.

I said, "My pretty fair maid, why do you so early rise?"
"I love to breathe the morning air, whilst the lark soars in the sky.
This spot is sweet to wander although the ocean roars;
It wakes the bosom of the deep," says Jenny of the Moor.

We both sat down together by a pleasant shady side
I said "My dear, with your consent, I'll make you my bride
I've plenty at my own command brought from a foreign shore
And proud's the man that wins the hand of (Janie) of the Moor."

"My true love was a sailor, and since he's gone to sea,
And true I'll be unto him whilst he is on the sea.
Our vows were fondly spoken as we parted at the door;
I'll wait for his return," says Jenny of the Moor.

"If your true love was a sailor, pray tell to me his name."
"His name was Dennis Rines; from New York Town he came.
With laurel I'll entwine him when he returns on shore
We'll join our hands in wedlock bands!" says Jenny of the Moor.

"If your true love's name was Dennis, I knew him very well.
Whilst fighting at the Armour by a cruel ball he fell.
Behold this is the token which upon his hand he wore."
She fell and fainted in my arms, sweet Jenny of the Moor.

"Since you have proved so good and true, stand up, my girl," I cried.
"Behold this is your Dennis, right here by your side.
Let us get united; we'll live happy on the shore,
The birds may sing and the bells will ring! I'll go to sea no more!"

One of numerous songs about the sailor's return, this includes the "token" which the sailor produces as proof of his identity. One cannot help but wonder at the circumstances which would have changed the fellow so much that she did not recognize him—he surely knows her when he sees her! The original broadside specifies "Dennis Ryan of Newry," (Northern Ireland) rather than New York, and "the Armour" is the Battle of Alma in the 1854 Crimean war. Broadsides of this song were published as early as 1855. The Barry collection has this from Mrs. Harding as well as "Janie of the Moor" from F. L. Tracy of Brewer, ME, 1932. The lyrics in italics are from the version published in the *Maine Woods Songster* (1939).

The Cruise of the *Lapwing*

John Radley, Jonesport, ME 1870
Jonesport Historical Society
Adaptation & tune © 2016 Stephen Sanfilippo
Transcription by Julia Lane 2018

The good schooner *Lapwing* from Jonesport bears away,
Being all spars and canvas from her bows she heaves a spray.
And as she passes through the Reach and down 'long Kelley strand;
We are going winter fishing to the Isle of Grand Manan,
The Isle of Grand Manan.
We are going winter fishing to the Isle of Grand Manan.

With her lofty spars and canvas, she nobly leaps ahead
And by the wind and on her course, looks up for Cutler head
And now in Cutler Harbor she safe at anchor rides
With plenty scope ahead of her to stem the winter tides.
To stem the winter tides, etc.

The sails they are so neatly furled and on the booms do lay,
And now my boys we will turn in, and await the dawn of day.
The girls on shore are handsome, noble-minded, true and kind
They are most jovial company to pass away the time.

Their cheeks are red and rosy; their teeth are pearly white,
To be within their company we take a great delight.
But now we're once more under way and standing out to sea
The billows foam under her bow and the wind is blowing free.

The foamy billows from the bow of the *Lapwing* they are spread,
And now, my boys she runs her course, down for the Northern head.
Now we are passing Northern head, and up by Swallows Tail,
The wind is fast a-canting, and a-blowing half a gale.

Now we see the *Essex*, Tall Barney* and his crew.
The Captain says, "Haul down your jib, and we will haul her to."
At last we have arrivéd, the fish aren't thick at all,
So we have made up our minds, we will not use a trawl.

But we will use our hand lines and see what we can do
Although it looks discouraging to try to put her through.
The ocean is but one white sheet, filled with snow and hail,
While we poor fearless fishermen are standing to the rail.

You little know the dangers that we undergo
As we are winter fishing, amid the ice and snow.
There was a schooner from the Deer Isle, her name was *Teniscott*,
The news she brought from Cutler will never be forgot.

The girls sent us their best respects, hoping we are well;
Then looking under our lea bow we saw the *Ocean Belle*.
She is built of white oak, and fastened through and through,
But lately she has got out-sailed by the *Mary O. Andrews*.

It was down by the Duck Islands, as you shall understand,
There they fell in company, not many miles from land.
For to out-sail each other, it was their whole intent,
With a heavy press of canvass their lofty spars were bent.

The *Ocean Belle* to windward of the *Mary O.* did lie
And just like a struck dolphin through the water she did fly;
But the *Mary O.* is coming on, either to win or lose,
And out from under her lea bow came the *Mary O. Andrews*.

The *Mary O. Andrews* is the winner of the race.
The *Ocean Belle*'s not satisfied 'til there's another race.
But you can search the state of Maine and the English waters through,
You cannot find a match there for the *Mary O. Andrews*.

And now our salt is wet my boys, our white wings they are spread,
And our color is a-flying at our main topmast head;
And as we go homeward rolling, a-rolling homeward bound,
We think it is of no disgrace to pass the bottle round.

Edited for singing by maritime historian Stephen Sanfilippo, this was composed in 1870 by fisherman John Radley of Jonesport, ME, a member of the *Lapwing's* crew. It was recited by Joshua Alley, age 93, of Jonesport, ME on September 16, 1937. Stephen & Susan Sanfilippo, together with Bill Plaskon of the Jonesport Historical Society, found the poem transcribed in the JHS archives. Steve created the melody and adapted the words for singing. They have graciously provided permission for inclusion in this collection. It is a wonderful account of a typical fishing voyage in Downeast Maine.

* "Tall Barney" (Beal) is a legendary hero in the Jonesport area.

Lowlands Low

Alonzo Lewis, York, ME 9/22/1947
Helen Hartness Flanders Collection
Transcription © 2015 Julia Lane

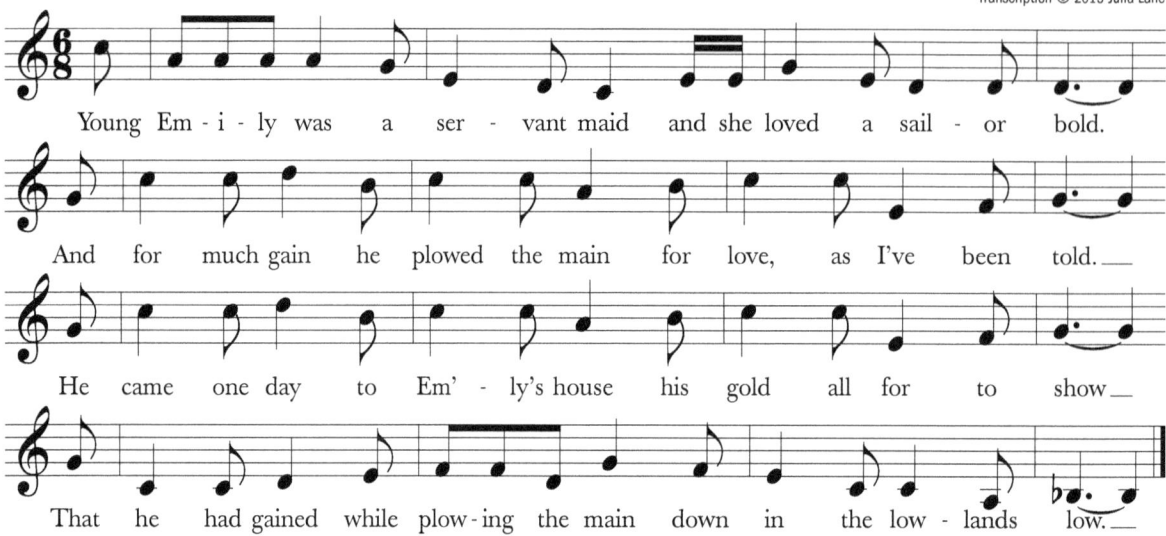

Young Emily was a servant maid and she loved her sailor bold.
And for much gain he plowed the main for love, as I've been told.
He came one day to Em'ly's house his gold all for to show
That he had gained while plowing the main down in the lowlands low.

"My father keeps a public house way down by yonder sea
Where you can go and tarry there until the morning be.
I'll meet you in the morning; don't let my parents know
That your name it is young Edmund Dell and you plow the lowlands low!"

He went unto her father's house, he calléd for a bed;
Now little did that young man think how sorrow crowned his head.
Says Emily's cruel father "Your gold will make a show
And I'll send your body sinking down in the lowlands low!"

He had but just got into bed; had scarcely fell asleep,
When Emily's cruel father into his room did creep.
He stabbed and dragged him from his bed, to the water side did go;
He sent his body floating down in the Lowlands low.

Young Emily on her pillow, she dreamed a troublesome dream.
She dreamed she saw her true love's blood down by some crystal stream.
She rose by day in the morning, to seek him she did go
Because she loved him dearly and he plowed the lowlands low.

"Oh, father, where's that stranger come here last night to dwell?"
"He's dead and gone," says the father, "and you no tale must tell!"
"Father, you'll die a public death besides a public show
 For murdering young Edmund Dell who sailed the lowlands low!"

She went before the counselor; her story she made known.
Her father was arrested; his trial it came on;
The jury proved him guilty and hanged he was also
For the murder of young Edward Dill who plowed the Lowlands low.

Now I'll go down to yonder harbor, 'tis there I'll spend my life
I never will be married, nor yet be made a wife.
The big ships on the ocean they go rolling to and fro
They remind me of my Edmund Dell who sailed the lowlands low.

The numerous international versions of this tragic tale are based on an early 1800's English broadside. Through the "folk process," the original hero, Edwin, morphs into Edmund, Edmond, Edmon, Edward and even Johnny and Henry! In addition, his occupation ranges from a sailor to a plowboy, a driver and even a diver. In 1847 a melodrama, *The Flowers of the Forest,* by English playwright John B. Buckstone, was produced at the Adelphi Theater in London and in Boston the same year at the National Theatre. Mrs. Eckstorm says, in her *British Ballads from Maine Vol. 2* (p. 155): "It is very likely that the vogue of the play, which continued to be performed for a number of years at the leading American theatres, had some effect on the diffusion of the ballad." Ten versions have been documented in Maine. Mr. Lewis's song is interesting in that it has the unusual feature of the surname "Dell," or "Dill" which only occasionally appears in Vermont, New Hampshire and in the Southwest U.S. We have combined his lyrics with those from Justin DeCoster's "Edward Dill" circa 1925, Buckfield, ME, whose lines are in italics.

Willie & Molly

Annie Syphers, Monticello, ME 9/30/1941
Helen Hartness Flanders Collection
Transcription © 2019 Julia Lane

Said Willie to Molly, "Why can't you agree
And now give consent and be married to me?"
Her cheeks they did flush like two roses in June,
Saying, "I'm afraid, William, we'll marry too soon."

They parted that night with kisses so sweet
To return the next morning before it was light.
He took her by the arm saying "Come along with me
Before we get married our friends for to see."

He led her through groves and through valleys so deep
Until this fair damsel began for to weep,
Saying. "I'm afraid William, you've led me astray
On purpose my innocent life to betray!"

"It's true dearest Molly, it's true that I have;
For all of last night I was digging your grave!"
She saw the grave dug and a spade standing by
"Is this your bride's bedding, young man?" she did cry.

"Oh Molly, dear Molly there's no time to stand!"
And instantly taking a knife in his hand
He piercéd her heart and the blood it did flow
And into the grave this fair body he threw.

He covered her up and then rode along
Leaving nothing but small birds to weep and to mourn.
He rode to the port, boarded ship and sailed free
Bound out for New Portland, bound out for the sea.

As William at night upon his bed lie
He heard the voice of an innocent cry,
Saying "Arise up, false William, arise up and fear
The voice of a fair one who once loved you dear!"

He opened his eyes and his blood it ran cold.
He saw a fair damsel stand in the ship's hold!
She had in her arms a baby so fair;
He went to embrace them but nothing was there.

And then there was nothing but screeches and cries
And flashes of fire flew out from his eyes!
There was nobody present to see this sad sight
He then fell distracted and died that same night.

Here is another variation from a song family known as "The Gosport Tragedy," which has its roots in the town of Gosport, near Portsmouth, England. Versions of the ballad appear throughout the English-speaking world titled variously "The Ship's Carpenter," "Polly," "Willie and Molly," or "The Dreadful Ghost." Professor David Fowler (University of Washington) surmised that the original 34 stanza ballad, printed about 1730, was based on an actual event. His essay on the subject, based on extensive research, appeared in *Southern Folklore Quarterly* in 1979. Professor Fowler found no substantial evidence of the crime but several elements which appear in the original ballad correlate with contemporary events and personages. Interestingly, Mrs. Eckstorm collected a version titled "The Gaspereaux Tragedy" from Horace Priest of Sangerville who heard it in a lumber camp in the late 19th century.

Bill Seymour

Alonzo Lewis, York, ME 9/22/1947
Helen Hartness Flanders Collection
Transcription © 2017 Julia Lane
Adapted by Fred Gosbee © 2019

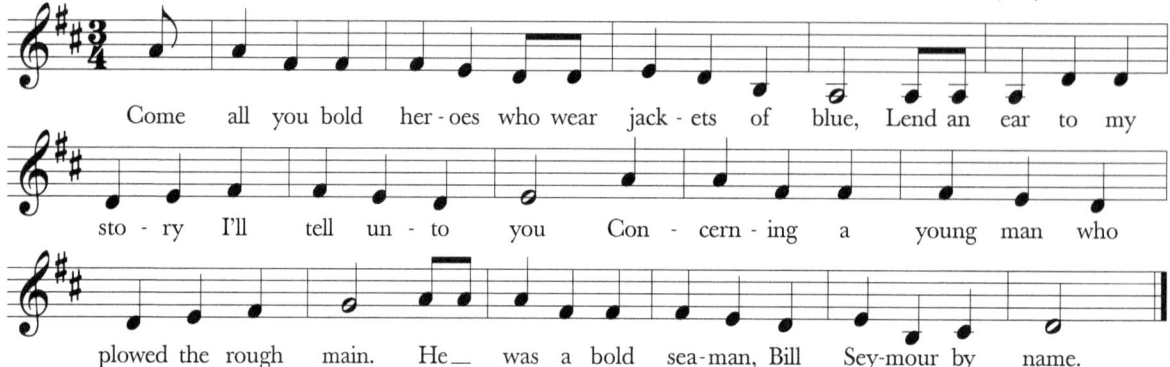

Come all you bold heroes who wear jackets of blue,
Lend an ear to my story I'll tell unto you
Concerning a young man who plowed the rough main.
He was a bold seaman, Bill Seymour by name.

A fierce fiery temper this young man possessed
While jealous proceedings deep wounded his breast
And the dark clouds of heaven took care of his soul
While his eyes sparkled fire like a bright burning coal.

He was a twin brother to Warren, by name,
Who was frank, open-hearted with honor and fame.
Born of the same mother, reared with the same care
Still chose the road down to ruin and despair.

There was a fair damsel who lived close at hand.
Sweet Clarey was courted by both of these men.
Warren succeeded and made her his wife.
Bill vowed revenge, though it cost him his life.

As he went a-walking one cold winter's day
He met his bold crew and to them he did say,
"Prepare for the conflict, no longer delay!
For the arrow is thrown and we may have foul play!"

He stole away Clarey, his own brother's bride
And over the ocean the Vulture *did ride.*
And the bold reckless captain led that bloody band
While he held a broad saybree and a cutslash in hand.   [saber and a cutlass]

You go down to the cabin and then you will see
The handsomest creature that ever could be;
Her cheek pale as marble and her eyes black as sloe
And a fountain of tears from them they do flow.

She's found a pistol and a dirk to her hand!
Clarey then vowed that she'd take her stand
And never give up to that hellish fiend
For the whole of his treatment was her to demean.

Next moment, a rap it was heard at the door
"Open!" cried Seymour, whom she did abhor,
And the bold buccaneer with a smile on his face
Rushed in—that fair lady he thought to embrace!

"Stand back, cruel monster!" she said to him straight
"Or the pistol shall teach you your own dismal fate!"
At the sight of those weapons he stepped back with surprise
While tiger-like vengeance did flash in his eyes.

"Must I be thus frightened of you, lady fair?
With your pistol you try my courage to dare?
Your weapons fair lady all them I'll defy—
My will I will have, on that you rely!"

Then, like a fierce lion on Clarey did spring
Resolvéd upon her dishonor to bring!
Her pistol it failed her in that trying hour
And he dashed it like lightning from her hand to the floor.

A dirk from her bosom she instantly drew;
"Stand back, cruel monster, or I'll run you through!"
She leaped forth to strike at the pirate so bold;
That made him fall back and relinquish his hold.

At that very moment was a most dreadful blast
As lightning descended and rent the mainmast!
He then from the cabin flew up to the deck
Maddened with rage and his vessel a wreck.

Oh, the words on his lips they had not scarcely died
When a call from the lookout a sail he espied.
He's taken his glass and the ocean did scan
To learn of this vessel and find out her plan.

It is, "Oh hell and fury!" he quick did exclaim,
"It is my brother's vessel, *Flying Arrow* by name
The Vulture's *a wreck! We can no longer run,*
And lightning has disabled four of our guns!"

He called for all hands as he shouted so loud
Which raised every pirate in that lawless crowd,
But that brave little schooner with terrible force
Kept boldly ahead and would not change her course.

At length the *Flying Arrow* was flown alongside
And the two grappling irons together were tied.
Then both springing forward, within a short space,
The two rival brothers they met face to face!

Next moment, the clash of the weapons did ring
As the two opponents their saybrees did fling.
So skilled in the heart and so nobly he played
Till on his own deck this bold pirate he lay.

"Now William, my brother, 'tis you I have slain
Unblessed and unhonored you'll sleep in the main
No home, friend or kindred shall riches repay
Let the white foaming billows your winding sheet be!"

We have not found this fascinating ballad anywhere else! This may have originally been a much longer song. Apparently, it is based on a novella *The Rival Brothers, or, The Corsair and Privateer; A tale of the last war* by Henry P. Cheever, Esq. (Boston, 1845). Perhaps Alonzo's father, who taught him the song, distilled the story to relate it to his children without benefit of an actual book. Some of the verses in Lewis's version don't make sense until you read the novella. To fill out the story and remove the plot discontinuities would mean introducing additional characters (and verses!) so we have edited several lines (in italics) to make the story scan. The song was recorded twice by Mrs. Flanders possibly in an attempt to rectify discrepancies. Lewis stuck with his lyrics but used a different tune each time. Coincidentally, Alonzo Lewis shares his name with a celebrated poet, known as "The Bard of Lynn" (MA) but we have not found any obvious connection between the two.

The Lightning Flash

John P. A. Nesbitt, St. Stephen, New Brunswick 1930
via Mary Smyth, Brewer, ME
Phillips Barry Collection
Transcription © 2019 Julia Lane

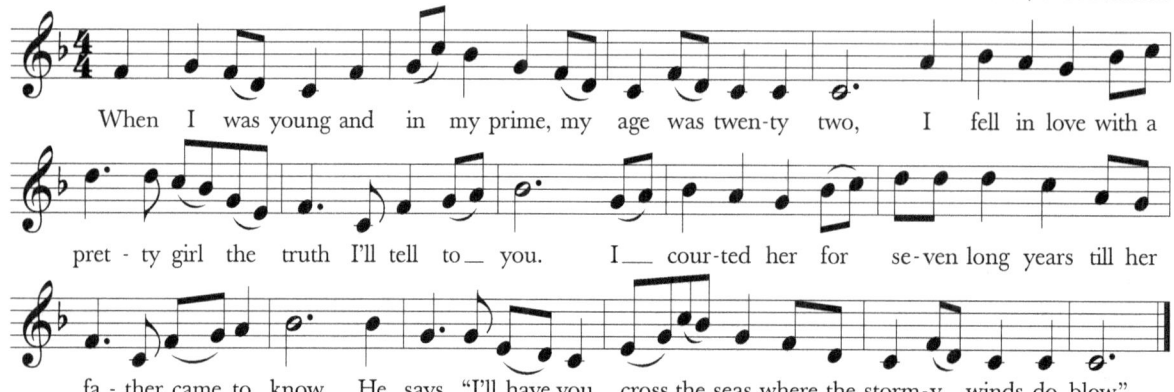

When I was young and in my prime, my age was twenty-two,
I fell in love with a pretty girl the truth I'll tell to you.
I courted her for seven long years till her father came to know.
He says, "I'll have you cross the seas where the stormy winds do blow."

On the fourteenth of September from Queen's Harbor we set sail.
Bound down to Gibraltar in a sweet and a pleasant gale
The wind blew fair, our course we steered, our ship before the wind
But still my heart was filled with love for the girl I left behind.

When we got to our distant port we stopped a short time there,
Our orders run to Milligar the weather being fair.
The very next day we sailed away, all with a cloud of sail
When the storms arose, eclipsed the sun, they blew a tremendous gale.

The wind it riz to a hurricane, it blew a tremendous gale
And the captain says, "My brave boys, go reef the top mainsail!"
No sooner when his order was given, up aloft we lay,
Like hearty tars to lay those yards, his orders to obey.

When we got to the main topsail, a horrid flash came on
Oh, God! How I remember the last eclipse of the sun!
The thunder rolled tremendously, and the lightning around us did flash,
The heavy sea rolled over us and on the deck did dash.

Early the next morning, wasn't we a sight to view!
Our captain was washed overboard and three men of the crew;
The thunder rolled tremendously, and by that veil of light,
I and three other sailors by that lightning we lost our sight.

But thanks be unto kind Providence that carried us back on shore,
Back to dear old Ireland to the girl whom I adore.
To me she did prove loyalty, constant and kind to me,
We join our hands in wedlock bands but her face I ne'er can see!

Generally found in Newfoundland and Nova Scotia, this is often sung to a tune variant of the Irish song "Erin's Green Shore." Another Maine song, similar to those and collected by Flanders from singer Charles Finnemore of Bridgewater, ME in 1941, was recorded by Dan Milner. This beautiful rendition was gathered earlier by Phillips Barry and Mary Smyth just over the Maine border in St. Stephen, NB. As a matter of record, Maine singer Carrie Grover, in her book *A Heritage of Song*, describes her father, a seaman, suffering lifelong trauma and vision damage from a similar event to that described in the song. "Milligar" is probably Malaga, a common destination of sailing ships.

The Sailor in the Boat

Lorenzo Hooper, South Berwick, ME 1941
Helen Hartness Flanders Collection
Transcription © 2016 Julia Lane

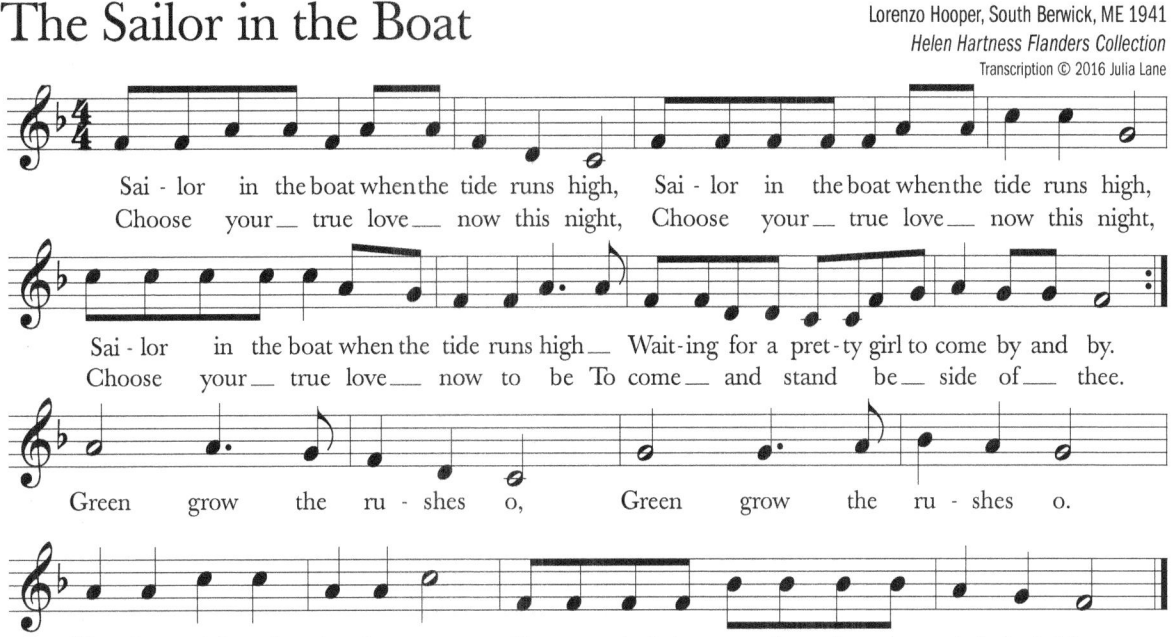

Sailor in the boat when the tide runs high,
Sailor in the boat when the tide runs high,
Sailor in the boat when the tide runs high
Waiting for a pretty girl to come by and by.

Choose your true love now this night,
Choose your true love now this night,
Choose your true love now to be
To come and stand beside of thee.

    Green grow the rushes o,
    Green grow the rushes o.
    Kiss her quick and let her go.
    Never mind the weather when the wind don't blow.

Here is a children's dance game which is probably a descendent of those popular in colonial times. The chorus reminds us of Robert Burns's song "Green Grow the Rashes," and so may point to a Scottish origin. The York & Berwick, Maine area received a large number of Scottish prisoners of war in the 18th century and Mr. Hooper's family also settled there. This game is similar to the "Jolly Sailors" dance previously mentioned. Mr. Hooper says: "To play this game, you form a circle with the boy in the center and you choose a girl when you sing 'Choose your true love now to be, to come and stand beside of thee!'"

Songs of Ships & Sailors

A Trip to the Grand Banks

Amos Hanson, Orland, ME
Phillips Barry Collection
Transcription © 2016 Julia Lane

Early in the spring when the snow is all gone
The Penobscot boys are anxious their money for to earn.
They will fit out a fisherman, one hundred tons or nigh,
For the Grand Banks of Newfoundland their luck for to try.

Sailing down the river, the weather being fine,
Our homes and our friends we leave far behind.
We pass by Sable Island, as we've oft' done before
Where the waves dash tremendous on a storm beaten shore.

Now the vessel is our quarters, the ocean is our home,
And islands, capes, and headlands we leave far astern.
We run to the eastward for three or four days
Then round to and sound upon the western edge.

Then we run for the shoals and we run for the rocks
Where the hagduls and careys, they surround us in flocks.
We let go our anchor where the sea runs so high
On the Grand Banks of Newfoundland the snapeyes for to try.

Early in the morn at the dawn of the day
We jump into our dories and we saw, saw away.
The snapeyes steal our bait and we rip and we rave,
If we ever get home again we'll give up the trade.

In this way we pass the summer, through dread and through fear
In fog mulls and gales of wind, and big ships passing near.
They sometimes run the schooners down and sink them in the deep
The thought of such scenery is horrid to repeat.

Now the salt is all wet but one half a pen.
The colors we will show and the mainsail we will bend.
Wash her down and scrub the decks, the dories we will stow
Then heave up the anchor! To the westward we go.

Until the 1960s fishing schooners sailed from Gloucester and the Maine coast to harvest the rich resources of the Grand Banks of Newfoundland. The crews were a hardy lot who understood the value of camaraderie as they shared their lives and fortunes with each other. Amos Hanson, the writer of this song and others, was a lifelong fisherman born in Penobscot, ME, in the mid 19th century. He was well known as a local "character" who made up verses and songs around town, some of which were less than complimentary to his neighbors. He disappeared at sea in the 1890s. Ralph Page, who printed this song in his periodical *Northern Junket*, notes: "Snapeyes are small codfish, so-named because they bite at fisheyes used for bait. 'Hagduls' or 'Hagdens' are jaegers or skuas; gulls that rob smaller species of their catch. 'Careys' are storm petrels or 'Mother Carey's chickens.'"

Songs of Ships & Sailors

The *Golden Vanity*

Harriet Gott Murphy, Rumford Center, ME 9/12/1942
Helen Hartness Flanders Collection
Transcription © 2017 Julia Lane

Oh, my father owns a ship all in the north country;
She goes by the name of the *Golden Vanity*.
And I fear she may be taken by some Spanish crew,
As she sails along the Lowlands, on the Lowlands,
As she sails along the Lowlands low.

The first one that spoke up was a saucy cabin boy,
"Say, what will you give me if I will her destroy?"
"I'll give you gold and silver, my daughter fair and gay
If you'll sink her in the Lowlands, in the Lowlands,
If you'll sink her in the Lowlands low."

The boy he bent his breast and then he plunged in.
The boy he bent his breast and then began to swim.
He swam alongside of this bold Spanish ship,
And he sank her in the Lowlands, in the Lowlands,
And he sank her in the Lowlands low.

Oh, some were playing cards and some were shaking dice,
And some were in their hammocks a-sleeping very nice.
He bored two holes in her broadside and let the water in,
And he sank her in the Lowlands, in the Lowlands,
And he sank her in the Lowlands low.

The boy he swam back unto the starboard side,
And being quite exhausted, so bitterly he cried,
"Oh, captain, take me in, for I'm going with the tide,
And I'm sinking in the Lowlands, in the Lowlands,
And I'm sinking in the Lowlands low."

"I will not take you in," our captain then replied,
"I will not give you gold nor my daughter for your bride.
I'll shoot you, I'll stab you, and send you with the tide,
And I'll sink you in the Lowlands, in the Lowlands,
And I'll sink you in the Lowlands low."

The boy then did swim under unto the larboard side
And being quite exhausted, so bitterly he cried,
"Oh, messmates, take me in, for I'm going with the tide,
And I'm sinking in the Lowlands, in the Lowlands,
And I'm sinking in the Lowlands low."

They threw the boy a rope and they drew him up the side.
They laid him on the deck and the boy he soon died.
They laid him in his hammock and they sent him in the tide,
And they laid him in the Lowlands, in the Lowlands,
And they laid him in the Lowlands low.

The *Golden Vanity*, designated #286 by ballad scholar Francis Child, is also known as "The *Sweet Trinity*," among other titles. It has been associated with Sir Walter Raleigh, as one of the ships named in his biography is the *Sweet Trinity* and there is a 1635 broadside titled "Sir Walter Raleigh Sailing in the Lowlands." The broadside's introduction describes "How the famous ship called the *Sweet Trinity* was taken by a false Gally & how it was again restored by the craft of a little Sea-boy who sunk the Gally." In that ballad, the young man does the deed and receives the promised gold, though not the bride, and does not drown. That is as far as any historic evidence goes in verifying the actual event.

Numerous Maine versions of this ancient ballad are published elsewhere. Mrs. Flanders printed Mrs. Murphy's lyrics in *Ancient Ballads Migrant to New England*, but the tune, though recorded by Flanders, was not included. Mrs. Murphy was the daughter of Captain Lewis Freeman Gott of Bernard, ME. Fannie Eckstorm collected the song from her in 1925 and included in her *British Ballads from Maine* (1929). The lyrics vary slightly, but again, there is no melody noted. We have transcribed Mrs. Murphy's tune from the Flanders recording and are happy to present the song intact.

The Oak and the Ash

Capt. Archie Spurling, Islesford, ME 11/1925
Phillips Barry Collection
Transcription © 2019 Julia Lane

The sailor being drowsy, he hung down his head.
He asked for a candle to light him to bed.
She lit him to bed as maidens ought to do
And he vowed and declared she must come with him too.

    Home, dearie, home, to your own counteree.
    Home, dearie, home, to your own counteree
    Where the oak and the ash and the bonny birch tree
    Are all a-growing green in North Amerikee.

She being young, she thought it no harm;
She jumped in beside him to keep herself warm.
He hugged her, he kissed her, he called her his dear,
She wished the short night had been a long year.

Next morning so early the sailor arose
And into her lap he heaped handfuls of gold
Saying, "Take this, my dear! 'Twill buy you milk and bread.
For that is what you get for lighting sailor lads to bed!"

"If it is a girl, she shall wear a gold ring
If it is a boy, he shall fight for his king
With his low quarter shoes and his jacket so blue
He shall walk the quarter deck as his daddy used to do."

Six variants of this song were collected in Maine with others titled "Home Dearie," "English Jackie," and "Rosemary/Raspberry Lane." Both lyrics and tune were recorded by Phillips Barry. There are several generally popular versions, some more socially acceptable than others. The chorus suggests a connection with the 17th century song, "The North Country Maid," which includes these lyrics: "The oak and the ash and the bonny ivy tree are all growing green in my own country." "The Servant of Rosemary Lane" appears circa 1820. The more benign later versions seem based on a poem "O, Falmouth is a fine town," by W. E. Henley (1878). Stan Hugill, in his book, *Shanties from the Seven Seas* (p. 365), says it was "obviously a shore song taken over by seamen for use at the capstan." He gives three variants plus alternate lines for several of the verses as shanty singing tended to be spontaneous. In the 20th century Navy sailors introduced new verses, some suggestive, and the song became the popular "Bell Bottom Trousers" published by Moe Jaffe ©1944.

The Sailor's Bride

Tune: Mrs. Sarah Lane, Hiram, ME 5/12/1942
Helen Hartness Flanders Collection
A composite of Lane, Young & Dunworth 1925
Phillips Barry Collection
Transcription © 2019 Julia Lane

It was early, early in the spring
Oh, how joyfully the birds did sing.
There's not a bird so happy as I
As when my sailor lad is nigh.

CHORUS:
    Tra la, la la, la la, la!
    Tra la, la la, la la, la!
    There's not a bird so happy as I
    When my sailor lad is nigh.

The moon rose o'er the silvery sea
The good ship rode right gallantly
The sailor left his sea-girt home
As lightly we rowed where the wild waves moan.

    Tra la, la la, la la, la!
    Tra la, la la, la la, la!
    The sailor left his sea-girt home
    As lightly we rowed, etc.

The eastern stars were shining too
Beneath the waves of the waters blue.
The sailor left his lovely bride
A-weeping by the ocean side.

'Tis scarce three months since we've been wed
Oh, how quickly the time has sped!
Tomorrow morning at the dawning of the day
The proud ship bears my lover away.

Time rolls on and he comes no more
To greet his bride on the ocean shore.
The ship went down in a howling storm
And the waves engulfed my sailor's form.

I wish that I were sleeping too
Beneath the waves of the ocean blue;
My soul with God, my body in the sea
And the blue waves rolling over me.

Five versions are found in Maine collections but none is complete, so we have combined them. The song is widespread, from Ohio to Orkney, with the earliest, "The Sailor's Bride," recorded by Rev. Franklin Eddy, Ashtabula, Ohio, in an album dated 1852. Variants have different titles but the texts are basically similar with slight differences in adjectives; for instance, the last lines describe the waves as blue, white, green, broad, cruel or wild. Some have a refrain and some don't. The tunes recorded in Maine are essentially the same and remarkably like that found both in England and Newfoundland. They may be sourced from an incongruously perky recording of "The Bride's Lament" by Frank Crumit released by Victor in 1928 though none of the Maine songs include his mermaid verse.

Songs of Ships & Sailors

Bung Yer Eye

Murchie Harvey, Houlton, ME 9/28/1941
Helen Hartness Flanders Collection
Transcription © 2016 Julia Lane

Oh, there was a young gentleman walking the street.
A very fine damsel he chanced for to meet.
And as she drew near him she says, "Will you buy?"
"Now what have you there?" and she said, "Bung Yer Eye!"
    Tura-la, Tura-la, Tura-la ran do day

"Oh, now to be serious, what have you got there?"
"It's good Holland gin, sir, I vow and declare;
It's good Holland gin, sir, it is, bye the bye
And an odd name they call it; it is Bung Yer Eye.
    Tura-la, etc.

"How much like a gentleman you do appear!
You can have my ginavy, you need never fear.
While talking with a neighbor who's just passing by
I'll leave you in care of this young Bung Yer Eye."

Now the woman being gone and I fully bent
To open the basket it was my intent.
When I opened the basket, I heard a child cry,
When up in my face popped this young Bung Yer Eye!

Now what has this jade of a woman got here?
Now fer my ginavy, I'm afraid I'll pay dear.
The girls they'll all poke me as I pass them by;
They'll say I'm the daddy of young Bung Yer Eye.

Now I took that child home as I heard people say
To get the child christened without more delay.
Said the parson, "I'll christen your child bye an' bye.
What name shall we call it?" Said I, "Bung Yer Eye."

"Bung Yer Eye," said the parson, "That is an odd name."
"An odd name it is, sir, and an odd way it came.
Instead of ginavy, as I thought to buy,
I opened the basket, out popped Bung Yer Eye."

Now the very next day I was walking the street.
This very same damsel I chanced for to meet.
Now I cried to policeman jest as hard's I could cry,
"Now stop that damned rascal! She's bunged both my eyes!"

Here is the age-old "bait & switch" routine as the clever damsel outwits the sailor on leave. Also known as "Quare Bungo Rye" it often includes a complex nonsense chorus, possibly as a lampoon of the Gaelic speech of Irish immigrants in the 1800s. Upon comparing this version with a broadside from the Bodleian library, the word "ginavy" appears to be a corruption of "Geneva" meaning "Dutch gin." "Geneva" was derived from the word *genever*, the Dutch word for juniper, a primary ingredient in the making of gin. Interestingly, a popular version of this song describes "the finest of whisky from High Germany" aka Holland.

Songs of Ships & Sailors

Lovely Lou

Gene Staples, Dixfield, ME 9/12/1941
Eloise Hubbard Linscott Collection
Transcription © 2013 Julia Lane

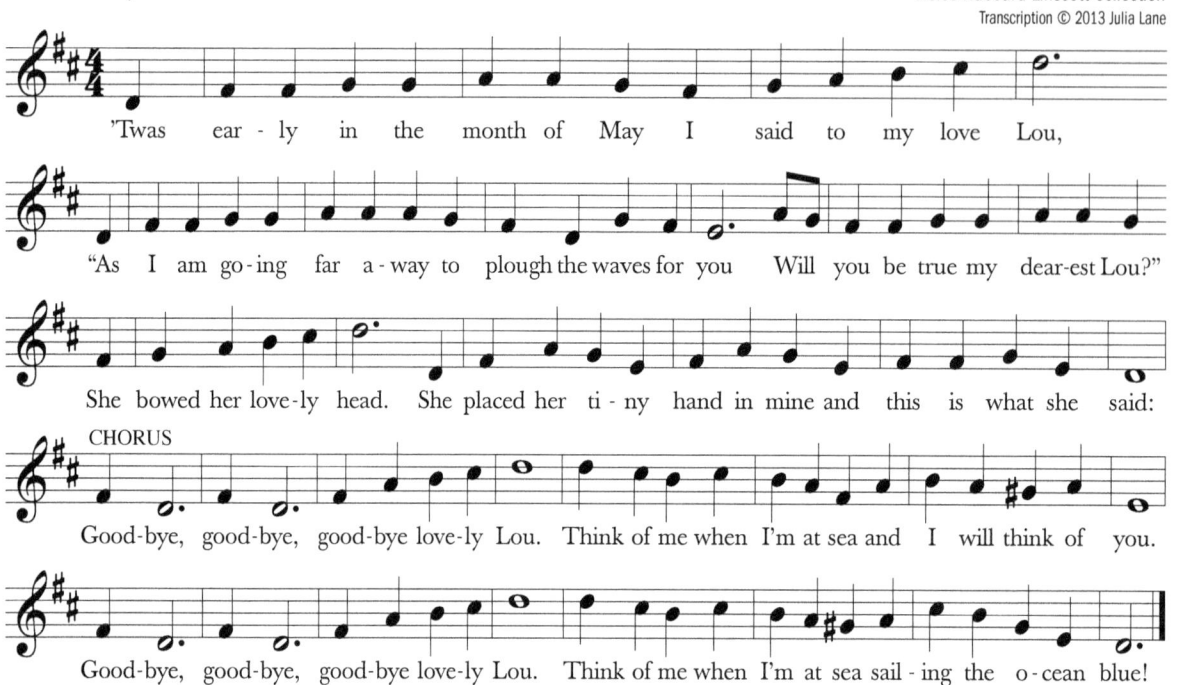

'Twas early in the month of May I said to my love Lou,
"As I am going far away to plough the waves for you
Will you be true my dearest Lou?" She bowed her lovely head.
She placed her tiny hand in mine and this is what she said:

CHORUS:
    Goodbye, goodbye, goodbye lovely Lou.
    Think of me when I'm at sea and I will think of you.
    Goodbye, goodbye, goodbye lovely Lou.
    Think of me when I'm at sea sailing the ocean blue!

"I will be true" said Lovely Lou "to do the same I ought.
But I've been told you sailors have a wife in every port!"
So goodbye, Lou, don't look so blue don't think me so unkind
I never shall forget the gal that first I left behind.

I've one thing, Lou, to tell to you before the seas I roam;
And that is of the presents I am going to bring you home.
An Indian shawl, a parasol, a tiny kangaroo;
A monkey and a parrot, yes, and they are all for you.

I bid adieu to lovely Lou. We parted on the shore;
And something seemed to tell me I should never see her more.
When I returned I quickly learned that she had gone away.
So now, as Lou has proved untrue, why, I can only say,

    Goodbye, etc.

"Goodbye, Lovely Lou" was "a popular comic song" written, composed and sung by John Read and published in 1878 both in London and the U.S. It does not seem to have significantly made its way into the oral tradition. Mr. Read also claims authorship of the song "Every Inch a Sailor."

Far, Far at Sea

Unidentified singer, Searsport, ME 1916
Roland Palmer Gray Collection
Music: C.H. Florio circa 1837
Transcription © 2017 Julia Lane

'Twas night when the bell had struck twelve
And poor Susan was laid on her pillow.
In her ear whisper'd some fleeting elf,
"Your love now lies tossed on a billow,
Far, far at sea."

All was dark, when she woke out of breath,
Not an object her fears could discover;
All was still as the silence of death,
Save fancy, which painted her lover
Far, far at Sea.

So, she whisper'd a pray'r; clos'd her eyes;
But the phantom still haunted her pillow;
While in terrors she echo'd his cries,
As struggling he sunk in a billow
Far, far at Sea.

In his book *Songs and Ballads of the Maine Lumberjacks*, Roland Palmer Gray says that a copy of this song, with a crude woodcut of a ship in one corner, was sent to him by "a retired seaman" in Searsport, ME, in 1916. Gray, a professor of English at the University of Maine, in turn gave it to the library there in 1917. He goes on to say that the words were printed as a broadside about 1835, apparently of English origin. The music, by C. H. Florio, is given in *The Vocal Companion* edited by John Parry (London, 1837). The song was in the repertoire of the famous singer Charles Incledon (1763–1826) and is printed in numerous early 19th century songsters.

The *Eastern Light*

Capt. Archie S. Spurling, Islesford, ME 10/1925
Fannie Hardy Eckstorm Collection
Tune; James Rice, Cape Broyle, NFLD 1951
Kenneth Peacock Collection
Transcription © 2018 Julia Lane

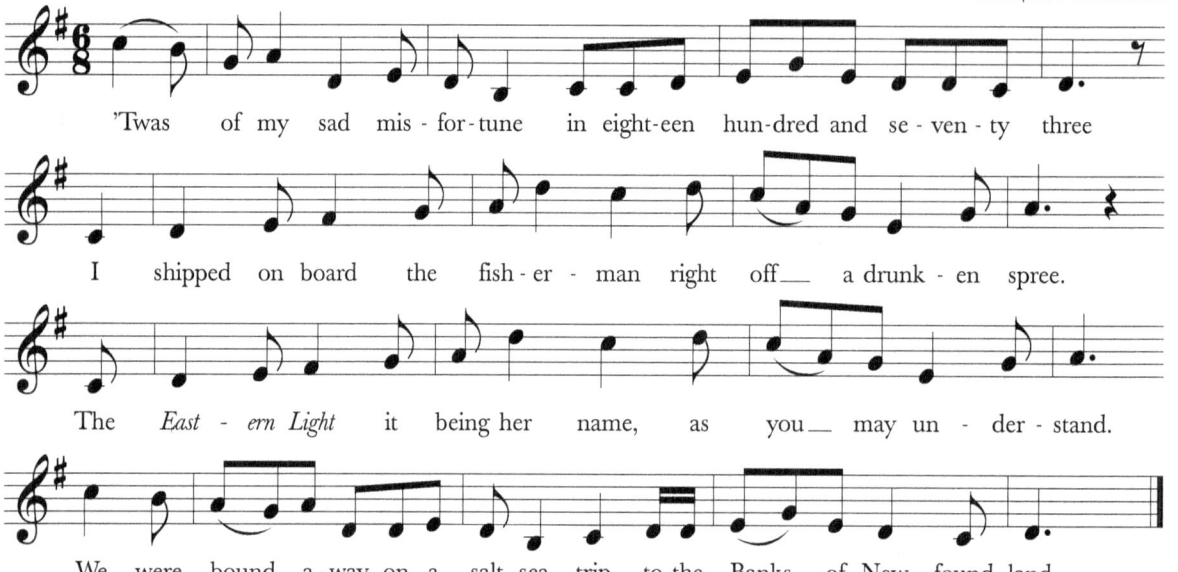

'Twas of my sad misfortune in eighteen hundred and seventy-three
I shipped on board the fisherman right off a drunken spree.
The *Eastern Light* it being her name, as you may understand.
We were bound away on a salt sea trip to the Banks of Newfoundland.

Our Captain's name being McCloud, the truth to you I'll tell,
He was a jolly Irishman, I s'pose you all know well.
He had a jug of rum on board that mustered the whole of our crew,
And we drank the health of the Gloucester girls when bidding them adieu.

Then Eastern Point we rounded by, left Thatcher's far behind,
We kept her east-southeast, my boys, the Grand Banks for to find.
And on our passage going out we were busily employed
Rigging up our fishing gear the halibut to decoy.

It's now we're anchored on the Banks our trials do begin,
The way the crew's all serving me I think it is a sin.
They had their choice of dories, and they chose their trawls likewise;
If I opened my mouth to say a word, 'twas "Damn!" and "Bugger my eyes!"

We cruised all o'er the foggy bank the space of eighteen days,
We boarded a couple of Frenchmen, no brandy could we raise.
The halibut they were getting scarce, we run our codfish gear,
McCloud, he says, "I'll fill her up, if it takes a half a year."

So early in the morning the cook he loudly bawled,
"Come, jump and get your breakfast, boys, and go and haul your trawls."
You'll have hardly time to light your pipe when over your dory goes.
You'll have to make three sets today no matter how it blows.

'Twas Saturday the tenth day of June, the Captain he loudly shouts,
"Come, jerk along your dories, boys, we'll break the anchor out.
Our provisions they are getting scarce, no longer can we stay,
So give her the big mainsail, we'll get her under way."

Now mind not lose a buoy line, an anchor or a knife,
For if you do it will be charged to you, now you can bet your life.
And when you stand your watch, my boys, be sure and stay on deck,
If anything should happen you'll find it on your check.

So now the anchor's on the bow and we are homeward bound,
And when we get in Gloucester we'll pass the glasses round.
We'll go down to Johnny the Lager* and have a regular tight,
We'll drink the health of the Gloucester girls, success to the *Eastern Light*.

A typical story of a fishing voyage, this was taken down in October 1925, from the singing of Captain Archie S. Spurling, of Islesford, ME, who learned it many years before on board a fishing vessel. The song is reminiscent of the bothy ballads made by the migrant workers of Scotland and Ireland. The workers would live together in a small house or bothy, similar to life onboard a fishing schooner or in a woods camp. They would make songs about their work, each other, and the boss, often with descriptions of and warnings about unfair treatment. The *Eastern Light*, 70 tons, was built in 1866 and was owned by Maddocks and Company, of Gloucester. Lyrics appear in *Minstrelsy of Maine* (1929); the tune is that sung by James Rice (1879–1958) of Cape Broyle, Newfoundland, collected in 1951 by Kenneth Peacock.

* Horace Beck says that this is actually "Johnny the Logger," whom he claims was a famous saloon owner and whisky tester (rectifier) but I have not found evidence of this.

Songs of Ships & Sailors

The Greenland Whale

Lyrics: Phebe Stanley, Baker Island, ME 9/1925
Fannie Hardy Eckstorm Collection
Tune: Carrie Grover, Gorham, ME 10/29/1943
Eloise Hubbard Linscott Collection
Transcription © 2016 Julia Lane

It was in the year eighteen hundred and one, on March the twentieth day,
We hoisted up all our topsails and for Greenland bore away, brave boys,
For Greenland bore away.

Greenland is a barren land there's nothing there grows green
But the ice and snow and the whale-fish he blows and the daylight's seldom seen, brave boys,
And the daylight's seldom seen.

The boatswain in the crosstrees stands with a spyglass in his hand.
"Here's whale! Here's whale! A whale-fish!" he cries, "And she blows on every span, brave boys,
And she blows on every span!"

Our Captain, he's walking the quarterdeck and a clever old man was he.
"Overhaul, overhaul and your davit tackle fall and launch your boats for the sea, brave boys,
Launch your boats all three."

Our boats being launched and the crew got in and all five of our jolly boat's crew.
Resolvéd was each seaman bold to steer where the whale-fish blow, brave boys,
To steer where the whale-fish blow.

The whale being struck, our lines played out; he gave us a fluke with his tail
Which caused us to lose our five jolly tars and we did not take that whale, brave boys,
And we did not take that whale.

When the sad news to our captain came, *he stamped his foot and swore,*
For the losing of his five jolly tars it grieved his heart full sore, brave boys,
It grieved his heart full sore.

Haul down, haul down our colors low and for Liverpool we'll sail,
Where we'll greet our friends and sweethearts dear and hunt no more for the whale, brave boys,
And hunt no more for the whale.

Commercial whaling in Greenland began around 1610 when the Dutch sent ships to exploit the resource there. The first recorded European whaling activity in North America was in Pemaquid, ME, though the indigenous people had been hunting whales for centuries. Maine was subsequently not very active in the whaling trade, though sporadic attempts were made to establish whaling companies along the coast. Certainly ships were built here for the trade and Maine sailors served onboard. In any case, there are very few whaling songs in the Maine tradition. We have combined the tune sung by Carrie Grover, who only gave one verse to Eloise Linscott, with lyrics from Mrs. Phebe Stanley of Mt Desert Island who was 85 when she sang this for Mary Smyth in 1925. Smyth published the words in *Minstrelsy of Maine,* noting that the date in this song (1801) is one of the earliest given in any version. We have mended her missing lines with those from another version (in italics).

The Rocks of Scilly

Mr. Adam Morris, Kingman, ME 9/18/1934
Fannie Hardy Eckstorm Collection
Tune: *Helen Creighton Collection*
Transcription © 2019 Julia Lane

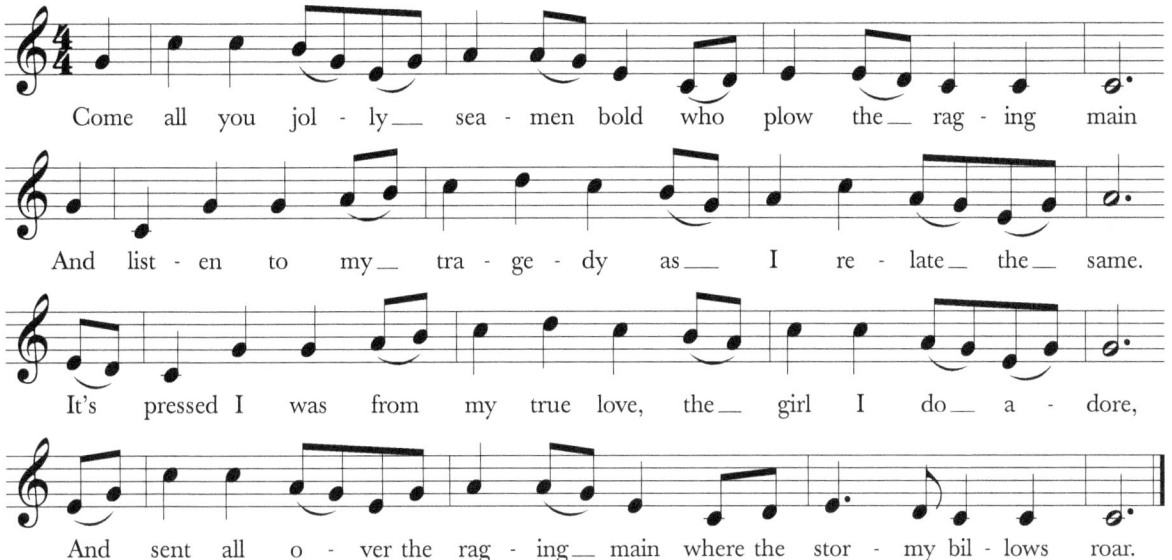

Come all you jolly seamen bold who plow the raging main
And listen to my tragedy as I relate the same.
It's pressed I was from my true love, the girl I do adore,
And sent all over the raging main where stormy billows roar.

It's to the West Indies we were bound, that dismal course to steer,
And all the way that we sailed on I thought of Polly dear.
Sometimes aloft, sometimes on deck and other times below,
But thoughts of Polly still ran in my mind, for Love commands it so.

We were not long upon the deep when a storm began to rise.
The wrestling waves got mountains high and dismal were the skies.
The wind it blew from the southeast and so dismal did appear
It made jolly seamen bold not know what way to steer.

The bos'n up the mast did go unto the main tops'l high.
He looked around with watery eyes, no land or light could spy.
"Bear off, bear off, before the wind and the Scilly Rocks keep clear!
On the ocean wide we must abide until daylight does appear!"

The very first stroke our good ship gave our captain loud did cry,
"The Lord have mercy on our souls, for in the deep we die!"
And out of fifty seamen only four reached the shore,
And our good-lye ship to pieces went and never was heard of more.

Bad news, bad news to Plymouth came that our good ship was lost.
It will cause many a pretty girl for to lament her loss
And Polly, dear, you must grieve for the love of your sweetheart;
It was the stormy winds and wrestling waves caused you and him to part.

The Scilly Islands lie off the southernmost tip of Cornwall, and their many dangerous shoals and currents make for tricky navigation, especially in rough weather. Mr. Morris's song is almost identical to an 1819 English broadside about being pressed to serve on a ship, probably military, bound for the West Indies. In the early 1800s various countries, including the U.S., sent military to the Caribbean to assert their desire for control of the islands. The Newfoundland and Nova Scotia variants have the action in the East Indies and describe the captain's desire to save the cargo, as well as several more verses detailing the anguish of the storm. These are likely later iterations inspired by the active trading routes to India in the mid 19th century. The tune is from James Young of East Petpeswick, Halifax County, NS, collected by Helen Creighton and published in *Traditional Songs From Nova Scotia* (pp. 200–201) in 1950.

The Poor Little Fisher Boy

Mrs. William Currie, West Enfield, ME, 1/1924
Fannie Hardy Eckstorm Collection
The Poor Little Sailor Boy
Oliver Jenness, York, ME, 9/18/1941
Helen Hartness Flanders Collection
Transcription © 2016 Julia Lane

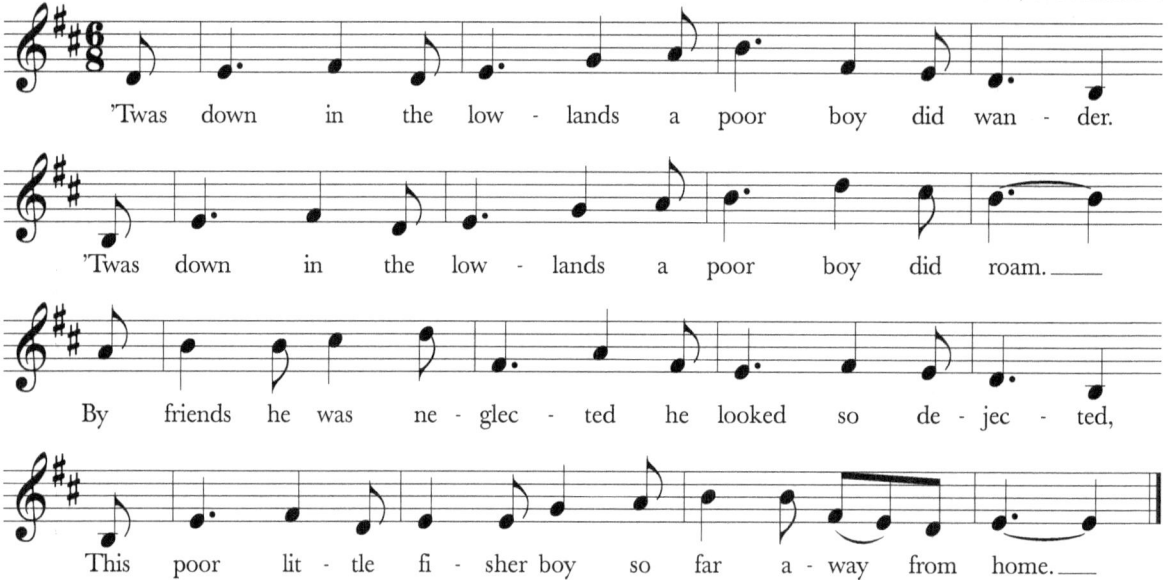

'Twas down in the lowlands a poor boy did wander.
'Twas down in the lowlands a poor boy did roam.
By friends he was neglected he looked so dejected,
This poor little fisher boy so far away from home.

Dark was the night and loudly rolled the thunder,
The lightning in each flash and the ship was overcome;
But at last he looked around for to seek his native ground,
In the deep he left his father so far away from home.

"Oh, where is my father? Where is my mother?
Where are the friends that were so dear to me?
My mother died on her pillow, my father on the billow!"
Cried the poor little fisher boy that roamed so far from home.

When the girl saw him, she opened wide her window
And to her father's house she desired the boy to go,
And the tears rolled from her eyes as she listened to the cries
Of the poor little fisher boy that roamed so far from home.

She begged of her father to seek him employment,
She begged of her father no longer to let him roam.
"Oh, daughter, dear, don't grieve me; the boy shall never leave
Dear lad, I will relieve thee, though far away from home."

And 'twas many long years that he stood up on the masthead
Many long years e'er he became a man.
And it's now he tells all strangers the hardships and the danger
Of the poor little fisher boy that roamed so far from home.

Many's the long year that he served his noble master.
Many the daily labor as he is not alone;
For now he is happy and is married to the daughter
And the poor little fisher boy at last has found a home.

The theme of the neglected and dejected orphan touched the hearts of Victorian England long before Dickens and continues to bring tears to eyes even today. We have combined two versions of the song with different titles but very similar lyrics. "The Poor Little Fisher Boy" was sung in 1924 by Mrs. William Currie, West Enfield, ME, who said she learned it in Ireland. In 1941, Oliver Jenness of York, ME, sang "The Poor Little Sailor Boy." Both songs developed simultaneously in the early 19th century and were extremely popular. "The Fisherman's Boy" appears in London in J. Catnach, *Catalogue of Songs* (1832), was quoted in *Dens of London Exposed* (1835), and is in the W&T Fordyce Catalogue (c1828–1837), *Ballad-Singer's Budget*. "The Poor Little Sailor Boy" broadside was "Sold Wholesale and Retail" by J. G. Hunt, at the Song Depot and Book Stand, South Side City Wharf in 1836. Both are found in collections of traditional singers throughout the British Isles, Ireland, Canada and the U.S., where we find both Fisher and Sailor with the later addition of a Soldier Boy! Our Maine variants each have unique features; the detail of the sailor on the masthead in verse 7 is from Oliver Jenness and the marriage at the end is from Mrs. Currie. Neither detail is found in any other version we have seen. There seem to be two tune families. The minor one here, from Mr. Jenness, is also used for the Southern and bluegrass versions of the song, whereas the major tunes appear in Ireland.

The Tailor and the Chest

Oliver Jenness, York, ME 9/23/1948
Helen Hartness Flanders Collection
Transcription © 2016 Julia Lane

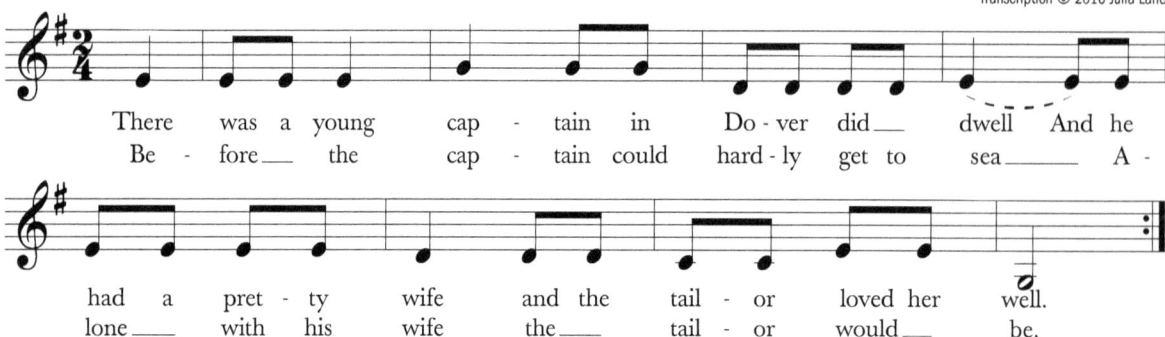

There was a young captain in Dover did dwell
And he had a pretty wife and the tailor loved her well.
Before the captain could hardly get to sea
Alone with his wife the tailor would be.

The tailor one evening was walking on the street
The captain's wife he chanced to meet
He stepped up to her, saying, "How do you do?"
And they sighed and said, "Love to lodge along with you."

They went home and about ten o'clock
Along came the captain and loudly did knock
Roused this couple right out of their sleep
"Oh, where shall I hide, and where shall I creep?"

She says, "I have a chest there by the closet side.
Where you can get in and cunningly can hide."
She opened the chest and she tumbled him in
And there was the tailor like a thief in the mill.

She opened the door and her husband stood there
Likewise the bos'un and seven men more.
She stepped up to him, and she gave him a kiss:
"My dear loving husband, what means this?"

"I did not come to disturb you of your rest
And I'm bound out to sea and come for my chest."
Then up stepped the boatsmen stout and strong
And they takes up the chest to carry it along.

And they had not carried it mor'n half through the town,
Than the weight of the tailor caused it swift to come down.
The boatsmen being tired, they set it down to rest
Says one to the other, "What the Devil's in the chest?"

They tried the key but they couldn't make them do.
And up stepped the bos'un and charged it with his shoe.
He opened the chest and showed to them all
And there was the tailor like a hog in the stall.

He shets the cover down, says, "We'll take him right along."
They locked the tailor in the hold and sailed off to Hong Kong!
They took him to China and sold him off for tea
And that was the last of the tailor to be seen.

This song has been widely collected in the Northeast with a number of titles: "The Jolly Boatswain," "The Boatswain and the Tailor," "The Randy Tailor." The story of the husband cleverly thwarting a wife's extramarital affair has been popular for centuries showing up in the 14th century writings of Boccaccio. Most versions are humorous, as here, and the interloper is severely discomfited while the wife's dignity is maintained. Although Mr. Jenness' tune is pretty basic, the song is clever and worth including.

The Banks of Brandywine

George Dalton, Brewer, ME 6/24/1941
Helen Hartness Flanders Collection
Transcription © 2018 Julia Lane

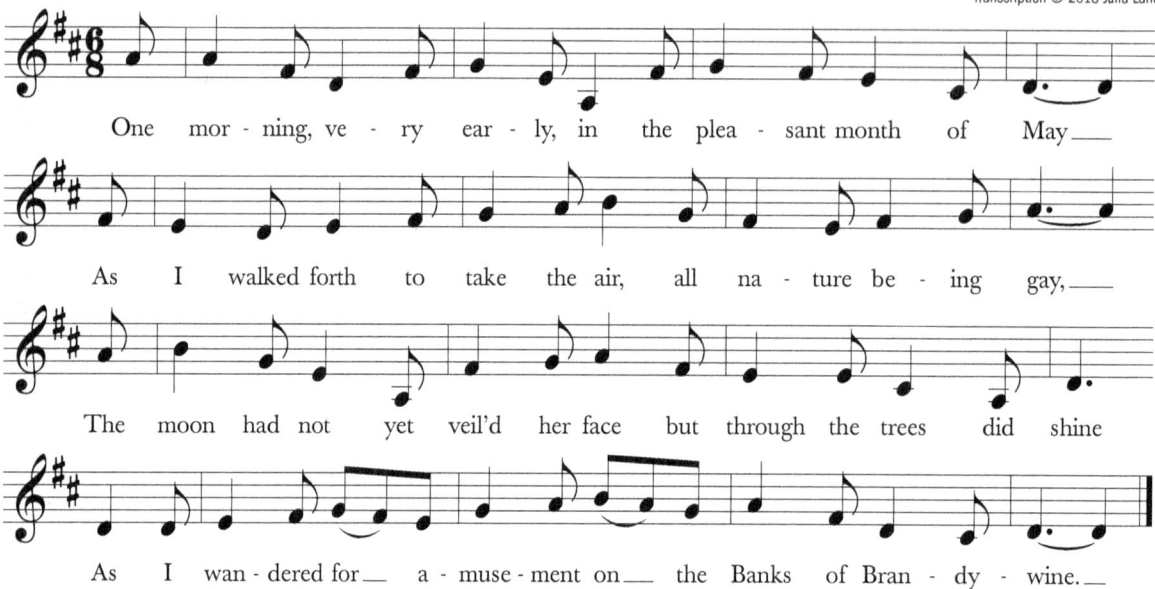

One morning, very early, in the pleasant month of May
As I walked forth to take the air, all nature being gay,
The moon had not yet veil'd her face but through the trees did shine
As I wandered for amusement on the Banks of Brandywine.

By many rough and cragged rocks, and bushes of small growth,
By many lofty ancient trees the leaves were putting forth;
I wandered up along those banks, where murmuring streams do join,
Where pleasant music caught my ear on the banks of Brandywine.

At such an early hour I was surprised to see
A lovely maid with downcast eyes upon those banks so gay.
I modestly saluted her, she knew not my design,
And requested her sweet company on the Banks of Brandywine.

"I pray, young man, be civil, my company forsake
For in my real opinion I think you are a rake,
My love's a valiant sailor; he's now gone to the main
While comfortless I wander on the Banks of Brandywine."

"My dear, why do you thus give up to melancholy cries?
I pray give up your weeping, and dry those lovely eyes,
For sailors in each port, my dear, they do a mistress find
Then they leave you still to wander on the Banks of Brandywine."

"O leave me, sir, do leave me. Why do you me torment?
My Henry won't deceive me, therefore I am content.
Why do you thus torment me and cruelly design
As to fill my heart with horror on the Banks of Brandywine?"

"I wish not to afflict your mind but rather for to ease
Such dreadful apprehensions, they soon your mind will seize.
Your love, my dear, to another girl in wedlock bands has joined."
'Twas then she fainted in my arms on the Banks of Brandywine.

The lofty hills and craggy rocks re-echoed back her strains
The pleasant groves and rural shades were witness to her pains.
"How often has he promised me in Hymen's chains to join?
Now I'm a maid forsaken on the Banks of Brandywine."

"O no, my dear, that ne'er shall be! Behold your Henry now!
I clasp you to my bosom, love, I've not forgot our vow.
It's now I know you're true, my dear, in Hymen's chains we'll join
And bless the happy morn we met on the Banks of Brandywine!"

This is a fragment recorded by Flanders (italics) which we have augmented with lyrics from an early broadside. The recording index names the singer as Annie Tate Moore, but it is an unidentified male voice which we believe to be George Dalton. Mr. Dalton's words appear in italics. This popular theme of the long absent lover returning in disguise to try his sweetheart's constancy reminds us of the ancient epic story of Ulysses.

The Handsome Cabin Boy

Charles Finnemore, Bridgewater, ME 10/28/1943
Helen Hartness Flanders Collection
Transcription © 2016 Julia Lane

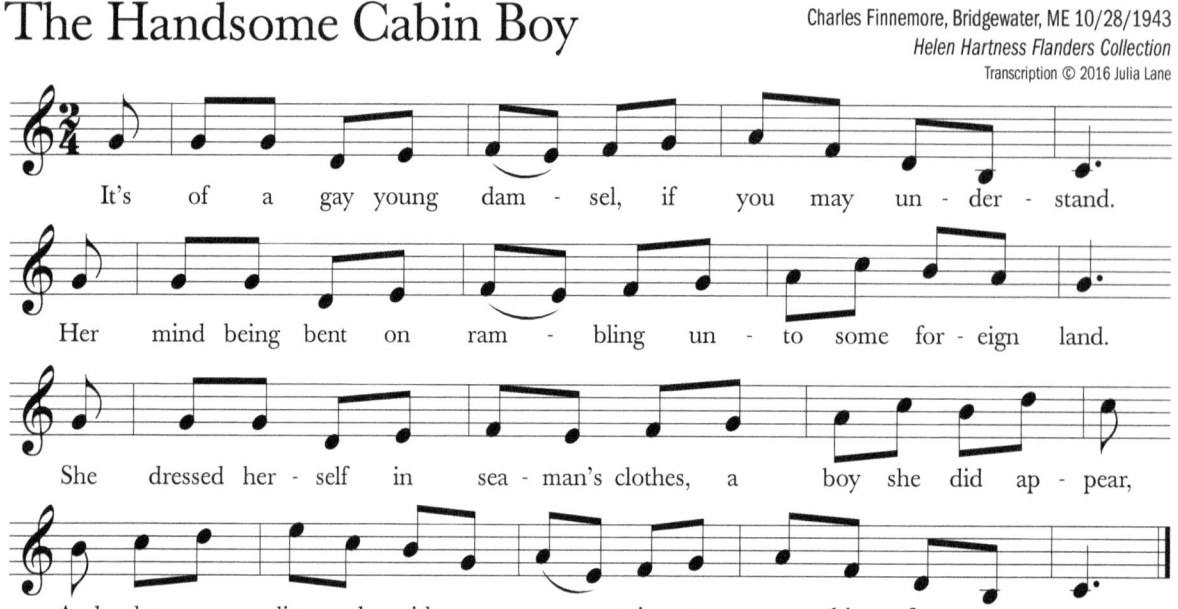

It's of a gay young damsel, if you may understand.
Her mind being bent on rambling unto some foreign land.
She dressed herself in seaman's clothes, a boy she did appear,
And she enlisted with the captain to serve him for a year.

She being spry and nimble, she done her duty well.
But mark what followed after, my song itself will tell.
The captain's wife, she being onboard, was overcome with joy
To think they had enlisted such a handsome cabin boy.

She being spry and nimble, her sidelocks they did curl.
The sailors often said that she looked just like a girl!
But eating cabin biscuits her color did destroy
And the waist did swell on pretty Nell, our handsome cabin boy.

Through the Bay of Biscay our gallant ship did plow
When down amongst the sailor boys there rose a bloody row!
The captain's wife was standing by and laughing at the fun
Just to think the cabin boy would have a daughter or a son!

Although the fantasy persists that women were not allowed onboard ship, the evidence of women at sea is pretty clear. Some women served as captain's servants, providing laundry and mending services as well as cooking and cleaning. Documents from the British battle known as "Glorious First of June" in 1794 include the award of a citation for valor to a sailor, Daniel Tremendous McKenzie, whose status was recorded as "Baby." This seaman was, in fact, a male infant born during the battle! Although the award was officially conferred, a request for a similar award for his mother, who was obviously present, was denied as it was said there would be "numerous other requests." There were, in fact, wives of seamen onboard who served as nurses and cooks receiving no pay, but sharing in that of their husbands. Tradition has it that the imminently expectant pregnant women were sometimes placed next to the firing cannons to induce labor thus coining the term "son of a gun."

Homeward Bound 1

Lyrics unattributed
Fannie Hardy Eckstorm Collection
Tune: Susie Carr Young, *Barry Collection*
Transcription © 2018 Julia Lane

Now to Blackwall Docks we bid adieu,
To Sukie, and Sal and Kitty too.
Our anchor's weighed, our sails unfurl'd,
We are bound to plow the watery world.
Huzza! We are outward bound.

And should we touch at Malabar,
Or any other port as far,
The purser he will tip the chink,
And just like fishes we will drink.
Huzza! We are outward bound.

Now the wind blows hard from the east-nor'east,
Our ship will sail ten knots at least!
The Purser will our wants supply,
And while we've grog we will ne'er say die.
Huzza! We are homeward bound.

And now our three years it is out,
It's very nigh time we back'd about,
And when we're home, and do get free,
Oh, won't we have a jolly spree!
Huzza! We are homeward bound.

And now we haul into the docks,
Where all those pretty girls come in flocks,
And one to the other they will say
"Oh! here comes Jack with his three years pay!"
Huzza! We are homeward bound.

And now we haul to the "Dog and Bell,"
Where there's good liquor for to sell.
In comes old Archer with a smile,
Saying "Drink, my lads, it's worth your while,
For I see you are homeward bound."

Ah! but when our money's all gone and spent,
And none to be borrowed nor none to be lent,
In comes old Archer with a frown,
Saying "Get up Jack! let John sit down.
For I see you are outward bound."

Versions of this appear in most 19th century songsters with varying titles. Although we are not certain of the source for these particular lyrics, on her copy of this song (titled "Homeward Bound") Eckstorm notes "Susie Carr Young knows this as 'St Catherine's Docks.'" We found Young's version of the tune with that title but with only the first verse among her manuscripts in Phillips Barry's collection transcribed by George Herzog. We had to remove two measures of Herzog's tune to make it fit Eckstorm's refrain. St. Catherine's Docks was a development project constructed in East London, 1825–28, to clear out a slum area and provide more dock space in the city. Some 11,000 residents lost their homes in the process but the area quickly became a place where denizens of the nautical community came to ply their various trades, including taverns like the "Dog and Bell" in the song.

Tip the chink = to pay the money owed

Homeward Bound 2

James Kneeland, Searsport, ME 1914
from *The Kneeland Miscellany*
Tune & Additional Lyrics: *Joanna Colcord Collection*
Transcription © 2019 Julia Lane

We're homeward bound up Liverpool Sound.
    Good-bye, fare ye well! Good-bye, fare ye well!
We're homeward bound up Liverpool Sound.
    Three cheers, my boys! We're homeward bound!

We're homeward bound, heave up and down,
Oh, heave on the capstan and make it spin round.

Our anchors we'll weigh and our sails we will set;
The friends we are leaving we leave with regret.

Oh, heave with a will and heave long and strong,
And sing a good chorus, for 'tis a good song.

We're homeward bound, you've heard them say,
Then hook on the catfall and run her away.

She's a flash clipper packet and bound for to go;
With the girls on the towrope she cannot say no.

We're homeward bound, and the winds they blow fair,
And there'll be many true friends to greet us there.

Probably used as a working shanty, this is often sung for entertainment as the tune and chorus invite participation. Frank Kneeland only gives one verse as sung by his father James in their 1914 genealogy *The Kneeland Miscellany*, but given that they lived in Searsport, home port of maritime song collector Joanna Colcord, it seemed appropriate to complete the song with the tune and additional lyrics from her book, *Songs of American Sailormen*.

Tossed Upon Life's Raging Billow

James Kneeland, Searsport, ME 1914
From *The Kneeland Miscellany*
Composer: George W. Bethune 1830
Transcription © 2017 Julia Lane

Tossed upon life's raging billow, sweet it is, Oh Lord, to know
Thou canst press a sailor's pillow and canst feel a sailor's woe.
Never slumb'ring, never sleeping, though the night be dark and drear.
Thou the faithful watch art keeping; "All is well!" Thy constant cheer.

And though loud the winds be howling, fierce though flash the lightnings red
And the storm clouds wildly lowering o'er the sailor's anxious head,
Thou canst calm the ocean billow and its noise and tumult still
Crush the tempest's wild commotion at the bidding of Thy will.

Thus, our hearts the hope will cherish, while to heav'n we lift our eyes,
Thou wilt save us ere we perish, thou wilt hear our faintest cries!
And, tho' mast and sail be riven, life's short voyage soon is o'er;
Safely moor'd in heav'n's wide haven, storms and tempests vex no more.

Frank Kneeland, the son of the singer, tells us "Father and Mother learned this last in the Fall of [18]66 while attending a singing school at the Roberts Schoolhouse run by a man named Tucker." Known as a "Sailor's Hymn," written by Pastor George W. Bethune, it appeared in the *Christian Lyre* (1830) and in the *Seamen's Devotional Assistant* the same year. It is "said to have been the Author's first and favourite hymn, having been written when he was on a voyage to the West Indies, for the benefit of his health, in the year 1825." (*Lyra Sacra Americana*, p. 297).

The Greenwood Tree

Hanford Hayes, Stacyville, ME 7/13/1941
Helen Hartness Flanders Collection
Transcription © 2020 Julia Lane

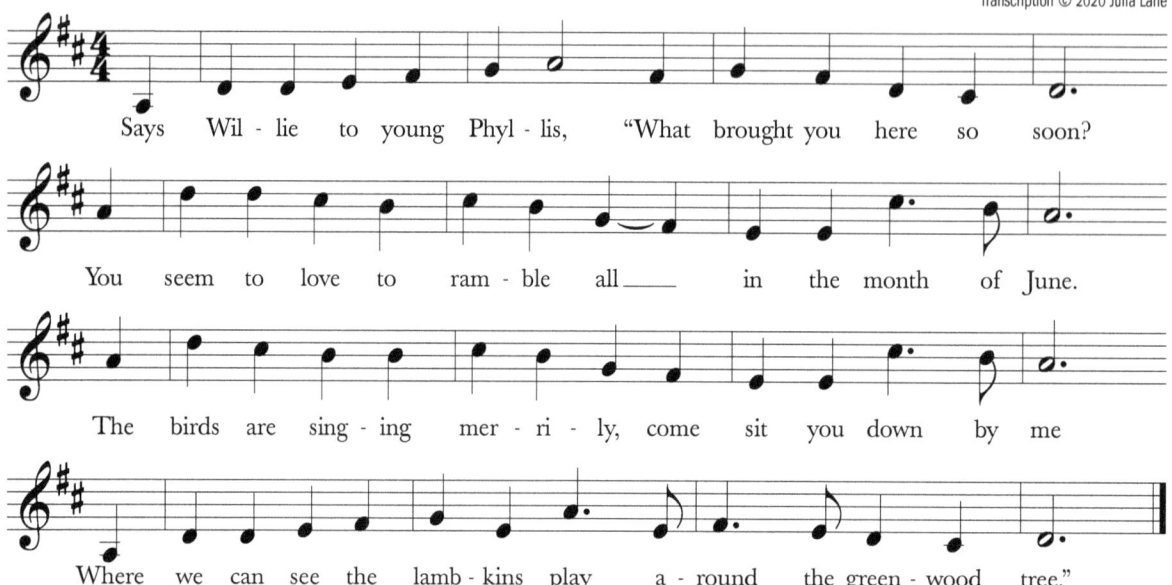

Says Willie to young Phyllis, "What brought you here so soon?
You seem to love to ramble all in the month of June.
The birds are singing merrily, come sit you down by me
Where we can see the lambkins play around the greenwood tree."

Says Willie to young Phyllis "Your parents would me blame
They say to wed too early, they say it was a shame.
Your father has declared that he'll prove my overthrow
Although I am a sailor boy that plows the ocean through."

Says she, "Don't mind my father although he threatens you.
For though I am his daughter such usage will not do,
I will venture with my sailor, no longer will I mourn.
For you seldom find a better when your old sweetheart is gone."

Said William, "Now the ocean has summoned me away,
I hope you'll change your notion, and with your parents stay.
It will hurt your constitution, and your fingers are so small.
So stay at home and do not roam our cable ropes to haul."

Said Phyllis, "I have clothing all ready for the sea,
So we will go together unto America,
And then we'll be united and live so happily.
And talk about our tales of love, likewise the greenwood tree."

They both did go together to sail the ocean wide,
Young Phyllis did her duty, for William was her pride.
But, mark their desolation, the wind began to blow.
The lightning flashed, the thunder roared, in flakes down fell the snow.

For three weeks on the ocean, they were tossed up and down.
The ship had lost her anchors and the masts away were blown.
When short of provisions and all prepared to die,
Young Phyllis hung around her love and bitterly did cry.

Young William let the small boat down, and in it they did go.
Poor Phyllis and young William all on the sea did row.
Their drink it was salt water and that alone was sweet;
They tore their clothing from their backs for they had nought to eat.

With thirst and cold and hunger they on their knees did pray,
Midst lightning, rain and thunder they passed their time away.
At length upon a dismal night they were cast upon a strand
On the coast of America, a good and friendly land.

They met with kind assistance; it did their health restore.
And now they are united all on that fruitful shore!
They are happy in America, all in prosperity.
Young Phyllis and young William who went away to sea.

Mr. Hayes only sang the first two verses of this rare ballad also known as "William and Phyllis." We found the rest in the 1906 *Journal of the Folk-Song Society of Great Britain* (p. 216) in which Ralph Vaughn Williams says: "I heard this song from my house in Barton Street, Westminster; it was sung by three men selling ballad sheets." He was delighted to find that folk and ballad music were alive in London in 1904. Although we have not found it in any other North American collections, and it is scarce in the U.K., it has been around for a while, being published early in the 1800s by Joseph Russell as a broadside in Birmingham. The details of the couple eating their clothing to stay alive and subsequent casting ashore in America, "a good and friendly land," are certainly unique.

Songs of Ships & Sailors

Mary's Dream

Carrie Grover, Gorham, ME
Heritage of Song 1953
Transcription and adaptation © 2014 Julia Lane

The moon had climbed the highest hill
Which rises o'er the river deep,
And from the eastern summit shed
Her silv'ry light on field and tree.
When Mary laid her down to sleep,
Her thoughts on Jamie far at sea,
When soft and low a voice she heard,
Saying, "Mary weep no more for me!"

CHORUS:
>Mary weep no more for me.
>Mary weep no more for me.
>Mary weep no more for me.
>Mary weep no more for me.

She from her pillow gently raised
Her head, to ask who there might be,
And saw young Jamie shivering stand,
With visage pale, and hollow e'e.
"O Mary dear, cold is my clay;
It lies beneath the stormy sea.
Far, far from thee, I sleep in death,
So, Mary weep no more for me!

"Three stormy days and stormy nights,
We toss'd upon the raging main;
And long we strove our ship to save,
But all our striving was in vain.
Even when horror chill'd my blood,
My thoughts were always on loving thee
The storm is past, and I at rest;
So, Mary, weep no more for me!

"O, maiden dear, thyself prepare;
We soon shall meet upon that shore
Where love is free from doubt and care,
And thou and I shall part no more."
Loud crow'd the cock, the shadow fled;
No more of Jamie could she see:
But soft the passing spirit said:
"Sweet Mary, weep no more for me!"

Romantic songs of sailor lovers abound in the tradition, as do tales of spectral visitation. "Mary's Dream" was written in Scotland by John Lowe in 1772 as a tribute to a friend. It became very popular in Maine in the early 19th century and appears in *Jack Downing's Songbook* (1840) published in Hallowell, as well as several songsters and broadsides of the time. More recently, Maine singer Carrie Grover published her parents' version in her book *A Heritage of Song* (1953) and Horace Beck includes it in *The Folklore of Maine*. Julia has added the chorus and changed the hero's name to Jamie to reflect a local story, circa 1826, which appears in the *History of Dresden, Maine* by Charles Edwin Allen (p. 858) as follows:

> Captain Samuel Lilly had the finest house in North Woolwich. He had it built for his wife who was an extremely aristocratic English woman. They adopted Mary Ann Goss, who had come from England, when her parents moved on to New York. They raised the child in style and she was known as the most beautiful girl in all the countryside. When she came of age, she became engaged to Captain James Henry Perkins who was said to be remarkably handsome and very well liked. Captain Perkins commanded the brig *Planter*, built in 1826. On a voyage to the West Indies, the crew were all taken ill with "ship fever." As there was no medicine chest onboard, the entire company succumbed including Captain Perkins. In his delirium he sprang overboard and drowned. The one man who was left to tell the tale ran the ship on the Florida Keys and abandoned her. She was later brought back by Redford Tallman of Dresden. After the death of Captain Perkins, Mary Ann Goss had a peculiar dream. In it, she saw his vessel sail up the Kennebec River and stop opposite their house. A plank was put out and, as she saw him start to walk ashore, she went to meet him. Before she could reach him, he disappeared saying, "Prepare to follow me." She afterwards became very melancholy and her friends tried without success to divert her. Less than a year after her strange dream, she was preparing for an outing when she fell lifeless to the floor. She was deeply mourned by her many friends who remarked that she was "still beautiful even in death."

The Little Sailor Boy

Frank Kneeland, Searsport, ME 10/1941
Helen Hartness Flanders Collection
Lyrics from *Kneeland Miscellany* 1914
Transcription © 2017 Julia Lane

There was once a little sailor who was both brisk and bold.
He courted a damsel worth thousands of gold.
Her father said, "Dear daughter, if this is your intent
To wed with this sailor boy I will never give consent!"

So she sat down and wrote and the letter she sent
To let her true love know her old father's intent,
Saying, "My heart is sincere; my love it will prove true
There is none in this world I can fancy but you!"

Then the little sailor wrote saying, "If you I can't obtain
I will cross the wide ocean and go into Spain.
Some craft there or project intending to try
To outwit your old father or else I must die."

So he bought him rich robes and in pearls he did appear
Disguised as a prince from Morocco he did steer
With a star upon his breast came to see his love again
And the old man was pleased with his young Prince of Spain.

So he said, "Most Noble Prince, if you will agree
To wed with my daughter your bride she shall be."
"'Tis with my whole heart," this young sailor boy did say,
"If she'll be my bride I'll get married today!"

So off to the church they were hurried with speed.
The old man gave up his daughter indeed
Which caused this old man with pride and joy to dance
To think that his daughter had wed with a prince.

Then up spoke the little sailor saying, "Don't you know me?
I am that little sailor boy you once turned away!
'Tis you I have outwitted by venturing my life
Gaining twelve thousand pounds and a beautiful wife."

"You may go to the devil!" the old man made reply,
"You have robbed me of my money and my daughter likewise
But if I'd once mistrusted that this had been your plot
Not one penny of my money nor my daughter would you got!"

Also called "The Prince of Morocco," the sailor's return is more elaborate than others in this genre. In this case, the disguise is contrived to dupe the girl's father and reminds us of the same motif in the story of Aladdin. Although it appears as a broadside in the early 19th century, it does not seem to be particularly popular in the tradition. One would think it would be, but the exotic ruse may have seemed less credible to the general New England public. This text, attributed to Amanda Crockett Kneeland, is from *The Kneeland Miscellany*, a genealogy of the family of James Kneeland, Searsport, ME (1914). The tune is as sung by his son Frank for Helen Flanders in 1941. Frank said, "Mother learned this of Hiram Hurd of Exeter, ME, about 1858."

Songs of Ships & Sailors

Glenaloon

Mr. Chas F. Alley, Jonesport, ME 1930
Phillips Barry Collection
Tune: Thomas Cleghorn, Harvey Station, NB 1964
Dr. Edward Ives Collection
Transcription © Julia Lane 2021

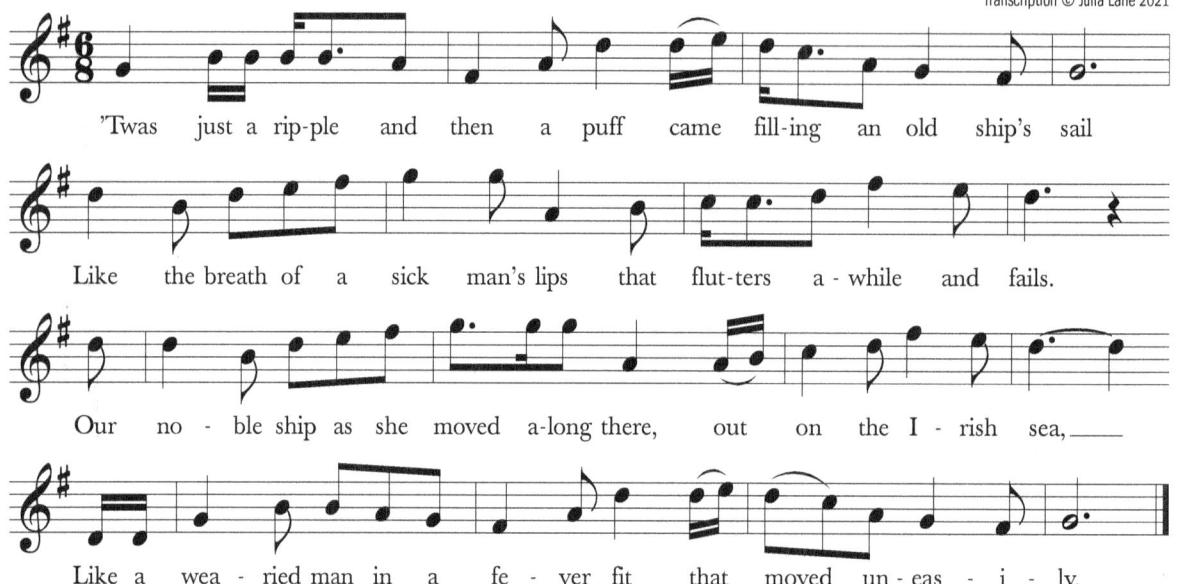

'Twas just a ripple and then a puff came filling an old ship's sail
Like the breath of a sick man's lips that flutters awhile and fails.
Our noble ship as she moved along there, out on an Irish sea,
Like a wearied man in a fever fit that moved uneasily.

No headway on our old ship now; she might have been log!
Three leagues away the land lay hid in a bank of cold gray fog
And two points on our starboard bow, 'twas a summer's night in June
Where the water and air seemed joined in one, rose up a red full moon.

O, bloody red, but it silvered soon with a faint and glimmering light
Stretched from our bark to the ocean's edge, wavering broad and bright
There's something in the shiny belt about a league away,
Like the shapeless mass of a rugged rock on the face of the water lay.

I got my charts; could see no rocks or reefs just thereabout
But I kept my eye on the ugly thing and could not make it out.
I looked through mine eyeglass steadily as I walked the quarter deck
I ordered my men to lower our boat thinking it was a wreck.

As we pulled away for that shapeless thing through the fitful light of the moon
We read the name on her starboard bow; it was the *Glenaloon*.
We hailed her but never no sound could hear; there was no one on her deck
We shipped our oars and touched the side and climbed on board of the wreck.

There was a rubbish of splintered spars, her fore and mainmast gone
Shattered boats on her littered decks, but of human beings none.
O, surely there is one human form crouching down on the wreck
In an old sou'wester and Guernsey frock – a ship mate, here on the wreck!

'Twas sadly I raised the old chap's hat – I remember the moon was full –
I startled back as the bright rays shone on a shimmering ghostly skull!
And making my way through the sails and spars muddled with shade and light
Five more skeletons we found bleached to a deathly white.

Then stepping off through splinters and spars, for the cabin I made my way
As in a trance, some figure there, the skeleton skipper lay.
In his boney hand had a paper clutched; I read what it said next day,
"We're wrecked, boat stove and food all gone. We can but watch and pray!"   [stove = smashed in]

As we rowed away from that mastless brig in the light of the pitiful moon
I read again that fatal name, that queer name Glenaloon.
And faster and faster into the water the blades of our stout oars fell
For her deck seemed swarmed with shadowed forms waving a wild farewell.

Next day the sun shone clear and bright, we buried her fleshless crew
All sheeted and shrouded one by one they sank in the waters so blue.
And oft, when I look in a summer's night through the clear light of the moon
It freshens the horrors I once beheld on the wreck of the *Glenaloon*.

Here's a wonderful creepy ghost ship song that almost got overlooked because of variations in the title and the spelling of the ship's name. The lyrics started their career as a poem created by Boston writer Francis Alexander Durivage (1814–1881). In addition to writing several popular histories and novels, he regularly contributed poetry, humorous articles and sketches to magazines and newspapers nationwide sometimes under the name "Old 'Un." His longer poems were, no doubt, memorized for recitation by students and entertainers. We found a transcript titled *Glenaloon* in Phillips Barry's papers at the Houghton Library indicating that it was "from the recitation of Mr. Chas F. Alley, Jonesport, ME." Upon close examination, a faint imprint appears on the page, probably from an additional page not included in the file. It says "'The Skipper's Yarn' by Francis Durivage printed in the *Calais Advertiser* February 1, 1873" with the note "founded on fact." There were several lines missing, so we have patched it with lyrics (in italics) collected from Neil O'Brien, Pictou, NS and printed in *MacKenzie's Ballads and Sea Songs from Nova Scotia* (1928). The tune, however incongruous, is from *Folksongs of New Brunswick* by Edward D. Ives where it is titled "The Wreck of the *Glenna Loon*." It was collected from Thomas Cleghorn of Harvey Station, NB. Durivage's original poem appears in a posthumous collection of his writing printed in 1881 by his daughter. Although we have not found any historic ship with the name "Glenaloon," that doesn't mean the story isn't true.

A Wet Sheet and a Flowing Sea

Susie Carr Young, Brewer, ME circa 1930
Phillips Barry Collection
Original transcribed by George Herzog
Transcription © 2019 Julia Lane

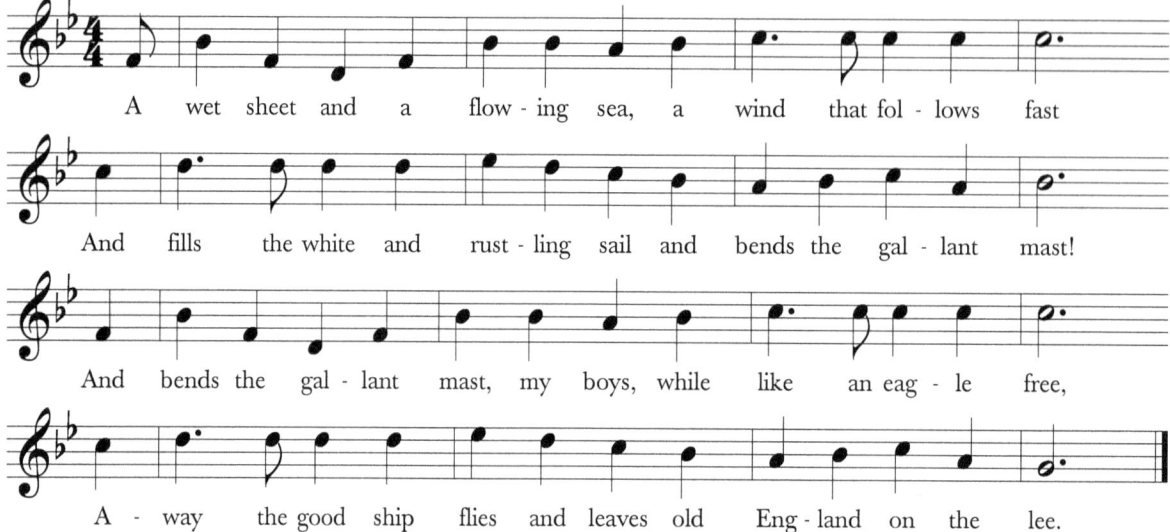

A wet sheet and a flowing sea, a wind that follows fast
And fills the white and rustling sail and bends the gallant mast!
And bends the gallant mast, my boys, while like the eagle free,
Away the good ship flies and leaves old England on the lee.

O for a soft and gentle wind! I heard a fair one cry;
But give to me the swelling breeze, and white waves heaving high:
The white waves heaving high, my lads, the good ship tight and free;
The world of waters is our home, and merry men are we.

There's tempest in yon hornéd moon, and lightning in yon cloud;
And hark the music, mariners! The wind is wakening loud.
The wind is wakening loud, my boys, the lightning flashes free;
The hollow oak our palace is, our heritage the sea.

The following fragment was collected from Susie Carr Young of Brewer, ME, circa 1930. A note from Mrs. Young says "These crazy words to a pretty air is a relic of my eighth year. The first line seems to be related to 'Reuben and Rachel,' the rest to the title."

Oh, far beyond the northern sea I hear a fair one cry
Oh, give to me the rolling breeze and the white waves heaving high
And the white wave heaving high, my boys, while like an eagle free
This world of waters is our home and merry men are we

The original lyrics were written by Allan Cunningham (1784–1842), a Scottish poet and author who was born at Keir, Dumfriesshire. His father was a neighbor of Robert Burns at Ellisland, and young Allan became friends with local ballad collector James Hogg and the writer Walter Scott. Cunningham tried his own hand at collecting and writing ballads which were eventually published and well received. "A Wet Sheet and a Flowing Sea" is considered one of the best British sea-songs, although written by a landsman. References to the song appear throughout 19th century literature. In 1827, it was adapted, arranged and "sung with distinguished applause" by Thomas Walton, who published it in Philadelphia. Another setting was made in 1850 by "M. S." of Baltimore, and published by G. Willig, Jr.

Peter Jones

Oliver Jenness, York Village, ME 9/18/1941
Helen Hartness Flanders Collection
Transcription © 2017 Julia Lane

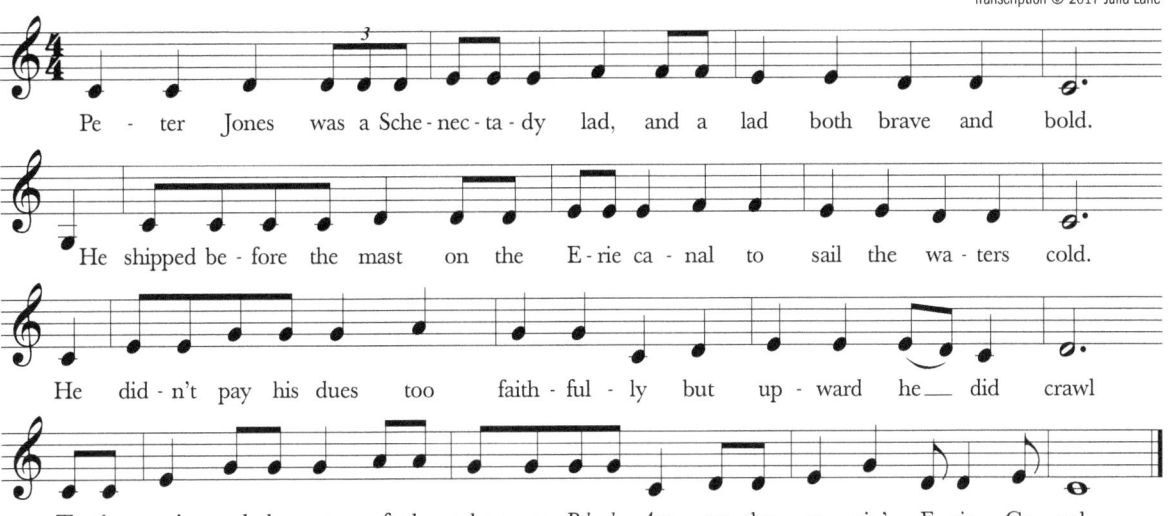

Peter Jones was a Schenectady boy and a lad both brave and bold.
He shipped before the mast on the Erie canal to sail the waters cold.
He didn't pay his dues too faithfully but upward he did crawl
To the cap'n and the mate of the schooner *Polly Ann* on the ragin' Erie Canal.

There was old Bill Smith on a pirate craft and a pirate too was he.
He never was known to spend a cent or to treat the company.
He gambled and was a brawler, too, and he stood near seven foot tall
And he haunted all the whisky shops on the ragin' Erie Canal.

But he had a daughter Ishabel, she was just sixteen years old.
She tumbled into love with Peter Jones, that gallant sailor bold.
She quickly deserted her father's craft and out of the stern did go
And sailed away with Peter Jones on the ragin' Erie Canal.

When Old Bill Smith found that his girl was gone, oh, he was much enraged!
He took a big drink of Schenectady rum and set off on his rampage.
He swore a big three-story oath as he staggered down the street
Saying, "Shiver my timbers and blast my eyes if I don't get square with Pete!"

Peter Jones was aboard at the stern of his craft and attending to his gear
Little did he think that old Bill Smith had got his dander reared.
But he crept aboard so sneakily, so lightly he did tread
And grabbed up the anchor in both of his hands and broke the young man's head.

Old Bill Smith was very much surprised when he see what he had done;
He then swore another oath and overboard he plunged.
Now old Bill Smith is dead and gone, forget him we never shall
For his body served to poison all the eels in the Erie Canal.

Although Mr. Jenness seemed uncertain in his singing of this canal ballad, changing tunes and forgetting lyrics, it was too good not to try and mend. We found no other songs like it anywhere we looked and so Fred did his best to complete the story.

Songs of Ships & Sailors

Peter Street

Charles Finnemore, Bridgewater, ME 10/29/1943
Helen Hartness Flanders Collection
Transcription © 2016 Julia Lane

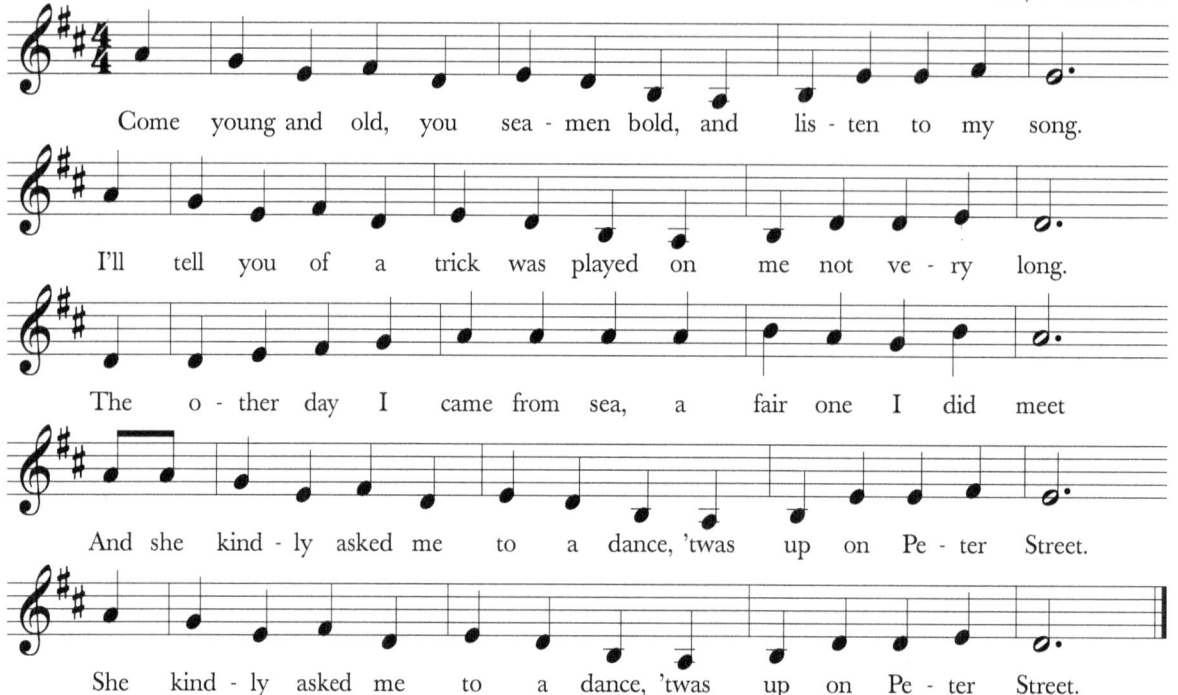

Come young and old, you seamen bold and listen to my song.
I'll tell you of a trick was played on me not very long.
The other day I came from sea, a fair one I did meet
And she kindly asked me to a dance, 'twas up on Peter Street.
She kindly asked me to a dance, 'twas up on Peter Street.

I said "My handsome fair one, I can't dance very well
For Weakinstown this night I'm bound where all my friends do dwell.
The other day I came from sea; I saved up fifty pounds.
My friends will be expecting me tonight in Weakinstown,
My friends will be expecting me tonight in Weakinstown."

"If you can't dance very well, surely you can have a treat
You can have a glass of brandy and something for to eat.
At ten o'clock this very night I'll meet you at the train
If you consent to give a call when you come to town again,
If you consent to give a call when you come to town again."

So finding her so friendly, I calléd on a car
To take us to the bar room; the distance was not far.
The girls all on the other side these words to me did say,
"Ah poor ol' chap, you'll lose your cap if you do go that way,
Ah poor ol' chap, you'll lose your cap if you do go that way!"

And when we reached the bar room, sure the liquor did come in,
When every man had drinked a round the dancing did begin.
Me and my love had dancéd all through a merry tune.
She said, "My dear, we will repair to a chamber all alone!"
She said, "My dear, we will repair to a chamber all alone!"

After the dancing had been o'er we straight to bed do go
But it's little did I think that she would prove my overthrow.
My watch, my chain, my fifty pounds – oh dear what will I do?
Now fair you well sweet Weakinstown, I never will see you.
Now fair you well sweet Weakinstown, I never will see you.

When I come to my senses, oh nothing could I spy
But a woman's shirt and apron upon the bed did lie.
I cursed, I swore, my hair I tore, oh dear what can I do?
Now fair you well sweet Weakinstown, I never shall see you,
Now fair you well sweet Weakinstown, I never shall see you.

When everything was silent, 'bout the hour of twelve o'clock,
I put on the shirt and apron and I headed for the dock.
The sailors saw me coming and these words to me did say,
"Ah poor ol' chap, you've lost your cap since you've been gone that way,
Ah poor ol' chap, you've lost your cap since you've been gone that way."

"Is this the new spring fashion, Jack, that lately came on shore?
Oh, where's the shop you buy them at? Oh, is there any more?"
The captain cried, "Why Jack, my boy, I thought in Weakinstown
You might have got a better suit than that for fifty pounds!
You might have got a better suit than that for fifty pounds!"

I might have done much better but I couldn't get the chance.
I was walking down from Peter Street when I was asked to a dance.
I danced my whole destruction! I was skinned from head to feet
So I take my oath I'll go no more to a dance on Peter Street!
So I take my oath I'll go no more to a dance on Peter Street!

Come, young and old, you seamen bold, a warning take by me
Be sure to shun bad company when you go on a spree.
Be sure to shun bad company or you'll end up like me
With a woman's dress and apron for to fit you out for sea,
With a woman's dress and apron for to fit you out for sea.

Variants of this song are well known and widespread. It would seem that even if sailors weren't always in danger of losing all their clothes on shore they still enjoyed singing about it. Given the Irish penchant for self-deprecating stories that make fun of adversity, the place of action might be Peter Street in Dublin, which saw a great deal of activity involving sailors in the 19th century. The location of Weakinstown, however, remains a mystery.

Grace Darling

Justin DeCoster, Buckfield, ME 1930
Fannie Hardy Eckstorm Collection
Tune from George Linley 1838
Transcription © 2018 Julia Lane

Oh, father lovéd the storm is raging and cold and heavy the night mist falls.
Some hapless crew, a prey to danger, for help, for help despairing calls.
Trim, trim the lamp, the boat launch quickly; though danger threatens the worst we'll brave.
The toil I heed not if we can rescue the shipwrecked wanderers from the grave!
Oh, father lovéd the storm is raging and cold and heavy the night mist falls.
The boat launch quickly! The boat launch quickly! Some hapless crew for help now calls!

"My gentle child, 'twere worse than madness to tempt the billow this fearful night;
Again to sleep, to rest betake thee! Await, await the morning's light."
"I cannot sleep, their shrieks appall me; Oh! Father, heard ye that piercing cry?
Arise ye, hasten, the day is breaking! Look out, look out, a wreck I spy.
Oh! Father lovéd, I fear no danger; with you I will boldly breast the wave.
The boat launch quickly, the boat launch quickly, the hapless crew we yet may save!"

The boat is launched through breakers roaring — like to some wild bird, the frail skiff flew —
That gentle girl, with love unshaken, has saved from death that hapless crew!
The danger past, her heart beats lightly, her silent transport no pride betrays.
Tho' grateful tears are round her falling, and hearts are throbbing to her praise.
The danger past, her heart beats lightly, her silent transport no pride betrays,
Tho' grateful tears are round her falling, and hearts are throbbing to her praise.

Grace Horsley Darling was the daughter of the keeper of the Longstone lighthouse on the Farne Islands off southeast Scotland. At age 23 she captured the imagination of the public when on Sept 7, 1838, accompanied by her father, she rowed out to rescue the crew of the steam freighter *Forfarshire* that had foundered on a nearby ledge. The media went wild with the story and she was subjected to much unwanted attention, including offers of marriage. She unfortunately died of tuberculosis four years later. Her boat was subsequently exhibited at the 1893 World's Fair in Chicago. The story was reported in detail in the newspapers, both in the U.K. and the U.S., which resulted in the composition of several very popular songs commemorating her exploits. This is a version of the George Lindley opus published in New York in 1838 soon after Grace's heroic effort. It was collected (circa 1930) by Fannie Eckstorm from Mr. Justin DeCoster, the "Bard of Buckfield," who used to say of himself, perhaps unguardedly, that "he knew and sung more songs than any person living!"

Mournful Tragedy!
Lines on the Drowning of Six Young Men in the Harbor of Portland, near Diamond Cove

William Withington, Portland, ME 1850
ME Historical Society
Transcription © 2018 Julia Lane

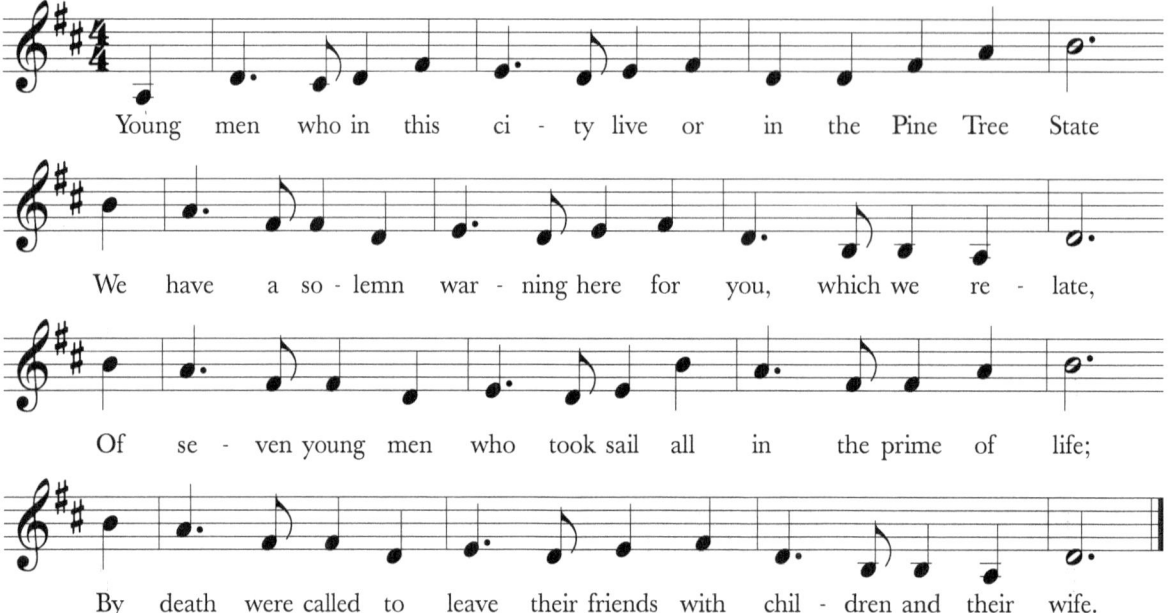

Young men who in this city live or in the Pine Tree State
We have a solemn warning here for you, which we relate,
Of seven young men who took sail all in the prime of life;
By death were called to leave their friends with children and their wife.

They went down Portland harbor for to take a pleasure sail,
The eighth day of October, when six perish'd in that gale.
There was but one who swam to shore, to tell the news to all
He said, near Diamond Cove, their boat was capsiz'd in a squall.

Since then their bodies have been found and brought up to this place
Where all their wives and children dear could once more see their face.
Their friends will long time mourn their loss here in the State of Maine;
But still, it may be said, our loss is their eternal gain.

But we, who now survive the dead, have got to follow soon;
It may be by the morning light at midnight, or at noon.
It may not be in the same way that these young men met their death
But when bold death calls us, we say we must yield up our breath.

Then to the judgment we must go where God will judge us all
And that will be when Gabriel's trump shall give us the last call.
Then we shall meet our friends again on Canaan's happy shore;
And spend a long eternity where death will be no more.

Here, men will sin, day after day from morning until night;
But in that world, we hear them say will be a glorious light.
The sting of death, we read, is sin, death now from that makes free;
But in the world we have not seen, there we must shortly be.

We now submit these lines to those who mourn the loss of friends,
And hope they'll seek a heaven of joy, where pleasure never ends.

Typical of a news broadside composed on a local event, this piece from 1850 was printed by Stephen Berry, Printer, 177 Fore Street, Portland, and could be purchased for three cents. It specifies the tune, "Auld Lang Syne," so we are able to include it in this collection using the version which was popular at the time. The original printed copy may be viewed at mainememory.net. It is illustrated with images of six coffins at the top of the page. Apparently, this morbid decoration was usual. Another composer of these broadsides, Thomas Shaw, made a decent living writing and publishing similar verses which he sold to survivors of the tragedies and their families and friends. Each of his creations has the appropriate number of coffins designating the body count. Unfortunately, he did not include the melodies in his publications.

The *White Squall*

Frank & James Kneeland, Searsport, ME
The Kneeland Miscellany 1914
Poem/ lyrics by Richard Johns 1832
Music by George Barker 1833
Transcription © 2015 Julia Lane

Oh, the sea was bright and the barque rode well.
The breeze bore the tones of the vesper bell.
'Twas a gallant barque with a crew as brave
As e'er was launched on the heaving wave.
As e'er was launched on the heaving wave
For she shone in the light of declining day.
Each sail was set and each heart was gay,
Each sail was set and each heart was gay.

They neared the land where in beauty smiles
The sunny shores of the Grecian isles.
All thought of home and the welcome dear
That soon should greet each wand'rer's ear.
That soon should greet each wand'rer's ear
And in fancy joined in the social throng
The festive dance and the joyous song,
The festive dance and the joyous song.

The *White Squall* glides through the azure sky
Hark! What means that despairing cry?
Farewell the transient dreams of home:
'Tis the cry for help where no help can come.
'Tis the cry for help where no help can come
For the *White Squall* glides o'er the surging wave
And the barque is 'gulfed in an ocean grave,
And the barque is 'gulfed in an ocean grave.

This was an extremely popular parlor song but, because the copyright laws of the time were very lax, there is some confusion about the authorship of both the original poem and the setting of the music. It seems that in 1832 Brevet-Major Richard Johns, while serving in the Mediterranean, wrote the poem "shortly after the mysterious disappearance of one of his Majesty's sloops of war in the Mediterranean, supposed to have been lost in a squall of this character which, sudden and violent in its coming, too often proves fatal." (*Ladies Magazine & Museum*, 1836). The lyrics appealed to George Barker, a well-known composer of the time. The sheet music was published and dedicated to a celebrated singer named John Braham, who included it in his repertoire. As time passed, numerous broadsides were also published with and without attribution. After Johns died in 1851, the song was published in the U.S. with another poet, Barry Cornwall, named as author and occasionally with Braham as composer.

The Battleship, The *Maine*

Oliver Jenness, Chase's Pond, York, ME 9/23/1948
Helen Hartness Flanders Collection
Last verse: Andrew B. Sterling 1898
Transcription © 2017 Julia Lane

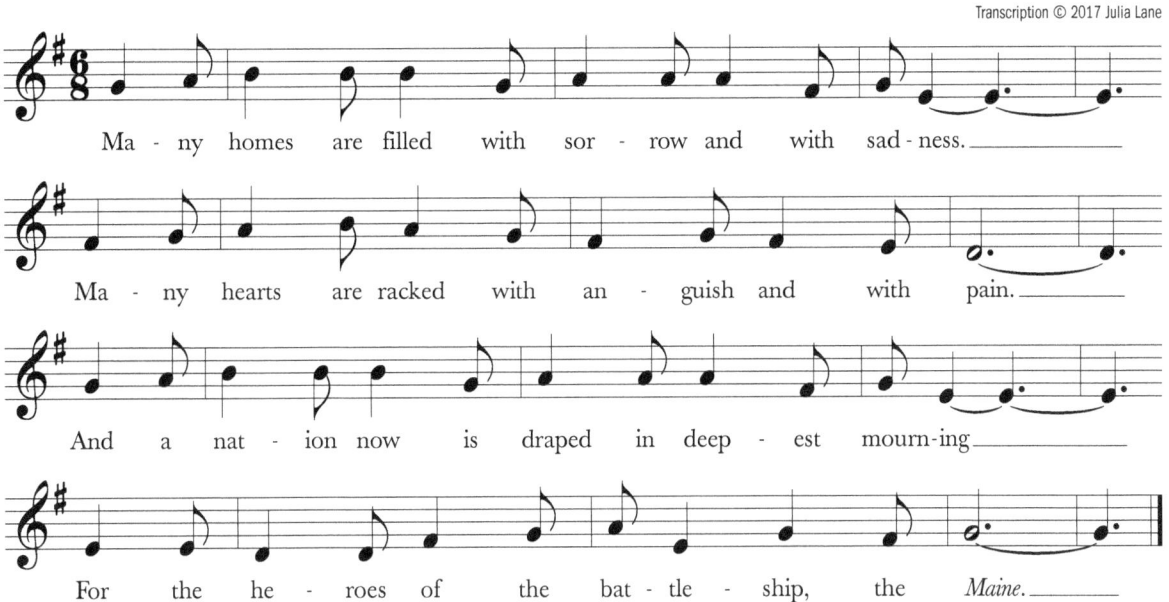

Many homes are filled with sorrow and sadness.
Many hearts are racked with anguish and with pain.
And a nation now is draped in deepest mourning
For the heroes of the battleship, the *Maine*.

Some sleep beneath the waters of the harbor;
Some repose beneath a mound of Spanish clay,
And their spirits seem to cry aloud for vengeance
On the shores of Havana far away.

Oh, the moon shines down tonight upon the waters,
Where the heroes of the *Maine* in silence lay;
May they rest in peace, the loved ones who are sleeping,
On the shores of Havana far away.

The American battleship USS *Maine* was sent to Havana Harbor in January 1898 to protect U.S. interests during the Cuban War of Independence from Spain. On February 15, 1898, the ship blew up and sank killing 260 officers and men on board. An investigation ensued with a U.S. Navy board of inquiry ruling that the ship had been sunk by the external explosion of a mine. Some U.S. Navy officers disagreed with the board, suggesting that the ship's magazine had been ignited by the spontaneous combustion of the coal locker. American newspapers capitalized on a volatile political situation to boost circulation, claiming that the Spanish were responsible for the disaster. "Remember the *Maine!*" became a rallying cry for action. As a result, the sinking of the *Maine* was a catalyst that accelerated the onset of the Spanish American War. This song appeared as an 1898 broadside written by Andrew B. Sterling and sung to the tune of the song "On The Banks Of The Wabash, Far Away" by Paul Dresser (1859-1906). It quickly became popular as the news of the tragedy spread.

Old Sailor's Song

Henry Hunter Chamberlain, Round Pond, ME circa 1920
Fannie Hardy Eckstorm Collection
Tune: Traditional
Transcription © 2018 Julia Lane

Come listen unto me awhile and I will tell you then
The hardships and the misery of life on a merchantman.
At four o'clock in the morning the mate will turn you to
To wash and scrub the paintwork if there's nothing else to do.

At seven bells the watch is called; our Captain comes on deck.
Then he is growling at the mate if the stun'sails are not set,
Then reeve your tack and halyards, your sail now hoist away
Or else you may expect no peace the remainder of the day.

At eight o'clock the watch below they all do come on deck
And arrange around the foremast a job of work to get.
Our second mate comes forward "Take this, take that!" you know
Then "Bear a hand, me hearties, and up aloft you go!"

The watch on deck they go below to try to get some sleep.
Our forecastle it leaks like hell our bunks are dripping wet.
You scarcely do get turned in and that you all do know
When there is three raps on the gangway, "Reef topsails there below!"

Then out we do turn without any delay.
The mate is calling "Bear a hand! the sails will blow away!"
Then we do get on deck to pull and haul like hell;
Then "Lay aloft, my hearties, and your earings hand out well!"

It is there upon the topsail yard the wind, it blows a gale.
The seas they do run mountains high, with snow and sleet and hail.
But it is no use in growling, boys, the sails they must be reefed
Although our fingers are so numb we hold on with our teeth!

It is there upon our weather yardarm there lies our striker and blower.
Saying "Watch the weather there to leeward; our sail you now light over!"
Then haul out to leeward. Oh, your points now knot away
Then jump into the rigging boys and down on deck you lay.

Our tops'l yard mast-headed the watch they go below
The watch on deck coils up the ropes and that you all do know
You scarcely do forward get to try to get some breath
When our mate he cries "Come pump her out, it is either life or death!"

Now 'tis seven years and over I have plowed the raging main.
But damn my heart and liver if you e'er catch me again!
For when I get into New York, I'll bid the seas farewell
And the captains, mates and second mates, I'll pitch them all to hell!

Here's a song from personal experience that dispels all romance about the life of a sailor at sea! Collected by Fannie Eckstorm, it was printed in *Songs of American Sailormen* by Joanna Colcord. Colcord suggested "You Gentlemen of England" as a possible melody, and indeed, the 17th century song works well with these lyrics which, like that song, also describe the trials of a sailor. Henry H. Chamberlain and his father were well known characters involved in local business and politics throughout the nineteenth century, particularly with coastal land surveys. A local village developed by Chamberlain bears his name. Mr. Chamberlain became the state senator from Bristol in 1897. His namesake ship, the three-masted schooner *Henry H. Chamberlain,* became stranded during the gale of 1898 in Pemaquid Harbor. Although this song clearly reflects the personal experience of someone who has worked on a sailing ship, we have not found clear evidence that Chamberlain did so. Perhaps a voyage or two as a young man was enough to put him off a career at sea.

Some of the terms used in this song are obscure, so we consulted our friend James Nelson, maritime historian and writer, who tells us:

> The [seventh] stanza is describing the process of reefing a topsail. The men would lay out on the yard and "light" or pull the sail to windward and "pass" or tie the reef earring (a small line used to fasten the upper corners of the sail). Then they would haul the sail back to leeward and do the same. "Your points now knot away" is an easy one; it means to tie the reef points around the yard (the reef points are short lengths of line passed through grommets in the sail and tied around the yard with a reef knot to hold the bulk of the sail.)
>
> When reefing, the weather yardarm was considered the place of honor (such honor I could do without). A friend of mine used to quote this bit of doggerel: "The tar who rides the Flemish horse (the footrope at the yardarm) and reeves the earring through, he sings his song from the windy tops, the best of all the crew."

Striker and blower: According to Stan Hugill, "The word 'blow' was a Packet Rat production meaning 'to knock' or, in a broader sense 'to knock a man down by means of fist, belayin' pin or capstan bar'. Chief Mates in the Western Ocean Packets were known as 'Blowers' Second Mates as 'Strikers' and Third Mates as 'Greasers.'" *Shanties from the Seven Seas* (1984, p. 154).

The House Carpenter (Child 243)

Lyrics: Capt. Lewis F. Gott, Bernard, ME 1926
Fannie Hardy Eckstorm Collection
Tune: Susie Carr Young, Brewer, ME 1928
Phillips Barry Collection
Transcription © 2019 Julia Lane

"I might have married a king's daughter fair,
And she would have married me,
But I've just returned from the salt, salt sea
All for the sake of thee,
All for the sake of thee."

"If you could have married a king's daughter,
I am sure you are much to blame;
For I have wed with a house carpenter,
And Johnnie it is his name,
And Johnnie it is his name."

"If you'll go leave your house carpenter,
And go along with me,
I'll take you where the trees grow tall
On the isle of sweet liberty,
On the isle of sweet liberty."

"If I go and leave my house carpenter,
And go along with thee,
What means have you provided for me
To keep me from slavery,
To keep me from slavery?"

"Oh, don't you see that good light ship
A-standing in to land,
With a hundred and fifty brave young men
Shall be at your command,
Shall be at your command!"

She went upstairs herself to dress,
Very beautiful she was to behold,
For when she walked along the streets
She shone as though she were gold,
She shone as though she were gold.

She took her babe upon her knee,
And she gave him kisses three,
Saying, "Stay at home with your father dear,
For to bear him company,
For to bear him company."

They had not sailed more than two weeks,
I am sure it was not three,
When this cruel mother began to weep,
And to weep most bitterly,
And to weep most bitterly.

"Oh, do you weep for your house carpenter,
Or the dangers of the sea?
Or do you weep for that sweet little babe
That you left when you came with me,
That you left when you came with me."

"I don't weep for my house carpenter,
Nor the dangers of the sea,
But I do weep for the sweet little babe
That I left when I came with thee,
That I left when I came with thee."

They had not sailed more than three weeks,
I am sure it was not four,
When this good ship sprung a leak
And she sank to rise no more,
And she sank to rise no more.

Come all you mothers far and near,
Take warning now by me,
And never sell your babe for gold,
Lest you sink in the salt, salt sea,
Lest you sink in the salt, salt sea.

Smyth and Eckstorm received a copy of this song written down in 1926 by Capt. Lewis F. Gott of Bernard, ME, "as sung by him for many years." These lyrics appear in *British Ballads from Maine* (1929). A tune was later noted and contributed to them by Susie Carr Young of Brewer, who says it was "traditional in her family." Francis Child found the song, also called "The Demon Lover," and published it as #243 in his collection, *The English and Scottish Popular Ballads*. It can be traced to a very popular 1685 ballad entitled "A Warning for Married Women, being an example of Mrs. Jane Reynolds (a West-country woman), born near Plymouth, who, having plighted her troth to a Seaman, was afterwards married to a Carpenter, and at last carried away by a Spirit, the manner how shall be presently recited." The Maine and New England versions leave out the dramatic references to "hell and damnation" or supernatural influences which appear in other variants. We have included an additional verse (in italics) collected by William L. Alderson, for the Library of Congress, from Allen Johnson which he learned in Calais, ME, which does imply an other-worldly quality. The ballad is often confused with another song, "The Ship's Carpenter" or "Handsome Harry" in which the sailor/lover seduces and then murders the unfortunate girl.

Songs of Ships & Sailors

The Rosy Banks of Green

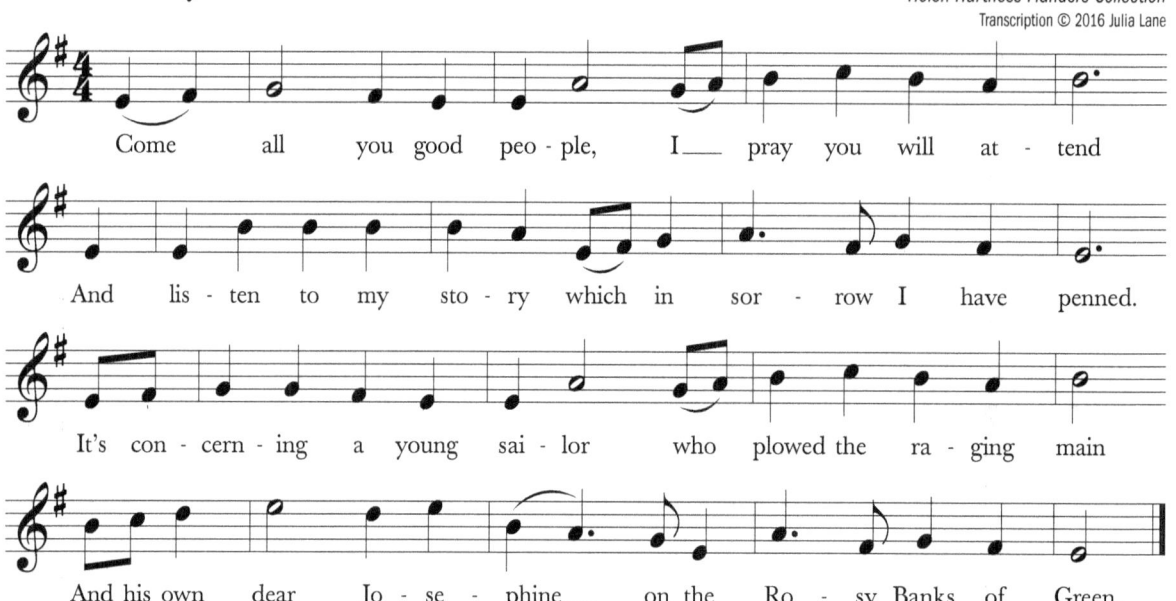

Come all you good people, I pray you will attend
And listen to my story which in sorrow I have penned.
It's concerning a young sailor who plowed the raging main
And his own dear Josephine on the Rosy Banks of Green.

This young couple they had been schoolmates when in early childhood's day
And only as a schoolboy he had stole her heart away.
She was admired by lords and squires but their love would prove in vain
For she dearly loved her sailor on the Rosy Banks of Green.

It was a Sunday evening down by her father's grove
This fair one sat conversing to the lad she dearly loved.
With his kisses and embrace he said "Poor Josephine
Tonight we'll be far from the Rosy Banks of Green."

Her old father was a-listening; 'twas more than he could stand.
He sprung upon those lov-e-yers with loaded gun in hand!
He said "Die, you cursed youth and no more you'll plow the main
For I'll make sure you never leave the Rosy Banks of Green!"

As he aimed the deadly pistol and the fatal trigger drew
Josephine like lightning to her lover's arms she flew!
As the bullet sped its course, so true its aim had been
And they both fell together on the Rosy Banks of Green.

While Josephine lay dying, these words she did say
"It's well my dear old mother did not live to see this day!
With her high seat in Glory a witness she has been
For the murder of her daughter on the Rosy Banks of Green!"

While Charlie he lay dying, these words he did say;
"It's soon I will be lying in the cold and dreary clay."
He embraced her to his heart and he kissed her cheek and chin
And they both died together on the Rosy Banks of Green.

So come all you young lovers I pray you lend an ear
For these two brave lovers and in sorrow shed a tear.
Beneath a marble tombstone down by yon purling stream
Slumber those two innocent lovers on the Rosy Banks of Green.

This seems to be a nautical variant of "The Constant Farmer's Son," in which the suitor is murdered by the girl's brothers, although she survives. Numerous versions of "Rosy Banks" are found in Northeastern Canada, particularly in Newfoundland, although the earliest version I have found there is 1952. Mrs. Flanders recorded four singers in Maine prior to 1945. The song may have migrated with itinerate fishermen and woodsmen. Emma Turner's melody is identical to that of Steve Barlow of Mars Hill, a fair distance away. We have combined their lyrics for a more complete story; Barlow's lyrics are in italics.

The Haven of Rest

Captain Archie Spurling, Cranberry Island, ME 1950
Horace Beck Collection
Original lyrics by H. L. Gilmour 1885
Music by George D. Moore
Transcription ©2019 Julia Lane

My soul in sad exile was out on life's sea,
So burdened with sin and distressed.
Then I heard a sweet voice saying, "Make Me your choice!"
And I entered the Haven of Rest.

CHORUS:
> I've anchored my soul in the Haven of Rest,
> I'll sail the wide seas no more.
> The tempest may sweep over wild, stormy deep;
> In Jesus I'm safe evermore.

I yielded myself to His tender embrace,
In faith taking hold of the Word,
My fetters fell off, and I anchored my soul;
The Haven of Rest is my Lord.

The song of my soul, since the Lord made me whole,
Has been the old story so blest,
Of Jesus, Who'll save whosoever will have
A home in the Haven of Rest.

How precious the thought that we all may recline,
Like John, the belovèd so blest,
On Jesus' strong arm, where no tempest can harm,
Secure in the Haven of Rest.

O come to the Savior, He patiently waits
To save by His power divine;
Come, anchor your soul in the Haven of Rest,
And say, "My Belovèd is mine."

Henry Lake Gilmour (1836–1920), a native of Northern Ireland, went to sea as a teenager to learn navigation. Emigrating to the United States around 1850, he worked as a house painter then served the Union in the Civil War in the 1st New Jersey Cavalry, being captured and imprisoned. After the war, he trained and practiced as a dentist. Joining the Methodist church, he became a Sunday School superintendent and choir director. Attending the many religious camp meetings of the day, Gilmour became in demand as a gospel song leader and worked in that capacity throughout the mid-Atlantic states. Of his compositions, "The Haven of Rest" (1885) is probably his most popular, with lyrics based on Hebrews 6:19 "We have this hope as an anchor for the soul, firm and secure." It appears in over 200 hymnals with music by George D. Moore. In Maine, Captain Spurling was recorded by both Fannie Eckstorm in the 1920s and just before he died in 1950 by Horace Beck. In his dissertation, Horace Beck says that after Spurling's death, he received numerous requests from the captain's neighbors for copies of this song as it was a favorite in the community.

Old Ironsides

Lyrics: H. Meyers 1950, *Horace Beck Collection*
Original poem: George Pope Morris 1802-1864
Music: Bernard Covert 1850
Transcription © 2019 Fred Gosbee

Old Ironsides at anchor lay in the harbor of Mahon.
A dead calm rested on the bay; the waves to sleep had gone
When little Al, the captain's son, a lad both brave and good,
In sport up shroud and rigging ran and on the main truck stood.

A shudder ran through ev'ry vein, all eyes were turned on high.
There stood the boy with dizzy brain, between the sea and sky.
No hold had he above or below; alone he stood in air.
To that far height none dare to go; no aid could reach him there.

We gazed, but not a man could speak, with horror all aghast
In groups, with pallid brow and cheek, we watched the quivering mast
The atmosphere grew thick and hot, and of a lurid hue,
As, riveted unto the spot, stood officers and crew.

The father came on deck, he gasped, "Oh Lord! Thy will be done!"
And suddenly a rifle grasped and aimed it at his son.
"Jump far out into the wave, boy! Jump or I'll fire!" he said,
"The only chance your life can save! Jump!" and he obeyed.

He sank, he rose, he lived, he moved, and for the good ship struck out.
On board we hailed the lad beloved with many a manly shout.
His father drew in silent joy those wet arms 'round his neck,
Then folded to his heart the boy, then fainted on the deck.

Collected from H. Meyers by Horace Beck around 1950, this melodramatic opus was published in 1850 by Oliver Ditson in Boston. According to the cover sheet it was sung "with great applause by Ossian E. Dodge at his fashionable Entertainments throughout the Union." Dodge's trademark was singing genteel, comic songs. He purportedly said, "I will write my own songs, and the public shall learn that a comic song is not necessarily a vulgar one." An earlier setting was made by by Henry Russell, Esq. and published by W. C. Peters in 1845 soon after the poem, titled "The Main Truck or A Leap of Life" was written, by George Pope Morris (1802–1864). The third verse (in italics) is from the original.

My Sailor Boy

Mrs. Fred W. Morse, Isleford, ME 1/22/1934
Mrs. William Currie, West Enfield, ME 1/3/1934
Fannie Hardy Eckstorm Collection
Tune: Susie Carr Young / *Phillips Barry Collection*
Transcription © Julia Lane 2019

The sailor's life is a roving life.
It robbed me of my heart's delight.
It caused me to lament and mourn
As I sadly wait for his return.

It was early, early all in the spring
When my true love sailed to serve the king.
The raging seas and the winds blew high
Which parted me from my sailor boy.

Oh, father, father build me a boat
Far on the ocean I mean to float
And every ship that will pass by
I'll hail and inquire for my sailor boy.

I had not sailed long over the deep
When a big ship I come by chance to meet.
"Oh, Captain, Captain, do tell me true
Is my dear Willie on board with you?"

"What color clothes did your Willie wear?
What sort of hair had your true love?"
"He had a short blue jacket and it trimmed all round
And his curly locks they were hanging down."

"Oh, indeed fair lady, he is not here
For he is drowned I sadly fear
For it's on that green isle that we passed by
I lost four more and your sailor boy."

She wrung her hands and tore her hair
Like one distracted or in despair.
She dashed her small boat against a rock
Saying "How can I live when my true love's lost?"

"I will go home and write a song;
I'll write it true and write it long
And at every line I'll shed a tear
And every verse I'll cry 'Willie dear!'"

"Go dig my grave both long and deep.
Place a marble stone at my head and feet
And on my bosom place a turtle dove
So the world may know that I died for love."

Come on now sailors, dress in black;
Come on, fair maids, we will dress alike
From the Captain's cabin to the mast so high
In mourning black for your sailor boy.

An early broadside of this song was printed in Limerick, Ireland, in 1780. The first and last verses are from a set of lyrics sent in to Fannie Eckstorm dated January 3, 1934, by Mrs. William Currie, West Enfield, ME, as sung by her mother in Ireland many years before. A note with the manuscript asked that Mrs. Currie's name not be printed in the newspaper. The first two lines of the second verse are the same as the song "Early, Early in the Spring" by Kneeland, though the storyline differs. Versions of "The Sailor Boy/ Sweet William" are found in collections throughout the U.S., U.K., and Ireland.

Songs of Ships & Sailors

The Female Smuggler

Charles Finnemore, Bridgewater, ME 9/30/1941
Helen Hartness Flanders Collection
Transcription © 2016 Julia Lane

Come lis-ten a-while and you'll soon hear, By the ra-ging seas lived a mai-den fair.

Her fa-ther fol-lowed a smug-gling trade, Like a war-like he-ro, like a war-like he-ro

That ne-ver was a-fraid.

Come listen awhile and you'll soon shall hear,
By the raging seas lived a maiden fair.
Her father followed a smuggling trade,
Like a war-like hero, like a war-like hero
That never was afraid.

In seamen's clothing young Jane did go,
Just like a sailor from top to toe.
In her belt two daggers prepared for war,
Went the female smuggler, went the female smuggler
That never feared a scar.

She had not sailed far from the land
When death's dark sail put her to a stand,
"Those saucy pirates," young Jane did cry
 Sayed the female smuggler, sayed the female smuggler,
"We'll conquer, boys, or die."

Then close alongside those two vessels came.
"Cheer up," sayed Jane, "Boys we'll board the same,
We'll take our chances to rise or fall,"
 Sayed the female smuggler, sayed the female smuggler,
"I never feared a ball."

We beat those pirates and took their store
And soon returned to Old England's shore;
Like a gay young dandy she marched along,
This young female smuggler, this young female smuggler
And sweetly sung a song.

She had not traveled far on the shore
Till she was met by the Commeedore
"Stand and deliver or you shall fall,"
But the female smuggler, but the female smuggler
Sayed, "I never feared a ball."

"What do you mean?" sayed the Commeedore
"I mean to fight, for my father's poor,"
She drew a dagger and ran him through.
This young female smuggler, this young female smuggler
Then to her father flew.

But she was followed by the blockade,
In iron strong they put this fair maid;
The day that she was to be tried,
This young female smuggler, this young female smuggler
Was dresséd like a bride.

The Commeedore against her did appear,
His health restored and from danger cleared
And when he saw to his great surprise,
It was a female smuggler, it was a female smuggler
That fought him in disguise.

The Commeedore to the jury sayed
"My heart won't let me persecute this maid
Pardon, I ask on my bended knee!
She's a valiant maiden, she is a valiant maiden,
So, pardon if you please."

"Why do you pardon?" said a gentleman,
"To make her my bride now it is my plan
And I'll live happy forevermore
With my female smuggler, with my female smuggler"
Then said the Commodore.

There are many variations on the story of the "female sailor." Although some are based on truth, others, like this, are pure fantasy. Seemingly related to the song, "Willam Taylor," this is a wonderful adventure of an intrepid young woman determined to live life her way. Although the ending is a bit of a letdown it is indicative of the time and culture in which the song thrived. This song was so popular that its tune was specified for numerous other broadsides. Special thanks are due to Steve Woodbury for his thorough research regarding the many variants of this song.

The Faithful Sailor Boy

Jack McNally, Staceyville, ME 9/25/1940
Helen Hartness Flanders Collection
Transcription © 2017 Julia Lane

'Twas a cold November day when snow lay on the ground,
A sailor boy stood on the deck of a ship that was outward bound.
A lassie, she stood by his side, shed many's a bitter tear
And when he pressed her to his heart he whispered in her ear:

CHORUS:
   "Goodbye, my love, my own true love, this parting gives me pain.
   You'll be my hope and guiding star till I return again.
   My thoughts will be on you, my love, when storms are raging high.
   So fare you well; remember me, your faithful sailor boy."

'Twas in a gale the ship set sail; the lass was standing nigh.
She watched the vessel out of sight till tears bedimmed her eyes.
She prayed to God, to Him above to guide him on his way;
Her loving prayers for him that night re-echoed on the main.

But sad to say, the ship returned without her sailor boy
For he had died while on the main; the flag was half-mast high.
And when his comrades come on shore and told her he was dead
They handed her the message that were the last words that he said:

FINAL CHORUS:
> "Goodbye, my love, my own true love, on earth we'll meet no more
> But I hope we'll meet in Heaven above on that eternal shore,
> Where we will be united so far above the sky
> You never will be parted from your faithful sailor boy."

A well-known parlor song from the 19th century, we have found versions of this throughout the English-speaking world. Although there are any number of "Faithful Sailor" ballads from earlier centuries, this particular song seems relatively new. Hugely popular even now, especially in the British Isles, the consistency across versions indicates its origins as a published song. The earliest we've found is a Scottish broadside, "The Sailor Boy," from 1880. Some sources say it was possibly written by Thomas Payne Westendorf (1848–1923) and G.W. Persley (1837–1894) Commercial audio recordings were released by "old-timey" artists on Okeh records as "The Sailor Boy's Farewell" in the 1920s which may also explain its popularity.

Songs of Ships & Sailors

Andrew Barden (Child 250)

Charles Finnemore, Bridgewater, ME 2/28/1948
Helen Hartness Flanders Collection
Transcription © 2017 Julia Lane

There was three bro-thers in old Scot-a-land, In old Scot-a-land did dwell.

And they did cast lots to see which of them Would go rob-bing all on the salt sea, sea, sea,

Would go rob-bing all on the salt sea.

There was three brothers in old Scot-a-land,
In old Scot-a-land did dwell.
And they did cast lots to see which of them
Would go robbing all on the salt sea, sea, sea,
Would go robbing all on the salt sea.

The lot it fell on Andrew Barden
The youngest of the three,
And he went a-robbing all on the salt sea
To maintain his two brothers and he, he, he
To maintain his two brothers and he

As he had sailed out one fine summer's morn
Just as the day did appear
He saw this large vessel a-sailing far off
And at length it come sailing quite near, quite near
Till at length it come sailing quite near.

"Whose ship, whose ship?" cried Andrew Barden
"Whose ship, I pray tell me?"
"I'm a rich merchant ship from old Eng-a-land.
Will you please to let me pass by, by, by,
Will you please to let me pass by?"

"Oh no, oh no," cried Andrew Barden
"That thing it never can be!
Your ship and your cargo I will take away
And your bodies I'll leave in the sea, sea, sea,
And your bodies I'll leave in the sea."

When the news to Eng-a-land came,
When King Hen-ery wore the crown
That his rich merchant ship it was taken away
And his merry men all they were drowned, drowned, drowned,
And his merry men all they were drowned.

"Go build me a ship," said Captain Charles Stuart,
"And make it of oak so sure,
 If I don't git that Andrew Barden
 I'll never come back on shore, shore, shore
 I'll never come back on shore."

 So, they built him a ship out of oak so strong
 And covered it over with brass
 With a hundred and ten of bold-hearted men
 To bear him companee, nee, nee,
 To bear him companee.

 As he had sailed out one cold winter's morn
 Just as the day did appear,
 He saw this large vessel a-sailing far off
 Till at length it come sailing quite near, near, near
 Till at length it come sailing quite near.

"Whose ship, whose ship?" cried Captain Charles Stuart
"Whose ship, I pray tell me?"
"I'm a bonny Scotch robber from old Scot-a-land.
 Will you please to let me pass by, by, by
 Will you please to let me pass by?"

"Oh no, oh no," cried Captain Charles Stuart,
"Oh no, that never can be.
 Your ship and your cargo I will take away
 And your bodies I'll heave in the sea, sea, sea
 And your bodies I'll heave in the sea."

"Come on, come on," cried Andrew Barden,
"I value you not one pin.
 If you're brass outside it makes a fine show;
 I am good steel within, within,
 I am good steel within."

 It was broadside for broadside each other did pour
 And cannons like thunder did roar
 And Captain Charles Stuart took Andrew Barden
 And he was hung on old Eng-a-land's shore, shore, shore
 He was hung on old Eng-a-land's shore.

One of many versions of Sir Andrew Barton (Child Ballad 167) and Henry Martin (Child Ballad 250) both of which have their origins in a song first printed in the early 17th century telling of the exploits of one Sir Andrew Barton and his two brothers, John and Robert. Although he carried a letter of marque from King James to act as a privateer, Barton allegedly flaunted this authority and engaged in outright piracy, much to the displeasure of His Majesty. The "Captain Charles Stuart" in this version of the song historically belongs circa 1812 as he was an American naval hero of that era. At least nine versions of this song have been recorded in Maine.

Songs of Ships & Sailors

The Loss of the *Albion*

Lydia Tenant, E. Orland, ME 5/12/1942
Helen Hartness Flanders Collection
Transcription © 2016 Julia Lane

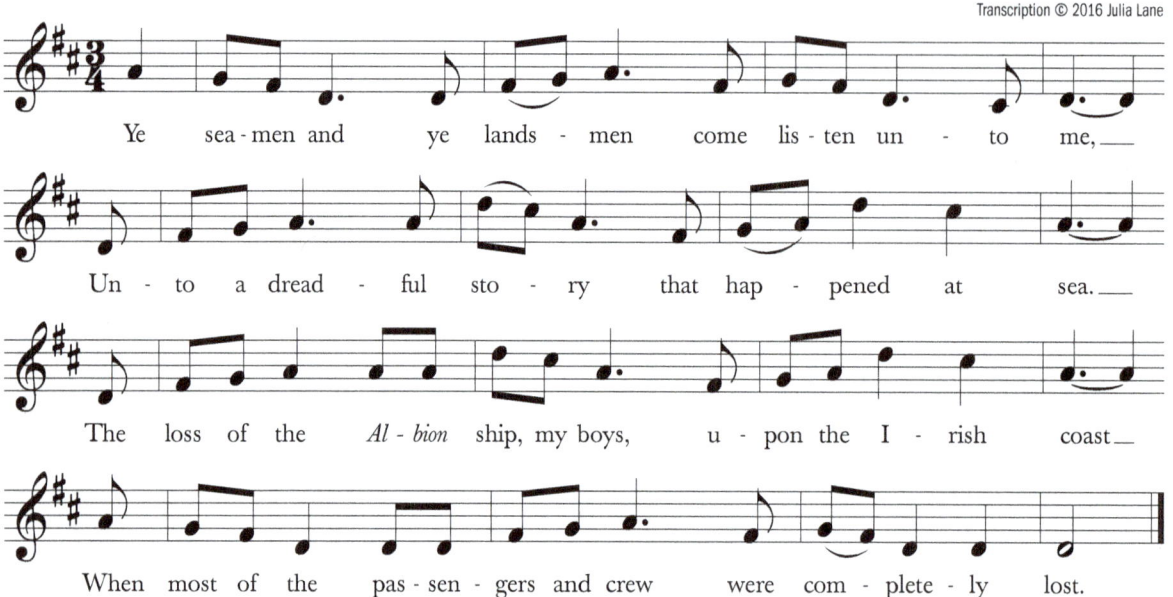

Ye seamen and ye landsmen come listen unto me,
Unto a dreadful story that happened at sea.
The loss of the *Albion* ship, my boys, upon the Irish coast
When most of the passengers and crew were completely lost.

'Twas on the first of April, when first we did set sail,
Kind Neptune did protect us with a sweet and pleasant gale,
Until about the twentieth a storm there did arise,
The raging billows loud did roar and dismal were the skies.

'Twas on a Sunday morning, the land we did espy;
At two o'clock, we make it clear, the seas were mountains high,
The outward wind began to blow and heavy squalls came on,
Which caused the passengers to weep and sailors for to mourn.

All prudent sail we carried to keep us clear from land,
Expecting every moment that our vessel she would strand.
Our foretops'l was split, my boys, our foreyard took away,
The mainmast by the deck was broke, and mizzen swept away.

Our Captain was washed overboard, into the boundless deep,
Which caused all there that was on board to lament and to weep.
Unto the pumps we lashed ourselves, most dreadful for to know,
And many a noble soul, my boys, they overboard did go.

We had a lady fair on board, Miss Powell was her name,
Whose name deserves to be engraved upon the list of fame;
She wished to take her turn at pump, her precious life to save,
No sooner was her wish denied, then she met with a wat'ry grave.

All night in this condition we were tossing to and fro,
At three o'clock in the morning we were in the midst of woe;
Full twenty-seven men on deck, with each a broken heart;
The *Albion* struck against a rock and midship, she did part.

Our passengers were twenty-nine, when from New York she sailed,
With twenty-five bold sailor lads as ever crossed the main;
Full fifty-four, she had on board, when first she did set sail
And only nine escaped the wreck to tell this dreadful tale.

So now that noble vessel, the *Albion*, she is lost,
Although the mighty ocean, she so often times had crossed;
Our noble captain, he is lost, a man, a sailor bold,
And many a noble soul are lost and many a heart laid cold.

The *Albion* was one of the first packet ships operated by the Black Ball Line offering trans-Atlantic crossings on a regular schedule. The ship, commanded by Captain John Williams, with a crew of twenty-five and carrying twenty-three cabin and six steerage passengers, sailed from New York on the 1st of April, 1822. After a pleasant passage with moderate weather, on the evening of April 21, 1822, she encountered a tremendous gale off the south coast of Ireland. In the initial blast, the masts were carried away, the hatches driven in and six of the crew swept overboard. Through the night the *Albion*, drowning in the relentless waves, was buffeted by the gale and drifted towards the craggy cliffs near the Head of Kinsale. At 3:00 a.m. she ran aground and broke up at the foot of the cliffs. As the day dawned, local people were forced to watch in horror as the survivors perished one by one, it being impossible for them to effect a rescue. Of the 54 people on board only nine survived. The wreck created a sensation as several of the passengers were notable personalities of the day. Horrific detailed eyewitness reports appeared in newspapers on both sides of the Atlantic, resulting in various poems and broadsides commemorating the tragedy. The place where the ship struck, in Garretstown, Kinsale Ireland, is still called Albion Rock. A lifeboat was subsequently established on this part of the coast to prevent further loss of life. The verse in italics is from another virtually identical version of the song that was collected by Fannie Eckstorm and appears in her *Minstrelsy of Maine* (1927). Mrs. Eckstorm remarks: "The song was immensely popular and still persists. We might have had numerous copies of it."

Hull's Victory

American Advocates, Hallowell, ME 1812
Transcription © 2019 Julia Lane

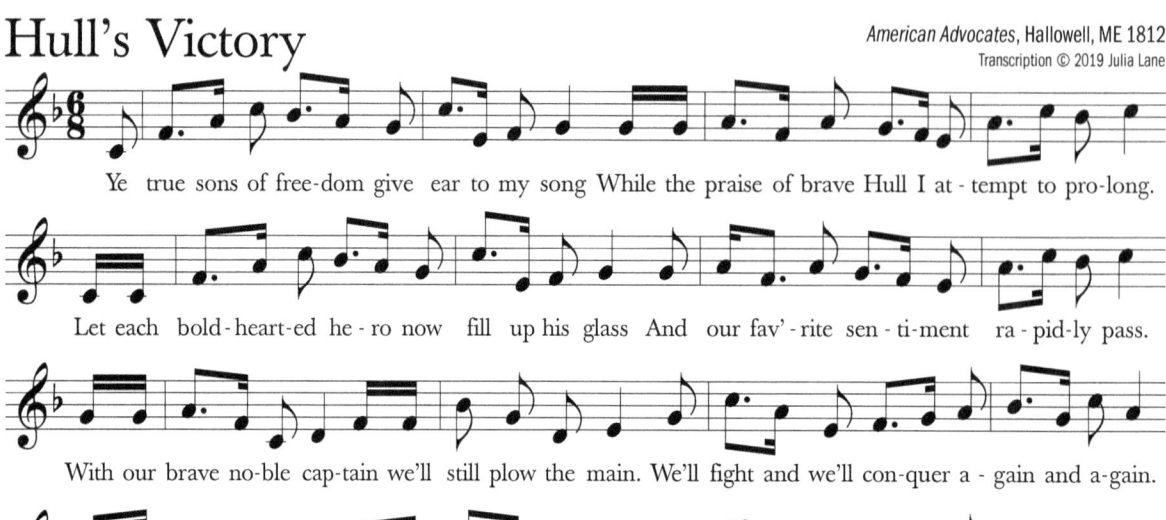

Ye true sons of freedom give ear to my song
While the praise of brave Hull I attempt to prolong.
Let each bold-hearted hero now fill up his glass
And our favorite sentiment rapidly pass.
With our brave noble captain we'll still plow the main.
We'll fight and we'll conquer again and again.
    With our brave noble captain we'll still plow the main.
    We'll fight and we'll conquer again and again.

With a fine springing breeze, our sails they were bent,
And with hearts full of joy to the ocean we went,
In the fam'd *Constitution* a taut and staunch boat,
As ever was seen on the water afloat.
With our brave noble Captain, we plow'd the deep main,
And when he commands, we are ready again.   [*repeat last two lines each time*]

On the twentieth of August, a sail we espied,
We hove to, and soon we came up alongside;
The drum beat to quarters, to quarters we run,
And each tar bravely swore to stand fast to his gun.
Our Captain so brave, as we sail'd on the main,
Now bid us a harvest of glory to gain.

A broadside the foe quickly into us pour'd,
We return'd 'em the favor dircct on the word,
Each heart was undaunted, no bosom knew fear,
And we car'd not a snap for the saucy *Guerriere*.
With our noble commander we fought on the main,
And we'll conquer with him when he bids us again.

The balls now flew thick, and quite warm was the play,
Their masts and their rigging was soon shot away,
We shatter'd their hull with all possible speed,
With our good spunky bulldogs, of true Yankee breed,
'Twas thus with our captain we fought on the main,
With him a rich harvest of glory to gain.

The blood from the enemy's scuppers run fast,
All hopes of subduing us now were quite past.
So, they wisely concluded, by hob or by nob
That 'twas best to give o'er what they thought a bad job
With our true noble Captain, we'll fight on the main,
And we hope that with him, we'll soon conquer again.

The Britons had seldom before seen the like,
For we rak'd 'em so clean, they'd no colours to strike;
So, a gun on their lee they were forc'd to let fly,
To inform us they didn't quite all wish to die.
'Twas thus with our captain we fought on the main,
And we're ready brave boys, to fight with him again.

In twenty-five minutes, the business was done,
For they didn't quite relish such true Yankee fun;
So, we kindly receiv'd 'em on board our good ship,
Many cursing the day when they took their last trip.
With our brave noble captain we'll still plow the main.
We'll fight and we'll conquer again and again.

Now homeward we're bound with a favoring breeze,
As full of good humor and mirth as you please,
Each true-hearted sailor partakes of the glass,
And drinks off a health to his favorite lass.
With our brave noble captain we've plow'd the deep main,
With him we the laurels of glory did gain.

Now success to the good *Constitution*, a boat
Which her crew will defend while a plank is afloat,
Who never will flinch, or in duty e'er lag,
But will stick to the last by the American flag.
So true to our colors we'll ever remain,
And we'll conquer for freedom again and again.

When again we shall plow old Neptune's blue wave,
May honors still circle the brows of the brave,
And should our bold foes wish to give us a pull
We'll show 'em the good *Constitution* and Hull.
And now with three cheers ere we sail to the main,
We will greet our brave Captain again and again.

The battle described here took place on August 19, 1812, some 600 miles east of Boston, when Captain Hull, commander of the USS *Constitution* in the new American Navy defeated Captain D'Acres who commanded HMS *Guerriere*, the pride of the British. The surprising victory inspired numerous commemorative songs, poems, dances and even a quilt pattern. A contemporary broadside published in the *American Advocates*, Sept. 17, 1812, was printed in Hallowell, MA (ME post 1820) as "Hull's Victory, or, Huzza for the *Constitution*" without reference to an appropriate tune. The text appeared in eleven songsters between 1813 and 1818.

  Although a "New Patriotic Song" by this name was composed by John Bray and there is dance tune named "Hull's Victory," which is popular among New England fiddlers to this day, neither was suitable for these lyrics. We considered using English composer William Boyce's song "Heart of Oak," which is coincidentally and ironically the official song of the Royal Navy, as it has a similar structure and refrain. We then discovered that the ballad was subsequently published in William McCarty's *American National Songbook of 1842* and specifies the tune: "Paul Jones Victory." The only music of this name that we could find was the broadside "Paul Jones Victory," which in turn specifies the tune "Stick a Pin There." This music does fit these "Hull's Victory" lyrics, and so we have transcribed it here. (see also The *Constitution* & the *Guerriere*)

Old Horse

Composite Eckstorm, Colcord & Hugill circa 1930
Set by Dick Swain to a traditional tune
Transcription © 2019 Julia Lane

FIRST VERSE & CHORUS:
Old horse, old horse, what brought you here
From Saccarap' to Portland Pier?
All worn out with sore abuse
Then salted down for sailors' use.

Old horse, old horse, both far and near,
You carted stone this many a year
Along the rough and dusty track
Where you fell down and broke your back.

In strongest brine you have been sunk,
Until you're hard and coarse as junk
And we poor sailors standing near
Must eat you though you look so queer.

Between the mainmast and the pump
I'm salted down in great big junks.
To eat such poor and wretched fare
You're food for every hard-worked tar

Old horse, old horse, we'd have you know
That to the galley you must go.
The cook without a sign of grief
Will boil you down and call you beef

The sailors they do me despise,
They turn me o'er and damn my eyes,
Cut off my meat and pick my bones
And throw the rest to Davy Jones.

Now if you don't believe this story's true
Look in the barr'l and you'll find his shoe

Also known as the "Sailor's Grace," this song, sung by sailors throughout the world, is thought to have originated in Maine. Saccarapa is the old name for Westbrook, where there was a quarry that provided ballast stones for ships on the Portland waterfront. Horses would pull the heavy cartloads until they died of exhaustion and then, according to tradition, they were slaughtered and their meat salted and sold as beef to feed sailors on board ship. According to Horace Beck, the casks that contained the meat had handle grips made of horseshoes. This is a composite of several variants noted down by Fannie Eckstorm, Joanna Colcord, and Stan Hugill set by historian/singer Dick Swain to an appropriately dismal old tune. Another version, called "Poor Old Man," (see page 74) has a shanty-type chorus and was collected by Roland Palmer Gray from Mr. Charles Creighton, of Thomaston, ME. A more recent recording of a fragment was made of Robert French in Franklin, ME, on March 10, 1962 by Sister Poulin, and is available from the Maine Folklife Center. The song is not to be confused with the shanty "Poor Old Horse," which was sung to accompany the "Dead Horse" ceremony performed when the sailors had worked the first month and paid off their advance wages. A landsmen's version, about an elderly farm horse, was collected by Eckstorm from Mary Hindle.

The *Nightingale*

Jack McNally, Stacyville, ME 5/10/1942
Helen Hartness Flanders Collection
Transcription © 2017 Julia Lane

My love, he was a rich farmer's son.
His come-lye person my heart had won.
When I think on him my courage fails
Since my love was lost in the *Nightingale*.

My parents were of a high degree
And my true love not so rich as they.
They sent a press gang who did not fail
For to press my love in the *Nightingale*.

Oh, the *Nightingale* was a vessel stout
Well rigged, well manned and well fitted out
With fifty guns the truth I do tell;
Five hundred on board of the *Nightingale*.

On the eighteenth day of November last
The wynds they blew a tremendious blast.
They lost their spars likewise every sail.
What a dismal wreck was the *Nightingale*.

Then a sea o'erwhelmed them both fore and aft,
Not many men on the decks was left.
Her sides stove in and her timbers failed;
To the bottom went the brave *Nightingale*.

And the very night that my love was lost
He appeared to me a frightful ghost.
He appeared to me being cold and pale
Just as he was lost in the *Nightingale*.

These words he spoke with lamenting cries,
"In the Bay of Biscay my body lies,"
Saying, "Nancy, dear love, you may bewail
For your love is lost in the *Nightingale*!"

To the mountain green I will make my way,
To the lonesome seashore myself I'll take
And every time that I see a sail
My heart will bleed for the *Nightingale*.

We believe this is not an American song, given the references to the press gang, the number of sailors (which suggest a war ship), and the Bay of Biscay. All these terms led us to look in the Royal Navy loss list which shows the wreck of HMS *Nightingale* in 1674. In 1707, a ship of this name was taken by the French then re-taken by the English and renamed *Fox*. We also found an HMS *Nightingale* circa 1805 during the Napoleanic wars but there is no record of a wreck. Several merchant ships have borne the name although we are reasonably sure, given the evidence, that the song is not about these vessels. In 1851 an extreme clipper dedicated to Jenny Lind, "The Swedish Nightingale," was built in Eliot, ME. The ship's interesting, if tragic, career includes duty as a tea clipper, the slave trade and as a supply ship for the Union, finally wrecking with all hands lost in 1893. Canadian songwriter Stan Rogers memorializes the wreck of an English coal transport with this name in his song "Flowers of Bermuda," but again, we are convinced the ship in question belongs to the 18th century British Royal Navy. Versions of the song appear as broadsides, in the 1835 *Forget-me-not Songster* and in collections in the U.K., the U.S., and particularly Northern Ireland. This song was recorded twice by Mr. McNally and this version is a combination of the two, plus speculative lyrics where the recording was indistinct, and additional lyrics from the *Forget-me-not Songster* (in italics).

The Prayer of the Soldier & the Sailor

Charles Finnemore, Bridgewater, ME 10/29/1943
Helen Hartness Flanders Collection
Transcription © 2016 Julia Lane

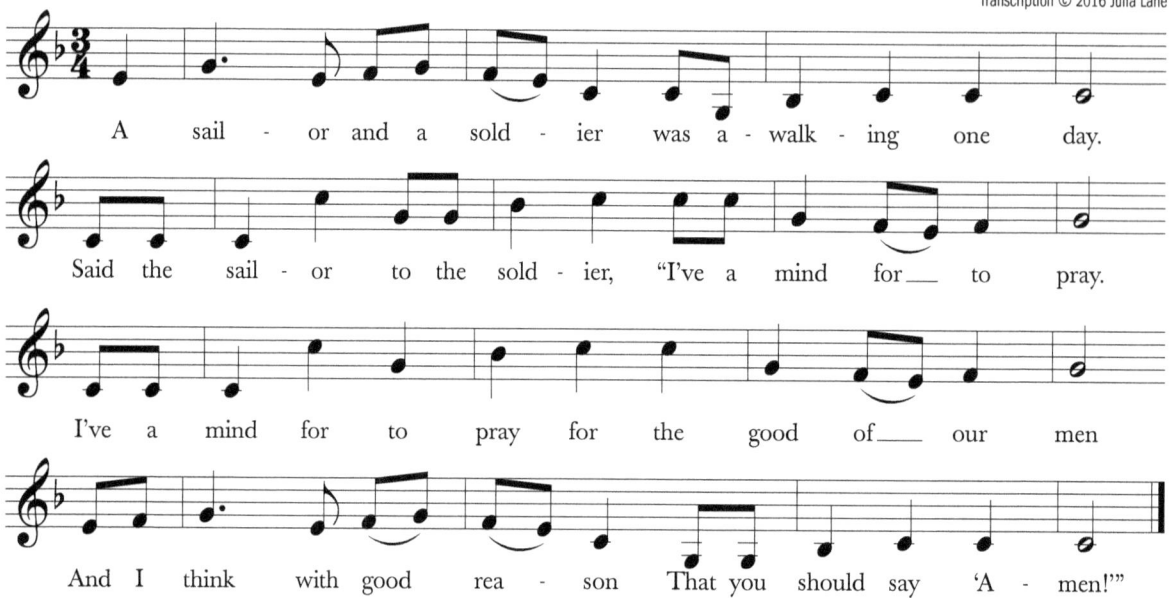

A sailor and a soldier was a-walking one day.
Said the sailor to the soldier, "I've a mind for to pray.
I've a mind for to pray for the good of our men
And I think with good reason
That you should say, 'Amen!'"

"The prayer of my petition is for you and me
May the heavens protect us wherever we be
And if we do meet a pretty girl we'll embrace
May the God of heaven bless us."
Said the soldier, "Amen!"

"It is for our justice they give for a fee
They give a case against you and a case against me
They will take away our money and they will treat us with disdain
May the hibble triple Devil damn them!"
Said the soldier, "Amen!"

"It is for our lawyer they plead for their fee
They plead a case against you and a case against me
And they'll leave us in the cold jail and there we'll remain
May the hibble triple Devil damn them!"
Said the soldier, "Amen!"

"It is for the doctor they ride for their fee
They give ague to you and blister to me
It's all to their money they care not for our pain
May the hibble triple Devil damn them!"
Said the soldier, "Amen!"

"It is for the minister, they preach and they pray
They take all your money and senses away
Send you to hell at last and there you remain
May the hibble triple Devil damn them!"
Said the soldier, "Amen!"

"It is for the cobbler they take them as they rise
For every pair of shoes they will tell full fifty lies
And the rest of the mechanics and that sort are not lame
So we'll rank them among the rest."
Said the soldier, "Amen!"

"It is for the merchant, they most of them cheat
As long as our cash lasts they'll flatter and treat
But when our purse is empty no favor we gain
May the hibble triple Devil damn them!"
Said the soldier, "Amen!"

"It is for the farmer that follows the plow
They get a nice living by the sweat of their brow
They have a wife and three children and a home for a friend
May the kind heaven bless them!"
Said the soldier, "Amen!"

This song is a commentary on the value of the working class and disdain for the professional class. There are several variations of the song, the most well-known being the "Topman and the Afterguard." It seems likely that our song is older than that since, like earlier variants, it includes complaints about other professions, whereas the characters in "Topman and the Afterguard" restrict their complaints to personnel on their ship. Mr. Finnemore garbles the original refrain, "May the Devil double triple damn them!" perhaps to try to reduce its profanity. A tangential version of the song has the sailor and soldier praying for pleasurable things like breweries and brothels and tends to be vulgar. The song has been collected in the Southern U.S. and appears in W. L. Fagan's *Southern War Songs* (1892). These may all be based on "The Mare and the Foal" which appears in the John Bell Song Collection from Northumberland, circa 1810–20:

The Mare and the Foal (excerpt)

A mare and a foal they ran in great speed,
The mare from the Bible began for to read,
"Stay," said the foal, "before you begin,
Whatever you pray for I'll answer, Amen."

"We'll pray for the millers who grind us our corn,
For they are the biggest rogues that ever were born;
Instead of one sackful they'll take two for toll,
May the devil take millers." "Amen" said the foal.

The *Lady of the Lake*

Charles Fennimore, Bridgewater, ME 9/1941
Helen Hartness Flanders Collection
Transcription © 2019 Julia Lane

As I walked out one evening down by the banks of Clyde,
It was near the town of sweet Dundee, a bonny lass I spied.
Her doleful lamentations did me greatly surprise
And her crysthal tears in torrents rolled from her tender eyes.

I being unobservéd to her I quickerlye drew near,
Not knowing that it was the voice of my Eliza dear,
Her doleful lamentations did me greatly surprise
And her crysthal tears in torrents rolled from her tender eyes.

I stepped up to this maiden and unto her did say,
"Why weep you here, my bonny lass, come tell to me, I pray,"
And turning 'round, "Young man," she sayed, "I pray don't trouble me,
When I'm in grief I find relief beneath this willow tree."

I said, "My pretty fair maid, now I would like to know,
What is the cause of all your grief, your misery and woe?"
"If this be all, young man," she sayed, "That you require of me,
My story I will tell to you beneath this willow tree.

"'Twas once I loved a sailor by the name of Willie Brown
And in the *Lady of the Lake* he left fair Belfast town,
With full five hundred emigrants bound for Amerikay
When on the coast of Newfoundland they were all cast away."

I says, "My bonny lassie, I in that vessel went
Along with your love, Willie Brown some happy hours I spent;
He was my loyal com-me-rade in the *Lady of the Lake*
When off the coast of Newfoundland his leave from me did take.

"It was out on the main ocean five hun-der-ed miles from shore
A northeast wind mountaineous high, down on our vessel bore;
The *Lady of the Lake* that night was into pieces rent
And all excepting thirty-four, down to the bottom went.

"Your Willie Brown among the rest, he too was cast away.
Before the ship in pieces went, those words I heard him say,
'Now fare you well, Eliza Gray, I fear your heart will break
When you get news that I am lost in the *Lady of the Lake*!'"

"If this be all, young man," she sayed, "If what you say is true,
Here's to all earthly pleasures, to them I bid adieu,
The rest of my life, a single maid I do intend to live,
So I pray, young man, don't trouble me beneath this willow shade."

I said, "My pretty fair maid, from weeping now refrain,
You see I'm spared once more to see my native land again
Here is a token you gave me when I left Belfast Cape
It bears the bonny likeness of my Eliza Gray."

Yet another song where the long-absent sailor tests the faithfulness of his true love. The "token" this time is not a ring, but a locket with her picture. Otherwise the song follows this very popular story line. It is a rather rare song, though it was also collected by Sam Henry in Ballymoney, Northern Ireland in 1938 and there is one undated broadside in the National Museum of Scotland. Interestingly, the ship's name is that of an immigrant brig that left Belfast, Northern Ireland, bound for Quebec on April 8, 1833. On May 11, the *Lady of the Lake* (later called "The *Little Titanic*") struck an iceberg and sank 250 miles east of Cape St. Francis, Newfoundland. Over 200 Irish immigrants died due to the negligence of the ship's intoxicated captain and crew who were miraculously able to save themselves. They and surviving passengers spent 75 hours in open boats before being picked up by passing ships. As tragic as this event was, it is curious that we could find no other song commemorating it. Another ship, also called *Lady of the Lake*, left Londonderry in June the same year and came safely to Wilmington, NC.

Songs of Ships & Sailors

Captain Fielding's Tragedy

Frank Tracy, Brewer, ME 10/7/1941
Tune: Hanford Hayes
Helen Hartness Flanders Collection
Transcription © 2016 Julia Lane

My name it is George Jones, sir, I'm from the county Clare.
I quit my aged parents; I left them living there.
I being inclined on roving at home I would not stay,
And much against my parents' will I shipped and went to sea.

My last ship was the *Salamdine*; I shudder at her name.
I joined her in Valperey, down on the Spanish Main.
I shipped as cabin steward, which proved a fatal day,
When a demon came on board of us and led us all astray.

He said he'd work his passage. The ship was homeward bound
With copper ore and silver worth many thousand pounds.
Besides, two cabin passengers on board of us did come:
The one was Mr. Fielding and the other one was his son.

'Twas on a Sunday morning when this horrid deed was done
When Fielding took his Bible, he swore us one by one
Thus, Fielding first induced us to do this horrid crime
Although we might have prevented it had we begun in time.

'Twas on a Monday morning I'm sorry to relate
We commenced our desperate enterprise when first we killed our mate.
Then next we killed our captain and overboard him threw,
Then next we killed our carpenter and three more of our crew.

The watch lay in their hammocks when the work of death begun;
We called them up; as they came up we killed them one by one.
Poor unexpected victims lay in their beds asleep,
We called them up and murdered them and threw them in the deep.

The firearms and weapons all we threw into the sea.
He said he'd steer for Newfoundland, to which we did agree.
We found with Captain Fielding, for which he lost his life,
A brace of loaded pistols, likewise a carving knife.

His son, he begged for mercy for he was all alone,
But his sad tale was soon cut short and overboard was thrown.
We served him as his father who met a watery grave;
We buried son and father beneath the stormy waves.

And next it was agreed upon before the wind to keep.
We had the world before us; we were on the trackless deep.
We ofttimes kept before the wind as we could do no more
And on the twenty-ninth of May were shipwrecked on shore.

To Newgate we were taken, bound down in iron chain,
Confessing to our deadly crimes and all whom we had slain.
So fare you well, my parents dear, I'll never see you more.
So fare you well, my own sweetheart, you're the girl that I adore.

On February 8, 1844, the British barque *Saladin* left Valparaiso with a crew of twelve, under the command of Captain Alexander Mackenzie, carrying a cargo of guano. Unbeknownst to the crew, she was also carrying over 7,000 silver dollars, a pile of 13 silver bars and 90 tons of copper. Two passengers, a Captain George Fielding and his twelve-year-old son, had engaged passage to London. On May 21, 1844, the ship was found stranded near Country Harbor, Nova Scotia, with only six men aboard, all drunk and acting suspiciously. The last entry in the ship's log was for April 14, 1844. Authorities soon realized that horrific events had taken place and investigations ensued that led to Canada's last piracy trial.

It seems that the passenger, George Fielding, was himself an unscrupulous man wanted by Peruvian authorities for smuggling. He had seen the valuable cargo and, through threats and promises of riches, seduced members of the crew into mutiny and the murder of Capt. Mackenzie and other crew members. Fielding took over as captain, but it soon became evident to the remaining crew that he was not to be trusted. They dispatched him and his son to the mercy of the Atlantic leaving only six men alive aboard *Saladin*. The mutineers then decided to ground the ship in Nova Scotia and abscond with the cargo but were apprehended almost immediately upon landing. As the truth of their adventure was revealed, the six were taken to trial in Halifax charged with piracy and murder. The jury was only out fifteen minutes before returning guilty verdicts for George Jones, William Johnston, John Hazelton and Charles Anderson on charges of mutiny, murder and piracy. The four were sentenced to hanging. Carr and Galloway, who, it seems, had been coerced by the others, were found not guilty of their part in the mutiny. It seems that the multitudes attending the execution were particularly impressed with George Jones's last speech and this song was made shortly afterwards. Collector Horace Beck has found another song about the *Saladin* called "George Augustus Anderson," which also recounts the heinous crime. The lyrics in italics are from *Folk Songs of Canada* by Edith Fowkes.

The Miser's Daughter

Mrs. Mary Hindle, Bangor, ME 9/12/1929
Fannie Hardy Eckstorm Collection
Tune from Walt Wermouth, Walton, NY
Norman Cazden Collection / Folksongs of the Catskills 1982
Transcription © 2018 Julia Lane

In London's fair city a miser did dwell.
He had one only daughter whom a sailor loved well.
Now when this old miser was out of the way
She was with her jovial sailor by night and by day.

When her old father came this for to know,
He swore his revenge on fair Sarah's beau,
He declared his fair Sarah should ne'er be his bride,
He transported the sailor out on the ocean wide.

Straightway to his captain, "Good news I have to tell,
I have a young sailor as a transport to sell,
Oh, send him a-sailing far over the sea,
And he'll never return to London the fair city to see."

"O daughter, O daughter, good news I have to tell,
I've been to the captain your sailor to sell;
I've sold him to the captain for guineas and gold,
He'll ne'er come back to London that city to behold."

Then swift to the captain this maiden did go,
Says she, "Where is my sailor that my father has sold?
I'll give you the guineas, I'll give you the gold
If you'll give me back my sailor that my father's just sold."

"Oh lady, fair lady, that never can be,
I've sent your young sailor far out o'er the sea,
I've sent him a-sailing, far over the main
And he'll ne'er return to London the fair city again."

Cursed be my father! He has ruined me
Blessed be my mother wherever she be
I will go down to my cottage and sit myself down
All for my young sailor I will sigh and moan.

A popular late 18th century broadside, this version became a favorite in Southern England into the 20th century but is not often found in the U.S. We have added the standard enigmatic last verse from the broadside (in italics) to complete the story. Another Maine version, titled "London's Fair City" collected by Ives, is only a fragment but the singer describes a tragic ending. Mrs. Hindle told the collector that she learned this from Eunice (Hamilton) Buck, of Monson and Parkman, who "learned her songs of the old settlers." Lacking a tune from Maine, we have used that sung by Walt Wermouth of Walton, NY called "There was an Old Miser" collected by Norman Cazden. The New York variant has a happy ending with the couple reunited.

The Banks of Newfoundland 2

Capt. George Henry Spurling, Isleford, ME 1925
Fannie Hardy Eckstorm Collection
Tune: Traditional
Transcription © 2019 Julia Lane

You rambling boys of Liverpool, I'll have you to beware.
When you go in a Yankee packet ship no dungarees to wear,
But have a big monkey jacket all unto your command,
For there blows some cold nor'westers on the Banks of Newfoundland.

CHORUS:
    We'll wash her and we'll scrub her down with holy stone and sand,
    And we'll bid adieu to the Virgin rocks on the Banks of Newfoundland.

We had one lady fair on board, Bridget Reilly was her name
To her I promised marriage and on me she had a claim.
She tore up her flannel petticoats to make mittens for our hands,
For she could not see the sea boys freeze on the Banks of Newfoundland.

Now, boys, we're off Sandy Hook and the land's all covered with snow.
The tugboat will take our hawser and for New York we will tow,
And when we arrive on the Black Ball dock the boys and girls will stand;
We'll bid adieu to packet sailing and the Banks of Newfoundland.

One of many songs with this title, this song is found more often than "The Banks of Newfoundland 1" (see page 31). It is an old Irish broadside ballad related to an earlier British song describing the tribulation of convicts transported to the penal colony of Van Diemen's Land (Tasmania). This song, adapted to describe the hardships of the voyage across the North Atlantic, became popular with emigrants sailing from Britain to America, and remains in the repertoire of singers from the Canadian Maritimes and New England. In *Minstrelsy of Maine* (p. 222), Mrs. Eckstorm describes another song of this name published in the *Boston Transcript* in May, 1926. This was allegedly written by a sailor from Sherkin Island, Ireland, and describes being stranded on the Banks of Newfoundland during the passage of the ship *Jane* from Baltimore in 1844. Twenty-two passengers and four seamen were lost in the incident. A tune composed by Newfoundland's Chief Justice Francis Forbes in 1820 became the Royal Newfoundland Regiment's official march during World War I.

Songs of Ships & Sailors

The *E. A. Horton*

Judson Carver, West Jonesport, ME 8/20/1942
Helen Hartness Flanders Collection
Transcription © 2016 Julia Lane

Ye sons of Uncle Samuel! come, listen for awhile.
I will tell you of the capture that was made in Yankee style
Of the schooner *E. A. Horton* by her bold undaunted band
Commanded by brave Knowlton, a true son of Yankee land.

The schooner *E. A. Horton* in a British harbor lies,
She was taken by the *Sweepstakes* while cruising in disguise;
Our Treaty they rejected, our Government they defy,
They have captured our fishermen – now, Johnny, mind your eye!

Says bold Knowlton to his comrades, "If you'll but follow me,
We'll take our vessel back again whatever the cost may be!
We are pledged to one another like brothers brave and true
And we'll show those British sailor lads what Yankee boys can do!"

On the first day of October in the year of seventy-one
Those bold undaunted heroes their daring work begun.
While Johnny's boys were sleeping with ruin on their brain
The sons of Uncle Samuel took their vessel back again.

Now the schooner *E. A. Horton* and her gallyant company
From Old Dominion sailed away and many miles to sea.
The cutters couldn't find them though they searched the ocean round
Those gallyant sons of freedom for their native land were bound.

Now there's going to be a bully time in Gloucester town tonight
The heavy guns are firing and the torches burning bright
The bands play Yankee Doodle and they make the bells to ring
Everyone is shouting "Boys, the *Horton* has got in!"

Now the sons of uncle Samuel they warn you to beware.
Come and join the treaty and settle this affair
And learn to do by others as they would do by you
And you'll never abuse your neighbors as old Johnny used to do!

An epic song amongst the New England fisherman, this story of daring escape had currency in the woods as well. On September 1, 1871, the Gloucester fishing schooner *Edward A. Horton*, was seized by the Canadian cutter *Sweepstakes* for fishing inside the three-mile limit. Escorted to Guysborough, Nova Scotia, she was stripped of her sails and secured to a wharf, to be held until a court could decide the case. Her owners had had a vessel seized the previous year and were not confident they could avoid lengthy litigation, but Captain Harvey Knowlton, himself a part owner in the vessel, was determined do all he could to free the schooner. Feigning defeat, he sailed back to Cape Ann, only to return to Canso, NS, three weeks later. Bold plans were laid with Captain "Spud" McDonald, a notorious smuggler, to recapture the *Horton* with a crew of Grand Banks fishermen enlisted in Canso for the venture.

The plan began to unfold October 3rd as the crew sneaked eighteen miles through the woods to hide in a barn outside Guysborough. Meanwhile, Captain Knowlton, in disguise, cased the town for several days locating the loft where the sails were stored and sounding the channel. A clear moonless night with a fresh northwest breeze on Sunday, October 8, favored an outbound vessel. Accordingly, the crew slipped into town in the middle of the night and quietly broke into the sail loft to liberate the *Horton's* suit of canvas. They hurried to the ship where they silently and skillfully restored the sails to spars and mast hoops. Remaining unmolested, as there were no guards and hence no alarm, they were even able to return some sails that had been taken by mistake. By 2:30 a.m. the *Horton* was on her way to Gloucester. On the morning of October 9, Guysborough townspeople gaped red-faced at the empty mooring.

Just before her capture, the *Horton* had been resupplied so there were plenty of provisions and fresh water aboard. Expecting pursuit by the Canadians, Captain Knowlton made for George's Banks, out of Canadian waters, where they rode out a severe easterly gale that had blown up. After the storm passed, the *E. A. Horton* set sail on course for Cape Ann. News of the escape had reached Gloucester and, fearing the Canadians might intercept the schooner on her way home, influential town officials petitioned the government to dispatch U.S. revenue cutters to escort her to safe harbor. The protection proved unnecessary. On October 18, the *Horton* sailed victoriously into Gloucester to the booming of cannon and the ringing of church bells. The next day, schools and businesses were closed as the whole town enjoyed a holiday. A torch-lit parade with brass band led the way to the town hall where Captain Knowlton and his volunteer crew were presented with a $1000 purse that had been gathered by the citizens of the town. The song, by William E. Lakeman, was printed in *Fisherman's Ballads and Songs of the Sea* in Gloucester, MA, in July 1874. Mrs. Eckstorm, in *Minstrelsy of Maine* speculates that the song is modeled on "Johnny Bull (Heenan & Sayres)" which was a favorite of both fishermen and woodsmen.

THE SCHOONER "E. A. HORTON" CUT OUT FROM BRITISH WATERS BY MASSACHUSETTS FISHERMEN.

Songs of Ships & Sailors

The Rambling Female Sailor

Jack McNally, Stacyville, ME 8/28/1942
Helen Hartness Flanders Collection
Transcription © 2016 Julia Lane

Come all you boys from far and near and listen to my ditty
Whilst I do tell of a come-lye maid and she was both young and pretty.
This maid's true love was pressed away and drownded in some foreign sea
Which caused this fair maid for to say, "I will be a rambling sailor!"

With the jacket blue and trousers white just like some sailor neat and tight
And the raging seas was the heart's delight of the rambling female sailor.
From stem to stern she would free-lye go, she braved all dangers and feared no foe
But soon you'll hear of the overthrow of the rambling female sailor.

This maiden gay did a wager lay she would go aloft with any.
Aloft she went, as they do tell, where she'd been ofttimes many.
In going aloft, as they do tell, she missed her hold and down she fell
And she careless-lye bid this world farewell did the rambling female sailor.

And when her snow white breast was seen they took her to be some foreign queen;
Miss Rebecca Young, it was the name of the rambling female sailor.
On the river Thames she was known right well and few of the pretty girls could her excel
But one fatal call was the sad downfall of the rambling female sailor.

You heros all from far and near just listen to this story.
Her body lies beyond the Clyde and her suffered soul in glory.

A true story, the newspaper *Bell's Weekly Messenger* (No. 1941, June 16, 1833) reports: "The sex of a female sailor named Rebecca Young was revealed in a tragic accident that arose because she was too confident of her ability to go aloft." Under the name of Billy Bridle she worked two years on a boat in the Thames. The story goes that she challenged a male sailor to a race up the rigging. Both reached the top, but upon descending, she tried to slide down a halyard, and, in her haste, burned her hands, releasing her grip and falling to her death. An inquest at Gravesend determined it to be an accident.

"The Rambling Female Sailor" was first printed by W. Fordyce, Newcastle, England most likely as a response to the news report. In spite of the verity of the story, the song is rare in the folk tradition, though it has been found in Australia. The tune, simply called "The Rambling Sailor," is Irish in origin and is a variant of a hornpipe called "The Chanter's Tune." Another song, "The Rambling Sailor," describes the sexual exploits of a sailor onshore and also uses this tune. Sam Henry, the celebrated collector of Ulster songs, believes this song originated as "The Rambling Suiler" or "beggarman" and is from the time of King James V of Scotland (1513–1542).

If I Was a Blackbird

Hanford Hayes, Stacyville, ME 5/1942
Helen Hartness Flanders Collection
Transcription © 2016 Julia Lane

If I was a black-bird I'd whis-tle and sing. I'd fly to the ves-sel my true love sails in.

I'd light on the top-mast and there build my nest and sing a sweet song to the one I love best.

FIRST VERSE & CHORUS:
    If I was a blackbird I'd whistle and sing.
    I'd fly to the vessel my true love sails in.
    I'd light on the topmast and there build by nest
    And sing a sweet song to the one I love best.

I am a young sailor and my story is sad
I once was carefree and a brave sailor lad.
I courted a lassie by night and by day
But now she has left me and sailed far away.

I promised to take her to Donnybrook Fair
And to buy her fine ribbons to tie up her hair.
I promised I'd tarry and to stay by her side
But she said in the morning she sailed with the tide.

If I were a writer and could handle the pen
One long loving letter to my true love I'd send
And I'd tell of my sorrow, my grief and my pain
Since she has left me and sailed o'er to Maine.

Her parents they chide me and do not agree
Saying me and my true love never married shall be,
But let them deprive me, let them do as they will
While there's breath in my body she's my true love still.

The first verse/chorus was sung by Hanford Hayes of Stacyville, ME for Helen Flanders in 1942. The earliest versions of this song were collected in Hampshire, England, in 1906. According to Colm O'Lochlann's *Irish Street Ballads* (1960), it was sung by Dublin street singers from 1920 and afterwards by J. M. Kerrigan, the Irish Ambassador to the United States. Irish singer Delia Murphy, wife of Mr. Kerrigan, recorded the song in 1939 and it was often played on radio. Hayes's tune is related but different. The gender of the narrator varies in different versions.

    The subject of the song has an interesting parallel with a story found in the *History of Bristol & Bremen, Maine,* by John Johnston (1873) and in local lore. Moses Young was an early settler to the area from Northern Ireland. A young lady of the family had a lover whom she favored despite the opposition of her father and family. To thwart the affair, she was sent in 1748 to Pemaquid in the Province of Maine to live with her uncle. Not to be denied, the young man, Alexander Fossett, determined to follow her. Landing first at Philadelphia, he soon made his way north, where legend says he sang beneath her window and gained the favor of her family. The couple were married and their descendants still live in Bristol. Because of this coincidence and the lack of additional lyrics provided by Hayes, Fred Gosbee has adapted the song and uses the first verse as a chorus.

Songs of Ships & Sailors

Bold Manning

Albert Cox, Sherman Mills, ME 5/1942
Helen Hartness Flanders Collection
Transcription © 2016 Julia Lane

Bold Mannin' went to sea one day, a dismal day 'twas too.
The air was thick as buttermilk all with the fog and dew.
And Mannin', like a hungry shark, he plowed the raging main
All of the forepart of the day until he reached the *Fame*.

Oh, when he came up to the ship he steered up alongside
And with loud speaking trumpet "Where are you from?" he cried.
"Speak up and give an answer; be sure you tell me true
For if you tell to me a lie, 'twill be the worse for you."

And then those frightened mariners, not knowing what to do,
Spoke up and gave an answer, made sure they told him true.
"We are the *Fame* from New York; to London we are bound.
And William Craig is our capting's name, a native of that town."

"O, darn your eyes," Bold Mannin' cries, "That tale will never do.
Just pull your foresails to the mast and let your ship lie to."
And then those wicked pirates took their broadswords in hand
And went on board of this merchant ship and murdered every man.

They searched the *Fame* all over; they searched everything
Till at length they came to a fair young girl down in her own cabin.
And she was playing on her harp, so merrily she did sing,
"Home, home, sweet home there's no place like home."

Oh, some did curse while others swore they'd have her for a wife
When up spoke bold Mannin' saying, "I'll put an end to all this strife."
He then took out his long broadsword without a fear or dread
And stepped up to this helpless maid and severed off her head!

And then those wicked pirates not caring what they'd done,
They went on board of their own ship and merrily cries, "Go on!"
With a bottle of grog in each hand, so merrily they did sing
And all the forepart of that night they caused the air to ring.

'Twas early the next morning just at the break of day,
"Forequarters, forequarters," Bold Mannin' he did say,
"I see a large East India ship, I know her to prevail,
We'll heist aloft our pirate flag and after her we'll sail."

Oh, when they came up to the ship they steered up alongside
And with loud speaking trumpet "Where are you from?" he cried,
"Speak up and give your answer, be sure you tell me true
For if you tell to me a lie 'twill be the worse for you!"

Bold Rodney stood on his quarterdeck, a surly man was he,
Not caring to give answer but kept straight on his way,
And Mannin' like a man was mad, he stamped his foot, said he,
"You surly old rascal, I'm ruler of the sea!"

When Rodney heard what he had said, he steered right in his face
Pulled up his painted canvas and showed two rows of teeth,
And gave to them a broadside which took them unawares
And caused those wicked pirates for to lament and swear.

Oh, broadside for broadside with grapeshot and round
And soon those wicked pirates saw that they were going down.
"Forequarters! forequarters!" Bold Mannin' he did cry.
"No quarters here, no quarters there," Bold Rodney made reply.

We gave to them another broadside of grapeshot and round
And soon those wicked pirates saw that they were going down
And then a band of music on Rodney's deck did play,
"We sons of old Brittaynia forever gain the day!"

A particularly graphic song of an encounter between a merchantman and a pirate, this seems to originate in Scotland, appearing in the Greig/Duncan Collection, and migrating to Ireland, Maritime Canada, and Maine. One feature which does not occur in all versions is that of the oblivious young lady below decks singing to the accompaniment of her harp or guitar. The ruthless pirate captain ends her concert with a stroke of his sword, apparently to prevent a fight amongst the sailors. The subject of her song "Home, Sweet Home" suggests the piece is no older than that ditty, namely 1828. Two other sets of lyrics, collected by Phillips Barry and Fannie Eckstorm circa 1924, are published in *Minstrelsy of Maine*. One of the singers, Horace Priest, learned songs from his father who, he says, escaped a British man-o'-war while off Boston due to harsh treatment and then came to the Maine woods (*Minstrelsy of Maine*, p. 259).

Two rows of teeth = the cannon ports in the ship's side. Sometimes ships would disguise themselves by covering their gunports with a canvas curtain.

Songs of Ships & Sailors

The *Union* of St John

Mrs. Seth Thornton, SW Harbor, ME 1926
Fannie Hardy Eckstorm Collection
Tune: Moses Harris, Lethbridge, NFLD 1976
Kenneth Peacock Collection
Transcription © 2018 Julia Lane

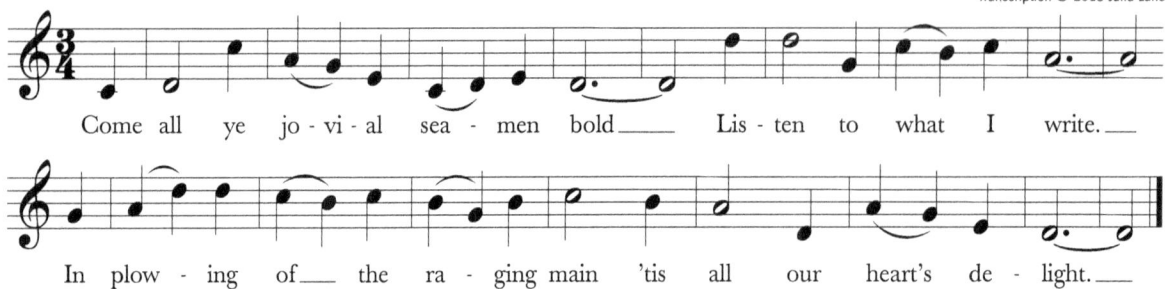

Come, all ye jovial seaman bold, listen to what I write.
In plowing of the raging main 'tis all our heart's delight.
While you landsmen safe on shore, no dangers do you know.
And we like jovial seamen bold go plow the ocean thro'.

You are always at home with your pretty girls telling them fine tales,
The hardest work that ever you done is down in your cornfields.
You have a roof to shelter you from all the showers of rain,
While we like jovial seamen bold go plow the raging main.

It was on the ninth of February, half past meridian,
The weather was tremendous cold and *clouds o'er cast the sun*.
The wind was north by east my boys, all mixed with snow and hail.
It was cold enough to take our lives exclusive of the gale.

The wind was north by east my boys, when first the gale come on
Then under a reefed foresail, my boys, three leagues to sea we run.
And then we reefed our topsail and strove to hand her in
Not knowing the awful danger the lee shore did attend.

We tried to take our courses in but that we could not do
For the frost with its congealing power wrought our rigging so.
When clearing off our foreyard, there came a dreadful squall
Which knocked our bark on her beam ends! Have mercy on us all!

It knocked her down on her beam ends, three minutes there she lay
Then Atkins to the forward went and the foresail cut away.
And saying, "We shall founder for I have no means to try!
The sea comes rolling o'er the wreck I see continually!"

And then to speak affectionately, Alas! His glass was run!
He lashed himself unto the pump whereafter he was seen.
There was one Captain Meader who beheld the dreadful shock
The *Union* on her beam ends three leagues off Mount Desert Rock.

We tried for to board her, but that could not be done
For the weather was tremendous cold and high the waves did run.
We sailed all around her and made what remarks we could
Her pumps before the foremast, her roundhouse painted red.

Her tiller reached over her roundhouse and that is very rare
With a goose's neck upon the end by which her men did steer.
Some more remarks our men did take, too many their fates I know
Her foresail cut from the yard, two swivels on her bows.

The next day they boarded her and to their sad surprise
While grief filled every heart, my boys, and tears ran from their eyes,
Saying " 'tis the *Union* of St John, my boys, full well I know them all.
When I think of their distresses it makes my blood run cold.

"When I think of their distresses it makes my heart to bleed
One lashed and frozen to the pump, one in the cabin dead."
Then, Atkins, the solemn truth to you and to your seaman was
By all your bold proceedings you have gainéd much applause.

And now you're gone forever, may God your soul receive,
But for your dear young widow; methinks I hear her grieve.
But do not grieve young widow, and think it thus so hard,
In the midst of all your trials, it's from the hand of God.

In the midst of your distresses, I'd have you remember this,
That God he is the widow's God, Father to the fatherless.
There's mothers too, who're crying aloud, "What have I done?
I am depriv'd of all my joys, alas, I've lost my son."

And maidens, too, have lost their choice, perhaps their only care!
Their aching hearts in sorrow break; down falls the briny tear.
The brig was manned by eight brave men as good as ever tried,
Like sons of men they lived and sons of heroes died.

Come all you brave sailors bold, come listen unto me
Come and place your dependence on God wherever you may be.
We will always have a jovial time when in God's name we trust
And him who slights his mercy will be laid in the dust.

Eckstorm and Smyth printed this without a tune in their book *Minstrelsy of Maine* (1927) declaring that it was the most difficult of any song to record. Even though it was allegedly one of the three most popular shipwreck songs in Maine in the nineteenth century, they said "nobody knew it, but only knew someone else who used to know it."

Their quest bore fruit in 1926 when Mrs. Seth Thornton of Southwest Harbor transcribed it from the singing of Mrs. Joan B. Moore, age 87, who learned it when she was 7, around 1840. Her lyrics are in plain text. In addition, a broadside titled "The Brig *Union*" was recovered by Mrs. Thornton in 1927 when she found it in an old scrapbook. She copied it exactly as it appeared and wrote: "The paper has the appearance of great age and there is a woodcut of a foundering ship on it and an elaborately designed border around the song, which is printed in very fine print. No name is given, but at the bottom of the sheet it says 'Sold wholesale and retail by J. G. Hunt at the Head of City Wharf, South Side'. The scrap book was evidently made during the Civil War, but the broadside gives evidence of being older than that" (p. 279). It is essentially identical to that found in *A Collection of American Songs and ballads, 205 in number* which is dated 1840 and includes a handwritten index. "The *Union* of St. Johns" appears on page 56.

The changes made over time to the original are fairly minor, such as the details of the storm, the hero being Atkinson, rather than Atkins, who cuts away the foresail rather than the foremast. Two verses of "remarks" made by the rescue crew, presumably about the identification of the ship, have been cut in the more modern version. The brave captain observing the wreck has been named Captain Meader, which may or may not be true.

There is some confusion regarding the identity of the ship partly because different versions name her home port as "St. John," which is in New Brunswick, or "St John's" which is in Newfoundland. In addition, there were many ships with the name "*Union*" and several were wrecked, though not in Maine. About 1904, Mr. Walter M. Hardy, Mrs. Eckstorm's brother, learned from Captain William Coombs of Islesboro that the *Union* was a brig wrecked off the Maine coast perhaps as early as 1837. (MM) It makes sense, then, that the broadside refers to this tragedy. Coincidentally, the *Northern Shipwrecks Database* shows the Dec 21, 1884 wreck of the schooner *Union*, registered at St John, NB, at Mt Desert Island en route from New York to St John 50 years after the published broadside! Not surprisingly, the song has been popular in Newfoundland and so we have used the tune of a version sung by Moses Harris of Lethbridge, NFD, recorded there in 1976 by Kenneth Peacock.

The lee shore = the shore upon which the vessel is in danger of drifting.
To take our courses in = In a square-rigged vessel, such as a brig, the courses were the sails bent to the lower yards.
Wrought our rigging = The rigging was so stiff with ice they could not take in their lower sails.
On her beam ends = the beams are the horizontal transverse timbers. On her beam ends is heeled over; almost capsized.

Songs of Ships & Sailors

The Merry Mackerel Catchers

Lyrics: Jacob S. Lord, Gloucester, MA 1882
Printed in *The Fisherman's Own Book* by Procter Bros.
Adapted by Julia Lane to a traditional tune
Transcription © 2018 Julia Lane

It's laugh, "Ha! ha!" and shout, "Hurrah!" we are bound for the coast of Maine.
Our hold's well stored with salt and food, in the boat we've a fine new seine.
As the sun goes down we round Eastern Point to Monhegan our course is turned,
And smoothly o'er the water skims our ship like a wild sea bird.

    Just like a wild sea bird, me boys, just like a wild sea bird.
    And smoothly o'er the water skims our ship like a wild sea bird.

The watch is set, the pipes are lit and a game of cards is on.
A lively lad has a song to sing; Uncle Ben has a yarn to spin.
So pleasantly passes the time away till eight bells, when all turn in
Hear the measured tramp of the watch on deck and the snoring of the men!

    The snoring of the men, me boys, the snoring of the men
    Hear the measured tramp of the watch on deck and the snoring of the men!

It's break of day, the sun peeps up, the morning's clear and cool,
Aloft the lookout makes his way to sight the early school.
"A school! A school!" from the foremast head is the lookout's exciting call
"On the weather bow! It's showing red! Can't say if it's large or small."

    "Can't say if it's large or small. Can't say if it's large or small
    On the weather bow! It's showing red! Can't say if it's large or small."

Now all is life on the schooner's deck, as she plows thro' the sparkling brine
Her crew in oiled clothes anxious wait for a chance to wet the twine
"Come down from aloft! Haul the dory out, and tumble up here, cook!
Work lively, lads, and cast her off! Pull out, and we'll have a look."

"Pull out, and we'll have a look. Pull out, and we'll have a look.
Work lively, lads, and cast her off! Pull out, and we'll have a look."

"Hold! Way enough—ah, there they rise—Good fish! I'd say they're fine
Now gently start her ahead, my boys, seine-master, give them twine!
Jump to the purse line, one and all! Give a long, strong steady pull;
The rings are up—yes, take them on—By Jove! I believe she's full!"

"By Jove! I believe she's full! By Jove! I believe she's full!
The rings are up—yes, take them on—By Jove! I believe she's full!"

And so it proved; of number twos right cheerily did we bail
Till the skipper cries, "We've got enough, she's full from rail to rail."
All night we worked at split and gib, next day they were salted down.
As the sun sank low in the ruddy west we made sail for Gloucester town.

We made sail for Gloucester town. We made sail for Gloucester town.
As the sun sank low in the ruddy west we made sail for Gloucester town.

Although this was not collected by any of the songcatchers, it appears in an 1882 publication popular among shoreline communities, *The Fisherman's Own Book*, (Procter Bros. Gloucester, MA, p. 169). It specifically mentions the destination as Maine and the description of the fishing process is accurate. The book also includes "Valuable Statistics of the Fisheries" and is a fascinating window into the life and times of the fishing community. Countless Maine fishermen joined the crews of the Gloucester schooners to reap the harvest of the Grand Banks. Julia has set the words to an old tune so it can be added to the tradition.

Number twos = mackerel at least 11" long
split = to cut the fish in half down the backbone
gib = to eviscerate the fish

Fair Phoebe & Her Dark-Eyed Sailor

Mrs. Guy R. Hathaway, Mattawamkeag, ME 1932
Phillips Barry & Fannie Hardy Eckstorm Collections
Transcription © 2018 Julia Lane

I'll tell you of a come-lye young lady fair
Who was walking out for to take the air.
She met a sailor upon the way
So I paid attention,
So I paid attention to hear what they might say.

"Fair maid," said he, "why roam you alone?
For the night is coming, and the day's far gone."
She said, while tears from her eyes did flow,
"For my dark-eyed sailor,
For my dark-eyed sailor, so manly true and bold!"

Cries William, "Drive him from off your mind!
As true a sailor as him, you'll find!
Love turns aside, and cold does grow,
Like a winter's morning.
Like a winter's morning when hills are clad with snow."

These words did Phoebe's fond heart enflame;
She cries, "On me you shall play no game!"
She drew her dagger, and then did cry,
"For my dark-eyed sailor,
For my dark-eyed sailor, a maid I'll live and die.

"It's seven long years since he left this land;
A diamond ring he took from off my hand;
He broke the token; left half with me,
And the other's rolling,
And the other's rolling at the bottom of the sea.

"His coal black eyes and his curly hair,
His flattering tongue did my heart ensnare;
Genteel he was, and no rake like you,
To advise a maiden,
To advise a maiden to slight the jacket blue.

"A tarry sailor I'll ne'er disdain,
But always I will treat the same;
To drink your health, here's a piece of coin,
For my dark-eyed sailor,
For my dark-eyed sailor still claims this heart of mine!"

When William did this ring unfold,
She seemed distracted midst joy and woe.
"You're welcome, William, I've lands and gold
For my dark-eyed sailor,
For my dark-eyed sailor, so manly true and bold."

In a cottage down by the riverside,
In unity and love, they now abide;
So, girls, be true while you lover's away,
For a cloudy morning,
For a cloudy morning oft brings a pleasant day.

"The Valiant Seaman's Return" (1703) seems to be the inspiration for a plethora of songs with this subject. There are at least seven variants recorded in Maine. Some include a "broken token" pledged between the two lovers as well as a disguise or lack of recognition to test the faith of the lovelorn lady. A landsman's variation is "The Claudy Banks" in which the hero is a soldier. The tune most often used for the "Dark Eyed Sailor" is called "The Female Smuggler" (see page 206). This version was recorded by Phillips Barry circa 1932 from the singing of Mrs. Hathaway who reported that she "learned it when a child from her aunt."

The Worn-Out Sailor

F. L. Tracy, Brewer, ME 1925
Phillips Barry Collection
First transcribed by S. L. Bayard
Transcription © 2019 Julia Lane

One Summer's eve as labor was o'er and the birds were singing gaily,
A poor old Tar, worn out with age, came through our village begging.
I pitied his sad mournful tale, of pity I'm no railer:
"I pray you bestow your charity on me, I'm a poor worn-out sailor.

"Despise not my hull, I pray, you don't, because I'm shabby rigging.
If I had my limbs, I'd rather work than I'd be seen a begging.
I am like a ship distressed at sea, without a friend to hail her;
I pray you, bestow your charity on me, I'm a poor old worn-out sailor.

"When false reports came home that I was dead, my poor wife died broken hearted.
My daughter roamed I know not where, and forever we were parted.
I was shipwrecked of all I held most dear: poor girl, I often wail her;
If I could find her, she would comfort me, I'm a poor old worn-out sailor."

And as he sang his mournful song, a female gaz'd upon him;
She burst in tears of frantic wild, and sank upon his bosom.
"Oh father!" she cried, (for it was his child, whose duty ne'er had failed her)
"Oh, come you home and live and die with me, you're a poor old worn-out sailor.

"I have a home, a husband dear, right welcome he will meet you;
Although you're poor and clad in rags, right welcome he will greet you;
And when you resign your parting breath, my duty ne'er will fail me;
I'll see you laid in your silent grave, you're a poor old worn-out sailor."

In the 19th century there was increasing social awareness about orphans and veterans especially during the Great Famine and after the Civil War in the U.S. The Shakers were famous for their work with these communities and everyone is familiar with these themes in the works of Charles Dickens. This song may be a result of that awareness, although it never became particularly popular. An English broadside of 1853, it was published in Henry De Marsan's *New Comic and Sentimental Singer's Journal*, Chatham Street, NY in 1871. It also appears in the Canadian Maritime collections of Helen Creighton and Edith Fowke.

Songs of Ships & Sailors

Yankee Tars

Dr. Darlington, Bangor, ME 1816
Tune: Traditional English, "Mrs. Casey"
Fannie Hardy Eckstorm Collection
Transcription © 2016 Julia Lane

Whenever the Tyrant of the main assaults Columbian Seamen
He'll find them ready to maintain the noble name of Freemen.
Long our Tars have borne in peace with British domineering,
But now they've sworn the trade shall cease, for vengeance they are steering.

CHORUS:
    Then toast the Brave for they will save
    Columbia's fame from sinking.
    The honor'd scars of Yankee Tars
    Are glorious themes for drinking!

First gallant Hull he was the lad, who sail'd a Tyrant hunting:
And swagg'ring D'acres soon was glad to honor striped Bunting!
Intrepid Jones next boldly sought the demons of oppression;
With a superior force he fought, and gave the knaves a threshing!

Then quickly met our nation's eyes the noblest sight in nature;
A first-rate Frigate, as a prize, brought in by brave Decatur.
Then veteran Bainbridge next prepar'd to wield his country's thunder:
In quest of foes he boldly steer'd, and drove the *Java* under!

And daring Lawrence next parades — from zone to zone he sought 'em
One boasting Briton he blockades, and sends one to the bottom!
Next see our gallant *Enterprize*, how nobly ocean rocks her!
There Burrows for his Country dies, but first subdues the *Boxer*.

With loud applauses next we greet the glorious news from Erie
Behold! a powerful British fleet, submits to gallant Perry!
Then Warrington, his Country's pride, steps boldly forth to serve her;
And quickly humbled by his side, we see the fierce *Epervier*!

From noble Blakely's dauntless force his vanquish'd foes in vain steer;
For he could stop the *Avon*'s course, and overhaul the *Reindeer*!
McDonough, hero of Champlain, next proved, that British seamen
With Yankee tars contend in vain — because those tars are freemen.

With "*Ironsides*" brave Stewart slips to sea on her third cruise, sir,
And, tired of flogging single ships, he drubs them now by twos, sir.
The *Penguin* next, with her bold crew, thought she to strike would scorn it
She sought a *Wasp* but found, in lieu, our Biddle and his *Hornet*.

Our Yankee tars to Afric's shore our heroes, lastly, led 'em
And Turkish banners bow before the starry flag of Freedom.
Come, push the flowing bowl around, and in Columbia's story
Long may such gallant names abound, to vindicate her glory.

Found in papers of Fannie Hardy Eckstorm at Fogler Library, University of Maine, Orono was a photocopy of a broadside "printed and sold at the Bangor Printing Office (1819)." A listing of American naval conquests and their heroes, it was later published in 1842 in *Songs, Odes and other Poems on National Subjects by Wm McCarty, Philadelphia Part Second-Naval* with this comment: "The following song was composed by Dr. Darlington, one of the representatives in Congress from Pennsylvania, and sung by him at the dinner given by the delegation from that state, to Commodore Decatur and Captain Stewart, at Washington, on the 8th of January, 1816." The guests of honor at that event, Stephen Decatur (1779-1820) and Charles Stewart (1778-1869), were both dashing and popular naval heroes during the early history of the United States with long careers of distinguished service in the post-Revolutionary conflicts in the West Indies, the Mediterranean and the War of 1812. The tune noted on the broadside, "Mrs. Casey," is a well-known English Morris dance tune.

Songs of Ships & Sailors

Andrew Rose

Frank Kneeland, Searsport, ME 10/1941
Helen Hartness Flanders Collection
Text from the *Kneeland Miscellany* 1914
Transcription © 2016 Julia Lane

Young Andrew Rose, the British sailor,
Whose hardships now I will explain;
'Twas on the passage from Barbados
All on board of the *Martha Jane*.

Wasn't that most cruel usage
Without a friend to interpose?
How they whipped and mangled, gagged and strangled
The British sailor young Andrew Rose.

'Twas up aloft the captain sent him
Naked beneath the burning sun
Whilst the mate he followed after
And flogged him till the blood did run.

Next in a water cask they put him
For seven long days they kept him there.
At last poor Andrew begged for mercy;
The captain swore and left him there.

The captain gave him stuff to swallow,
Such stuff to you I will not name,
When all the crew were sick with horror
While on board the *Martha Jane*.

'Twas on the quarterdeck they laid him,
Gagged him with an iron bar;
Wasn't that most cruel usage
To put upon a British tar?

For thirty days they did ill use him
When into Liverpool they did arrive
And the Judge who heard the story
Said, "Captain Rogers, you must die!"

Come all ye friends and near relations,
And all ye friends to interpose;
Never treat a British sailor
Like they did young Andrew Rose.

This gruesome song was much sung among sailors, and, apparently, the incident about which it was written resulted in legislation for better treatment of seamen. A true story of terrible conditions on board some British ships, the event took place in 1857. The ship, called the *Martha and Jane*, was short a crewman and a captain. They signed seaman Andrew Rose and Captain Henry Rogers at Barbados to achieve a full complement. The two had a history of despising each other even on shore. On board, the hatred escalated and Capt. Rogers abused his authority to order the merciless torture of Rose until he died. When the ship arrived in Liverpool, the story came to the attention of the authorities.

Captain Rogers was tried, found guilty and executed at Liverpool on September 11, 1857, in the presence of a crowd of 50,000 people. As punishment for their complicity in the affair, the first and second mate were sentenced to transportation and penal servitude for life. The gory details of the crime are described in *The Annual Register, Or, A View of the History and Politics of the Year 1857, Volume 99* (London: F. & J. Rivington, 1858, p. 158) which begins: "Another instance of the brutal excesses into which the possession of unlimited power will lead men of ill-regulated minds, and of the need which British seamen may sometimes have of the protection of the law against the violence and tyranny of their own officers, has been exhibited by the circumstances which led to Henry Rogers, William Miles, and Charles Edward Seymour being indicted for the murder of Andrew Rose, between the 11th of May and the 5th of June in this year."

Mr. Kneeland says this song used to be a favorite of George A. Bowen in Searsport in 1914. In Joanna Colcord's *Songs of American Sailormen* she says she heard her father, a sea captain from Searsport, ME, sing it and found it in a notebook after his death. We have added her last verse here (in italics). Edna Floyd of Jonesport, recorded by Flanders in 1942, says that her father sang this ballad which was popular when she was growing up.

Johnny German

Hanford Hayes, Staceyville, ME 8/28/1942
Helen Hartness Flanders Collection
Transcription © 2017 Julia Lane

As I arrived in London I had the joyful news.
I will relate them on to you if you will not refuse.
"It is all for the sake of a sailor lad who's gone far o'er the main;
He's left me here heartbroken if he never returns again."

"He sails on board of the *Rainbow*; he's a mate for Captain Low.
His name, 'tis Johnny German; is that the man you know?"
She clasped her hands with joyfulness, saying, "That's the very man.
Pray tell me is he a-living yet and do no longer stand."

I said, "Leave off your joyfulness, for very well I know,
Your darling Johnny German, he died five months ago."
'Twas then she wrung her lily-white hands; lamenting she did cry,
A-shedding many the bitter tear and wishing that she could die.

She went unto her chamber her heart was filled with woe,
But straight way following after this young man he did go,
Saying, "Mary, arise and open the door and leave all sorrow behind;
I have come here for to comfort you and it's comfort you shall find."

Miss Mary she was surprised to hear and rose to open the door;
"Oh Johnny, how could you deceive me so when you were here before?"
"I done it to try your constancy, to see if you hadn't proved true,
And I never met with a maid in my life that could compare with you!"

So, fare thee well to the *Rainbow*, since Mary's gained my heart,
No one shall have her from me, till death it does us part;
She is fairer than the morning sun, she is sweeter than the rose,
Or any other flower that in the garden grows.

"Johnny German/Jarman" is relatively rare in the Northeast. The ship name causes the song to be sometimes confused with "Captain Ward and the *Rainbow*," #287 in the Francis Child ballad collection. We have added the last two verses which were recorded by Eckstorm from Mrs. Emery Howard of North Blue Hill, ME, in 1932. These appear in *British Ballads from Maine Vol. 2.* (pp. 97–103).

Songs of Ships & Sailors

The Isle of Man Shore

Mrs. Annie V. Marston, West Gouldsboro, ME 1930
Phillips Barry Collection
Transcription © 2016 Julia Lane

On the Isle of Man shore as I carelessly wandered
One Saturday's evening when calm was the air,
I saw a fair maid with a child in her ar-ems   [arms]
Inclined to the rocks, her grief to declare.

With sorrowful accents I heard her complaining
Saying: "Willie, dear Willie, come back unto me!"
Then again she exclaimed "Oh, no more shall I see him,
My own dearest Willie lies under the sea."

From the Quays of Den Darken a steamboat packet sailed away
Bound unto Liverpool, last Wednesday set sail.
The weather being fair as the land disappearéd
Our hearts they were merry, both gentle and gay.

But the night coming down, both darksome and dreary,
The wind had increased to a terrible storm.
"Look out for the lighthouse!" the captain he called out
"I fear that this night we shall all suffer harm."

The seas rolled like mountains, no shelter to fly to.
The ship by the billows was tossed to and fro!
Two men were swept over into the main foaming ocean
While women and children were crying below.

Some fell on their knees, Heaven's mercy imploring
And some lay insensible or sunk in despair.
The seas loudly roaring, the sailors all swearing
And when that they heard us they mocked at our prayer

But my Willie stood by me to cheer and protect me
While my helpless infant I pressed to my breast.
We shouted for aid but no help come near us
So now, tender Christians, think of our distress!

The boats were launched out in the main foaming ocean;
In one of them was my infant and I.
But before they reached shore they were all overwhelmed
And soon in the deep forty bodies did lie.

But my Willie, being brave, to the ship he returned again
And I was safely landed on the Isle of Man shore.
But to save his old father his own life he ventured
Now, alas, I am doomed to behold him no more.

And now I am left a poor desolate widow,
Scarce one year in wedlock as you plainly see,
To beg for my bread among hard-hearted strangers
May heaven smile down on my infant and me.

Variants of this British broadside are popular in the northeastern tradition, appearing in Maine and the Canadian Maritimes as "The Quay of Dundocken," "The Desolate Widow," and "The Wild Shore." We believe the name of the quay is meant to be Dundalk, Ireland, which is on the Irish Sea halfway between Dublin and Belfast, and an obvious place for a ship to embark for Liverpool via the Isle of Man. Strangely, the song seems to be unknown on the actual Isle of Man and we could not find a specific shipwreck by which it was inspired.

The *Enterprise* and the *Boxer*

Printed in "The Bird of Birds," Boston 1818
Tune: Portsmouth, circa 1812
Revised Lyric & Transcription © 2013 Fred Gosbee

Come all ye sons of Freedom, come listen unto me.
I'll tell of an engagement that happened on the sea
Between the *Enterprise* and *Boxer*, two noble ships of fame.
Although the *Enterprise* is small she made the *Boxer* tame.

We sailed out of Portland harbor in a sweet and pleasant gale,
The saucy *Boxer* hovering round, she proudly spread her sail.
It being about Meridian when we to her drew near,
We hoisted Yankee colors, and gave to them three cheers.

It was on the fifth of September, it being a glorious day,
The *Enterprise* and *Boxer*, they had their bloody fray.
The *Enterprise* soon box'd her, and quickly made them see
That we were Yankee heroes all from America.

When we came on board the *Boxer* 'twould grieve your hearts full sore
To see all those proud Englishmen lying in their gore
And there upon the quarterdeck where officers do tread
Their young captain, Samuel Blyth, was found among the dead.

So now we've gain'd the victory, my Yankee hearts of steel,
But, oh, the heavy price we paid, to force our foes to yield
For in the fight was Burrows hit, he got his mortal blow,
Alas, our young commander shall see Portland town no more.

In a Portland cemetery those two young heros lie.
God bless Lieutenant Burrows, and Captain Blyth likewise
Far from the roaring din of battle, the province of the brave,
They slumber for eternity in the silence of their grave.

During the War of 1812, the waters off the coast of Maine were particularly active due to proximity with English Loyalist territory in Canada and the business of smuggling. On September 5, 1813, the U.S. brig *Enterprise* and the British brig *Boxer* fought a fierce battle just off Monhegan Island in midcoast Maine. The day was very clear, and the engagement was witnessed by onlookers from Boothbay to Matinicus over 10 miles away. Both captains were under thirty years old and in their first command. Although the *Enterprise* clearly had the advantage, the *Boxer* was unable to strike her colors and surrender as her confident captain had nailed them to the mast. The British suffered 21 casualties to the Americans' 12. Both captains were killed in the forty-five-minute engagement and are buried side by side in Portland. The youth of the fallen commanders caught the public imagination and thousands of people witnessed the elaborate double funeral. Many songs were written about the battle but none reference the burial place of the captains. Fred Gosbee edited and adapted this version, which was printed in *The Bird* (Boston, 1813). His additions are in italics. There was no tune specified so he set it to "Portsmouth," a popular tune of the times.

THE ENTERPRIZE AND BOXER.

Songs of Ships & Sailors

The Silvery Tide

James Kneeland, Searsport, ME 1914
Tune from Wesley Smith, PEI, Canada 1963
Dr. Edward Ives Collection
Transcription © 2018 Julia Lane

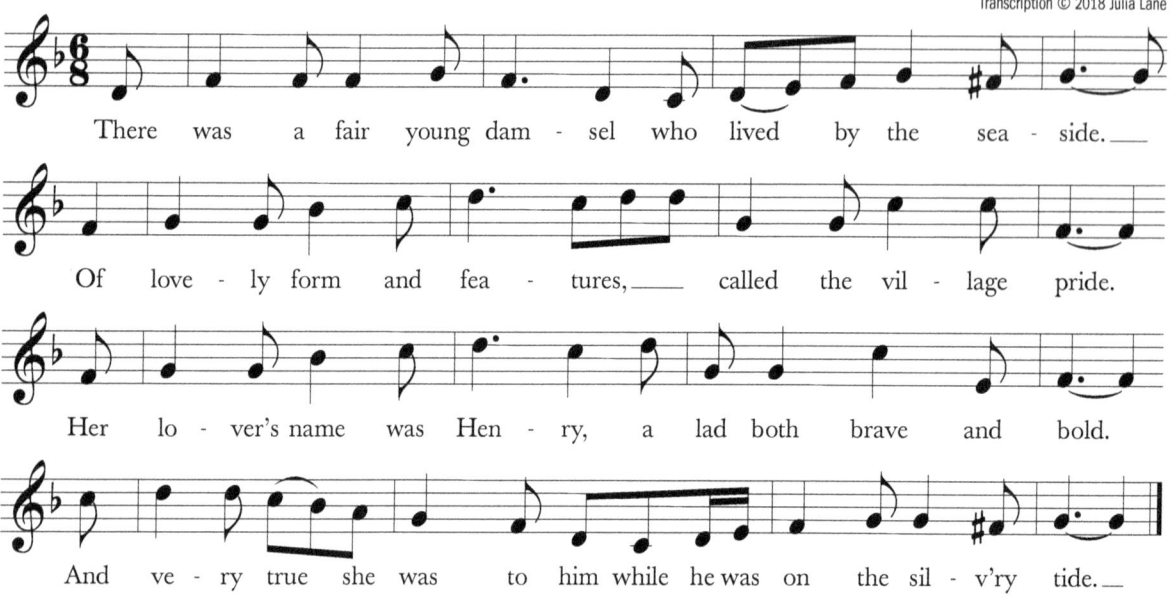

There was a fair young damsel who lived by the seaside.
Of lovely form and features, she was called the village pride.
Her lover's name was Henry, a lad both brave and bold.
And very true she was to him while he was on the silvery tide.

In young Henry's absence a young nobleman there came
Who tried with all his powers young Mary's love to gain.
Young Mary, she repulsed him with all her power and strength
Saying, "My lover, and I have but one, is on the silvery tide."

Then near to desperation this nobleman did say,
"To prove the separation I'll take her life away!
I'll watch her late and early and in some silent place
I'll send her body floating out on the silvery tide."

As this nobleman was walking one morn to take the air
Down by the silvery waters he spied this maiden fair.
Then said the saucy villain, "Consent to be my bride
Or you'll sink or swim far, far from him who's on the silvery tide!"

With trembling lips said Mary, "My vows I ne'er can break
My Henry I love dearly and I'll die for his sweet sake."
With his handkerchief he bound her arms and plunged her o'er the side
And shrieking, she went floating out upon the silvery tide

It happened a few days after young Henry he came home
Expecting to be happy and fix the wedding day.
"We fear your true love's murdered!" her aged parents cried,
"Or she's caused her own destruction out on the silvery tide!"

That night in his bed chamber, young Henry could find no rest;
The thoughts of pretty Mary disturbed his aching breast.
He dreamed that he went walking down by the ocean side
And his own true love sat weeping on the banks of the silvery tide.

Young Henry rose from his chamber for to search the sea banks o'er;
'Til four o'clock next morning he roamed from shore to shore;
At four o'clock in the morning pretty Mary's corpse did find,
That to and fro went floating out on the silvery tide.

He knew it to be his own true love by a gold ring on her hand,
And when he untied the handkerchief it brought him to a stand;
The name of her base murderer was there before his eyes,
Who had put an end to Mary out on the silvery tide.

This nobleman was taken, the gallows was his doom
For murdering pretty Mary all in her youthful bloom;
Young Henry was so dejected that he wandered 'til he died.
And his last word it was "Mary!" who died on the silvery tide.

The Kneeland Miscellany, in which these lyrics appear, did not specify a tune, so we have used one from Wesley Smith of PEI recorded by Dr. Edward (Sandy) Ives in 1963. Dr. Ives says in his book *Folksongs from Prince Edward Island* (*Northeast Folklore vol 5*), "'The Silvery Tide' seems to be best known in the northern tradition (particularly in the Northeast)." Flanders found it in Maine, Vermont, and New Hampshire. It was collected by composer Percy Grainger in England, Helen Creighton in Nova Scotia and Alan Lomax in Michigan. Numerous broadsides were printed dating from 1813 (J. Catnach London) and the song can still be heard in the repertoire of several contemporary musicians. We have two versions from Maine; in addition to Kneeland, it was also sung by Carrie Grover, of Gorham, ME, in 1953 and appears in her book *A Heritage of Song*.

Mary & Willie

Mrs. John S. Russell, Bangor, ME, 2/14/1934
Fannie Hardy Eckstorm Collection
Tune first transcribed by Samuel Bayard 1939
Transcription© 2019 Julia Lane

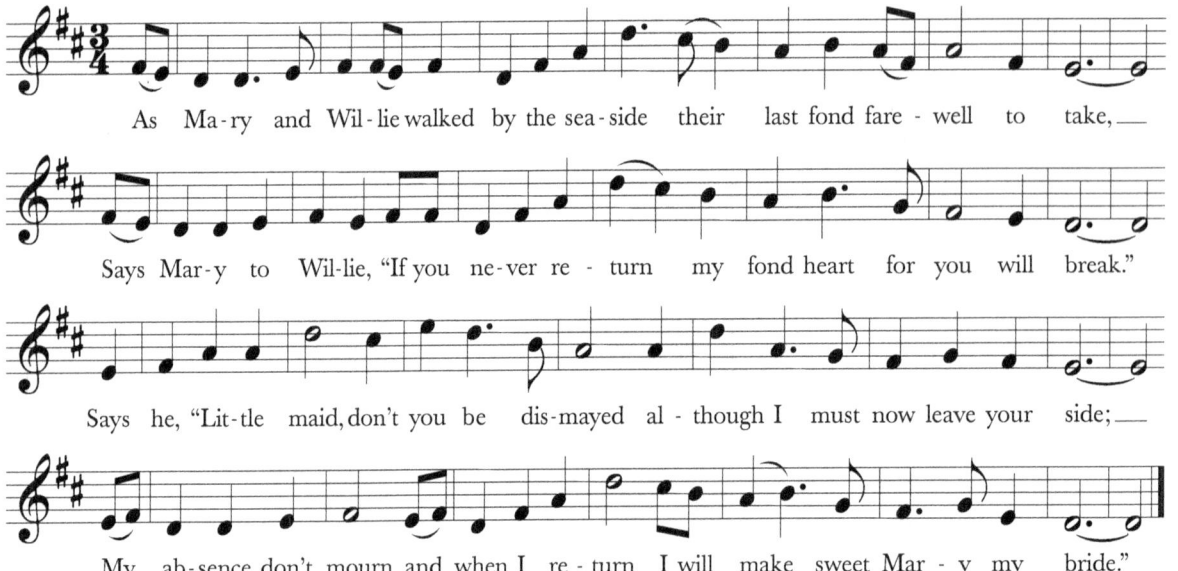

As Mary and Willie walked by the seaside their last farewell to take,
Says Mary to Willie, "If you never return, my fond heart for you will break."
Says he, "Little maid, don't you be dismayed although I must now leave your side;
My absence don't mourn and when I return I will make sweet Mary my bride."

Seven years had gone past, no news came; at last she stood in her own father's door,
When a beggar passed by, with a patch on his eye, and begged a charity bestow.
Saying, "If you will bestow on to me charitee your fortune I'll tell you; beside
The lad that you love will never return to make little Mary his bride."

This fair maid, being frightened, and trembled with fear, cries, "All that I own I will give,
If one thing I ask you, come tell to me true. Tell me if my Willie still lives."
"He liveth," said he, "but in great povertee. He is shipwrecked and careworn beside,
And because he is poor, he will never return to make little Mary his bride."

"Oh, God only knows the joys I do feel, though over his losses I mourn;
But he is welcome to me in his great povertee, let his jacket be tattered and torn."
Then the beggar threw by the patch from his eye, threw away his old crutch and his cane;
In a suit of blue clothes and his cheek like a rose, he appeared to his Mary again.

[To last two lines of music:]
Says he, "Little maid, don't you be afraid. 'Twas only your love for to try,
To the altar straightway, without more delay," and he made little Mary his bride.

The earliest version of this popular song seems to be a broadside presented by J. Evans of Long Lane, Smithfield, England, in 1794. Many subsequent variants appeared and it remained a favorite into the 20th century, being collected from traditional sources throughout the U.K., U.S., Canada, and Ireland. Another of the "returned sailor" songs, it lacks the "broken token" proving the identity of the hero. Perhaps it is the disguise motif that makes it so appealing. There are three versions recorded in Maine, one of which appears as "Little Mary, the Sailor's Bride" in Phillips Barry's *Maine Woods Songster* (1939). The Maine tunes seem most like those found in Northern Ireland.

Sail On, O Ship of State

Poem by Henry. W. Longfellow 1849
Adapted for song by Charles William Bardeen 1888
Arrangement © 2016 Julia Lane

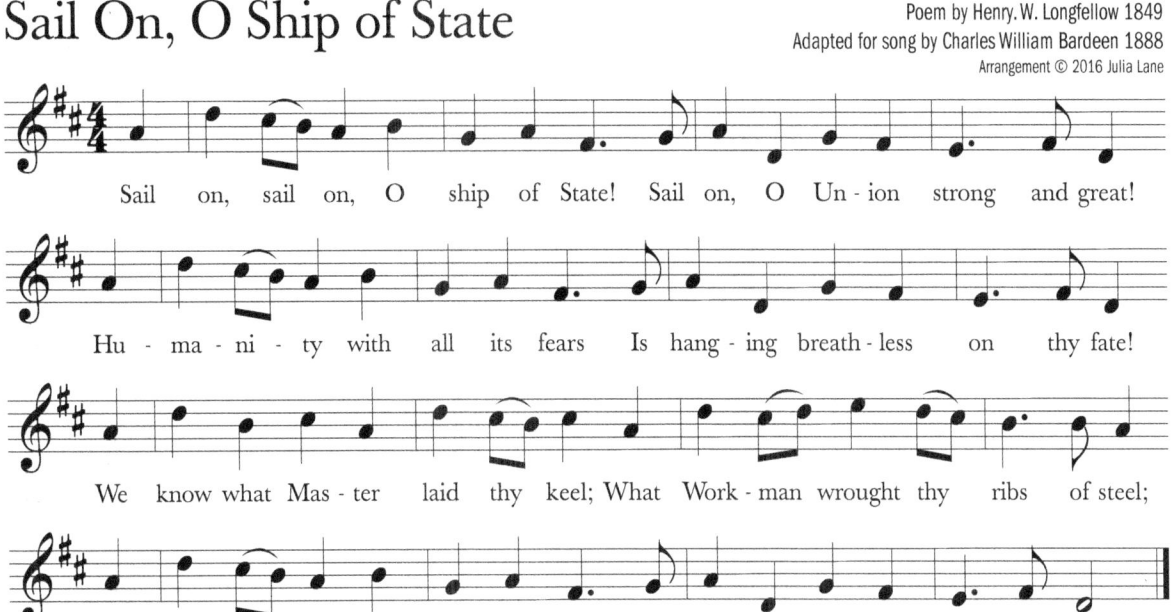

Sail on, sail on, O ship of State!
Sail on, O Union, strong and great!
Humanity with all its fears
Is hanging breathless on thy fate!
We know what Master laid thy keel;
What Workman wrought thy ribs of steel;
Who made each mast, and sail, and rope;
What anvils rang, what hammers beat.

Fear not each sudden sound and shock,
'Tis of the wave and not the rock;
'Tis but the flapping of the sail,
And not a rent made by the gale!
In spite of rock and tempest's roar,
In spite of false lights on the shore,
Sail on, nor fear to breast the sea!
Our hearts, our hopes, are all with thee.

Our hearts, our hopes, our prayers, our tears,
Our faith triumphant o'er our fears,
The anchors of our hope were shaped
In what great forge and what great heat
Sail on, Sail on, O Ship of State!
Sail on, O Union, strong and great!
Humanity with all its fears,
Is hanging breathless on thy fate!

We will not doubt, we will not fear
But sail right on with hearts of cheer.
Our hearts, our fortunes go with thee
Sail on, nor fear to breast the sea.
Our hearts, our hopes are all with thee
Our hearts, our hopes, our prayers, our tears
Our faith triumphant o'er our fears
Are all with thee; are all with thee!

The original poem, "Sail On, O Thou Ship of State," written by Longfellow in 1849, ended on a pessimistic note describing the demise of the ship, an inevitable end for the wooden ships of the day. However, on the eve of publication, he decided to change the verse, emphasizing the metaphor of the United States as a well-crafted "Ship of State" and adding the more inspiring lines. It was received with great enthusiasm and has been much quoted by statesmen and politicians ever since. It became part of the required elocution repertoire in schools and was set to various tunes for use in dramatic patriotic programs as well as in hymnals. The tune here is from a rousing traditional English song set by noted educator Charles William Bardeen, who was editor of *The School Bulletin* published in Syracuse, NY. His *Song Budget* series included hundreds of songs for use in schools. "The Ship of State" appears in *The Song Patriot* (1888) on page 23.

Songs of Ships & Sailors

The Jolly Sailor

Arthur Walker, Littleton, ME, 8/30/1942
Helen Hartness Flanders Collection
Transcription © 2016 Julia Lane

As I went a-walking up New York street,
I had made it my business my true love to meet.
"Oh," said I, "brother sailor pray tell me your name."
"I belong to the *Nancy*, from London she came."

"Oh, it's I am no sailor as you understand;
I am no sailor, but if you want a hand;
Oh, it's I am no sailor, but if you want a man,
For my passage over, I'll do what I can."

Now the ship was got ready at sunset we sailed,
And the wind from the nor'western it blowed a fine gale.
And it's as we were a-sailing with our own heart's content,
Our ship sprang a leak; to the bottom she went.

There was twenty-four of us, we was in a long boat,
And soon on the wild ocean we were forced there to float,
Till it's hungry came on, and death drawéd nigh,
So we ordered cast lots for to see who would die.

Now the lots were got ready and in a bag put
To see who would die for to feed the ship's crew.
One fair innocent young creature a short one she drew,
And she rose for to die, for to feed a ship's crew;

It was then that this young man his bold move did make
With tears in his eyes and his heart like to break.
With tears in his eyes and his heart like to burst,
"For the sake of your sweet life, love, I will die first."

Now the lots were turned over and in a bag put,
To see who this young man's butcher would be.
"Be quick and be ready; Let your offer be done."
And before there's a blow struck, we all heard a gun.

"Oh, stay your hand, butcher," the captain did cry,
For to ship ocean harbor we are now drawing nigh.
And as we were sailing with a fair wind and tide,
We came to the city close by the seaside

Now this couple they got married the very next day.
This couple they got married and the music did play
For the maidens all danced and the sailors did sing
Such singing and dancing this wedding did bring.

A version of "The Silk Merchant's Daughter," the original song describes the young man's encounter with a young woman who wishes to go with him to New England. The cannibalism motif and the narrow escape echo an actual event involving a 1740 ship called the *Sea Flower* which became disabled in a hurricane and drifted for weeks, causing the survivors to resort to the unthinkable. The ship was rescued and brought into Boston where the authorities were in a moral quandary about how to deal with the survivors. A Nova Scotia song, "The Starved Ship," also describes this event, and there is some speculation that a survivor of the original tragedy made his way there and settled.

Songs of Ships & Sailors

The *Bridget Ann*

Mr. D. H. Ham, Islesford, ME, c. 1925
Lyric Phillips Barry Collection
Transcription © 2021 Fred Gosbee

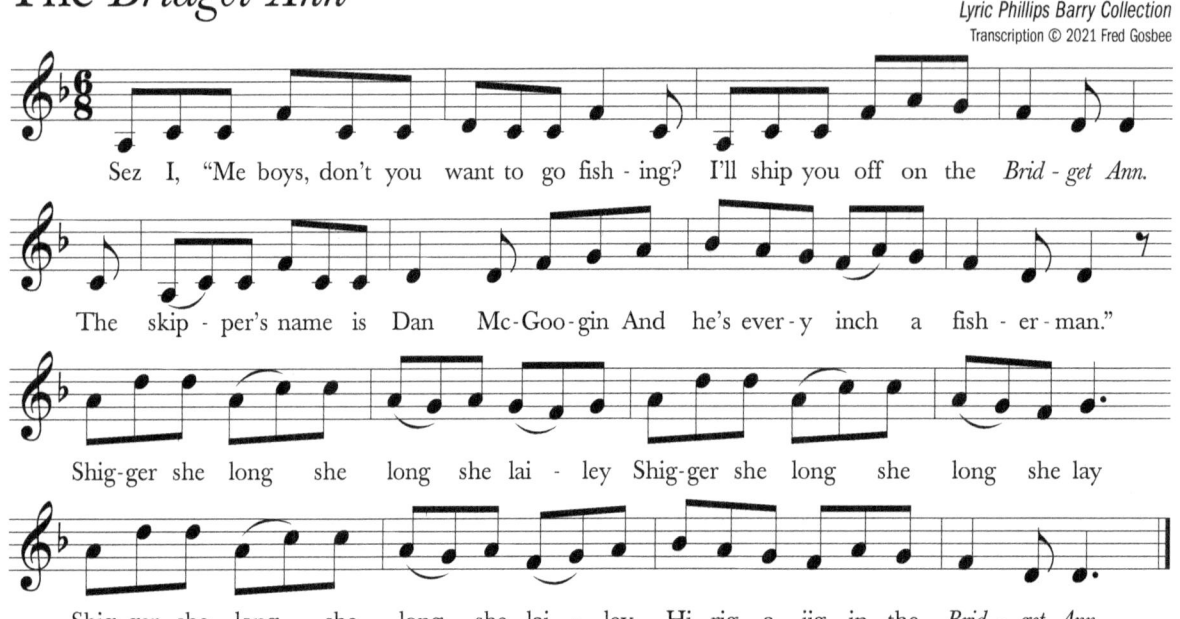

Sez I, "Me boys, don't you want to go fishing?
I'll ship you off on the *Bridget Ann*.
The skipper's name is Dan McGoogin
And he's every inch a fisherman."

CHORUS:
    Shigger she long she long she lailey
    Shigger she long she long she lay
    Shigger she long she long she lailey
    High rig a jig in the *Bridget Ann*.

A captain, cook and a crew of ten
Tried and true and trusty men,
It makes no odds what kind of weather
They fish all the time and heave together.

Halibut, cod and haddock and hake
From their trawls they catch and take
These they dress and salt in the hold
And have lots of money when the fish are sold

It don't take long for the *Bridget Ann*
To catch a trip for every man
Is trying to do the best that he can
To fill her as full as a caravan.

The cook knows how to dish up the grub
And fill each man as round as a tub
Good old scouse and cod's head chowder
Is what the crew calls extra fodder.

They take what is called fisherman's luck
A cold wet skin and a hungry gut
To every man's woe and each other's sorrow
Hard luck today but plenty tomorrow.

The winds may blow and the seas may be rough
Each of the crew hangs hard and tough,
Fishing in sunshine, also in fog
Without any milk or without any grog.

At last the hold's full; they leave from the banks
Topside out showing showing only two planks.
Burgee is hoisted to main topmast truck
With a fair wind home and a tide to buck.

It only takes a week to get back home
Fish are discharged, the skipper's alone.
He wants a good crew to go to the Banks;
Good old Downeasters, New England Yanks.

Mr. Ham said that the song goes back in his family to about 1800. This is unlikely, as trawl fishing didn't come into use until around 1840. Only the lyric was found in the Barry collection so we have used a slightly adapted version of a traditional tune, "The Connaughtman's Rambles," as the melody.

Burgee = a pennant, unique for each boat. When returning to port the burgee would identify the boat to those watching on shore.

A version of this song appears in the James Madison Carpenter Collection AFC 1072/001 MS (p. 09180) "Forecastle Songs and Chanties," Ph.D Thesis, Harvard University, 1928, pp. 185–186. Collected from Charles Snellen, Marblehead, MA. The verses are completely different.

We were sitting in the parlor
Thinking over every plan
When in came Palmer in a hurry
To ship us on the *Bridget Ann*.

CHORUS:
    Chitty shelong shelong shelah
    Hilo chitty shelong shelah

We went down to see the skipper
And finding him a nice young man
We told him we could go a-fishing
If he'd ship us on the *Bridget Ann*.

If you want to go a-fishing
Do your duty like a man.
Oil down the shrouds and gigging
All on board the *Bridget Ann*.

When we left old Cape Cod harbor
Plenty tobacco we had on hand;
When we reached the gut of Canso
Narry a chew on the *Bridget Ann*.

Here's the tar, now take a bucket
Rub it in on every strand.
You will strand upon the rigging
All on board the *Bridget Ann*.

We stopped awhile in the Gut of Canso
There lived the skipper's doxie, Ann.
Clear away, boys, get everything ready
To lower a boat from the *Bridget Ann*.

Working on the Railroad

Frank Stanley, Cranberry Island, ME 11/1927
Fanny Hardy Eckstorm Collection
Transcription © 2021 Julia Lane

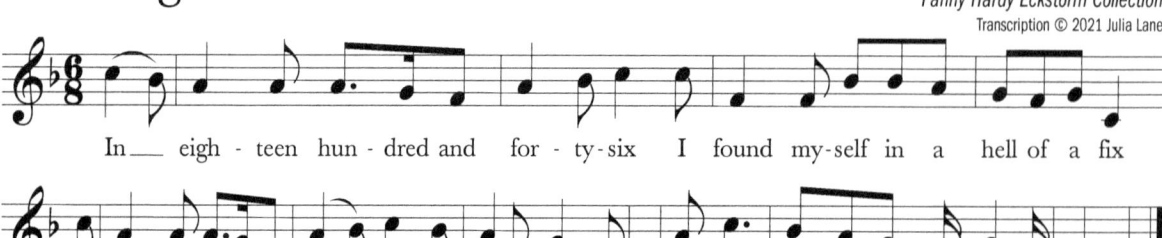

In eighteen hundred and forty-six
I found myself in a hell of a fix
A-working on the railway, the railway, the railway.
Poor Paddy works on the railway.

In eighteen hundred and forty-seven
When Dan O'Connell went up to heaven
He worked upon the railway, the railway, the railway.
Poor Paddy works on the railway.

In eighteen hundred and forty-eight
I found myself bound for the Golden Gate
A-working on the railway, the railway, the railway.
Poor Paddy works on the railway.

I eighteen hundred and forty-nine
I passed my time on the Black Ball line
A-working on the railway, the railway, the railway.
Poor Paddy works on the railway.

Here's a song describing the experience of the immigrant Irish who arrived just in time to build the railroads around the Northeast and into the west for the California gold rush. The rail lines in Portland were established in 1842 and laid the foundation for a development scheme ten years later. Entrepreneur John A. Poor sought to rival Boston by making Portland a major world port connecting ocean shipping with the inland markets by rail. Canadian cities such as Quebec and Montreal were a key focus as the cities were essentially land-locked in the winter. In 1853 a rail link was created to Montreal by the Atlantic & Saint Lawrence (later known as the Grand Trunk) Railway. Portland became a major port for the export of Canadian grain. The city was now teeming with Irish dockworkers newly arrived by ship as refugees from the famine conditions in Ireland. Incidentally, these men displaced the Black longshoremen who had previously worked on the waterfront. Portland was also a major importer of molasses and had a sugar refinery. The alcoholic by-products of this and the grain created both a legal distillery in McGlinchey's Brewery and a trade in bootleg booze. Tradition says that the term "Paddy Wagon" was coined there as the men had drinking issues and were often on the wrong side of the law, causing the officers to remove the inebriated men in wagons. The opportunity to work building the new railway system was an alternative opportunity for the ambitious. Many of these men did eventually leave Maine to work their way westward and try their luck in California.

The "Black Ball line" is the name of several British shipping companies. The original Black Ball line of trans-Atlantic packet ships was established in 1818 and ran between Liverpool and NY. A rival company, also called Black Ball, was the Saint John-Liverpool Packet Line which existed in the 1850s. In addition, the Liverpool/Australia line started in 1852 was also called the Black Ball! The inclusion of the company name in the song implies a collaboration, or maybe a rivalry, between the rail and shipping businesses. The song is classified as a working shanty in *Minstrelsy of Maine* (p. 238) and Mrs. Eckstorm says that Mr. Stanley sang additional verses filling in later years. The tune is from Joanna Colcord whose verses range from 1861–1864.

Willie-O

Lyrics: Carrie Grover, Gorham, ME 1955
Melody adapted from Franz Blanchard, Brewer, ME
Phillips Barry Collection
Transcription © 2021 Julia Lane

"Come all fair maidens, both comely and handsome,
Come list to me while a song I sing;
It's all concerning my true love Willie
Who has gone away for to serve his king.

Oh, he has sailed away on the good ship *Falcon*
And where he is I do not know.
May the angels guard and thus protect him
And bring to me my Willie O."

As Mary was sleeping, Willie came a-creeping
And knocked so softly at the bedroom door,
Saying, "Mary dear, don't be so frightened.
It is the voice of your Willie O."

Oh, they sat down, and were long conversing
While down her cheeks the tears did flow.
"Oh, Willie, dear, what has changed your color
From what it was long years ago?"

"Oh, Mary, dear, the clay has changed it.
I am the ghost of your Willie O.
Now Mary, dear, I must be going
For soon the cocks will begin to crow.

The cocks they're crowing, and I must be going,
Back to my grave I now must go.
One last embrace, then farewell forever.
You will see no more of your Willie O."

This is a version of a broadside ballad from the mid-19th century called "Sweet William's Ghost." It also appears in the Northern Irish traditional repertoire as "My Willy-O," "The Bay of Biscay," or "The Cruel Grave." The theme of the revenant lover is common in many traditions, with the break of dawn and the crowing of the cock signaling the final parting. A related song, "Lady Margaret," collected by Francis Child (#77), as well as "The Lover's Ghost" or "The Grey Cock," do not include the nautical element. These versions seem to date to the early 18th century.

This beautiful tune was recorded by Phillips Barry from Mr. Blanchard but the recording is badly compromised and the lyrics are unintelligible. Fortunately, Blanchard's melody was transcribed by Bayard, presumably before the recording was damaged. Carrie Grover also sang a version of "Willie-O" and transcribed it in a musical ledger which she planned to pass on to her children. Julie Mainstone Savas has created a wonderful resource, "The Carrie Grover Project," which contains Carrie's entire collection, including this song. We have adapted her lyrics to Blanchard's melody.

Songs of Ships & Sailors

Glossary of Nautical Definitions and Common Expressions

above board	the part of the ship that is visible, or that which is on deck
as the crow flies	Crows were caged at the top of the mast (Crow's nest) to be released when visibility was poor; they would fly straight for land
at the helm	to steer
back your topsail	to adjust the sail to bring the wind to the opposite side in order to slow down or stop (heave to)
belaying pin	a wooden or iron rod 15"–24" long, 1" or more in diameter. Used to tie off lines on a sailing vessel, they were easily accessible and made effective weapons
between wind and water	that which is vulnerable, i.e. the hull
bitter end	the end of the rope attached to a deck fastening called a bitt
bearing down	a bearing is a course; bearing down is an approach from the windward
by the reel	the speed of a sailing ship was determined by casting a float (log) astern and counting the knots on the log line as they passed through the navigator's hand for a specific time; hence the term knots meaning speed
catfall	the tackle used to lift the anchor to the cathead
cathead	a large wooden beam where the anchor is secured while at sea
chain shot	two half cannon balls joined by a length of chain used to cut the rigging and spars of an enemy ship
corvette	the smallest class of rated warships, ranking above a sloop of war and below a frigate.
courses	on a square-rigged ship the lowest sail on each mast
cut and run	to cut the anchor cable and run before the wind to escape an enemy
deep six	the ocean depths; to jettison overboard
go to wrack and ruin	wrack is seaweed, hence, a shipwreck or disaster
go by the boards	to be swept away as in off the deck
grapeshot	ammunition consisting of many small iron balls fired together from a cannon
gunpowder and good brandy	legend has it that before battle sailors were given a ration of rum mixed with gunpowder to impart additional courage
Guinea	a british gold coin valued from £1–£1.5
handspike	A stout wooden bar, 4'–5' long, used to turn a windlass or capstan
hard and fast	to be unmoveable; to make something fast is to attach it securely
hit the deck	to assemble ready for work, also to duck down
holy stone	a block of soft sandstone used in scrubbing the decks of a ship. It may be called this because the work was done while kneeling
hooker	a small sailing vessel used to service ships in harbor
in the doldrums	the doldrums are a region near the equator where there is frequently no wind, hence boring and depressed
jury rig	a temporary rigging or solution; from the French "jour"(day)

Songs of Ships & Sailors

landlord's quarter-day	in English and Irish tradition quarter days were the four dates in each year on which accounts had to be settled, ensuring that debts were not allowed to linger on
let it ride	allowing the ship to remain riding at anchor
mast	a vertical pole on a ship that supports the spars, sails, and rigging. On a square rigged ship there are three; the foremast, mainmast, and mizzenmast. A barque has three or more masts, a brig has two masts
monkey jacket	a short, close fitting jacket worn by sailors
nine-pounders	the cannon on a ship were rated by the weight of the cannon balls they shot
onboard	present on or in the ship
pipe down	the bos'n's signal for silence
plumb the depths	to drop a lump of lead or "plumb" line overboard to determine the depth
poop	aft deck of a ship; quarterdeck
pooped	when the sea washed over the poop deck, or stern, the ship would wallow and slow down
quarterdeck	the aft deck of a ship, usually raised above the main deck. Common seamen were not allowed on the quarterdeck except when performing their duties
run afoul	to be in trouble as a ship sailing or running into bad weather
scuttle-butt	a cask with a hole in the top holding drinking water. Sailors would gather to pass news or gosssip (like at a drinking fountain)
shipshape and Bristol fashion	all in order; the Bristol ships were known for their efficient crews
sound out	the leadsman would take a sounding of unfamiliar water by dropping a weight over the side to determine the depth
speaking trumpet	megaphone
spinning a yarn	sailors separated fibers from old rope to be used for caulking. Telling stories during this boring job helped pass the time
stud sail (studding sail, stu'ns'l)	on a square rigged ship an auxillary sail rigged on a boom extended from the end of a yard
swig	a very short haul on the halyard
switchel	a drink made of water mixed with vinegar
topgallant yard (t'gans'l yard)	the yards above the topmast yard on a full-rigged ship
taken aback	occasionally, a gust of wind may blow the sails back against the mast causing surprise and consternation
truck	a wooden disk or square that caps a mast; the main truck is the highest point on a ship. On the *Constitution* the main truck is 220' above the deck
weather gauge	the advantageous position of a fighting sailing vessel relative to another
whistle up a storm	sailors believed that whistling would cause a storm
yards	the horizontal spars on a square rigged ship that support the sails. The lowest yard held the course, the second held the topsail, the third the topgallant sail, the fourth the royal. From about 1850 the topsails and topgallant sails were split into upper and lower, adding two more yards. Some ships also had additional yards above the royals; skysails and moonrakers

Index of Song Titles

Song titles used in this book are in **bold**.
Alternate titles are in plain text.

Adieu Ye Banks & Braes of Clyde	9
Andrew Barden (Child 250)	210
Andrew Rose	240
Bagaduce Bay	34
The Ballad of the Oysterman	90
The Banks of Brandywine	172
The Banks of Newfoundland 1	31
The Banks of Newfoundland 2	225
The Basket of Eggs	28
The Battleship, The *Maine*	195
Bill Seymour	150
Black-Eyed Susan	24
The Black Cook	12
Blow Ye Winds, Aye-O	100
The Boatswain and the Tailor	170
Bold Daniels	47
Bold Dighton	14
Bold Manning	230
Bold McCarty	96
The Bold Northwestmen	118
The Bold Pirate	80
The Bold *Princess Royal*	40
The Bold Privateer	35
Bound Away	104
Bracey on the Shore	32
The Brave Boys of Bristol	10
The Brave Seaman	72
The Bridget Ann	252
Bright Phoebe	120
The British Man-O'-War	38
Bung Yer Eye	160
By the Edge of the Sea	122
By the Edge of the Sea	122
The Captain and the Squire	66
Captain Fielding's Tragedy	222
Captain Kidd	98
The Capture of the *Crown*	10
Caroline & Her Young Sailor Bold	140
The *Cedar Grove*	136
The *City of Baltimore*	96
The Colic	66
Come All You Sailor Boys	30
The *Constitution* and the *Guerriere*	110
The Crocodile	17
The Cruel Ship's Carpenter	48
The Cruise of the *Lapwing*	144
The *Cumberland*'s Crew	114
The Dark Eyed Sailor	236
The Deceitful Young Man	108
The Demon Lover	198
The Desolate Widow	242
Domeama	132
The Downeast Maid	120
The Dreadful Ghost	148
The *Dreadnaught*	104
The Drowned Sailor	52
Dublin Bay	44
The *E. A. Horton*	226
Early in the Spring	159
The *Eastern Light*	164
English Jackie	158
The *Enterprise* and the *Boxer*	244
The Evergreen Shore	138
Fair Lady Leroy	92
The Fair Maid All in Her Garden	5
Fair Phoebe & Her Dark-Eyed Sailor	236
Fair Susie	38
The Faithful Sailor Boy	208
False Nancy	36
Far, Far at Sea	163
Farewell Song of Enoch Arden	84
The Fate of Franklin	68
The Fate of *Rena Lee*	112
The Female Smuggler	206
Fifteen Ships on Georges Banks	62
The *Flying Cloud*	6
The Gallant Brigantine	50
The Gay Spanish Maid	78
The Gentle Boy	37
George Reily	20
The Girls of Bagaduce	102
Glenaloon	184
The *Golden Vanity*	156
Goodbye, Annie Darling	84

Songs of Ships & Sailors   259

The Gosport Tragedy	148
The Gosport Tragedy	48
Grace Darling	**190**
The Great Sea Snake	17
Green Beds	**130**
The Greenland Whale	**166**
The Greenwood Tree	**178**
The Handsome Cabin Boy	**174**
The Handsome Girls of Bagaduce	102
Handsome Harry	**108**
The Haven of Rest	**202**
Hearts of Gold	4
Henry Martin	210
Home Dearie	158
Homeward Bound 1	**175**
Homeward Bound 2	**176**
The House Carpenter (Child 243)	**198**
Hull's Victory	**214**
If I Was a Blackbird	**229**
The Indian Lass	42
In London Lived a Merchant	19
In the Year of '39	**133**
The Irish Rover	142
Isabeau S'y Promène	121
The Isle of Jamaica	50
The Isle of Man Shore	**242**
It's of a Rich Lady	64
I'll Sail the Seas Over	**84**
Jack, the Jolly Tar	**132**
Jacket of blue	
The Jacket of Blue	**105**
Jack Simpson, the Sailor	26
Jack Tar's Frolic	**30**
James Bird	**134**
Janie of the Moor	143
Jenny of the Moor	**143**
John Maynard	**106**
Johnny German	**241**
Johnny Jarman	241
John Riley's Farewell	**139**
The Jolly Boatswain	170
The Jolly Roving Tar	**89**
The Jolly Sailor	**250**
The Jolly Sailor Boys	**16**
The Jolly Sailors	3
The Jovial Sailor & His Beautiful Queen	**64**
Lady Franklin's Lament	68
The *Lady of the Lake*	**220**
The Lass of Mohea	42
The Lass of Mohee	**42**
The Lightning Flash	**152**
Lines on a vessel	45
The Little Sailor Boy	**182**
London's Fair City	224
Long Lost Johnny Reilly	5
The Loss of the *Albion*	**212**
Lovely Lou	**162**
Lovely Susan	38
Lowlands Low	**146**
Lowlands Low	156
The Lowlands of Holland	**53**
The Main Truck or A Leap of Life	204
Mary & Willie	**248**
The *Mary L. McKay*	124
Mary's Dream	180
The Merman	100
The Merry Mackerel Catchers	**234**
The Miser's Daughter	**224**
The Missing Ship	**45**
The *Monitor* and the *Merrimack*	116
Mournful Tragedy!	**192**
My Sailor Boy	**205**
The *Nightingale*	217
The Oak and the Ash	158
Old Horse	**216**
Old Ironsides	**204**
Old Sailor's Song	**196**
Our Ship Lays in the Harbor	**19**
Paul Jones	**128**
Peter Jones	**187**
Peter Street	**188**
Polly	148
The Poor Little Fisher Boy	**168**
The Poor Little Sailor Boy	168
Poor Old Man	**74**
The Prayer of the Soldier & the Sailor	**218**
Pretty Polly	130
Pretty Polly	48
Pretty Polly of Topsham	**60**
The Prince of Morocco	182
Pull the String	132
Quare Bungo Rye	160
The Quay Of Dundocken	242
The Questioner	37
The Rambling Beauty	36
The Rambling Female Sailor	**228**

Title	Page
The Randy Tailor	170
Raspberry Lane	158
Robin Hood's Bay	**52**
The Rocks of Scilly	**167**
Rockweed	**18**
Root, Hog, or Die	**58**
Rosemary Lane	158
The Rose of Breton's Isle	**88**
The Rose of Britain's Isle	88
The Rosy Banks of Green	**200**
Roving Jack Tar	**25**
Roving Jack Tar	25
The *Roving Lizzie*	**47**
Sail Away	**34**
Sail On, O Ship of State	**249**
The Sailor and the Ghost	108
The Sailor and the Sea Captain	**26**
The Sailor Boy	208
The Sailor in the Boat	**153**
Sailor Song	28
Sailor Song	30
The Sailors' Alphabet	**75**
A Sailor Walking in His Garden	**5**
The Sailor's Bride	**159**
The Sailor's Child	37
The Sailor's Come-All-Ye	**4**
The Sailor's Grace	216
The Sailor's Grave	**56**
Sailor's Love Song	120
The Sailor's Tale	**55**
Scarborough Sands	52
The Schooner *Fred Dunbar*	**102**
The Seaman's Sorrowful Bride	53
Sea Song	52
The Ship of Revolution	**86**
The Ship That Never Returned	**82**
The Ship's Carpenter	148
The Ship's Carpenter	**48**
The Ship's Crew of Sailors	105
The Silk Merchant's Daughter	250
The Silvery Tide	**246**
The Sinking of the *Royal George*	**76**
Sir Andrew Barton	210
The Sons of Liberty	**94**
The Spanish War	**57**
The Squire's Lost Lady	132
The *Stately Southerner*	**126**
St Catherine's Docks	175
Stow Brow	52
Sur le Bord de L'ile	**121**
Sweet Caroline	120
Sweet Mary Jane	120
The Sweet Trinity	156
The Tailor and the Chest	**170**
The Tall Young Oysterman	**90**
The Tarry Sailor	36
The Tarry Sailor	**73**
Ten Thousand Miles Away	**70**
Tit for Tat	26
Tossed Upon Life's Raging Billow	**177**
A Trip to the Grand Banks	**154**
True Lovers Bold	**22**
The *Union* of St John	**232**
The United Lovers	22
The Valiant Seaman's Return	236
A Wet Sheet and a Flowing Sea	**186**
The *White Squall*	**194**
Why Does My Father Stay So Long Away?	37
Why Don't My Father's Ship Come In?	**37**
The Wild Shore	242
William and Phyllis	178
Willie & Molly	**148**
Willie-O	**255**
The Wonderful Crocodile	17
Working on the Railroad	**254**
The Worn-Out Sailor	**237**
Yankee Tars	**238**
Ye Parliament of England	94
Young Edmund	146
The Young Squire's Frolic	66
'Twas Early, Early in the Spring	**85**

Index of First Lines

Adieu, ye banks and braes of Clyde	9
A gay Spanish maid at the age of sixteen	78
A is the anchor to our gallant ship	75
All on the Downs the fleet lay moored, their streamers waving in the wynd	24
An American frigate, a frigate of war	128
A sailor and a soldier was a-walking one day	218
A sailor bold and undaunted stood	68
A sailor walking all in his garden	5
As I arrived in London I had the joyful news	241
As I roamed on shore one Sunday from my gallant brigantine	50
As I walked out one ev-ening down by the banks of Clyde	220
As I went a roving for pleasure one day	42
As I went a-walking up New York street	250
As Jack walked out of London city	132
As Mary and Willie walked by the seaside their last farewell to take	248
A wet sheet and a flowing sea, a wind that follows fast	186
Bold Mannin' went to sea one day, a dismal day 'twas too	230
Come all British seamen that plows the rough main	14
Come all fair maidens, both comely and handsome	255
Come all good people far and near and you shall quickly hear	88
Come all jolly sailors I pray give attention	12
Come all jolly sailors, wherever you be	26
Come all ye bold Northwestmen who plow the raging main	118
Come all ye bold seamen, pray now attend	112
Come all ye fair gallants, fair gallants attend	60
Come all ye fair ladies and gentlemen bold	64
Come, all ye jovial seaman bold, listen to what I write	232
Come all ye pretty fair maids, if ye did but know	4
Come all ye sons of Freedom, come listen unto me	244
Come all you bold heroes who wear jackets of blue	150
Come all you bold undaunted ones who brave the winter cold	62
Come all you boys from far and near and listen to my ditty	228
Come all you good people, I pray you will attend	200
Come all you Irish stowaways and listen to what I tell	96
Come all you jolly-hearted sailors who on the foaming oceans roam	36
Come all you jolly seamen bold who plow the raging main	167
Come all you landsmen list to me, to tell you the truth I'm bound	17
Come all you sailor boys	30
Come listen awhile and you'll soon shall hear	206
Come listen unto me awhile and I will tell you then	196
Come old folks! Come young folks! Come and listen unto me	25
Come young and old, you seamen bold and listen to my song	188
Early in the spring when the snow is all gone	154
Goodbye Annie Darling, I leave you in sorrow	84
Here comes one jolly, jolly sailor boy	46
Her mighty sails the breezes swell and fast she leaves the less'ning land	45
I am a sailor by my right	108
I came on shore in the month of May	73
I dearly love the hearts so bold and the truth to you I'll write	3
If I was a blackbird I'd whistle and sing	229
I'll tell you of a come-lye young lady fair	236
I'm going to sing a song	116

I might have married a king's daughter fair	198
In Chamberlain Street two sailors were walking	28
In Dalston, fair city, in Dalston fair town	48
In eighteen hundred and forty-six	254
In London's fair city a miser did dwell	224
In Robin Hood's bay a fair damsel did dwell	52
In the year of our Lord fourteen hundred sixty six we set sail from the cove of Cork	142
Isabeau s'y pro-mèn-e le long de son jardin	121
It ofttimes has been told that the British seamen bold	110
It's a ship's crew of sailors you all now shall hear	105
It's a story, it's a story, it's a story of one	130
It's laugh, "Ha! ha!" and shout, "Hurrah!" we are bound for the coast of Maine	234
It's of a gay young damsel, if you may understand	174
It's of a noble steamer, the Cedar Grove by name	136
It's of a sea capting, a sea capting of late	66
It was down by Colvin's garden for pleasure I did stray	38
It was early, early in the spring	159
It was in the town of Liverpool, all in the month of May	89
It was in the year eighteen hundred and one, on March the twentieth day	166
It was of a young sea captain, on Cranberry Isle did dwell	32
It was on a fair morning, a fair morning in May	92
It was on Lake Erie's broad expanse one bright midsummer's day	106
It was on one summer's evening as I lay down to sleep	37
It was on the fourth of January down in the southern sea	100
Last Easter I was married, that night I went to bed	53
Many homes are filled with sorrow and sadness	195
My bark was far, far from the land	56
My love, he was a rich farmer's son	217
My name is Edward Hallahan as you may understand	6
My name it is George Jones, sir, I'm from the county Clare	222
My soul in sad exile was out on life's sea	202
Now to Blackwall Docks we bid adieu	175
Oh, come all you hardy haddockers, who winter fishing go	124
Oh, father lovéd the storm is raging and cold and heavy the night mist falls	190
Oh Mary, darling Mary, since you and I must part	35
Oh, my father owns a ship all in the north country	156
Oh my name was Captain Kidd when I sailed, when I sailed	98
Oh, shipmates come gather and join in my ditty	114
Oh, Sildin he brings rockweed to A, B, and C	18
Oh, there was a young gentleman walking the street	160
Oh, the sea was bright and the barque rode well	194
Old horse, old horse, what brought you here	216
Old Ironsides at anchor lay in the harbor of Mahon	204
On a bright summer's morning, the weather being clear	20
On a pleasant morn as the waves that rippled	82
One morn for recreation as I wandered along the seaside	143
One morning, very early, in the pleasant month of May	172
One Summer's eve as labor was o'er and the birds were singing gaily	237
On the fifteenth of April we sailed from the strand	40
On the Isle of Man shore as I carelessly wandered	242
On the twenty-sixth of April, or so it does appear	10
Our ship lays in harbor just ready for to sail	19
Peter Jones was a Schenectady boy and a lad both brave and bold	187
Said Willie to Molly, "Why can't you agree	148
Sail on, sail on, O ship of State!	249

Sailor in the boat when the tide runs high	153
Says Willie to young Phyllis, "What brought you here so soon?	178
Sez I, "Me boys, don't you want to go fishing?	252
Sing Ho! for a brave and a valiant bark and a brisk and lively breeze	70
The day of our sailing is fast drawing nigh	104
The good schooner Lapwing from Jonesport bears away	144
The moon had climbed the highest hill	180
Then sail away, sail o'er the ocean so blue	34
There was a fair young damsel who lived by the seaside	246
There was an old man came riding along	74
There was a tall young oysterman, lived by the river side	90
There was a young captain in Dover did dwell	170
There was once a little sailor who was both brisk and bold	182
There was three brothers in old Scot-a-land	210
The sailor being drowsy, he hung down his head	158
The sailor's life is a roving life	205
The waves dash high against the rocks with a mighty thund'ring roar	72
They sailed away in a gallant bark, Roy Neill and his fair young bride	44
'Tis a hundred years, so I've been told, since I was a boy at sea	55
'Tis of a ship of revolution, a ship of great fame	86
'Tis of a Stately Southerner that carries the Stripes and Stars	126
Toll for the brave, the brave that are no more	76
Tossed upon life's raging billow, sweet it is, Oh Lord, to know	177
'Twas a cold November day when snow lay on the ground	208
'Twas down in the lowlands a poor boy did wander	168
'Twas early, early in the spring	85
'Twas early in the month of May I said to my love Lou	162
'Twas in the month of September from St. Daniels we set sail	47
'Twas in the pleasant month of May	120
'Twas just a ripple and then a puff came filling an old ship's sail	184
'Twas night when the bell had struck twelve	163
'Twas of a rich nobleman's daughter, so lovely and handsome a girl	140
'Twas of my sad misfortune in eighteen hundred and seventy-three	164
'Twas on a dark and stormy night I heard a fair one say	139
'Twas on the eighteenth day of March we sailed from Bristol Town	80
'Twas on the twenty-fourth of March we got underway	58
We are joyously voyaging over the main bound for the Evergreen Shore	138
We're homeward bound up Liverpool Sound	176
Whenever the Tyrant of the main assaults Columbian Seamen	238
When I was a young man in the year of thirty-nine	133
When I was young and in my prime, my age was twenty-two	152
Yankee Dewey sailed away	57
Ye Parliament of England, ye Lords and Commons too	94
Ye seamen and ye landsmen come listen unto me	212
Ye sons of Uncle Samuel! come, listen for awhile	226
Ye true lovers bold, come listen unto me	22
Ye true sons of freedom give ear to my song	214
You darling girls of Bagaduce who live along the shore	102
You may all bless your happy lots that you are safe on shore	31
Young Andrew Rose, the British sailor	240
Young Emily was a servant maid and she loved her sailor bold	146
Young Isabel went a-walking all in her garden green	122
Young men who in this city live or in the Pine Tree State	192
You rambling boys of Liverpool, I'll have you to beware	225
You sons of freedom listen to me	134

Subject Index

ADVENTURE

The Banks of Newfoundland 2	225
The Bold Northwestman	118
The *Dreadnaught*	104
The *E. A. Horton*	226
The *Flying Cloud*	6
The Greenland Whale Fishery	166
The *Mary L. McKay*	124
The *Stately Southernor*	126

FALSE LOVERS

False Nancy	36
The Green Bed	130
Handsome Harry	108
The House Carpenter	198
The Lass of Mohee	42
Lovely Lou	162
Pretty Polly of Topsham	60
Roving Jack Tar	25
The Sailor's Bride	159
The Ship's Carpenter	48
'Twas Early, Early in the Spring	85

FEMALE SAILORS

Caroline and Her Young Sailor Bold	140
The Fair Lady Leroy	92
The Female Smuggler	206
Grace Darling	190
The Greenwood Tree	178
The Handsome Cabin Boy	174
The Jolly Roving Tar	89
My Sailor Boy	205
The Rose of Breton's Isle	88
True Lovers Bold	22

FISHING

The *Bridget Ann*	252
The Cruise of the *Lapwing*	144
The *E. A. Horton*	226
The *Eastern Light*	164
Fifteen Ships on George's Banks	62
The *Mary L. McKay*	124
The Merry Mackerel Catchers	234
Root, Hog, or Die	58
The Schooner *Fred Dunbar*	102
A Trip to the Grand Banks	154

GIRLS LEFT BEHIND

The Banks of Brandywine	172
The Basket of Eggs	28
The Captain and the Squire	66
Fair Phoebe and Her Dark-eyed Sailor	236
The Fate of Franklin	68
The Gay Spanish Maid	78
George Reily	20
Green Beds	130
Johnny German	241
The *Lady of the Lake*	220
The Lass of Mohee	42
The Lowlands of Holland	53
Mary's Dream	180
The *Nightingale*	217
The Oak and the Ash	158
Our Ship Lays in the Harbor	19
Roving Jack Tar	25
The Tarry Sailor	73

HEROES

Bold Dighton	14
Bold McCarty	96
The Bold *Princess Royal*	40
The Bold Seaman	72
The Capture of the Crown	10
The *Constitution* and the *Guerriere*	110
The *Enterprise* and the *Boxer*	244
Grace Darling	190
Hull's Victory	214
John Maynard	106
Paul Jones	187
The Sailor's Come All Ye	4
The Ship of Revolution	86
The Spanish War	57

Songs of Ships & Sailors

The *Stately Southernor*	126
Yankee Tars	238

HUMOR

The Basket of Eggs	28
The Black Cook	12
Blow Ye Winds Aye-O	100
Bracey on the Shore	32
Bung Yer Eye	160
The Captain and the Squire	66
The Crocodile	17
The *Irish Rover*	142
Jack the Jolly Tar	132
Peter Jones	187
Rockweed	18
The Sailor and the Sea Captain	26
The Sailor's Tale	55
The Tailor & the Chest	170
The Tall Young Oysterman	90

HYMNS

The Evergreen Shore	138
The Haven of Rest	202
Tossed Upon Life's Raging Billows	177

JACK ON SHORE

The Basket of Eggs	28
The Black Cook	12
Bung Yer Eye	160
The Gallant Brigantine	50
Green Beds	130
Jack, the Jolly Tar	132
Jack Tar's Frolic	30
The Jovial Sailor and his Beautiful Queen	64
The Lass of Mohee	42
The Oak and the Ash	158
Peter Street	188
Roving Jack Tar	25
The Sailor and the Sea Captain	26
The Tailor & the Chest	170

LOVE THWARTED

Lowlands Low	146
The Miser's Daughter	224

My Sailor Boy	205
The Rosy Banks of Green	200
The Silvery Tide	246

OTHER TRAGEDIES

Captain Fielding's Tragedy	222
The Faithful Sailor Boy	208
Far, Far at Sea	163
The Fate of Franklin	68
The *Golden Vanity*	156
James Bird	134
John Maynard	106
John Reilly's Farewell	139
Lowlands Low	146
The Missing Ship	45
Mournful Tragedy!	192
The Rambling Female Sailor	228
The Rosy Banks of Green	200
The Sailor's Grave	56
The Ship That Never Returned	82
The Silvery Tide	246
Sur le Bord de L'ile	121
Why Don't My Father's Ship Come In?	37

PIRATES & ROGUES

Andrew Barden	210
Andrew Rose	240
Bill Seymour	150
Bold Manning	230
The Bold Pirate	80
The *Bold Princess Royal*	40
Captain Fielding's Tragedy	222
Captain Kidd	98
The *Flying Cloud*	6
The *Roving Lizzie*	47
The Ship of Revolution	86

POLITICS & PATRIOTS

The Battleship, The *Maine*	195
The Capture of the *Crown*	10
The *Constitution* and the *Guerriere*	110
The *Cumberland's* Crew	114
The *E. A. Horton*	226
The *Enterprise* and the *Boxer*	244
Hull's Victory	214

The *Monitor* and the *Merrimack*	116
Paul Jones	128
Sail On, Oh Ship of State	249
The Sons of Liberty	94
The Spanish War	57
The *Stately Southernor*	126
Yankee Tars	238

A SAILOR'S LIFE

The Black Cook	12
The *Bridget Ann*	252
The Cruise of the *Lapwing*	144
The *Eastern Light*	164
Homeward Bound 1	175
Homeward Bound 2	176
The Jolly Sailors	3
The Merry Mackerel Catchers	234
Old Horse	216
Old Sailor's Song	196
Poor Old Man	74
The Prayer of the Soldier & the Sailor	218
Root, Hog, or Die	58
The Sailor's Alphabet	75
The Sailor's Come All Ye	4
The Sailor's Grave	56
The Schooner Fred Dunbar	102
A Wet Sheet and a Flowing Sea	186
Working on the Railway	254
The Worn-out Sailor	237

THE SAILOR'S RETURN

The Banks of Brandywine	172
The Bold Privateer	35
The Gay Spanish Maid	78
George Reily	20
Green Beds	130
Jenny of the Moor	143
Johnny German	241
The *Lady of the Lake*	220
The Little Sailor Boy	182
Lowlands Low	146
The Rosy Banks of Green	200
Roving Jack Tar	25
A Sailor Walking All in HIs Garden	5
The Silvery Tide	246
'Twas Early, Early in the Spring	85

SEA BATTLES

Andrew Barden	210
The Battleship, The *Maine*	195
Bold Dighton	14
The *Constitution* and the *Guerriere*	110
The *Cumberland's* Crew	114
Fair Lady Leroy	92
Hull's Victory	214
In the Year of '39	133
The *Monitor* and the *Merrimac*	116
Paul Jones	128
The Ship of Revolution	86
The Spanish War	57

SHIPWRECKS

The Banks of Newfoundland I	31
The *Cedar Grove*	136
Dublin Bay	44
The Fate of Franklin	68
The Fate of *Rena Lee*	112
Fifteen Ships on George's Banks	62
The Gay Spanish Maid	78
Glenaloon	184
The Greenwood Tree	178
The *Irish Rover*	142
The Isle of Man Shore	242
John Riley's Farewell	139
The Jolly Sailor	250
The *Lady of the Lake*	220
The Loss of the *Albion*	212
Mary's Dream	180
The *Nightingale*	217
Robin Hood's Bay	52
The Rocks of Scilly	167
The Sinking of the *Royal George*	76
The Union of St. John	232
The *White Squall*	194

SONGS OF PARTING

Adieu Ye Banks & Braes of Clyde	9
Black-Eyed Susan	24
The Bold Privateer	35
The British Man-O-War	38
The Downeast Maid	120
The Faitfhul Sailor Boy	208

Songs of Ships & Sailors   267

The Gay Spanish Maid	78
Goodbye Annie Darling	84
Homeward Bound 1	175
Homeward Bound 2	176
John Riley's Farewell	139
The Lass of Mohee	42
Lovely Lou	162
The Lowlands of Holland	53
Mary & Willie	248
Sail Away	34
Ten Thousand Miles Away	70

SUPERNATURAL

Blow Ye Winds Aye-O	100
Far, Far at Sea	163
Glenaloon	184
Handsome Harry	108
The House Carpenter	198
Mary's Dream	180
The *Nightingale*	217
The Ship's Carpenter	48
Willie & Mollie	148
Willie-O	255

TRUE LOVERS

The Banks of Brandywine	172
Caroline and Her Young Sailor Bold	140
Fair Phoebe and Her Dark-eyed Sailor	236
The Fate of Franklin	68
The Gay Spanish Maid	78
George Reily	20
The Greenwood Tree	178
If I Was a Blackbird	229
The Jacket of Blue	105
Jenny of the Moor	143
Johnny German	241
John Riley's Farewell	139
The Jolly Roving Tar	89
The Jolly Sailor	250
The Jovial Sailor and his Beautiful Queen	64
The *Lady of the Lake*	220
The Lass of Mohee	42
The Lightning Flash	152
The Little Sailor Boy	182
Mary & Willie	248
My Sailor Boy	205

The *Nightingale*	217
Our Ship Lays in the Harbor	19
Robin Hood's Bay	52
The Rose of Breton's Isle	88
The Rosy Banks of Green	200
Sur le Bord de L'ile	121
The Tall Young Oysterman	90
The Tarry Sailor	73
True Lovers Bold	22

MISC

The Jolly Sailor Boys	46
Old Ironsides	204
Rockweed	18
The Sailor in the Boat	153

Index of Song Sources

This list consists of all titles of sea songs noted as being in collections made of Maine singers pre-1950. Some have been lost and are noted a such. We have undoubtedly missed some songs as titles vary and are sometimes misleading. In addition, not all the collections were accessible for complete examination.

KEY TO SOURCES

BBM1 – *British Ballads from Maine Volume 1*, Barry/Eckstorm/Smyth, Yale Univ. Press, 1929

BBM2 – *British Ballads from Maine Volume 2*, Barry/Eckstorm/Smyth, Pauleena MacDougall, (ed.) Northeast Folklore Volume XLIV, University of Maine, 2011

CGHS – Carrie Grover, *A Heritage of Song*, Norwood Press, 1955, also https://carriegroverproject.com

CGMM – Carrie Grover Maine Manuscript, https://carriegroverproject.com

ELC – Eloise Linscott Collection, American Folklife Center, Library of Congress, Washington, DC

FHE – Fannie Hardy Eckstorm Collection, Fogler Library, Orono, ME

FHE/HHF/BDN – songs in articles from *Bangor Daily News*, 1933, by Fannie Hardy Eckstorm & Helen Hartness Flanders

FHE/MM – Fannie Eckstorm & Mary Smyth, *Minstrelsy of Maine*, Houghton Mifflin Co, Riverside Press, 1927

HB – Horace Beck Collection

HB/FM – Horace Beck, *The Folklore of Maine*, J.B. Lippincott, 1957.

HHF – Helen Hartness Flanders Collection, Middlebury College, Middlebury, VT

HHF/BM – Helen Hartness Flanders, *Ballads Migrant in New England*, Books for Libraries Press, 1968.

HHF/AB – Helen Hartness Flanders, *Ancient Ballads Traditionally Sung in New England*, University of Pennsylvania Press, 1960

JC/SAS – Joanna Colcord, *Roll and Go: Songs of American Sailormen*, Bobbs-Merrill Co, 1924

LO – Lomax Collection, American Folklife Center, Library of Congress, Washington, DC

KM – *The Kneeland Miscellany, Genealogy of the Kneeland Family, Songs of James & Amanda Kneeland* by Frank & Bertha Kneeland, 1917

MFC – Maine Folklife Center, University of Maine, Orono, ME

PB/BFSSNE – *Bulletin of the Folk Song Society of the North East*

PB/H – Phillips Barry Collection, Houghton Library, Harvard

PB/MWS – Phillips Barry, *The Maine Woods Songster*, Powell Printing, 1939

PB/LOC – Phillips Barry Collection, Library of Congress

RP/KJ – Ralph Page Collection, University of NH, Durham, NH, *Kitchen Junket Magazine*

RPG – Roland Palmer Gray, *Songs and Ballads of the Maine Lumberjacks*, Harvard University Press, 1924

SB – Samuel Bayard, Folk tunes from the Phillips Barry Collection, transcribed from Dictaphone recordings for Harvard College Library, June, 1942

SCY – Susie Carr Young tunes transcriptions in Barry Collection, Houghton Library, Harvard

SRC – Sidney Robertson Cowell Collection, Library of Congress, Washington, DC. Recorded in Teaneck, New Jersey

SOURCES

(Tune Name / Source Singer / Location / Date / Collector / Specific publication or recording code)

A

A St-Malo Beau Port de Mer – Margarita L. Bartley, Jackman, ME, 1954, **HHF**, T15A N/A

A St-Malo Beau Port de Mer – M. Joseph LeClair, Jackman, ME, 8/17/1954, **HHF**, T05B @ 25:25

Adieu, Ye Banks & Braes of Clyde – Frank/James Kneeland, Searsport, ME, 10/1941, **HHF**, D14A side A @ 31:56; *text:* **KM**

Adieu to Nova Scotia – **CGMM**

Andrew Barden (Sir Andrew Barton, Child 167, 250) – Charles Finnemore, Bridgewater, ME, 2/28/1948, **HHF**, D70B side B @ 00:12

Andrew Barton (Child 167, 250) – Mrs. S.M. Harding, Hampden Highlands, ME, **PB/LOC**

Andrew Batting (Sir Andrew Barton, Child 167, 250) – Frank/James Kneeland, Searsport, ME, 10/1941, **HHF/AB**, Dl3B side B @ 8:50; *text:* **KM**

Andrew Briton / The Three Brothers (Sir Andrew Barton, Child 167, 250) – Lamont Forbuss, Monson, ME, **PB/MWS**

Andrew Marteen (Sir Andrew Barton, Child 167, 250) – Hanford Hayes, Stacyville, ME, 9/22/1940, **HHF**, D06B side A @ 7:46, 5/5/1942, D19B side A @ 32:46, **HHF/AB4** p24, **HHF/BM** p72

Andrew Martine (Sir Andrew Barton, Child 167, 250) – Eliza Ostinelli, Portland, ME, 1859, **BBM1**, p226, **HHF/AB4**

Andrew Rose – Mrs. Edna Floyd, West Jonesport, ME, 8/20/1942, **HHF**, D33B side A @ 23:05

Andrew Rose – Frank/James Kneeland, Searsport, ME, 10/1941, **HHF**, D13B side A @ 43:00; *text:* **KM**

Andrew Rose – *tune:* Susie Carr Young, Brewer, ME, 1930, **PB/H**

As We Drew Near Old England – P. Dunn, Brewer, ME, **PB/LOC**

B

Bagaduce Bay (Sail Away) – *text fragment:* Hattie Hanson Soper, Orland, ME **PB/H**, **PB/BFSSNE**

The Ballad of Nantucket (Pretty Maggie, Maggie in the Rain) – *text:* from "Adventure" by Robert W. Gordon, 8/1927, **FHE**

Banks of Clyde, The (Lady of the Lake) – Charles Finnemore, Bridgewater, ME, 9/1941 **HHF**, D16B side A @ 34:15, D16B side A (cont.) @ 28:10

Banks of Inverness, The – Carrie Grover, Gorham, ME, 1955, **CGHS**

Banks of Brandywine, The – George Dalton, Brewer, ME, 6/24/1941, **HHF**, **FHE/MM**, D11A @ 25:07

Banks of Brandywine, The – *text:* Mrs. Annie V. Marston, West Gouldsboro, ME, 1926, **FHE**

Banks of Newfoundland 1, The – *text:* Mrs. Annie V. Marston, West Gouldsboro, ME, 1926, **FHE/MM**, **PB/H**

Banks of Newfoundland 1, The – The Banks of Newfoundland, Mabel Worcester, Hanover, ME, 1967, **MFC**

Banks of Newfoundland 2, The – *text:* Capt. George Henry Spurling, Isleford, ME, 1925, **FHE/MM**

Banks of Newfoundland 2, The – *text:* Mrs. Fred Morse, Isleford, ME, 1926, **FHE/MM**

The Basket of Eggs (Sailor Song) – Sadie S. Harvey, Houlton, ME, 9/30/41, **HHF**, D15A side A @ 16:40

The Battleship, the Maine – Oliver Jenness, York, ME, 9/28/1948, **HHF**, D52A side B @ 7:25

Bill Seymour (Jacket of Blue) – Alonzo Lewis, York, ME, 9/22/1947, **HHF**, D50A side B @ 10:30, 10/01/1948, D52A side B @ 36:42

Billy Taylor (William Taylor) – *text fragment:* Miss Clara E. Harrison, Penobscot, ME, **BBM2**

Black Cook, The – Charles Finnemore, Bridgewater, ME, 5/8/1942, **HHF**, D25A18–19 @ 13:45

Black-Eyed Susan – Mrs. G. C. Erskine, Cheshire, CT, (Dixfield, ME) **HHF**, C09A side B @ 5:13

Black-Eyed Susan – Charles Finnemore, Bridgewater, ME, 10/29/1943, **HHF**, D39B side B @ 19:20, 26:51

Blow, Boys, Blow – David Kane, Searsport ME 10/1941, **HHF**, D60B side A @ 19:49

Blow, Boys, Blow – Wynifred Staples Smith, Dixfield, ME, 11/12/1941, **ELC** sr034asl

Blow the Man Down – Hanford Hayes, Stacyville, ME, 7/1941, **HHF**, D60B08 @ 22:55

Blow the Man Down – David Kane, Searsport, ME, 10/1941, **HHF**, D60B side A @ 17:08

Blow the Man Down – *text:* James Kneeland, Searsport, ME 1917, **KM**

Blow Ye Winds – Carrie B. Grover, Gorham, ME, 10/29/1943, **ELC** sr282bsl

Blow Ye Winds, Aye - O (The Merman) – Annie Tate Moore, Ellsworth Falls, ME, 6/22/1941, **HHF**, D11A side A @ 15:50 & @16:18

Blow Ye Winds, Aye - O (The Merman) – *text:* R.M.Davids, **JC/SAS**

Boatswain's Honest Wife, The (The Tailor and the Chest) – Susie Carr Young, Brewer, ME, 1925, **BBM2**

Bold Abandeersman, The (Capt. Bunker) – *text:* Mrs. Edwin F. Robbins, NE Harbor, ME, 1928, **FHE/HHF/BDN**, **PB/BFSSNE** 6:14-15, 1933; *tune:* George Herzog

Bold Caroline, The – *text:* Mrs. E.C.P. Bangor, ME, **FHE/HHF/BDN**

Bold Daniels (The Rovin' Lizzie) – Charles Finnemore, Bridgewater, ME, 10/28/43, **HHF**, D39B side B @ 42:28

Bold Dighton – Albert Cox, Sherman Mills, ME, 5/10/1942, **HHF**, D26A side B @ 4:14

Bold Dighton – Charles Finnemore, Bridgewater, ME, 5/7/1942, **HHF**, D25A side B @ 00:35, D68B side A @ 23:45

Bold Dighton – William Merritt, Ludlow, ME, 1941, **HHF**, D68B side A @ 15:50

Bold Fisherman, The – Charles Finnemore, Bridgewater, ME, 5/7/1942, **HHF**, D25B side A @ 27:25, BM

Bold Fisherman, The – Carrie Grover, Gorham, ME, 1941, **LO**

Bold Fisherman, The – Susie Carr Young, Brewer, ME, 1926; *tune:* George Herzog 1928, **BBM2**, **PB/H**

Bold Manan the Pirate – *text:* Capt. Lewis Freeman Gott, Bernard, ME, 1926, **FHE/MM**

Bold Manan the Pirate – *text:* Mr. Horace E. Priest, Sangerville, ME, 1924, **FHE/MM**

Bold Manning (Bold Manan the Pirate) – Albert Cox, Sherman Mills, ME, 5/10/1942, **HHF**, D26A side B @ 11:43

Bold Manom (Bold Manan the Pirate) – *text:* Charles Finnemore, Bridgewater, ME, 2/24/1952, **HHF**

Bold McCarty (The City of Baltimore) – *text:* Charles F. Alley, Jonesport, ME, 10/1927, **PB/H**

Bold Northwestman (Come All Ye) – Frank/James Kneeland, Searsport, ME, 10/1941, **HHF**, D14A side A @12:45; *text:* **KM**, **FHE/HHF/BDN**, **PB/LOC**, **PB/BFSSNE** 10, 1935, pp. 17–18

Bold Northwesternman, The – Charles Finnemore, Bridgewater, ME, 5/7/1942, **HHF**, D25B side A @ 6:42

Bold Northwesternman, The – John P. A. Nesbitt, St. Stephen, NB, **PB/BFSSNE** 4, 1932, pp. 13–14

Bold Pirate, The – *text:* Joseph Gilley via Mrs. Nathan S. Stanley, 8/1924, Mrs. Harriet Taylor & Mrs. Phoebe Stanley, 9/1926, Baker & Little Cranberry Islands, ME, **FHE/MM**

Bold Prince of Royal, The (The Bold Princess Royal, Prince of Regent) – *text: Springfield Sunday Union*, 8/19/24, **FHE**

Bold Princess Royal, The – *text:* Frank Matthews, Eastport, ME, 10/1927, **PB/H**

Bold Privateer, The – *tune:* Susie Carr Young, Brewer, ME, 1930, **PB/H**

Bold Sea Captain, The (Capt. Wedderburn's Courtship, Child 46) – **CGMM**

Boney was a Warrior – Wynifred Staples Smith, Dixfield, ME, 11/12/1941, **ELC**, sr034

Bos'n's Tale, The (The Sailor's Tale) – David Kane, Searsport, ME, 1945, **HHF**, D54A side A @ 41:23

Bracey on the Shore – *text:* Mrs. Enoch Bulger, Big Cranberry Island, ME, 9/3/1926, **FHE/MM**

Brave Seaman, The – *text:* Kathleen Clark, Pembroke, ME, 1928, Pembroke, ME, Historical Society

Bridget Ann, The – *text:* M. G. A. Ham, Bath, ME, 1930, **PB/H**

British Man o' War, The (Lovely Susan) – Charles Finnemore, Bridgewater, ME, 10/28/1943, **HHF**, D39B side B @ 00:40

British Man o' War, The (Lovely Susan) – Jack McNally, Stacyville, ME, 9/25/1940, **HHF**, C12A side A @ 17:35, C11B side A @ 26:28 (This cut is labelled "Hanford Hayes" and introduced as such by the technician. The recordist, however introduces McNally. It is a continuation) 5/9/1942, D24A side A @ 15:36

British Sailor, Andrew Rose, The – Susie Carr Young, Brewer, ME, **PB/H**

Bung Yer Eye – Murchie Harvey, Houlton, ME, 9/28/1941 **HHF**, D15A side A @ 10:42

Burial at Sea (The Sailor's Grave) – *text:* Albert Garland, Ellsworth, ME, 7/19/1936, **PB/H**

C

Cap'n Paul – *text:* Mrs. Mary O. Tinum, Kennebunk, ME, 7/24/1941, **HHF/BM**

Captain and the Squire, The – *text:* Dale Potter, Kingman, ME, 1947, **HB**

Captain Bunker (The Bold Abandeersman) – *text:* Mrs. Edwin P. Robbins, NE Harbor, ME, 1928, **FHE/HHF/BDN**, **PB/BFSSNE** 6:14–15, 193; *tune:* George Herzog

Captain Fielding (Fielding's Tragedy, Charles Augustus Anderson, The Saladin) – Hanford Hayes, Stacyville, ME, 8/26/1942, **HHF**, D29B side A @ 3:50

Captain Kidd – Carrie Grover, Gorham, ME, 1955, **CGHS**

Captain Kidd – *text:* Justin Decoster, Buckfield, ME, 1925, **FHE**

Captain Kidd – **JC/SAS**

Captain Ward and the Rainbow (Child 287) – Capt. Lewis Freeman Gott, Bernard, ME, 10/1924, with tune via Mrs. H. R. Murphy 1928, **BBM1**, **HHF/AB**

Captain Ward and the Rainbow (Child 287) –fragment with *tune:* Edward Holt, St Andrews, NB, 9/27/1927, **BBM1**

Captain Ward (Child 287) – Ralph Lewis, York, ME, 9/22/1947, **HHF/AB**, **HHF/BM**

Captain Ward (Child 287) – *text:* Lincoln Shorey, Carmel, ME, 3/31/1928, **BBM1** (Tune sent 6/1930, **BBM2** p310)

Captain Wasgatt – *text:* Mrs. Phoebe Stanley, Baker Island, ME, 10/1926, **FHE/MM**

Captain's Chest, The – Mrs. Eileen Finnemore, Portland, 11/4/1941, **ELC** – N/A

Captain Wedderburn's Courtship (Child 46) – *tune:* Mrs. S. M. Harding, **PB/LOC**, **BBM1**; *tune:* **SB**

Capture of the Crown, The (The War of 1812) – *text:* Mr. Henry H. Chamberlain, Round Pond, ME, 11/1929, **PB/H**

Songs of Ships & Sailors

Capture of the Crown, The – *text:* "The Life of Commodore Samuel Tucker," by John H. Sheppard, Boston, 1868

Caroline and Her Young Sailor Bold – *text:* Henry Bunker, Cranberry Isles, ME, 5/1926, **PB/H**

Caroline and Her Young Sailor Bold – *text:* Mr. John S. Russell, Bangor, ME, 2/17/1934, **FHE**, **PB/H**, **PB/BFSSNE** 2:9–10

Cedar Grove, The – Stephen Barlow, Mars Hill, ME, 8/30/1942, **HHF**, D29A side B @ 13:20

Charles Augustus Anderson (Captain Fielding, Fielding's Tragedy) – *text:* Mrs. Dalton Raynes, Matinicus, ME, **HB/FM**

Charming Lass of Mohea, The – Alonzo Lewis, York, ME, 9/22/1947, **HHF**, D52A side B 00:30

Church and Chapel (Pull Down) – *text:* Capt. William Coombs, Isleboro, ME, 1904, vis Walter M. Hardy, Brewer, ME, **FHE/MM**

City of Baltimore, The (Bold McCarty) – *text fragment:* Harry Meyers, Matinicus, ME, **HB/FM**

Coast of New Barbary, The (High Barbary/Child 285) – Jack McNally, Stacyville, ME, 8/26/1942, **HHF/AB**, D30B side A @ 26:10

Constitution and the Guerriere, The – *text:* Justin De Coster, Buckfield, ME, 9/1935, **PB/H**

Constitution and the Guerriere, The – *text:* Lewis Freeman Gott, Bass Harbor, ME, 10/1924, **PB/H**

Constitution and the Guerriere, The – Harry Wass, Addison, ME, 8/18/1942, **HHF**, D31A side A @ 13:58

Cork Harbor (The Lightning Flash) – Charles Finnemore, Bridgewater, ME, 9/22/1941, **HHF**, D16B side B @ 13:08, D17A side A @ 00:40 (cont.)

Crocodile, The (Rummy Crocodile, The Sea Serpent) – Frank Tracy, Brewer, ME, 10/7/1941, **HHF**, D15B side A @ 32:43, **PB/H**

Crocodile, The (Rummy Crocodile, The Sea Serpent) – Carrie Grover, Gorham, ME, 1955, **CGHS**

Crocodile, The (The Great Fish) – *fragment:* Susie Carr Young, Brewer, ME, 1929; *tune:* George Herzog

Cruel Ship's Carpenter, The (Pretty Polly) – F.E. Buzzell, Freedom, ME, **PB/LOC**; *tune:* **SB**, 1942

Cruise of the Lapwing, The – *text:* John Radley, Jonesport, ME, 1870, Jonesport, ME, Historical Society

Cruise of the Nancy Banker, The – *text:* Mrs. Oliver K. Joyce, Gott Island, ME, 1924, Capt. Archie S. Spurling, Isleford, ME, 1926, **FHE/MM**

Cruising Down Barbary (High Barbary, Child 285) – Frank/James Kneeland, Searsport, ME, 10/1941, **HHF/AB**, D13B side B @ 11:55–12:12; *text:* **KM**

Cumberland's Crew, The – *text:* James Kneeland, Searsport, ME, 1917, **KM**

Cumberland's Crew, The – Dr. Edward "Sandy" Ives, "Folksongs of Maine," Smithsonian Folkways, 1959

Cutter Water Lily, The – *text:* Capt. Samuel P. Cousins, Trenton, ME, 1870, **FHE/MM**

D

Dark-Eyed Sailor, The (Fair Phoebe & Her Dark-eyed Sailor) – *text:* M. Howard, S. Getchell, St. Stephen, NB, 1930, **PB/H**

Dark-Eyed Sailor, The (Fair Phoebe & Her Dark-eyed Sailor) – Carrie Grover, Gorham, ME, 1955, **CGHS**

Dark-Eyed Sailor, The (Fair Phoebe & Her Dark-eyed Sailor) – Mrs. Guy Hathaway, Mattawamkeag, ME, 6/14, 25, 26/1932, **PB/LOC**

Dark-Eyed Sailor, The (Fair Phoebe & Her Dark-eyed Sailor) – Jack McNally, Stacyville, ME, 5/5/1942, **HHF**, D07A side A @ 15:47, @ 25:20, @ 29:34, @ 32:06

Dark-Eyed Sailor, The (Fair Phoebe & Her Dark-eyed Sailor) – *text:* Mrs. Joan B. Moore, Seawall, Southwest Harbor, ME, 8/1927, **PB/H**

Dark-Eyed Sailor, The (Fair Phoebe & Her Dark-eyed Sailor) – *text:* Mrs. Fred Morse, Isleford, ME, 1926, **PB/H**

Dark-Eyed Sailor, The – *text:* Mrs. Rosalie Chick Wood, Bangor, ME, 1899, **FHE**

Death of Captain Friend, The – *text:* Mrs. Oliver K. Joyce, Gott Island, ME, 8/1924, **FHE/MM**

Death of Captain Samuel Spurling, The – *text:* Broadside, 1837, **FHE/MM**

Death of Captain Smith C. Spurling, The – *text:* Mrs. Evelyn F. Hamor, Bar Harbor, ME, 1926, **FHE/MM**

Death of Herbert Rice, The – *text:* Capt. Archie S. Spurling, Isleford, ME, 10/1925, Mrs. Enoch Bulger, Cranberry Isles, 1925, also Broadside written by Charles Stanley 1868 Cranberry Island, ME, **FHE/MM**, **HB/FM**

Death of William Cilley – *text:* Mrs. Emeline Spurling Bulger, Big Cranberry Island, ME, Mrs. Phoebe Stanley, Baker Island, ME, 9/3/1926 (Original broadside provided) **FHE/MM**

Desolate Widow, The (Isle of Man Shore) – Carrie Grover, Gorham, ME, 1955, **CGHS**

Desolate Widow, The (Isle of Man Shore) – Susie Carr Young, Brewer, ME, 1925, **PB/H**
Dixey Bull – *text:* Mr. T. R. McPhail, Thomaston, ME, 1925, **FHE/MM**
Down by the Seaside – Carrie Grover, Gorham, ME, 1955, **CGHS**
Downfall of Pyracy, The – *text:* **FHE**
Downeast Maid, The (Bright Phoebe, Sweet Caroline) – *fragment & tune:* Susie Carr Young, Brewer, ME, **PB/BFSSNE** 3:16, **PB/H**
Dreadnaught, The – Oliver Jenness, York, ME, 9/19/41, **HHF**, D13A side A @ 34:47–35:02
Dreadnaught, The – *text fragment:* Harry Meyers, Matinicus, ME, **HB**
Drunken Sailor, The – *text fragment:* **FHE/MM**
Dublin Bay (Roy Neill/Neal) – *text:* Mrs. Rosalie Wood, Bangor, ME, 1875, **PB/H**
Dying Californian, The – Oliver Jenness, York, ME, 9/18/1941, **HHF**, D13A side A @ 27:48, 31:58
Dying Californian, The – Sarah Lane, Howland, ME, 5/11/1942, **HHF**, D25B side B @ 11:14
Dying Californian, The – Hanford Hayes, Stacyville, ME, 8/25/1942, **HHF**, D29B side A @ 21:05
Dying Californian, The – *text:* **HB/FM**

E

E. A. Horton, The – Judson Carver, Jonesport, ME, 8/20/1942, **HHF**, D33B side A @ 29:35
E. A. Horton, The – Harriet Gott Murphy, Rumford, ME, 9/12/1942, **HHF**, D31B side B @ 0:55
E. A. Horton, The – *text:* Mrs. Oliver K. Joyce, Gott Island, ME, 1924, **FHE/MM**
E. A. Horton, The – *text:* Mrs. Phoebe Stanley & Captain King, Baker Island, 1926, **FHE/MM**
Early in the Spring (The Sailor's Bride) – Sarah Lane, Hiram, ME, 5/12/42, **HHF**, D25B side B @ 14:14
Early, Early in the Spring (The Sailor's Bride) – Susie Carr Young, Brewer, ME, 1925, **PB/H**
Eastern Light, The – *text:* Capt. Archie S. Spurling, Islesford, ME, 10/1925, **FHE/MM**; *text:* **HB/FM** 1950
Edwin and Emma (Young Edwin in the Lowlands Low) – *text:* Mrs. David Libbey, Newport, ME, 1916, **BBM2**
Edward Dill (Young Edwin in the Lowlands Low) – *text:* Justin DeCoster, Buckfield, ME, 1925, **BBM2**
Eighteen Fine Seamen (The Silk Merchant's Daughter) – *text fragment:* Dale Potter, Kingman, ME, 1947, **HB**
English Jackie (Home Dearie Home, The Oak and the Ash) – *text:* Mrs. Mary Hindle, Bangor, ME, 9/1929, **FHE, PB/H**
Enterprise and the Boxer, The – *text:* Printed in "The Bird of Birds", 1818
Evergreen Shore, The – *text:* Amanda Crockett Kneeland, Searsport, ME, 1917, **KM**

F

Fair Lady Leroy – Carrie Grover, Gorham, ME, 10/29/1943, **ELC** sr033asl
Fair Maid by the Seahore, The – Mrs. Annie V. Marston, West Gouldsboro (Charlestown), ME, 1929, **PB/MWS, PB/BFSSNE** 7:12, **BBM2**
Fair Maid by the Shore, The – *text:* Horace Priest/Charles Porter, Sangerville, ME, 8/1925, **BBM2**
Fair Maid on the Shore, The – Carrie Grover, Gorham, ME, 1955, **CGHS, LO**
Fair Phoebe and Her Dark-eyed Sailor – Mrs. Guy Hathaway, Mattawamkeag, ME, 6/1932, **FHE, PB/MWS, PB/BFSSNE** 6:8–10, **PB/LOC**
Fair Susie (Lovely Susan/The Yankee Man o' War) – *text:* Horace Priest/Mr. Everett York, Sangerville, ME, 8/1925, **BBM2**
Faithful Sailor Boy, The – Hanford Hayes, Stacyville, ME, 12/7/1940, **HHF**, D24A side B @ 15:40, 24B, side A @ 00:30
Faithful Sailor Boy, The (The Two Sailors) – William Irish, Sherman, ME, 1941, **HHF**, D15A side B @ 9:50
Faithful Sailor Boy, The – Jack McNally, Stacyville, ME, 9/25/1940, **HHF**, C12A side A @ 12:48
Faithful Sailor Boy, The – Edward Rand, Sherman Mills, ME, 8/28/1942, **HHF**, D28A side B @ 12:58
False Nancy – Annie Marston, West Gouldsboro, ME, circa 1925, **PB/H**
Far, Far at Sea – *text:* Unidentified singer, Searsport, ME, 1916, **RPG**
Farewell and Adieu, You Fair Spanish Maidens – Carrie Grover, Gorham, ME, 5/1941, **SRC**
Fatal Dream, The – *text:* **FHE** (noted but not found)
Fate of Franklin, The – Will Merritt, Ludlow, ME, 1941, **HHF**, D14B side A @ 14:20, 18:24

Fate of Rena Lee (The Fate of Ramilles) – Frank/James Kneeland, Searsport, ME, 10/1941, **HHF**, D13B side B @ 0:10; *text:* **KM**

Female Smuggler, The – Charles Finnemore, Bridgewater, ME, 9/30/1941, **HHF**, T14B side A @ 9:05, D16B side B @ 10:18 (cont)

Fielding's Tragedy (The Saladin) – Frank Tracy, Brewer, ME, 10/7/41, **HHF**, D15B side B @ 00:35

Fifteen Ships on George's Banks – *text:* Mr. Henry Bunker, Cranberry Island, ME, 1924, **FHE/MM**

Fifteen Ships on George's Banks – *text:* Mrs. Mary L. Cotton, Orland, ME, 1926, **FHE/MM**, **HB/FM**

Fifteen Ships on George's Banks, Margaret Hallett, Lubec, ME, 1963, **MFC**, Digital Commons

Fight Between the Monitor and the Merrimack, The – *text:* Henry Hunter Chamberlain, Round Pond, ME, 1920, **FHE**

First to California, Oh, Fondly I Went (Row, Bullies, Row) – *text:* Capt. J. A Creighton, Thomaston, ME, 1925

Fishermen's Song, The – *text:* Robert Holbrook manuscript, April 1851, Boothbay Historical Society, Boothbay, ME

Fishermen's Song, The – *text:* Mrs. John B. Moore, Seawall, Southwest Harbor, ME, 8/18/1927, **PB/H**

Fishes, The – Carrie Grover, Gorham, ME, **CGMM** 230

Flyering Cloud, The (The Flying Cloud) – Frank L. Tracy Brewer, ME, 7/11/1932; 6/10/1934, **PB/LOC**; *tune:* **SB**

Flying Cloud, The – Asa Brown, Carthage, ME, 11/12/1941, **ELC** afs6059bsl (Distorted recording)

Flying Cloud, The – *text:* Mr. Harry Cole, Springfield, ME, 3/1934. **FHE**

Flying Cloud, The – Jerry Desmond, Island Falls, ME, 7/11/1940, **HHF**, C10B side B @ 1:01

Flying Cloud, The – Jack McNally, Stacyville, ME, 8/28/1942, **HHF**, D30A side A @ 24:35, 28:51, 33:18

Flying Cloud, The – *text:* Mr. Harry Peters, Rebel Hill, Clifton, ME, 6/17/1936, **PB/H**

Flying Cloud, The – Dale Potter, Kingman, ME, 1940, **HHF**, C10A side B @ 6:49, 13:50, **HB/FM** 1947

Flying Cloud, The – *text:* Capt. Archie S. Spurling, Isleford, ME, 5/1925, **FHE/MM**

G

Gallant Brigantine, The (The Isle of Jamaica) – George Dalton, Brewer, ME, 6/28/1941, **HHF**, D11A side A @ 27:10,

Gallant Ship, The (1759) – *text:* Mrs. Seth Thornton, Southwest Harbor, ME, 4/9/1928, **PB/H**

Gaspereaux Tragedy, The (Gosport Tragedy) – *text:* Horace Priest, Sangerville, ME, 8/1925, **BBM2**

Gay Spanish Maid, The – *text:* Mrs. Mary Cotton, Orland, ME, 1927, **PB/H**

Gay Spanish Maid, The – *text:* Mrs. Pearle M. Crory, Portage, ME, 1/31/1934, **FHE**

Gay Spanish Maid, The – Hanford Hayes, Stacyville, ME, 5/5/1942, **HHF**, D59B side A 03:04 (N/A), D20A side A @ 00:34

Gay Spanish Maid, The – *text:* Mr. Edward Holt, St, Stephen, NB, **PB/H**

Gay Spanish Maid, The – *text:* Mr. Fremont Lee, Second Falls, NB, 1929, **FHE**

Gay Spanish Maid, The (Sweet Nancy) – *text:* Mrs. Annie Marston, West Gouldsboro, ME, 9/1929, **FHE**

Gay Spanish Maid, The – *tune:* Mrs. Annie Marston, West Gouldsboro, ME, 9/1929, **PB/H**

Gay Spanish Maid, The – *text fragment:* Mr. David Preble, Guilford, ME, 9/27/1928, **PB/H** tune by Herzog

Gay Spanish Maid, The – *text:* Miss Sittara Thomas, Blue Hill, ME; *tune:* Susie Car Young, Brewer, ME, 1930, **PB/MWS**

George Reily/Riley – *text:* **ELC** Hiram Virgin, Mexico, ME, 11/13/1941

George's Banks – Susie Carr Young, Brewer, ME, 1925, **PB/H**

Glenaloon – *text:* Mr. Chas F. Alley, Jonesport, ME, 1930, **PB/H**

Gloucester Gale, The (George's Banks) – *text:* Mrs. Seth Thornton/M.C.Gilley, 10/1926, **FHE/MM**

Ghost of Willie-O (My Willie-O) – Franz Blanchard, Brewer, ME, 1941, **PB/LOC**; *tune:* **SB**

Ghostly Fishermen, The (Ghostly Crew) – **HB/FM** w. tune

Golden Vanity, The (Sweet Trinity, Child 286) – *fragment text & tune:* Mrs. Sarah Robinson Black, Southwest Harbor, ME, 1928, **BBM1**

Golden Vanity, The (Sweet Trinity, Child 286) – *text:* Capt. Lewis F. Gott, Bernard, ME, 1926, **BBM1**

Golden Vanity, The (Sweet Trinity, Child 286) – *text:* Mr. Howard Getchell, St. Stephen NB/Capt. George E. Sanborn, 1888, **BBM1**

Golden Vanity, The (Sweet Trinity, Child 286) – Carrie Grover, Gorham, ME, 1955, **CGHS**

Golden Vanity, The (Sweet Trinity, Child 286) – Mrs. Guy Hathaway, Mattawamkeag, ME, 6/1932, **PB/LOC**, **PB/BFSSNE** 5, 1933 pp.10–11

Golden Vanity, The (Sweet Trinity, Child 286) – Leonard M. Patterson, Newport, ME, 6/23/1936, **PB/LOC**, **PB/BFSSNE** 5:10–11; *tune:* **SB**

Golden Vanity, The (Sweet Trinity, Child 286) – Mrs. Rose Robbins, Northeast Harbor, ME, 1928, **BBM1**

Goodbye, Annie Darling – Annie Tate Moore, Ellsworth Falls, ME, 6/22/1941, **HHF**, D11A side A @ 13:47

Gosport Tragedy, The (The Ship's Carpenter) – Carrie Grover, Gorham, ME, 1955, **CGHS**

Gosport Tragedy, The (The Ship's Carpenter) – *text fragment:* Mrs. Fred (Sarah?) Lane, Howland, ME, **HHF**

Gosport Tragedy, The (The Ship's Carpenter) – Mrs. Annie Marston, West Gouldsboro, ME, 8/1929, **BBM2**

Grace Darling – *text:* Justin Decoster, Buckfield, ME, 1925, **FHE**

Grace Darling – *text:* Mr. George Omar, St. Stephen, NB, circa 1930, **FHE**

Great Fish, The (The Crocodile) – *text:* Thomas Edward Nelson, Union Mills, NB, 1/1929, **FHE**

Green Bed, The (Polly) – *text:* James Kneeland, Searsport, ME, 1917, **KM**

Green Beds – *text fragment:* Mrs. James (Margaret) McGill, Chamcook, NB, 11/28/1928, **BBM2**

Green Beds (Johnny the Sailor) – Arthur Walker, Littleton, ME, 8/31/1942, **HHF**, D28B side A @ 8:41

Greenland Whale Fishery, The – Carrie B. Grover, Gorham, ME, 9/29/1943 **ELC** sr282asl, **LO**, **CGMM**

Greenland Whale Fishery, The – Leonard M. Patterson, Newport, ME, 6/23/1936, **PB/LOC**, **PB/BFSSNE** 6:14; *tune:* **SB**

Greenland Whale Fishery, The – *text:* Mrs. Phoebe Stanley, Baker Island, ME, 1925, **FHE/MM**

Greenland Whale Fishery, The (The Bold Abandeersman, Capt. Bunker) – *text:* Mrs. Edwin P. Robbins, NE Harbor, ME, 1928, **FHE/HHF/BDN**, **PB/BFSSNE** 6: pp 14–15, 1933; *tune:* George Herzog

H

Handsome Cabin Boy, The – Charles Finnemore Bridgewater, ME, 10/28/1943, **HHF**, D39B side B @ 9:10

Handsome Girls of the Bagaduce, The – Miss Annie Dunbar, North Castine, ME, 4/20/1924, **FHE**; *tune:* **PB/H** 1934

Handsome Harry (The Demon Lover) – *text:* Susie Carr Young, Brewer, ME, 1930, **PB/H**

Handsome Harry (The Demon Lover) – Jack McNally, Stacyville, ME, 5/9/1942, **HHF**, D24A side A @ 21:53

Haven of Rest, The – *text:* Archie Spurling, Cranberry Island, ME, 1950, **HB**

Heart Rending Boat Ballad (The Sailor Boy) – *text:* **FHE**

Hello, Somebody (Hilo) – *text:* Laura E. Richards, Gardiner, ME, 3/1926, **FHE/MM**

Henry Martyn (Sir Andrew Barton, Child 167) – Fred Brackett, Stacyville, ME, 5/10/1942, **HHF/AB**, D 26B side A @ 14:00

High Barbary (Child 285) – *text:* Capt Lewis Freeman Gott/Capt. John Dawes Bernard, ME, 1925, **BBM1**, **HHF/AB**x4

Highland Laddie – *text:* Susie Carr Young, Brewer, ME, 1926, **FHE/MM**

Home Boys, Home (Home Dearie Home) – *text:* Colonel Smith, **HB**

Home Dearie, Home (English Jackie, The Oak & the Ash) – Eunice Perry, Dexter, ME via Mary Hindle, Bangor, ME, 9/12/1929, **PB/H**

Home Dearie, Home – Capt. Archie Spurling, Isleford, ME, 1926, **HB/FM**

Home Dearest, Home – Carrie B. Grover, Gorham, ME, **CGMM**

Homeward Bound1 – Susie Carr Young, Brewer, ME, 1925, **FHE**, **PB/H**

Homeward Bound2 – *text:* James Kneeland, Searsport, ME, 1917, **JC/SAS**, **KM**

Horton's In! The – *text:* Mrs. Oliver K. Joyce, Gott Island, ME, 1924, **FHE/MM**

Horton's In! The – *text:* **HB/FM**

House Carpenter, The (Child 243) – *text:* Capt. Lewis F. Gott, Bernard, ME, 1926; *tune:* Susie Carr Young, Brewer, ME, 1928, **PB/H** , **BBM1**

Hull's Victory – *American Advocates*, Hallowell, ME, 1812

Hyannis on the Cape – *text:* D. H. Ham, Islesford, ME, 1932, **PB/H**

I

If I was a Blackbird – Hanford Hayes, Stacyville, ME, 5/5/1942, **HHF**, D24B side A @ 25:25

I'll Go Back from Whence I Came (Saucy Sailor) – Carrie Grover, Gorham, ME, 10/29/1943, **ELC** sr283b,

In the Brig: Air "Rake from Kildare" – Clifford Henry, North Bucksport, ME, **PB/H**, **PB/LOC**; *tune:* **SB**

In the Year of '39 – Alonzo Lewis, York, ME, 10/1/48, **HHF**, D52A side A @ 25:19

In Fair Salem Town (The Valiant Seaman's Return) – Mr. Thomas Edward Nelson, Union Mills, NB, 9/28/1927, **BBM2**

In London Lived a Merchant (Our Ship Lays in the Harbor) – Graham Wilson, Cherryfield, ME, 09/25/1940, **HHF**, C11B side A @ 0:55

Irish Rover, The – David Kane, Searsport, ME, 10/1941, **HHF**, D67A side A @ 27:07

Isle of Am-e-o, The – *text:* Capt. William Quinn, Orrington, ME, via Mrs. Avery Olmstead, Brewer, ME, 2/18/1924, air noted, **FHE**

Isle o' Holt (Highland Laddie) – *text:* Capt. William Coombs, Isleboro, ME, 1904, vis Walter M. Hardy, Brewer, ME, **FHE/MM**

Island of Jamaica, The (The Gallant Brigantine) – *text:* Hanford Hayes, Stacyville, ME, 9/1940, **HHF**, D60 side A lyrics sent/recording unclear

Isle of Man Shore, The (The Desolate Widow) – Carrie Grover, Gorham, ME, 1955, **CGHS**

Isle of Man Shore, The (The Wild Shore) – Albert Cox, Sherman Mills, ME, 5/10/1942, **HHF**, D26B side A @ 7:40

Isle of Man Shore, The – Charles Finnemore, Bridgewater, ME, 5/7/1942, **HHF**, D25B side A @ 00:50

Isle of Man Shore, The – Hanford Hayes, Stacyville, ME, 5/9/1942, **HHF**, D24A side B @ 12:21

Isle of Man Shore, The (The Desolate Widow) – Mrs. Annie V. Marston, West Gouldsboro, ME, 1925, **PB/BFSSNE** 1:8–9, **RP/KJ**

Isle of Mo-whee (Lass of Mohea) – *text:* Mrs. John Craig, Eastport, ME, via Mr. John S. Russell, Bangor, ME, 3/8/1934, **FHE**

J

Jack Tar (The Saucy Sailor) – tune & fragment: Susie Carr Young, Brewer, ME, 1925, **PB/H**

Jack Tar (Domeama) – Fred Fowler/Susie Carr Young, Hampden, ME, **PB/BFSSNE** 3:10–11

Jack Tar (Domeama) – Mr. George H. Spurling, Southwest Harbor, ME, 1927, **FHE/MM**

Jack Tar's Frolic (Come all you sailor boys) – David N. Poor, Portland, ME, 1842 (manuscript) via Sue Bicknell

Jack the Jolly Tar – *text fragment:* Mrs. G. C. Erskine, Cheshire, CT (Dixfield, ME) 1939

Jack Simpson the Sailor (The Sailor and the Sea Captain) – *text:* Dale Potter, Kingman, ME, 1947, **HB/FM**

Jack Williams (I am a boatman) – Susie Carr Young, Brewer, ME, 1925, **PB/H**

Jacket of Blue – *text:* Miss Annie L. Dunbar, North Castine, ME, 1925, **FHE**

Jacket of Blue (Ship's Crew of Sailors) – Jack McNally, Stacyville, ME, 1942, **HHF**, D07A side A (cont) @ 7:00, side B @ 7:40 is the beginning. Neither is noted on index; side B is incorrectly identified by the technician as Hanford Hayes

Jacket of Blue – *tune:* Annie Marston, Gouldsboro, ME, **PB/H**

Jacket of Blue (Bill Seymour) – Alonzo Lewis, York, ME, 10/01/1948, **HHF**, D52A side B @ 36:42

Jacket so Blue, The – *text:* **RPG**, Broadside (1835), Searsport, ME, 1916

Jacket so Blue (Ship's Crew of Sailors) – *text:* Dale Potter, Kingman, ME, 1937, **HB/FM**

James Bird – Susie Carr Young, Brewer, ME, 1925, **PB/H**

James Bird – John Hutchinson, Berry's Mills, ME, November 12, 1941, **ELC** sr 6071b 2:40 fragment, sr125 a

James and Florence (True Lovers Bold) – Carrie Grover, Gorham, ME, 1955, **CGHS**

Janie of the Moor – Frank L. Tracy Brewer, ME, 6/10/1934, **PB/LOC**

Janie on the Moor – Carrie Grover, Gorham, ME, 1955, **CGHS**

Jennie of the Moor – Mrs. S.M. Harding, Hampden Highlands, ME, **PB/LOC**

John Maynard – Charles Finnemore, Bridgewater, ME, 10/2/1945, **HHF**, D42A side A @ 37:36

John O'German – Mrs. Emery Howard, North Blue Hill, ME, 6/9/1932, **BBM2**, **PB/LOC**

John Riley (John Riley's Farewell) – *text:* Mrs. Pearle M. Crory, Portage, ME, 1930, **FHE**

John Riley's Farewell – Hanford Hayes, Bridgewater, ME, 9/22/1940, **HHF**, 5/10/1942 D06B side A @ 27:03 retake @ 40:05, D06B side B @ (cont) 00:37

Johnny, Fill up the Bowl – *text fragment:* Capt. Rufus H. Young, Hancock, ME, 1925 **FHE/MM**

Johnny German – Jack McNally, Stacyville, ME, **HHF**, D29B side B @ 29:45

Johnny German – Susie Carr Young, Brewer, ME, 1925, **BBM2**, **PB/H**

Johnny Jarman – Hanford Hayes (Index says McNally), Stacyville, ME, 8/28/1942, **HHF**, D29B side A @ 29:39, side B @ 1:58

Johnny's Been to London (The Green Bed) – Mrs. Susie Carr Young, Brewer, ME, 1925, **BBM2**

Jolly Hearted Sailors – **PB/BFSSNE** 1:7

Jolly Roving Tar, The – Carrie Grover, Gorham, ME, 1941, **ELC/LOC** sr327asl, **CGMM**

Jolly Sailor, The (The Silk Merchant's Daughter) – Arthur Walker, Littleton, ME, 8/30/1942, **HHF** D28B, side A @ 4:20

Jolly Sailors, The – Oliver Jenness, York, ME, 1941, **HHF**, D16A side B @ 7:15

Jovial Sailor and His Beautiful Queen, The – Susie Carr Young, Brewer, ME, 1925, **PB/H**

Jyacus – *text:* Colonel Smith, 1945, **HB**

L

Lady Leroy – Murchie Harvey, Houlton, ME, 5/7/1942, **HHF**, D24B side B @ 12:40, D25A side B @ 00:45

Lady of the Lake, The (The Banks of Clyde) – Charles Finnemore, Bridgewater, ME, 9/1941, **HHF**, D16B side A @ 34:15 D16B side A (cont.) @ 28:10

Lass of Mohea, The – Carrie Grover, Gorham, ME, 1941, **LO**

Lass of Mohea, The – *text:* Mrs. L.C. Foster, Carmel, ME, 1925, **FHE/MM**

Lass of Mohea, The – Oliver Jenness, York, ME, 9/20/1947, **HHF**, D47B side B @ 15:05, and @ 18:00

Lass of Mohea, The – Eugene Leach, Surry, ME, 8/20/1942, **HHF**, D31A side A @ 23:44

Lass of Mohea, The – Jack McNally, Stacyville, ME, 8/26/1942, **HHF** D29B side B @ 10:12

Lass of Mohea, The – *text:* Mrs. Annie Marston, Gouldsboro, ME, 1926, **FHE/MM**

Lass of Mohea, The (Little Mohea) – Perley Quigg, Island Falls, ME, 7/10/1940, **HHF**, C10B side A @ 19:50, **PB/LOC**

Lass of Mohea, The – Sadie Gray Smith, (Mrs. W. H.) Houlton, ME, 9/23/1940, **HHF**, D06B side B @ 2:19

Lightning Flash, The (Cork Harbor) – John P. A. Nesbitt, St. Stephen, NB, 1930 via Mary Smyth, Brewer, ME, **PB/H**, **PB/BFSSNE** 10:11, 3:14–15

Lion's Den, The – Mrs. Sarah Robinson Black, SW Harbor, ME, 9/1928, **BBM2**

Lion's Den, The – *text:* Mrs. Joan B. Moore, Seawall, SW Harbor, ME, 8/1927, **BBM2**

Lion's Den, The – *text:* Mr. T. Edward Nelson, St. Stephen, NB, 10/1927, **BBM2**

Lion's Den, The – Mr. John Sprague, Milltown, NB, 9/27/1928, **BBM2**

Lion's Den, The – *text:* Mrs. Phoebe Stanley, Baker Island, ME, 1/16/1926, **BBM2**

Little Mary the Sailor's Bride – Frank L. Tracy, Brewer, ME, 1939, **PB/MWS**

Little Mohea – Herbert Merry, Thorndike, ME, 9/12/1934, **PB/LOC**

Little Nell of Narragansett Bay – Frank L. Tracy Brewer, ME, 7/11/932, 6/10/1934, **PB/LOC**

Little Sailor Boy, The (Prince of Morocco) – Frank/James Kneeland, Searsport, ME, 1941, **HHF**, D14A side A @ 00:48; *text:* **KM**

Liza Ann – *text:* Colonel Smith, 1945, **HB**

Long Time Ago, A – *text:* Laura E. Richards, Gardiner, ME, 3/1926, **FHE/MM**

Loss of the Albion, The – Mrs. Lyddie Tennant, E. Orland, ME, 5/12/1942, **HHF**, D26A side B @ 0:26

Loss of the Albion, The – *text:* Susie Carr Young, Brewer, ME, 1926, **FHE/MM**, **PB/H**

Loss of the Due Dispatch, The – Carrie Grover, Gorham, ME, 1955, **CGHS**

Loss of the New Columbia, The – Carrie Grover, Gorham, ME, 1955, **CGHS**, **LO**

Loss of the Sarah, The – *text:* Mrs. Oliver K. Joyce, Gott Island, ME, 1924, **FHE/MM**

Loss of the Schooner Minerva, The – *text:* Broadside by Ebenezer Eaton, Cranberry Island, ME, ca. 1821, **FHE/MM**

Lovely Lou Gene Staples, Dixfield, ME, 11/12/1941, **ELC** afs6062bsl

Lovely Susan (The British Man o' War) – Susie Carr Young, Brewer, ME, 1925, **BBM2**, **PB/H**

Lovely Susan (The Yankee Man o' War) – *text:* Capt. Lewis Freeman Gott Bernard, ME, 1924

Lowlands – *text fragment:* Mr. Frank Stanley, Cranberry Island, ME, 11/1925, **FHE**

Lowlands of Holland, The (Child 93) – Carrie Grover, Gorham, ME, 1955, **CGHS**, **LO**

Lowlands of Holland, The (Child 93) – *text:* Mrs. James (Margaret) McGill, Chamcook, NB, 9/28/1928, **PB/H**

Lowlands Low (Lowlands of Holland) – *text:* Murray, Holden, ME, 1917, **RPG**

Lowlands Low (Golden Vanity/Sweet Trinity/Child 286) – Hanford Hayes, Stacyville, ME, 5/10/1942, **HHF**, D24B side A @ 11:14

Lowlands Low (Golden Vanity/Sweet Trinity/Child 286) – *text:* Mrs. Harriet Gott Murphy, Rumford Center, ME, 1942, **HHF/AB**

Lowlands Low (Young Edwin in the Lowlands) – Alonzo Lewis, York, ME, 9/22/1947, **HHF**, D50B side A @ 0:05

Lowlands Low (Edmund & Emily, Young Edwin in the Lowlands) – Susie Carr Young, Brewer, ME, 1925, **BBM2**

M

Maggie May – *text:* Franz Blanchard, Brewer, ME, 6/1934, **FHE**

Maria T. Wiley, The – *text:* Mrs. Laura E. Richards, Gardiner, ME, 1/1926, **FHE/MM**, (air noted but not found)

Mary & Willie (The Sailor's Bride) – Annie Syphers, Monticello, ME, 9/22/1947, **HHF**, D14B side B @ 1:00

Mary & Willie (The Sailor's Bride) – Mrs. J.S. Russell, Bangor, ME, **PB/LOC**; *tune:* **SB**

Mary L. McKay, The – Frederick William Wallace 1913, Helen Creighton Collection

Mary's Dream – Carrie Grover, Gorham, ME, 1955, **CGHS**

Mary's Dream – *text:* Mrs. Nina Starboard, **HB/FM**

Mermaid, The (Child 289) – *text:* Capt. Charles Donovan, Jonesport, ME, 1929 (as a shanty)

Mermaid, The (Child 289) – *text:* Capt Lewis Freeman Gott Bernard, ME, 1924, **BBM1**

Mermaid, The (Child 289) – *text:* John T. White, Brewer, ME, (PEI), **BBM1** (familiar tune noted)

Merman, The (Blow Ye Winds Aye-O) – *text:* Capt. L. Freeman Gott, Bernard, ME, 1925, **PB/H** 234

Merman, The (Blow Ye Winds Aye-O) – Annie Tate Moore, Ellsworth Falls, ME, 6/22/1941, **HHF**, D11A side A 15:50 and 16:38

Merry Mackerel Catchers, The – *text:* Jacob S. Lord, Gloucester, MA 1882, *The Fisherman's Own Book*, Procter Bros., Gloucester, MA

Miami Lass, The (Little Mohea) – Frank L. Tracy Brewer, ME, 7/11/1932, 6/10/1934, **PB/BFSSNE** 6:15–18, **PB/LOC**; *tune:* **SB**

Miser's Daughter, The – *text:* Mrs. Mary E. Hindle, Bangor, Sept. 12, 1929, **FHE**

Missing Ship, The – *text:* Harold W. Castner (journal), Skidompha Library, Damariscotta, ME

Mobile Bay (Clear the Track) – *text:* Mrs. Seth Thornton, Southwest Hbr, ME, 11/1926, **FHE/MM**

Molly and Willie (Cruel Ship's Carpenter) – Annie Syphers, Monticello, ME, 9/22/1947, **HHF**, D14B side A @ 29:00

Monitor and the Merrimack, The – *text:* Mr. Justin DeCoster, Buckfield, ME, 1925, **PB/H**

Mournful Tragedy – William Withington 1850, Broadside, Maine Historical Society, Portland, ME

My Lost Sailor Lad (Sailor's Bride/Early in Spring) – *text:* Dr. R.L. Grindle, Mount Desert, ME, 8/1924, **FHE**

My Sailor Boy – *text:* Mrs. Fred W. Morse, Isleford, ME, 1/22/1934, **FHE**

My Sailor Boy – *tune:* Susie Carr Young, Brewer, ME, 1930, **PB/H**

My Willie's on the Deep Blue Sea – Carrie Grover, Gorham, ME, 1955, **CGHS**

N

Nancy – Frank L. Tracy Brewer, ME, 7/11/1932, 6/10/1934, **PB/LOC**; *tune:* **SB**

Nellie Greer – Carrie Grover, Gorham, ME, 1955, **CGHS**

New Barbary (Child 285) – Wellman J. Delano, Gassets, VT, 1930, **HHF/AB**

New Barbary (Child 285) – fragment: Adam Morris, Kingman, ME, 1940, **HHF/AB** C10A side A @ 32:08

Nightingale, The – Jack McNally, Stacyville, ME, 5/10/1942, **HHF**, C10B side A @ 31:16, D23B side B @ 8:23

O

Oak and the Ash, The (Home Dearie Home, English Jackie) – *tune:* Mrs. James (Margaret) McGill, Chamcook, NB 1928, **PB/H**

Oak and the Ash, The (Home Dearie Home, English Jackie) – *text:* Capt. Archie Spurling, Islesford, ME, 11/1925, **PB/H**; *tune:* Herzog 1928, **HB**

Oak and the Ash, The (Home Dearie Home, English Jackie) – *text:* Phoebe Stanley, Baker Island, ME, via Maud King, Baker's Island, ME, 11/9/1925, **PB/H**

Ocean Burial, The (The Sailor's Grave) – *text:* **HB/FM**

Off the Magdelin Isles – Leonard M. Patterson, Newport, ME, 6/23/1936, **PB/LOC**; *tune:* **SB**

Old Horse (Sailor's Grace) – *text:* Mrs. Lewis Gott, Bernard, ME, Mrs. Seth Thornton, SW Harbor, ME, Joan B. Moore, Seawall, SW Harbor, ME, 1926, **FHE/MM**

Old Horse (Sailor's Litany) – *text:* Harry Meyers, Matinicus, ME, **HB/FM**

Old Ironside s – *text:* Harry Meyers, Matinicus, ME, **HB**

Old Sailor's Song – *text:* Henry Chamberlain, Round Pond, ME, 1920, **JC/SAS**

Old Redskin, The – *text:* Chaney Ripley, Matinicus Island, ME, **HB/FM**

Old Sea Song (The Mermaid, Child 289) – M.A.A. Young, Brewer, ME, 7/1930, **BBM2**

Old Ship of Zion, The – *text:* **FHE**

Old Woman on the Seashore, The – **PB/BFSSNE** 10:10

On a Bold Privateer – *fragment & tune:* Susie Carr Young, Brewer, ME, 1925, **PB/H**

On Board the Arethusa – Carrie Grover, Gorham, ME, **CGMM**

On Yonder Green Mountain – Carrie Grover, Gorham, ME, 1955, **CGHS**

Our Captain Says: "Away" – Carrie Grover, Gorham, ME, 5/1941, **SRC**

Our Gallant Ship (The Mermaid, Child 289) – Mrs. James (Margaret) McGill, Chamcook, NB, 4/1928, **BBM1**

Our Ship Lays in the Harbor (In London Lived a Rich Merchant) – Graham Wilson, Cherryfield, ME, 09/25/1940, **HHF**, C11B side A @ 0:55

P

Paddy Doyle – *text fragment:* Mr. Frank Stanley, Cranberry Island, ME, 11/1925, **FHE**

Paul Jones – *text:* Mrs. J. H. Fernald, Islesford, ME, 1932, **PB/H**

Paul Jones – *text:* James Kneeland, Searsport, ME, 1917, **KM**

Penobscot River Chantey – Wynifred Staples Smith, Dixfield, ME, 11/12/1941, **ELC** sr034asl

Peter Jones – Oliver Jenness, York, ME, 1941, **HHF**, D13A side B @ 3:54

Peter Street – Charles Finnemore, Bridgewater, ME, 10/29/1943, **HHF**, D39B side B @ 4:48

Phoebe and Her Dark-eyed Sailor – Susie Carr Young, Brewer, ME, 1925, **PB/H**

Pirate Crew, The – *text:* Mr. D. H. Ham, Isleford, ME, 1880, **PB/H**

Pirate's Serenade, The – *text:* Mrs. Harry Rowe, Patten, ME, **FHE/HHF/BDN**

Polly (The Green Bed) – *text:* James Kneeland, Searsport, ME, 1917, **KM**

Poor Little Fisher Boy, The (The Poor Little Sailor Boy) – Carrie Grover, Gorham, ME, 1955, **CGHS**

Poor Little Fisherman's Boy, The (The Poor Little Sailor Boy) – Susie Carr Young, Brewer, ME, 1925, **PB/H**

Poor Little Sailor Boy, The (The Poor Little Fisher Boy) – Oliver Jenness, York, ME, 1941, **HHF**, D13A side B @ 0:16–0:38, 9/25/1947, D60B side A @ 00:22

Poor Old Horse – Susie Carr Young, Brewer, ME, 1925, **PB/H**

Poor Old Man (Poor Old Horse) – **JC/SAS**

Prayer of the Sailor and the Soldier, The – Charles Finnemore, Bridgewater, ME, 10/29/1943, **HHF**, D39B side B @ 4:33

Pretty Maggie (Ballad of Nantucket) – *text:* Mr. C.E. Roe, 8/1927, **FHE**

Pretty Mohea, The – *text:* Mr. Chandler Moore, Bingham, ME; *tune:* Susie Carr Young, Brewer, ME, 1939 **PB/BFSSNE** 6:15–18, **FHE/MM**, **PB/MWS**

Pretty Mohea, The – *text:* Mr. C. A. Carpenter, Surry, ME, 3/25/1942, **HHF**

Pretty Polly (The Green Bed) – Mrs. Annie Marston, West Gouldsboro, ME, 9/1926 **BBM2**

Pretty Polly (Gosport Tragedy) – *text fragment:* Dale Potter, Kingman, ME, 1947, **HB**

Pretty Polly (Gosport Tragedy) – *text fragment:* Mrs. Nancy Smith, **HB**
Pretty Polly of Topsham – Susie Carr Young, Brewer, ME, 1930, **PB/H**, **PB/BFSSNE** 2:16–17
Princess Royal, The – Carrie B. Grover, Gorham, ME 10/29/1943, **ELC** sr164asl

R

Ramble Away – Chaney Ripley, Matinicus Island, ME, **HB/FM**
Rambling Female Sailor, The – Jack McNally, Stacyville, ME, 8/28/1942, **HHF**, D30B side A @ 6:50
Riley's Farewell (John Riley) – Leonard Gilks, Bridgewater, ME, 1945, **HHF**, D54A side B @ 7:16
Rio Grande, The – David Kane, Searsport, ME, 1941, **HHF**, D14A side B @ 7:27
Rio Grande, The – *text:* Harry Meyers, Matinicus, ME, **HB/FM**
Robin Hood's Bay – *text:* Frank Matthews, Eastport, ME, 1927, **PB/H**
Rocks of Scilly, The – *text:* Mr. Adam Morris, Kingman, ME, 9/18/1934 **FHE**, **HB/FM**
Rockweed – *fragment & tune:* Susie Carr Young, Brewer, ME, 1925, **PB/H**, **PB/BFSSNE** 3:18
Rolling John (Blow Boys, Blow) – *text fragment:* Mr. Frank Stanley, Cranberry Island, ME, 11/1925, **FHE**
Root, Hog, or Die – *text:* Capt. Archie Spurling, Isleford, ME, 1925, **FHE/MM**, **HB/FM**
Rose of Breton's Isle – John West, Harmony, ME, 1970
Rose of Britain's Isle, The – Jack McNally Stacyville, ME, 5/9/1942, **HHF**, D20B side A @ 15:10
Rosy Banks of Green, The – Steven Barlow, Mars Hill, ME, 8/30/1942, **HHF**, D29A side B @ 10:00
Rosy Banks of Green, The – William LeClair, S. Brewer, ME, 9/29/1945, **HHF** D42A side A @ 19:50
Rosy Banks of Green, The – Emma Turner, Bucksport, ME, 10/4/1941, **HHF**, D15A side B @ 15:30
Rosy Banks so Green, The – Frank Tracy, Brewer, ME, 10/7/1941, **HHF**, D15B side A @ 28:40, 6/10/1934 **PB/LOC**
Roving Jack Tar (The Saucy Sailor) – *text:* Mrs. Avery Olmstead, Brewer, ME, 3/1934, **FHE**
Rovin' Lizzie, The (Bold Daniels) – Charles Finnemore, Bridgewater, ME, 10/28/43, **HHF**, D39B side B @ 42:28
Rovin' Lizzie, The (Bold Daniels) – *text:* Mr. Horace E. Priest, Sangerville, ME, 1924, **FHE/MM**
Royal Prince Regent, The – *text:* Susie Carr Young, Brewer, ME, 1926, **FHE/MM**

S

Sail Away – *tune:* Mrs. Hattie H. Soper, Orland, ME, 1940, **PB/LOC** AFS 20,253, **PB/H**; *tune:* **SB**
Sail On, Oh, Ship of State – Henry Wadsworth Longfellow, Portland, ME, 1850, Adapted for song by Charles William Bardeen, 1888
Sailor and the Sea Captain, The – Charles Finnemore, Bridgewater, ME, 5/1942, **HHF**, D25B side A @ 15:55
Sailor Boy, The – Susie Carr Young, Brewer, ME, 1939, **PB/MWS**
Sailor Boy, The (The Prince of Morocco) – Frank/James Kneeland, Searsport, ME, 10/1941, **HHF**, D14A side A @ 0:09; *text:* **KM**
Sailor in the Boat, The – Lorenzo Hooper, S. Berwick, ME, 1941, **HHF**, D13B side A @ 16:55
Sailor Song, The (The Basket of Eggs) – Sadie S Harvey, Houlton, ME, 9/30/41, **HHF**, D15A side A @ 16:40
Sailor Song, The (Jack Tar's Frolic) – *tune:* Susie Carr Young, Brewer, ME, 1925, **PB/H**
Sailor Walking all in His Garden, A – Albert Conray, Ellsworth, ME, 5/14/1942, **HHF**, D26B side A @ 22:00
Sailor's Alphabet, The – Oliver Jenness, York, ME, 1941, **HHF**, D16A side B @ 3:08
Sailor's Alphabet, The – *text:* Mr. Fred Phippen, Isleford, ME, 5/1925, Capt. Archie S. Spurling Isleford, ME, 5/1925, **FHE/MM**
Sailor's Bride, The (Early in the Spring) – *text:* Miss Grace Dunworth, Machias, ME, 1924, **PB/H**
Sailor's Bride, The (Early in the Spring) – *text:* Mrs. Annie Marston, Gouldsboro, ME, 9/29/1929, **PB/H**
Sailor's Bride, The (Early in the Spring) – *tune:* Susie Carr Young, Brewer, ME, 1925, **PB/H**
Sailor's Come-all-ye, The – *text:* Susie Carr Young, Brewer, ME, 1926, **FHE/MM**, **PB/H**
Sailor's Grave, The – *text:* **KM** James Kneeland, Searsport, ME, 1917
Sailor's Grave, The – Mrs. Edna Floyd, W Jonesport, ME, 8/20/1942, **HHF**, D31A side A @ 9:40
Sailor's Grave, The – Hanford Hayes, Stacyville, ME, 9/25/1940, **HHF** C11A side A 02–03, D24A side B @ 3:56
Sailor's Grave, The – Annie Tate Moore, Ellsworth Falls, ME, 6/22/1941, **HHF**, D11A side A @14:40
Sailor's Grave, The – *text:* Mrs. Nina Starboard, **HB/FM**

Sailor's Grave, The – *text:* Dale Potter, Kingman, ME, 1947

Sailor's Love Song (The Downeast Maid, Bright Phoebe, Sweet Caroline) – Susie Carr Young, Brewer, ME, 1925, **PB/H**

Sailor's Tale, The – David Kane Searsport, ME, 1945, **HHF**, D54A side A @ 41:23

Sailor's Wooing, The – *text:* Mrs. Annie Marston, West Gouldsboro, ME, 10/1929, **BBM1**

Sailor's Wooing, The – *text:* Mr. McLellan Gilchrist, Thomaston, ME, 10/1929, **BBM2**

Santy Anna – Dr. Edward "Sandy" Ives, "Folksongs of Maine," Smithsonian Folkways, 1959

Saucy Sailor, The – Vernon Mayo, Menardo, ME, 9/1/1942, **HHF**, D31B side A (recording N/A)

Saucy Caroline, The – *text:* Mrs. Pattee, **FHE/HHF/BDN**

Schooner Fred Dunbar, The – *text:* Composed by Amos Hanson, Orland, ME, c. 1850, Mrs. Emory Howard, North Blue Hill, ME, 1932, Miss Annie Dunbar, North Castine, ME, 4/20/1934, **FHE**, **PB/BFSSNE** 5:15–16

Schooner Medora, The – **PB/BFSSNE** 11:19–20

Scilly Rocks, The – *text:* Mr. Ed Morris, Kingman, ME, **HB/FM**,

Sea Serpent, The (The Crocodile) – Frank L. Tracy, Brewer, ME, 7/11/1932, 6/10/1934, **PB/LOC**

Sea Symphonies (poem) – *text:* **FHE**

Sealers, The – *text:* Captain John T. White, Brewer, ME, 7/1925, **FHE/MM**

Shenandoah – David Kane, Searsport, ME, 10/1941, **HHF**, D54A13 @ 40:30

Ship Carpenter, The (Gosport Tragedy) – Arthur Walker, Littleton, ME, 9/1/1942, **HHF**, D28B side A @ 14:40, 19:01

Ship That Never Returned, The – *text:* James Kneeland, Searsport, ME, 1917, **KM**

Ship That Never Returned, The – Judson Carver, W. Jonesport, ME, 8/20/1942, **HHF**, D30B side B @ 10:45

Ship of Revolution, The – Albert Conray, Ellsworth, ME, 5/15/1942, **HHF**, D26B side A @ 28:45

Shove 'er Up – *text:* Susie Carr Young, Brewer, ME, 1926, **FHE/MM**

Simple Ballad (The Fisherman's Tale) – *text: Eastport Sentinel*, Eastport, ME, 1/4/1871, **FHE/MM**

Silk Weaver's Daughter, The – Carrie Grover, Gorham, ME, 1955, **CGHS**, **CGMM**

Silk Merchant's Daughter, The (Jolly Sailor) – *text fragment:* Dale Potter, Kingman, ME, 1947, **HB**

Silvery Tide, The – Carrie Grover, Gorham, ME, 1955, **CGHS**, **CGMM**

Silvery Tide, The – *text:* James Kneeland, Searsport, ME, 1917, **KM**

Single Sailor, The – *text:* Mrs. Annie Marston, Gouldsboro, ME, 1927, **BBM2**

Single Sailor, The – *text:* Mrs. Fred Morse, Isleford, ME, 1927, **BBM2**

Single Sailor, The – *text:* Mr. W.H. Venning, Sussex, NB, 1904, **BBM2**

Sinking of the Cumberland, The (The Cumberland's Crew) – *text:* Lewis F. Gott, Bernard, ME, 11/6/1925, **PB/H**

Sinking of the Royal George, The – *text:* James Kneeland, Searsport, ME, 1917, **KM**

Sinking in the Lowlands Low (Golden Vanity, Child 286) – *text:* Justin De Coster, Buckfield, ME, 1925, **BBM1**

Sinking in the Lowlands Low (Golden Vanity, Child 286) – *text:* Mrs. Maude King/Phoebe Stanley, Baker Island, ME, 1927, **BBM1**

Sons of Liberty, The (Ye Parliament of England) – Wynifred Staples Smith, Dixfield, ME, 11/12/1941, **ELC** sr034asl

Spanish War, The – *text:* Mr. Henry H. Chamberlain, Round Pond, ME, 1925, **FHE**

Stately Southerner, The – *text:* Capt Archie S. Spurling, Isleford, ME, 5/1925, **FHE/MM**, **HB/FM**, **RP/KJ**

Stately Southerner, The – Dr. Edward "Sandy" Ives, "Folksongs of Maine," Smithsonian Folkways, 1959

St. Catherine's Dock (Homeward Bound) – Susie Carr Young, Brewer, ME, 1925 **PB/H**

Sur le Bord de L'ile – Margarita L. Bartley, Jackman, ME, 1954, **HHF**, T04A @ 21:50

Sweet Caroline (Sweet Phoebe, The Downeast Maid) – Carrie Grover, Gorham, ME, 1955, **CGHS**

Sweet Nancy – Mrs. Annie V. Marston, West Gouldsboro, ME, 1939

Sweet Trinity (Golden Vanity) – Frank L. Tracy, Brewer, ME, 7/11/1932, 6/10/1934, **PB/LOC**

Sweet William of Plymouth – David S. Libbey, Newport, ME, 1904, **BBM2**

Sweet William of Plymouth – *reference:* Miss Florence E. Mixer, Greenwood Mountain, ME, **BBM2**

T

Tab Scott – *text:* Mrs. Dalton Raynes, Matinicus, ME, **HB/FM**

Tacking Ship Off Shore – *text:* Poem by William Palmer, Bath, ME, sent by J.A. Stevens, East Boothbay, ME, 1926, **FHE/MM**

Tailor and the Chest, The – Oliver Jenness, York, ME, 9/23/1948, **HHF**, D52B side A @ 12:06, T07A side A @ 26:10

Tall Young Oysterman, The – Johnson, 1925, **PB/H**; *tune:* **SB**

Tarry Sailor, The – Carrie Grover, Gorham, ME, 1955, **CGHS**

Tarry Sailor, The – Charles Finnemore, Bridgewater, ME, 5/7/1942, **HHF**, D25B side A @ 21:11

Tarry Sailor, The – *text:* Alonzo Lewis, York, ME, 9/22/1947, **HHF**

Tempest, The – Carrie Grover, Gorham, ME, 1955, **CGHS**

Ten Thousand Miles Away – *tune:* Capt. Archie Spurling, SW Harbor, ME, 1926, **PB/H**

There Was an Old Sailor – *text:* James Kneeland, Searsport, ME, 1917, **KM**

There's a Light in the Window – Carrie Grover, Gorham, ME, **CGMM**

Three Brothers of Merry Scotland (Sir Andrew Barton, Child 167) – Mrs. Annie Marston, Gouldsboro, ME, 1927, **BBM1**

Tilton's Fight (1722) – *text:* **FHE**

Tom's Gone Away – *text:* Laura E. Richards, Gardiner, ME, 3/1926, **FHE/MM**

Too-Li-Aye (John Kanakanaka) – *text:* Capt. J.A. Creighton, Thomaston, ME, 1925

Tossed Upon Life's Raging Billow – *text:* James Kneeland, Searsport, ME, 1917, **KM**

Trip to the Grand Banks, A – Amos Hanson, Orland, ME, 1860, PB, **PB/BFSSNE** Vol. 4, **RP/KJ**, 1932

Trip to the Grand Banks, A – Dr. Edward "Sandy" Ives, "Folksongs of Maine," Smithsonian Folkways, 1959

True Lovers Bold (James and Florence) – Carrie Grover, Gorham, ME, 1955, **CGHS**

True Lovers Bold – *text:* Mrs. Guy R. Hathaway, Mattawamkeag, ME, 6/14/1932, **FHE**, **PB/BFSSNE** Vol. 8, tune by Barry

Turkish Shore, The – Mrs. Herbert D. (Betty Gaye) Farnham, **ELC** afs6067bsl (tune discernible but not lyrics)

'Twas Early, Early in the Spring – Frank/James Kneeland, Searsport, ME, 10/1941, **HHF**, D14A side A @ 16:17; *text:* **KM**

Two Little Girls in a Boat – **PB/BFSSNE** 12: 10

Two Sailors (Faithful Sailor Boy) – William Irish, Sherman, ME, 1941, **HHF**, D15A side B @ 9:55

U

Union of St. John, The – *text:* Mrs. Seth Thornton/Joan Moore, SW Harbor, ME, 10/21/1926, **FHE/MM**

V

Valiant Seaman's Return, The – *tune:* Mr. D.A. Nesbitt, St, Stephen, NB, 1/1930, **BBM2**

W

Water of the Ocean, The – **PB/BFSSNE** 1:6

We are the Jolly Sailor Boys – Lorenzo Hooper, S Berwick, ME, 1941, **HHF**, D13B side A @ 11:52

A Wet Sheet and a Flowing Sea – *text fragment:* Susie Carr Young, Brewer, ME, 1930, **PB/H**; *tune:* Herzog

What Makes My Father Stay So Long – *text:* James Kneeland, Searsport, ME, 1917, **KM**

What Makes My Father Stay So Long – George Dalton, Brewer, ME, June 28, 1941, **HHF**, D11A side A @ 32:08

White Squall, The – *text:* James Kneeland, Searsport, ME, 1917, **KM**

Why Don't My Father's Ship Come In – Charles Finnemore, Bridgewater, ME, 10/29/1943, **HHF**, D39A side B @ 1:45

Wild Barbaree (High Barbary, Child 285) – Carrie Grover, Gorham, ME, 1955, **CGHS**

Wild Shore (Isle of Man Shore) – Albert Cox, Sherman Mills, ME, 5/10/1942, **HHF**, D26B side A @ 7:35

Will Reilly the Fisherman – Rose Davis, Brewer, ME, **PB/LOC** AFS 20,247

William & Mary (The Sailor's Bride) – Carrie Grover, Gorham, ME, 1955, **CGHS**

William Taylor – *tune:* Mrs. Josephine Collins, Hebron, ME, 8/6/1910, **BBM2**

William Taylor – *text:* Mrs. Annie Marston, Charleston, ME, 1929, **BBM2**, (tune N/A)

William Taylor – *tune:* Susie Carr Young, Brewer, ME, 4/9/1928, **BBM2**, **PB/H**

Willie & Mollie (The Ship Carpenter, Gosport Tragedy) – *text:* Mr. J.P.A. Nesbitt, St. Stephen, NB, 1927, **BBM2**

Willie & Molly (The Ship Carpenter, Gosport Tragedy) – Annie Syphers, Monticello, ME, 9/30/1941, **HHF**, D14B side A @ 29:14

Willie-O (The Ghost of Willy, The Bay of Biscay) – Carrie Grover, Gorham, ME, 1941, **CGMM**, **LO**

Willie-O, My (The Ghost of Willy, The Bay of Biscay) – Franz Blanchard, Brewer, ME, PB; *tune:* **SB** (text N/A)

Wind Sou'west, The – Carrie Grover, Gorham, ME, 1955, **CGHS**

While Strolling Through Norfolk (Cruising 'round Yarmouth) – *text:* Colonel Smith, **HB**

Whiskey Johnny – Mr. Frank Stanley, Cranberry Island, ME, 11/1925, **FHE**

Working on the Railway – *text:* Mr. Frank Stanley, Cranberry Island, ME, 11/1925, **FHE**

Worn-out Sailor, The – Frank L. Tracy Brewer, ME, 7/11/1932; 6/10–11/1934, **PB/LOC**; *tune:* **SB**

Wreck of the Ross, The – *text:* Thomas Gibbs, 1/13/1910, **PB/H**

Wreck of the Thomas, The – *text:* Skidompha Library archive, poem by Alonzo Lewis "The Bard of Lynn" 1843

Wreck of the Turkish Empire, The – *text:* Captain O.B. Hall, Jonesport, ME, 10/1927, **PB/H**

##

Yankee Tars – Copy of broadside, **FHE**

Ye Parliament of England – Frank/James Kneeland, Searsport, ME, **HHF**, D13B side B @ 2:30–2:52; *text:* **KM**

You Parliament of England – *text fragment:* Mrs. Clara Harriman, Sandy Point, ME, 1926, **PB/H**

Young Edmund (In the Lowlands) – Carrie Grover, Gorham, ME, 1955, **CGHS**

Young Edwin in the Lowlands – *text:* Mr. Oakes Alders/Aldus, Belfast, ME, 5/1925, **PB/H**, **BBM2**

Young Edwin in the Lowlands – *tune:* Mr. Edward Holt, St. Stephen, NB, 1929, **BBM2**

Young Edwin in the Lowlands Low – Mrs. Annie Marston, West Gouldsboro, ME, 1926, **BBM2** tune N/A

Young Emily (Young Edwin in the Lowlands) – *text:* Leonard M. Patterson, Newport, ME, 1937, **PB/BFSSNE** 12:12–13

Young Fisherman, The (The Bold Fisherman) – *text:* Mrs. Phoebe Stanley, Baker Island, ME, 1926, **BBM2**

Young Mary and Willie (Sailor's Bride) – Arthur More, Island Falls, ME, **HHF**, C11B 07 side B 1:40

Young Sailor Bold – Carrie Grover, Gorham, ME, 1955, **CGHS**

Songs of Ships & Sailors

Biographies of Collectors and Major Sources

Phillips Barry (1880–1937) was an American academic and collector of traditional ballads in New England. In 1914 Barry married Kate Fairbanks Puffer of Framingham, MA and began an association with the Ebert School in 1921. They enjoyed a pastoral life on their 70-acre Prospect Hill Farm near Groton, MA where he cultivated fruit trees. The farm included an orchard of some six hundred trees and the house was one of the oldest structures in town, dating from 1680 or before.

Barry studied at Harvard University, earning degrees in folklore, theology, and classical and medieval literature. After graduating, he began collecting variations of both American and Anglo-American ballads in the northeast United States. In 1930 he founded the Folk-Song Society of the Northeast. He edited and regularly contributed to the group's *Bulletin* which printed twelve issues from 1930 until his death in 1937. Barry's theory of "communal re-creation" (a process by which songs created by individuals were passed down by tradition, becoming changed by the people who sang them) was regarded by colleagues, such as Louise Pound, as a significant contribution to the study of ballads in the field, although it was not without critics.

Barry's collaboration with Fanny Hardy Eckstorm of Maine greatly enhanced his work with ballads as she and her associates provided him with a great body of field recordings. Phillips Barry's collections at Harvard and the Library of Congress contain a significant amount of material actually collected by Mrs. Eckstorm and her partner Mary Smyth. Together, they published *British Ballads from Maine* in 1929. His book *The Maine Woods Songster*, published posthumously, contains many of their collections edited by him. After his untimely death, Mrs. Barry retained this material, refusing to relinquish it to Mrs. Eckstorm, causing her to turn her attention to other interests. Barry also collaborated with Helen Hartness Flanders and Marguerite Olney in finding "Child Ballads" (those documented by Francis Child) in New England. He supported the work of Eloise Linscott as well. Barry's later work moved beyond British ballads to study original vernacular American songs. His work is archived both at Harvard University and the Library of Congress.

Horace Palmer Beck, Jr. (1920–2003), American folklorist, sailor, and Professor of American Literature at Middlebury College in Vermont, was born on September 27, 1920. He received his Ph.D. from the University of Pennsylvania in 1952, studying under esteemed folklorists MacEdward Leach and Frank Speck. His interest in American ballads led him to collecting songs in Virginia, Rhode Island, and Maine and seeking their context in history and lore. His recordings are archived in the American Folklife Center at the Library of Congress. His dissertation "Ballads and Songs from Down East" is archived in the Portland, ME Public Library special collections.

A traditional storyteller and a master of folklore, Beck was fluent in five languages. He began sailing at age three, subsequently logging 28 transatlantic crossings. The first white man allowed on the whaling ships in the West Indies and in Tonga in the South Pacific, he wrote a lengthy article about his experiences for the 1987 edition of *Folklife Annual: A Publication of the American Folklife Center at the Library of Congress*. The article contains photos taken by his wife, Jane. Horace Beck wrote numerous books, including *Folklore of Maine* (1957), *The American Indian as a Sea-Fighter in Colonial Times* (Marine Historical Association Publication, No. 35) 1959, and *Folklore and the Sea* (1973). His knowledge of and respect for seafaring and its denizens imbues his work with authenticity.

Beck's robust and enthusiastic lifestyle was the subject of many anecdotes and made him one of the most popular professors ever to teach at Middlebury College. He was also well regarded by his colleagues, who wrote a tribute biographical anthology in 1985, *By Land and By Sea*. He married Middlebury alumna Jane Webster Choate in August 1965. Together, they researched and presented programs on folklore. A celebrated folklorist in her own right, Jane Beck founded the Vermont Folklife Center, which continues to be a vital resource. They lived with their family in their mountain home in Ripton, VT. Horace Beck died in 2003.

Joanna "Nan" Carver Colcord (1882–1960) was born to Capt. Lincoln Alden Colcord and Jane French Sweetser Colcord, from Searsport, onboard the bark *Charlotte A. Littlefield* in the South Seas as they sailed around the world. Joanna spent much of her childhood and adolescence at sea. She photographed some of the family's adventures, including one trip in 1899 when Joanna accompanied her father on a voyage to China aboard the ship *State of Maine*. She eventually became a University of Maine graduate, earning an undergraduate degree in Chemistry (1909) and a master's degree in Biological Chemistry (1909). She then studied at the New York School of Philanthropy and became a social worker, publishing several books on the subject. She worked for the Russell Sage Foundation and other philanthropic organizations in New York City between 1911 and 1944.

Her family stories were never forgotten, however, and with her brother, Lincoln, she published *Roll and Go: Songs of American Sailormen* in 1924, re-issued in 1938 simply as *Songs of American Sailormen*. This book documents the songs and shanties she heard sung by the sailors on her father's ships. She did complain that her sources tended to self-edit when reporting the songs, due to her gender. Her dictionary of words and phrases originating in nautical culture, *Sea Language Comes Ashore*, was published in 1945. Joanna Colcord married widower Frank J. Bruno, her longtime colleague and professor, in Bangor in 1950. Bruno died in 1955 and personal health issues caused Joanna to move to Indiana to live with her stepson. She died there in 1960. Her papers and photographs are archived at the Penobscot Marine Museum in Searsport, ME.

Fannie Hardy Eckstorm (1865–1946) Born in Brewer, ME, she was the daughter of Maine's most famous fur trader, Manly Hardy. He traded the furs he obtained from the Penobscot tribal community to European markets. Fanny accompanied her father on his wilderness excursions and became interested in the people and wildlife they encountered. Inspired by her father, she became adept at taxidermy and woods lore such as trail-blazing. The folklore and culture of the people also fascinated her and informed her later study of them. She attended local school and in 1888 graduated from Smith College, majoring in anthropology.

Fanny met Norwegian-American Reverend Jacob Eckstorm in 1893 and they were married in Portland, Oregon. Moving to Eastport, ME to be closer to her family, Jacob and Fanny soon had two children, a daughter, Katherine Hardy, in 1894 and a son, Paul Frederick, in 1896. The family moved to Rhode Island two years later where Jacob died. The widowed Fanny moved back to Brewer with her two young children where they lived in the same neighborhood in which Fanny was born and raised. Two years later Fanny suffered the devastating loss of her daughter, Katherine Hardy, who died in 1901 at the age of seven.

Fanny Eckstorm's writings are diverse, including historical articles about the lumber and fur industries, ornithology, the Penobscot tribe, and several collections of ballads examining their social significance. In 1901, Eckstorm published *The Woodpeckers* and *The Bird Book,* two scientifically accurate children's books on ornithology. She gained respect for her meticulous research on the history of the Penobscot Indians when she published *The Penobscot Man* in 1904, building on her experiences with her father. Her accurate documentary stories of the lumbermen making their log drives down the Penobscot River resulted in the book *David Libbey: Penobscot Woodsman and River Driver* in 1907. In addition to her research and writing, Fanny was active in her community, volunteering for the Red Cross in World War I, establishing a public library in Brewer, and participating in women's suffrage activities.

Having heard the songs of the people in her travels, Fanny Eckstorm was passionate about documenting them and placing them in social context. Fanny, with her friend Mary Smyth, set about collecting from the people around them and telling the stories of the songs' inspiration. They enlisted the help of family members and friends to discover community members who remembered old songs. This resulted in the 1927 publication, *Minstrelsy of Maine*, which featured the vernacular creations of working people. Unfortunately, neither woman was musically trained and the book only contains lyrics. They did, however, attract the attention of the folklorist Phillips Barry at Harvard and he facilitated the transcription of the tunes by connecting them with ethnomusicologist George Herzog. Their collaborative effort *British Ballads from Maine* (1929) includes his musical transcriptions. Her association with Barry put Fanny in contact with other collectors including Helen Hartness Flanders and Marguerite Olney. They established a newspaper column to create awareness of the old songs and solicit contributions from the public. Although a second volume of *British Ballads* was planned, Mary Smyth and Phillips Barry both died in 1937. Barry's wife refused to release the material collected by Eckstorm and Smyth that was in his custody. Discouraged by this, Fanny turned her attention back to examining the Indian heritage of Maine, publishing *Indian Place-Names of the Penobscot Valley and the Maine Coast* in 1941.

A further blow came in 1943 when her son, Paul, died at the age of forty-eight. Her own health failing, Fanny did live to see the publication of her most well-known book, *Old John Neptune and Other Maine Indian Shamans* in 1945. Fanny Hardy Eckstorm died in 1946 of heart failure, and is buried in Oak Hill Cemetery in Brewer. *British Ballads from Maine (Second Series)*, which contains material retained by Mrs. Barry, was published in 2012 by her biographer, Dr. Pauleena MacDougall, after it was discovered in Phillips Barry's collections at Harvard. Fanny Eckstorm's personal papers are archived at the Fogler Library at the University of Maine in Orono. Among them is a plan for a "Maine Sea Songster" which was one inspiration for this book.

Helen Hartness Flanders (1890–1972) was born into a prominent Vermont family. Her father, James Hartness, served as the Governor of Vermont from 1921 to 1923. In 1911 she married industrialist and U.S. Senator Ralph Flanders. They had three children.

Helen Flanders began collecting traditional Vermont songs in 1931 as a result of her membership on the Committee on Traditions and Ideals of the Vermont Commission on Country Life. Flanders understood the connection between folksong and history and, with the Committee's support, she set about finding and collecting traditional songs to create an overview which became the Vermont Archive of Folk Song. Unfortunately, the focus of the Commission's mission was on eugenics, preventing her from collecting a complete ethnic representation of songs. However, armed with address books, she would drive herself to each interview using a dictaphone, sometimes powered by the car battery, and looseleaf notebooks to record her findings. She published *A Garland of Green Mountain Song* (1934) and *Country Songs of Vermont* (1937) with material from these early collections. Through her patient, generous and respectful approach, Helen Flanders developed a special personal relationship with her informants. These often grew into life-long associations which included additional visits and the exchange of gifts and letters. She invited willing singers to participate in her many public programs.

Realizing her personal limitations and lack of training regarding folklore or folk songs, she engaged Vermont musician George Brown, and leading folklorist author and scholar, Phillips Barry. Flanders soon connected with Barry's colleague, Fannie Eckstorm of Brewer, ME. The two women discovered the song links between Vermont and Maine and collaborated on collecting by developing a newspaper column for that purpose. Flanders met Marguerite Olney in 1939 through Olney's parents, who lived near Flanders in Springfield, Vermont and who had contributed songs to the Vermont Archive of Folk-Song. Recognizing Olney's musical and organizational strengths, Flanders invited Olney to join her collecting field recordings in the spring of 1940. Their fruitful relationship resulted in tremendous growth for the collection which by now was completely under Flanders' personal jurisdiction and renamed The Helen Hartness Flanders Ballad Collection.

Flanders donated the collection to Middlebury College in 1941 with Olney as curator. In addition, she gifted annual funds to cover maintenance of a car, purchase collection equipment, and pay for the bulk of the curator's salary. Flanders wrote articles, published, lectured and made contacts with singers. Olney nourished those relationships and helped grow the collection to include close to 5000 recordings from around the northeast states. There are also a myriad of other related materials.

In the early 1950s, Olney and Flanders published *Ballads Migrant in New England* (1953) based on their collected resources. That same year, they published an LP recording "Eight Traditional British-American Ballads." Their final published work together was the culmination of all Flanders' three decades of song collection: *Ancient Ballads Traditionally Sung in New England* (1961–65), a 4-volume set of the New England Child Ballads.

In recognition of her accomplishments as a ballad collector, Middlebury College awarded Flanders an honorary Master of Arts in 1942. She was a member of the National Committee of the National Folk Festival Association and vice president of the Folksong Society of the Northeast established by Phillips Barry. In 1966, the Vermont House of Representatives added Flanders's name to the state's Roll of Distinction in the Arts.

After a long period of deteriorating health, Helen Hartness Flanders died in 1972. Her grand-daughter, Nancy-Jean Ballard Siegel, is currently working on a biography of her grandmother. Flanders' collection is housed in the Special Collections of the Davis Family Library at Middlebury College in Middlebury, VT and is accessible both in person and online.

Roland Palmer Gray (1868–1962) was born in New York City in 1868 to Corydon Leonard and Jane Fowler Amerman Gray. In his biography, published in the 1915 *Who's Who*, it is noted that his grandfather, on the paternal side, was "of Scotch descent" from Martha's Vineyard. He attended private and public schools in New York, graduated from Colgate College in 1889. Continuing on to Columbia University, he received a BA in English in 1893, and, as class orator, won the Kingsford prize in public speaking. He married Nettie Patterson of Hamilton, NY on December 21, 1893. After college, Gray became Head of the Department of English at Marmaduke Military Academy (1893–94), Instructor of English at the University of Nebraska (1894–5), Instructor of English at the University of Rochester (1895–1902), and an assistant Professor there from (1902–5). Roland Palmer Gray did graduate work at Harvard, Yale, Oxford and the British Museum in London. He then became Professor of English and Librarian at Arcadia University (1905–8), an Assistant Professor of English, Indiana University and finally Professor of English and Head of the Department, University of Maine (1909–17).

He was President of the Maine State Teachers Association (1911–12), President of the Maine State Council of Teachers of English and a member of the Modern Language Association of America, the American Dialect Society, the

Press Club of Indiana and the National Society of Teachers of English. Active in Phi Kappa Phi and Delta Upsilon fraternal organizations, he was also an extension lecturer on Shakespeare, Tennyson and Browning.

We know very little about his interest and work with ballads except that, unlike Phillips Barry, Gray espoused the theory of "communal ballad origin" according to which ballads originated through improvisation by a group working together, which he claims to have witnessed in the Maine lumber camps. Although Fanny Hardy Eckstorm and her brother Walter M. Hardy allegedly contributed material which he published in *Songs and Ballads of the Maine Lumberjacks* (1916), according to her correspondence she was not appreciative of his efforts.

His publications include translations of Beowulf from Anglo-Saxon with an introduction and notes as well as several English text books. *Songs and Ballads of the Maine Lumberjacks* was produced through the Harvard University Press in 1924. In 1936 an article entitled "Balladry of New York State" appeared in *New York History* 18 (April): pp 147–155.

Carrie Blanche Spinney Grover (1879–1959) was born July 13, 1879 in Black River, Nova Scotia, to George Craft Spinney and Eliza Long, the youngest of nine children. The family lived and worked a homestead farm on the shores of Sunken Lake ten miles south of Port Williams. Her father, born in 1837, had been a mariner on merchant vessels, and, coming from a long line of singers, sang many of the songs he had learned from other sailors. Her mother sang the songs from her Irish father and Scotch-English mother as well as those her brothers brought home from the lumber camps.

In the early 1890s, when Carrie was 12, the family came to Newry, Maine where her older brother had purchased land. After attending a one room primary school in Newry, she went to Gould Academy High School in nearby Bethel. It was there she met her husband, Almon Roy Grover, whom she married in 1896 at the age of 17. They had three children: Gertrude, Ethel, and Roy.

Carrie continued her family's tradition of singing their songs throughout her life. In the 1940's she was invited to sing at folk festivals in Washington, D.C. and Boston, attracting the attention of prominent song collectors Eloise Linscott, Sydney Robertson Cowell, and Alan Lomax. Grover had heard Alan Lomax on a nationally distributed folk music radio show broadcast on WGAN in Portland, Maine, in December 1940. She wrote to him at the Library of Congress introducing herself and describing her family's songs. Their correspondence, which became quite friendly, led to a recording session for Lomax's collection in April 1941 when she traveled to visit her niece in Washington, DC. She continued on to visit her son in New Jersey and was recorded by Sidney Robertson (Cowell) at her son's home there. Eloise Linscott later recorded and photographed Carrie Grover. Those materials are all archived at the Library of Congress.

Inspired by her experiences in Washington, Grover decided to share her songs by publishing a book including tunes for every song. She remembered hearing her father remark to her mother that, once they passed on, the old family songs would disappear. Carrie resolved to learn as many as she could and, although she had already written out the words of many of them, she understood the importance of preserving the tunes with the lyrics. She shared her idea with Alan Lomax who was very enthusiastic and willing to help. Unfortunately, they were never able to fully collaborate due to distance and ill health, and the book was not published by the Library of Congress. Carrie's husband, Almon, passed away in 1948 causing her to retreat further.

Grover did not give up and, more than ten years later, she was able to accomplish her dream. Although she could both read music and play the fiddle, she was not able to write the music in manuscript. Determined that the songs be transcribed exactly as she sang them, she engaged the help of Ann Griggs, music instructor at her alma mater Gould Academy. The school published Carrie Grover's *A Heritage of Song* in 1955 when Carrie was 75. Intended as a family keepsake to be passed on to future generations, it is divided between her father's and mother's songs with commentary on the sources of many of them. The book was reprinted in 1973 by Norwood Press. Copies of both editions are extremely rare, but folklorists and musicians, understanding the book's importance, have shared copies among their community. Folklorist Sandy Paton was given a copy when he performed a program at Gould Academy. He shared it with several prominent musicians who soon began to interpret and record her songs particularly the song "Arthur McBride". This song garnered the attention of Irish singer Paul Brady as well as Bob Dylan and Roseanne Cash.

Carrie assembled a second songbook in 1957, which also includes other folkways — recipes, remedies, stories and dances, transcribed by her daughter Ethel. She contributed the manuscript to a local music society where she lived in Gorham, Maine. While seeking resources for a biography, this manuscript was discovered by Julie Mainstone Savas who includes this previously unpublished material as "The Maine Manuscript" on her website carriegroverproject.com. Carrie Grover's total musical collection contains 242 songs and nearly 50 fiddle tunes. It is a truly unique and valuable collection which provides a cultural window into an ordinary northern New England family's musical legacy.

Carrie Blanche Spinney Grover died in 1959 at the age of 79 at her son's home in New Jersey. She is buried at the Eastern Cemetery in Gorham, Maine beside her husband.

Frank Elmer Kneeland (1870–1948) was born on July 27, 1870 in Searsport, Maine to James Henry Kneeland (1843–1917) and Amanda Crockett Kneeland (1849–1932). His early life is not clear, but according to various documents, and his own account, he worked in Bogota and La Guaira Columbia in 1899 and spent three years in "the west and Old Mexico" from 1902–5. In 1904 he lived in Torreon, Mexico, and Silver City, New Mexico and was supportive of that territory's entrance into the United States.

On December 24, 1910, in Brooklyn, NY, Frank E. Kneeland married Bertha Louise Junkins (1875–1971). While living in Brooklyn their daughter Helen Elizabeth Crockett Kneeland was born Dec. 24, 1911, and daughter Frances Hichborn Kneeland on June 20, 1916. The family then moved to Searsport where the children attended grades one through eight in a one-room schoolhouse. Their second son, Frank Henry, was born in Belfast, Maine in 1921. They continued living in Searsport through 1940. After serving in the military, both Helen and Frank H. moved to Napa, California. Frances trained as a nurse at Mass. General Hospital in Boston and continued living in the area.

In 1914, while they were living in Brooklyn, NY, Frank E. Kneeland and his wife Bertha produced *The Kneeland miscellany; a heterogeneous collection consisting of father's and mother's songs, genealogical notes of the Crockett and Heagan families and incidents of family history, together with extracts from the first census, historical notes regarding the Porter district, &c.* This 400 page tome includes a treasure trove of information about the Kneeland and Crockett families including the lyrics to 100 songs sung by his father James and his mother Amanda, which apparently inspired the project. Although he is very thorough in reporting about previous generations he does not give much information about himself. The *Miscellany* describes at length the lives of his parents and other relatives of their generation, including the context in which the songs that he documents were sung. In 1916 he published *A Mexican diary: An intimate relation of a composite year's experiences in Mexico* which may have more information about himself.

Frank Kneeland's work in documenting his family songs came to the attention of Fanny Eckstorm and then Helen Flanders who recorded him in October 1941 singing 28 of the 100 songs that he included in the *Miscellany*. This is wonderfully valuable as the *Miscellany* only includes the lyrics. The Flanders index identifies the singer as James, but in fact it was Frank who was recorded singing his parents' songs. Kneeland's interest in genealogy continued throughout his life and in 1942 he produced "The Staples genealogy: An abridged record showing the direct line of descent from Peter Staple of Old Kittery to Nelson P. Staples of Searsport, Me. and his descendants."

Frank E. Kneeland died April 2, 1948 in Boston, MA, survived by his wife and children.

Dr. Edward D. "Sandy" Ives (1925–2009) was born Sept. 4, 1925, in White Plains, NY, the son of Warren L. and Millicent (Dawson) Ives. He married "Bobby" Barbara Ann Herrel in 1952 and they had three children, Stephen, Nathaniel, and Sarah.

After serving in the Marine Corps, Ives graduated from Hamilton College with a bachelor's degree in English and History, and received his Master of Arts degree in Medieval Literature at Columbia University. Sandy's long and varied teaching career began as an English instructor at Illinois College (1950 to 1953). He then taught at The City College of New York from 1953 to 1954, and finally at the University of Maine, where he taught first in the English Department and later in the Department of Anthropology.

Sandy Ives' supplemental work as a folk singer led him to explore the songs of the Maine woods camps and the Northeast oral traditions which would inform his subsequent career. He interviewed hundreds of people creating lasting relationships as a result of his genuine respect for his subject. His recording "Folk Songs of Maine" was released in 1959 on Smithsonian Folkways. Realizing the value of personal experience in the study of folklore, Ives guided his university students in "community-engaged scholarship," encouraging them to do research within their own network. Continuing his own pioneering work in oral history methodology, he attained his Doctorate in Folklore from Indiana University in 1962, and became a guest lecturer at the University of Edinburgh, Scotland, and the University of Sheffield, England.

Archiving the papers collected from students over several years, Ives created the Northeast Archives of Folklore and Oral History, and co-founded the Northeast Folklore Society with his colleague Bacil Kirtley in 1957. Since 1958, the Society has continuously published the journal *Northeast Folklore* with all 33 volumes being edited by Ives. In 1992 the Northeast Folklore Society and the Archives, which the Society the Council of Library and Information resources described as "perhaps the finest regional archive of its kind," merged to become the Maine Folklife Center. In 2011, original materials from the Archives were sold to the Library of Congress in Washington, DC for preservation.

Backup copies as well as materials accessioned since 2011 were transferred to the Fogler Library Special Collections at the University of Maine Orono in 2016.

In addition to the many papers and articles that Sandy Ives contributed to scholarship and to periodicals, his first book, *Larry Gorman, The Man Who Made The Songs*, was published in 1964, being reprinted in 1977 and 1993. He also authored *Lawrence Doyle, The Farmer-Poet of Prince Edward Island* (1971), *Joe Scott, the Woodsman Songmaker* (1978), *George Magoon and the Downeast Game War* (1988 and 1991), *Folksongs of New Brunswick* (1989), *The Bonny Earl of Murray: The Man, the Murder, the Ballad* (1997) — which was published both in Scotland and the United States — and, in 1999, *Drive Dull Care Away: Folksongs from Prince Edward Island*. His handbook *The Tape Recorded Interview: A Manual for Field Workers in Folklore and Oral History* (1980 and 1995), and instructional video, "An Oral Historian's Work" (1987) have become standard for courses throughout the country.

Dr. Edward D. Ives received numerous awards and honors throughout his career. These include a Guggenheim Fellowship, a Maine State Award from the Maine Council on the Arts and Humanities, the first Harvey A. Kantor Memorial Award for Outstanding Achievement in Oral History from the New England Association of Oral History, the Marius Barbeau Medal from the Folklore Studies Association of Canada, the Kenneth Goldstein Award for Lifetime Academic Leadership from the American Folklore Society, the Award of Honour for Lifetime Achievement from the Prince Edward Island Museum and Heritage Foundation and a Presidential Public Service Award from the University of Maine. Sandy was also awarded honorary degrees from the University of Prince Edward Island and Memorial University of Newfoundland. He served as a Folk Arts panelist for the National Endowment for the Arts, a Fellow of the American Folklore Society, a member of the Maine Arts Commission and was appointed to the Acadian Cultural Preservation Commission by the Secretary of the Interior.

After teaching in the English and Anthropology Departments of the University of Maine for 44 years, he retired in 1999 and died peacefully Aug. 1, 2009 at his home. His many students and colleagues will remember him as an inspiring and dedicated educator, as well as a supportive and generous friend.

Eloise Hubbard Linscott (1897–1978) was born and raised in Taunton, MA with her two sisters and three brothers. She graduated Radcliffe College in 1920 with a Bachelor of Arts in English Literature and married Charles Hardy Linscott in 1921. They made their home in Needham, Massachusetts, spending summers in Wolfeboro, New Hampshire. Their one son, John Hubbard Linscott, was born in 1929.

Linscott began fieldwork in folksongs in an effort to preserve her own family's legacy of songs which she hoped to pass on to her only son. As she gathered material, she began to realize that there was a wealth of this music which was in danger of disappearing. Using her own money, saved in a tin can, she arranged her own contacts and interviews ranging throughout New England. A tireless and enthusiastic collector, her field notes are detailed and interesting, revealing a respect and fondness for her informants. Her efforts were unfortunately not appreciated by her fellow collectors and her correspondence with Helen Flanders, particularly, reveals a territorial rivalry. Her lack of connection with any institution initially prevented her from receiving any official fellowships or logistical support. Although she did not generally associate with other scholars and was not active in the American Folklore Society or the Folksong Society of the Northeast, she was encouraged by Phillips Barry who invited her to use his library, contributed personal material from his collections and and helped edit her manuscript. Ten years of work yielded her book *Folk Songs of Old New England* (1939). It was described by John Lee Brooks, professor of American Folklore at Southern Methodist University, as an "American equivalent of Bishop Percy's 1765 work *Reliques of Ancient English Poetry*." Though she created several other manuscripts, this was her only publication.

Linscott began presenting lectures on folk music at music societies, camps, women's clubs, and arts organizations. She would sing and occasionally she would include other musicians to help present the music. In 1940, she received sponsorship from the Musicraft Record company and then, in 1941, from the Library of Congress. Alan Lomax, head of the Library's Archive of American Folk Song, allowed Linscott to borrow equipment for field research and within two weeks she delivered 36 glass-core master acetate discs of folk songs. Ultimately Eloise Linscott collected 2500 recordings, on cylinders, discs, and tapes. They include not not only songs in English, French, and Penobscot, but also a range of fiddle and dance tunes. One of her unpublished manuscripts, "Square Dances and Fiddle Tunes of New England," presents representative dances and tunes that she found at New England dance halls while doing her field research. In the 1940's Eloise Linscott became a volunteer coordinator for New England musicians at the National Folk Festival and helped organize regional festivals. Later in her life, Linscott suffered from ill health and sometimes had to limit her travels. However, she maintained her interest in folk music until her death in 1978.

The Eloise Hubbard Linscott collection is currently housed at the Archive of Folk Culture in the American Folklife Center at the Library of Congress in Washington, DC.

Marguerite Olney (1897–1976) of Springfield, VT received a Bachelor of Music degree, with a concentration in Public School Music, from the Eastman School of Music, Rochester, NY, in 1928. She also attended Washington University, the New York School of Social Work, and the Dalcroze School of Music. In 1940, she spent three months at Houghton Library, Harvard University under the auspices of Fanny Eckstorm, assisting with documentation and indexing of New England folk music cylinder recordings acquired from the late collector-scholar Phillips Barry. Mrs. Helen Hartness Flanders recognized her talents after meeting her during a collecting trip in Olney's home town. They collaborated for nearly 20 years with Olney transcribing, analyzing and organizing the field recordings they collected together. She also curated the Helen Hartness Flanders Ballad Collection at Middlebury College, in Middlebury, Vermont from 1941 until 1960, when the college eliminated Olney's position due to financial constraints. Olney and Flanders co-authored the book *Ballads Migrant in New England* in 1953. They also released the LP "Eight Traditional British-American Ballads" and Olney played a major role in the preparation of *Ancient Ballads Traditionally Sung in New England*, a 4-volume set edited by Flanders (1961-65).

Ralph George Page was born in Munsonville, New Hampshire, on January 28, 1903. His ancestry included Irish minstrels and a grandfather who was an Irish dancing master. His uncle was a square dance caller, and his father played the fiddle.

Based in Keene, New Hampshire, Ralph started calling contradances in 1930, when, while playing fiddle in a dance orchestra, he was asked to substitute for a caller who was ill with laryngitis. Dancers enjoyed his choice of music, the elegance of his dances and his clever remarks while on the microphone. He subsequently became one of the country's first full-time professional callers, known as the "Singing Caller of New England," and was a featured caller at the 1939 New York World's Fair.

In 1945, Ralph married Ada Novak of New York City, having met her at Camp Merriewoods in Stoddard, where she was assistant camp director. Their daughter, Laura Susan, was born in 1946.

Ralph had begun leading weekly square and contra dance evenings at the Y.W.C.A in Boston, MA in 1943 which continued for the next 25 years. One of three founders of the Natick, Massachusetts, New England Folk Festival Association (NEFFA), Page was the Master of Ceremonies at their first festival on October 28 to 29, 1946. He served as its president for many years.

After establishing his own square and folk dance camps, the first in New Hampshire in 1950, Page was invited to teach at dance camps throughout New England, in Georgia, and parts of Canada. Traveling west, Page taught the dances of New England to West Coast folk and contra dancers, particularly in California. He became a recording artist in 1946 on the *Disc* label for Moe Ash, in 1951 for Michael and Mary Ann Herman's *Folk Dancer* record label and on the *F&W* label. His original tune compositions have been featured by a myriad of folk dance groups. The English Folk Dance Society produced a recording by The Southerners Orchestra of Kent, England, titled "Southerners Plus Two Play Ralph Page." The album contains 11 of Ralph's original tunes and includes a book titled *The Ralph Page Book of Contras*.

Ralph Page revived many 18th and 19th century dances by interpreting obscure dance directions from old books and manuscripts found in the Library of Congress and other archives. Some fifty of these dances appeared in his periodical *Northern Junket* and his books, *Heritage Dances of Early America* and *An Elegant Collection of Contras and Squares*. *Northern Junket* magazine was published from 1949 to 1984. Ralph single-handedly produced 165 mimeographed issues which contained not only music and instructions for folk dances, but also editorials, recipes, stories, as well as sheet music for many folk songs.

Ralph Page was considered one of the leading dance callers of his time and an important figure in the history of traditional dance in America. He maintained a busy lifelong schedule running many dances in New England and abroad. Page died on February 21, 1985, in Keene, New Hampshire, where he had been living for many years and was buried in the family cemetery plot in Munsonville.

In 1986, the accumulated papers of Ralph George Page were purchased from the family jointly by the University of New Hampshire Library and the New England Folk Festival Association. The 36 boxes of material contain files which include information on folk song and dance, festivals and folk culture as well as memorabilia, programs and photographs from New England dance camps and festivals. His library consists of approximately 600 books and periodicals, sheet music, instructional notebooks, films, and 1,600 recordings. In 1988, these materials were donated to the Special Collections, Dimond Library, University of New Hampshire in Durham, NH.

Mary Winslow Smyth (1873–1937) was born in Bangor, Maine on March 26, 1873. She was graduated from Smith College in 1895, earning her Master's degree in 1897, and her Ph.D. in English from Yale University in 1905. She was an associate professor of English at Elmira College from 1922–1924. Her father was Rev.Newman Smyth, the minister of Center St. Congregational Church in New Haven, CT and her grandfather a professor at Bowdoin College. Her mother, Anna Marston Ayer, was from an old Bangor family who spent summers in the village of Islesford on Little Cranberry Island, ME near Mt Desert. Mary Smyth began independently collecting folksongs from the people around her, but soon established a working relationship with fellow folklorist Fannie Hardy Eckstorm. Smyth gathered songs from Maine's coastal areas while Eckstorm concentrated on those of woodsmen and other inland people. Together they created the 1927 book *Minstrelsy of Maine: Folk-songs and Ballads of the Woods and the Coast*.

When their work came to the attention of Phillips Barry, they invited him to collaborate and published their second book, *British Ballads from Maine: The Development of Popular Songs with Texts and Airs* (1929), with Barry listed as an editor. Mary Smyth objected to Barry's inclusion on the title page as she felt that, although he was a valuable contributor, his gender and reputation were being held in inappropriately high regard. She became the secretary of the Folk-song Society of the Northeast in 1930 and remained in that position until her death. Other publications include "Biblical Quotations in Middle English Literature Before 1350" (1911) and "Contemporary Songs and Verses About Washington," an article in the *New England Quarterly* (April 1932). Smyth had planned another volume of Maine songs to be titled *Lovelorn Ballads* which was never published.

Both Smyth and Eckstorm valued the vernacular material they had collected beyond the British ballads codified by Francis Child. A successful song collector and conscientious researcher, Mary described in an article to the *Bangor Daily News* the patience, persistence and luck necessary to establish the relationships and trust that would encourage informants to share their songs. She said that she would sometimes intentionally sing a song incorrectly knowing that few could resist correcting her with their version.

Mary Winslow Smyth died, unmarried, in 1937 at the age of 64 and was survived by her mother, brother and two sisters. Her papers are included in the Fanny Hardy Eckstorm collection at the Fogler Library at the University of Maine, Orono.

Susie Carr Young (1862–1933) Although Susie Carr Young is not recognized as an author of any publication, she was a significant contributor to the collections of both Philips Barry and Fanny Eckstorm. Her contributions appear in both *British Ballads from Maine* 1 and 2 as well as several of Phillips Barry's articles for the BFSSNE. Her family members were all well known as singers in the Bangor area and in 1900 she began documenting their songs. Her grandmother Mary Soper's ancestors came to Massachusetts in the mid 1600's and many of the 68 ballads that Susie documented from her date back to that era. In addition to her own family, she collected from friends including Mary Hindle of Brewer who had come from Nova Scotia to Brewer as a small child with her widowed mother. Hindle's ancestors had been loyalists who fled to Halifax from North Carolina during American Revolution.

Young's handwritten manuscripts, with her attempts at musical transcription, contain "Songs traditional in the Carr, Soper, Viles and Fowler families of Orland, Me & Hampden, Me." The four folders include children's songs, ballads, jokes and rhymes. There don't appear to be any from her husband, M.A.A. Young, who was born in England. Bayard made some attempts at interpreting her transcriptions, but some remain inscrutable. In spite of this, her dedication to documenting the songs of her family and acquaintances provides an invaluable record. These manuscripts are archived in the Phillips Barry Collection at the Houghton Library, Harvard.

Bibliography

Anonymous. *A Collection of American Songs and Ballads, 205 in number*. Handwritten manuscript with index. The British Library, 1840.

Anonymous. *The Forget Me Not Songster: Containing a Choice Collection of Old Ballad Songs as sung by our Grandmothers*. New York, NY: Nafis and Cornish, 1840.

Anonymous. *The Sailor's Song Book, or, Music of the forecastle: containing patriotic, nautical, naval, moral and temperance songs, adapted to popular and familiar tunes Music arranged in two parts, by Uncle Sam*.

Anonymous. *The Songster, being a choice collection of new and popular patriotic, comic, sentimental and descriptive songs*. New York, NY: 1841.

Ashton, John. *Real Sailor-Songs*. London: Leadenhall; New York, NY: Charles Scribner's, 1891.

Barry, Phillips. *The Maine Woods Songster*. Cambridge, MA: Harvard University Press, 1939.

Barry, Phillips, Eckstorm, Fanny Hardy & Smyth, Mary Winslow. *British Ballads from Maine*. New Haven, CT: Yale Univ. Press, 1929.

Barry, Phillips; Eckstorm, Fanny Hardy; Smyth, Mary Winslow; MacDougall, Pauleena (editor). *British Ballads from Maine Second Series*. Orono, ME: Northeast Folklore Volume XLIV, University of Maine, 2011.

Barry, Phillips. "The Transmission of Folk-song." *The Journal of American Folklore*, Volume 27:67-76, 1914.

Barry, Phillips. "Communal Re-Creation." *Bulletin of the Folk-Song Society of the Northeast*, 5:4-6. 1933.

Bayard, Samuel P. *Folk Tunes from the Phillips Barry Collection (unpublished transcriptions)*. Cambridge, MA: Harvard College Library, 1942.

Beck, Horace. *Downeast Ballads and Songs* PhD Thesis, Univ. of PA, 1952. Advisor: MacEdward Leach (Portland ME Public Library Special Collections)

Beck, Horace. *The Folklore of Maine*. Philadelphia and New York: J.B. Lippincott, 1957.

Beck, Horace. *Folklore of the Sea*. Middletown, CT: Wesleyan Univ. Press, 1973.

Bonyun, Bill & Gene. *Full Hold and Splendid Passage: America goes to sea. 1815–1860*. New York, NY: Knopf, 1969.

Bronson, Bertrand Harris. *The Singing Tradition of Child's Popular Ballads*. Princeton, NJ: Princeton University Press, 1976. Northfield, MN: Loomis House Press, 2009.

Campbell, Olive Dame and Sharp, Cecil J. *English Folk Songs from the Southern Appalachians*. New York and London: G. P. Putnam's Sons, 1917.

Cazden, Norman; Haufrecht, Herbert; Stude, Norman, *Folk Songs of the Catskills*. Albany, NY: State University of New York Press; Annotated edition 1983.

Chappell, William. *Popular Music of the Olden Time. 2 vols*. 1859; rpt. New York, NY: Dover, 1965.

Child, Francis James, *The English and Scottish Popular Ballads, Volumes 1–5. (1884–1898)* rpt. Mineola, NY: Dover Publications Inc, 1965, 2003.

Coffin, Tristram Potter. *The British Traditional Ballad in North America* (revised edition, with a supplement by Roger de V. Renwick). Austin, TX: University of Texas Press, 1977. American Folklore Society Bibliographical and Special Series, 2 (revised).

Cohen, Norm.

Colcord, Joanna. *Roll and Go; Songs of American Sailormen*. Indianapolis, IN: Bobbs-Merrill Co, 1924.

Cooper, David. *The Musical Traditions of Northern Ireland and Its Diaspora: Community and Conflict*. London, UK: (Ashgate Popular and Folk Music Series) Routledge, 2009.

Creighton, Helen, & Peacock, Kenneth. *Folksongs from Southern New Brunswick*. Ottawa, ON: National Museums of Canada 1971.

Creighton, Helen. *Maritime Folk Songs*. Toronto, ON: Ryerson Press, 1962.

Creighton: Helen Creighton. *Songs and Ballads from Nova Scotia*. Toronto, ON: J. M. Dent & Sons, 1932. Reprinted, New York: Dover Publications, 1966.

De Pauw, Linda Grant. *Seafaring Women*. Boston, MA. Houghton Mifflin, 1982.

Dooilver, Thomas. *The National Songster*: containing a collection of the most modern and admired patriotic, sentimental, anacreontic, comic and masonic songs, original and selected: to which is added a number of selected toasts and sentiments. Philadelphia: 1808.

Dibdin, Charles and Dibdin, Thomas. *Songs, Naval and National, of the late Charles Dibdin* : with a memoir and addenda. London: William Clowes and Sons, 1841.

Dibdin, Charles and Hogarth, George. *The Songs of Charles Dibdin*.

Dibdin, Charles and others. *Sea Songs and Ballads*. London UK: Bell and Daldy, 1863

Doerflinger, William Main. *Shanteymen and Shanteyboys: Songs of the Sailor and Lumberman*. New York: Macmillan, 1951. Reprinted as *Songs of the Sailor and Lumberman*, 1972.

Duncathail. *Street Ballads, Popular Poetry, and Household Songs of Ireland*. Second edition, 1865.

Eckstorm, Fanny Hardy & Smyth, Mary Winslow. *Minstrelsy of Maine*. Cambridge, MA: Houghton Mifflin Co, Riverside Press, 1927.

Edes, Peter. *The Warbler;* a collection of the most popular ancient and modern songs: in four numbers. Printed at Augusta [Me.] : for Ezekiel Goodale, 1805.

Firth, C. H. (Charles Harding). *Naval Songs and Ballads*. London, UK: Naval Records Society, 1908

Flanders, Helen Hartness. *Ancient Ballads Traditionally Sung in New England; 4 volumes*. Philadelphia, PA: University of Pennsylvania Press, 1960.

Flanders, Helen Hartness & Olney, Marguerite. *Ballads Migrant in New England*. Freeport, NY: Books for Libraries Press, 1968.

Flanders, Helen Hartness, and Brown, George. *Vermont Folk-Songs and Ballads*. Brattleboro, VT: Stephen Day Press, 1931.

Ford, Ira W. *Traditional Music of America*. New York, NY: E. P. Dutton, 1940. Reprint ed., Hatboro, PA: Folklore Associates, 1965.

Gilje, Paul A. *To Swear like a Sailor: Maritime Culture in America, 1750–1850*. Cambridge, UK: Cambridge University Press, 2016.

Gillespy, Edward. *The Columbian Naval Songster:* being a collection of original songs, odes, etc. composed in honour of the five great naval victories... New York, NY: Edward Gillespy, 1813.

Gordon, Robert W. *Folk-Songs of America*. New York: WPA Federal Theater Project, National Service Bureau, 1938. Reprinted from author's manuscript for articles in New York Times, January 2, 1927–January 22, 1928.

Gordon, Robert W., "Old Songs That Men Have Sung," *Adventure*, 1923–26, passim.

Annual Report: "Archive of American Folk Song from the report of R. W. Gordon, in charge," *Annual Report of The Librarian of Congress for the Year Ending June 30th, 1932*. Washington: Government Printing Office, 1932.

Gray, Roland Palmer. *Songs and Ballads of the Maine Lumberjacks*. Cambridge, MA: Harvard University Press, 1924.

Grover, Carrie B. *A Heritage of Songs*. First printed privately, Bethel, ME: Gould Academy Press, 1953, Norwood Editions (Norwood, Pa) 1973.

Holloway, John & Black, Joan. *Later English Broadside Ballads*. London, UK & NY: Routledge, 1975.

Hugill, Stan. *Shanties from the Seven Seas*. London, UK: Routledge & Kegan Paul, 1961.

Hullah, John, *The Song Book*. London, New York: Macmillan & Co., 1884.

Huntington, Gale (editor) *Sam Henry's Songs of the People*. Athens, GA: University of Georgia Press, 1990.

Huntington, Gale. *Songs the Whalemen Sang*. Mystic, CT: Mystic Seaport Museum Press, 1970.

Ives, Edward Sandy. *Folksongs of New Brunswick*. Fredericton, NB: Goose Lane Edition, 1989.

Ives, Edward Sandy. *Folksongs of Maine* (Folkways, 1959) Recording.

Karpeles, Maud. *Folk Songs from Newfoundland*. London, UK: Faber & Faber, 1971

Kennedy, Peter. *Folksongs of Britain & Ireland*. London & NY: Oak Publications, 1975.

Kidson, Frank. *Traditional Tunes*. Oxford, UK: Charles Taphouse & Son, 1891.

Kneeland, Frank and Bertha. *The Kneeland Miscellany*. Private Publication, 1914

Laws, G. Malcolm. *Native American Balladry*. American Folklore Society Bibliographical and Special Series, 1 (revised). Philadelphia, PA: American Folklore Society, 1964

Leach, MacEdward. *Folk Ballads & Songs of the Lower Labrador Coast*. Ottawa: National Museum of Canada, 1965.

Linscott, Eloise Hubbard. *Folk Songs of Old New England*. New York, NY: Macmillan Co, 1939.

Lodge, Henry Cabot and Ford, Worthington Chauncey. *Broadsides and Ballads Printed in Massachusetts 1639–1800, Volume 75*. Boston, MA: Massachusetts Historical Society, 1922.

Lomax, Alan. *The Folk Songs of North America*. Garden City, NY: Doubleday & Co, 1960.

Lomax, John. *American Ballads and Folk Songs*. New York, NY: Macmillan & Co, 1934.

Lovette, Leland P. *Naval Customs, Traditions and Usage*. Annapolis, MD: United States Naval Institute, 1939.

Luce, Stephen Bleeker. *Naval Songs: A Collection of Original, Selected, and Traditional Sea Songs.* New York, NY: Wm. A. Pond, 1918.

M., D. H. (editor) *Heroic Ballads with Poems of War and Patriotism.* Boston, MA: Ginn & Company, 1890.

MacDougall, Pauleena. *Fannie Hardy Eckstorm and Her Quest for Local Knowledge.* Lanham, MD: Lexington Books, 2013.

Mackenzie, William Roy. *Ballads and Sea Songs from Nova Scotia.* Cambridge, MA: Harvard Univ. Press 1928.

Mozley, Henry. *The British Melodist Or National Song Book.* London: 1822.

Mozley, J.M. *The Jovial songster; or, Sailor's delight: A collection of chearful and humourous songs, sung by the brave tars of Old England, and other merry companions, who over a cann of flip are disposed for mirth and good humour.* Gainsborough, 1792.

Newell, William Wells. "Early American Ballads. II." *Journal of American Folklore,* Volume 13, 1900.

Paton, Sandy. *New England Traditions in Folk Music (Recording notes)* Recorded Anthology of American Music, Inc. New York, NY: New World Records, 1977.

Post, Jennifer C. *Music in Rural New England Family and Community Life, 1870-1940.* Lebanon, NH: University of New Hampshire Press, 2004.

Pound, Louise Pound. *American Ballads and Songs.* New York: Charles Scribner's Sons, 1922. Reprint ed., 1972.

Price, Franklin. *Acadia Maritime Cultural Resources Inventory.* Bernard, ME, 2009

Procter Bros. *Fishermen's Ballads and Songs of the Sea. Compiled by Procter brothers. and respectfully dedicated to the hardy fishermen of Cape Ann.* Gloucester, MA: Procter Brothers, 1874.

Procter Bros. *The Fisherman's Own Book.* Gloucester, MA: Procter Brothers, 1882.

Quinn, Jennifer Post, *An Index to the Field Recordings in the Flanders Ballad Collection at Middlebury College.* Middlebury, VT, 1983.

Sandburg, Carl. *The American Songbag.* New York: Harcourt, Brace & Co., 1927.

Sharp, Cecil. *Folk-songs of England, Volume 1 & 2* London: Novello, 1908–12.

Shay, Frank. *American Sea Songs and Chanteys from the Days of Iron Men & Wooden Ships.*(Original publication 1924) New York: W.W. Norton and Company, Inc., 1948.

Shuldham-Shaw, P. and Lyle, E. B., (Editors). *The Greig-Duncan Folk Song Collection, vols 1-8.* Aberdeen, Scotland: Aberdeen University Press, 1981–2002.

Smith, Seba. *Jack Downing's Song Book.* Hallowell, ME: 1836.

Stone, Christopher. *Sea Songs and Ballads,* with introduction by Admiral Sir Cyprian Bridge G.C.B. Oxford: Clarendon Press, 1906.

Whall, W. B. *Sea Songs and Shanties.* Glasgow, Scotland: Brown, Son & Ferguson, 1910.

Whitten, Jeanne Patten.

Williams, Ralph Vaughan, & A. L. Lloyd. *The Penguin Book of English Folk Songs.* Baltimore: Penguin, 1969.

About the Authors

Julia Lane has loved, sung, researched and created folk music since childhood. She and her older brother learned and sang sea shanties to accompany his passion for sailing ships. Hearing her mother sing traditional English songs she became interested in their origins and began library research at age 10 learning more songs to sing herself. She became active in madrigal and Renaissance music groups as well as performing as a soloist. In addition, she was inspired by the literary works of J.R.R. Tolkien and his sources in the ancient ballad tradition. After graduating from Phillips Exeter Academy in 1974, her interest in traditional folk music and lore led her to study in Oxford, England. For over thirty years, she has conducted in-depth research into the social history and folkways of the Celtic lands and her native New England which has resulted in multi-media programs blending history and myth with both traditional and original music. Julia has studied piano, classical and flamenco guitar, and voice. A self-taught player of the Celtic folk harp, her unique style has won three international competitions. Lane is also a fine vocalist whose voice has been compared favorably with Loreena McKennitt, Jean Redpath and Judy Collins.

Julia collaborates with her husband, Fred Gosbee, who has also collected and performed folk music for over thirty years. As a child in central Maine, he heard his older relatives, who had worked in the lumber woods, singing the old woodsmen's songs and playing fiddle and accordian. Through high school, he became fully conversant with several band instruments, including the tuba, but also dabbled in folk instruments building himself a banjo from scrap wood panelling and an old bedpost. At the University of Maine, he was inspired by the folk music he heard in a college folklore class with Dr. Sandy Ives who became Fred's advisor. Dr. Ives became influential in Fred's awareness and appreciation for his own heritage of folk music and gave him the assignment of documenting songs sung by John West, his grandfather who worked in the woods from an early age. Fred was also encouraged to begin serious lutherie, building several guitars and a lute. Having had wide experience with community theater, both onstage and in production, Fred combined his theatrical experience with his knowledge of folk music when he arranged, composed, and performed new incidental music for a production of "A Spoon River Anthology." Gosbee has continued to write original songs in the traditional style, celebrating human experience. Having spent many years as a shipfitter and maritime engineer, the lives and heritage of those who follow the maritime trades are of particular interest. He is currently volunteering on a crew that is constructing a conjectural replica of Virginia, "Maine's First Ship," originally built in 1607 at the mouth of the Kennebec river. Fred sings and plays classic and 12-string guitar, viola, fiddle, and woodwinds and enjoys experimenting with both traditional and ethnic instruments. A skilled woodworker and technician, having learned from his resourceful and inventive father and grandfather, he designs and builds Celtic harps played by his wife, Julia, as well as other unusual and historic stringed instruments. In addition, Fred engineers and produces recordings for both the couple's musical entity, Castlebay, and other local musicians.

Castlebay maintains a commitment to cultural education and, since 1987, they have toured the Eastern U.S., Maritime Canada, Ireland, England and Scotland providing socio-historically informed music programs for festivals, folk clubs, schools, museums, libraries and arts centers as well as on radio and TV. The duo has also composed musical works as memoirs of travels in the UK and Ireland and celebrating journeys across the Atlantic. The Skye Suite, a cycle of musical impressions of the Isle of Skye in northwest Scotland, has been performed both in the U.S. and Scotland and released on CD. While researching Scottish music which has come to Maine, "Sang o' the Solway (The Galloway Suite)" evolved from an ongoing exchange with "Stravaig," a group from Galloway. The full length piece, which also include poetry and traditional music, has been performed several times there under the auspices of the Scottish Arts Council. Most recently, the duo created "Grand Design," a multi-media musical historical docudrama which chronicles the 1740 journey of women from Northern Ireland who were abandoned on a Maine island and rescued by Native Americans. A full production includes a chamber orchestra, video imagery and a cast of 20 with original and traditional music and dance. Castlebay has released numerous recordings which include both instrumental and vocal selections. Their music has been used for video soundtracks and as support for historical presentations. (www.castlebay.net).The duo has made their home in coastal Maine where they live in a post and beam home surrounded by rock gardens which they built themselves. They have raised three children and have one grand-daughter.

For more information, visit www.castlebay.net or contact castlebay@castlebay.net / phone 207-529-5438.

www.ingramcontent.com/pod-product-compliance
Lightning Source LLC
Chambersburg PA
CBHW060230240426
43671CB00016B/2903